Less Frequently Used Research Methodologies
in Applied Linguistics

Research Methods in Applied Linguistics (RMAL)

ISSN 2590-096X

The *Research Methods in Applied Linguistics* (RMAL) series publishes authoritative general guides and in-depth explorations of central research methodology concerns in the entire field of Applied Linguistics. The hallmark of the series is the contribution to stimulating and advancing professional methodological debates in the domain. Books published in the series (both authored and edited volumes) will be key resources for applied linguists (including established researchers and newcomers to the field) and an invaluable source for research methodology courses.

Main directions for the volumes in the series include (but are not limited to): Comprehensive introductions to research methods in Applied Linguistics (authoritative, introductions to domain-non specific methodologies); In-depth explorations of central methodological considerations and developments in specific areas of Applied Linguistics (authoritative treatments of domain-specific methodologies); Critical analyses that develop, expand, or challenge existing and/or novel methodological frameworks; In-depth reflections on central considerations in employing specific methodologies and/or addressing specific questions and problems in Applied Linguistics research; Authoritative accounts that foster improved understandings of the behind the scenes, inside story of the research process in Applied Linguistics.

For an overview of all books published in this series, please see *benjamins.com/catalog/rmal*

Editor

Rosa M. Manchón
University of Murcia

Editorial Board

David Britain
University of Bern

Gloria Corpas Pastor
University of Malaga

Marta González-Lloret
University of Hawai'i

Laura Gurzynski-Weiss
Indiana University Bloomington

Juan Manuel Hernández-Campoy
University of Murcia

Ute Knoch
University of Melbourne

Anthony J. Liddicoat
University of Warwick

Brian Paltridge
University of Sydney

Diane Pecorari
City University of Hong Kong

Luke Plonsky
Northern Arizona University

Li Wei
University College London

Volume 6

Less Frequently Used Research Methodologies in Applied Linguistics
Edited by A. Mehdi Riazi

Less Frequently Used Research Methodologies in Applied Linguistics

Edited by

A. Mehdi Riazi
Hamad Bin Khalifa University

John Benjamins Publishing Company
Amsterdam / Philadelphia

The paper used in this publication meets the minimum requirements of the American National Standard for Information Sciences – Permanence of Paper for Printed Library Materials, ANSI z39.48-1984.

DOI 10.1075/rmal.6

Cataloging-in-Publication Data available from Library of Congress:
LCCN 2023041692 (PRINT) / 2023041693 (E-BOOK)

ISBN 978 90 272 1442 3 (HB)
ISBN 978 90 272 1441 6 (PB)
ISBN 978 90 272 4921 0 (E-BOOK)

© 2024 – John Benjamins B.V.
No part of this book may be reproduced in any form, by print, photoprint, microfilm, or any other means, without written permission from the publisher.

John Benjamins Publishing Company · https://benjamins.com

Table of contents

CHAPTER 1. Introduction   1
A. Mehdi Riazi

CHAPTER 2. The multiperspectival approach to Applied Linguistic research: Exploring principles, questions, and orientations   9
Jonathan Crichton & Darryl Hocking

CHAPTER 3. Implementing the multiperspectival approach (MPA): A study of art and design communication   30
Darryl Hocking & Jonathan Crichton

CHAPTER 4. Multimodality: A systemic-functional semiotic perspective   49
Yixiong Chen, Csilla Weninger & Fei Victor Lim

CHAPTER 5. Applying multimodal analysis: Embodied teaching and textbook analysis   68
Csilla Weninger, Fei Victor Lim & Yixiong Chen

CHAPTER 6. Conversation analysis   83
Numa Markee

CHAPTER 7. Doing conversation analysis: Investigating avoidance strategy   111
Numa Markee

CHAPTER 8. Grounded theory   127
Gregory Hadley & Hiromi Hadley

CHAPTER 9. Applications of Grounded Theory in the field of Extensive Reading   149
Gregory Hadley & Hiromi Hadley

CHAPTER 10. Phenomenology   162
Seyyed Ali Ostovar-Namaghi

CHAPTER 11. Phenomenology: A showcase of EFL learners' experience of foreign language proficiency maintenance   180
Seyyed Ali Ostovar-Namaghi

CHAPTER 12. Narrative inquiry 191
Sabina M. Perrino

CHAPTER 13. Narrative inquiry: Case studies from Senegal
and Northern Italy 206
Sabina M. Perrino

CHAPTER 14. Repertory grids 224
Myles Grogan

CHAPTER 15. Repertory grids: A showcase of repertory grid technique 246
Myles Grogan

CHAPTER 16. Challenges and contributions of less frequently used
methodologies 264
A. Mehdi Riazi

Index 273

CHAPTER 1

Introduction

A. Mehdi Riazi
Hamad Bin Khalifa University

This introductory chapter is organized into two sections. The first section, the introduction, discusses research methodology in Applied Linguistics (AL), considering recent methodological debates. Each of the methodologies included in this volume is presented in two chapters, a theoretical and a showcase practical chapter. The second section, therefore, provides a synopsis of each of the chapters. The two sections of the introductory chapter provide a context for the readers so that they develop a general idea of what will follow in the body of the book.

1. Introduction

Research methodology has benefited from rigorous discussion in recent years in Applied Linguistics (AL) and, more broadly, in other disciplines. These discussions have led to methodological awareness (Plonsky, 2017) and were stated more rigorously by Byrnes (2013, p. 825) as a "methodological turn." Many books in AL are published wholly dedicated to research methodology, so listing them here will take up a lot of space. In addition, AL and second language-related journals have published papers on various aspects of research methodologies. A search in Google Scholar with the key terms "research methodology" AND "Applied Linguistics" on 3rd Feb. 2023 returned 20900 records for 2000–2023. Notwithstanding the growth of published books and articles, some methodological approaches and procedures still need more comprehensive discussion. There is, therefore, a crucial need to bring into the foreground less frequently used methodological approaches in AL research, given their affordances to contribute to knowledge production, theory development, and implications for practice. The current edited volume introduces, explains, and discusses some of those methodological procedures that are less frequently seen in the AL methodological discussion. Furthermore, the methodological approaches included in this volume respond to the recent conceptual and methodological debates in second language acquisition (SLA) and more broadly in AL (see. e.g., Douglas Fir Group, 2016;

https://doi.org/10.1075/rmal.6.01ria
© 2024 John Benjamins Publishing Company

Firth & Wagner, 2007; Hiver et al., 2023; King & Mackey, 2016; Li & Prior, 2023; Ortega, 2013).

At a conceptual level, there have been debates around cognitively oriented vs. socially oriented approaches to second language studies. Gao (2019), for example, raised the question of whether second language studies "should attribute primacy to the individual brain or the social world when exploring language learners' learning processes" (p.161). The cognitive approaches to second language studies have predominantly used quantitative approaches, whereas when it comes to social orientations to language studies, the predominant methodology has been qualitative. Ortega (2013), for example, observed that:

> As part of the social turn, diverse empirical qualitative and interpretive methodologies were needed that would be appropriate for the study of not just language development but also social dimensions of L2 learning, including conversation analytical, ethnographic, and microgenetic methods, as well as combinations of them. (p.5)

On the other hand, there has been a debate on whether disciplinary and interdisciplinary approaches to knowledge production should shift to transdisciplinary to solve real-life problems or continue to develop frontiers of knowledge. According to Ortega (2013), "transdisciplinarity ensues when scholarly communities attempt to solve complex knowledge problems with social impact by working across multiple disciplinary boundaries as well as with social actors outside academia" (p.3).

As noted above, the conceptual debates have had crucial implications for research and what counts as legitimate research and the produced knowledge. For example, the Douglas Fir Group (DFG) framework presents ten research themes that underpin holistic inquiries into "language learning and teaching" by "taking into account forces beyond individual learners" (DFG, 2016, p.20). One of these research themes is theorizing language cognition in context. This research theme has implications for research methodology and urges researchers to investigate how individual cognition interacts and builds on contextual factors. New orientations to the conceptualization of research problems have urged Applied Linguistics researchers to look for more innovative approaches to data collection and analysis. Accordingly, new methodological orientations like the ones discussed in this volume, although less frequently used, are appropriate candidates to address more complex research problems.

Drawing on Bigelow (2014), the Douglas Fir Group (2016) encourages transdisciplinary and solving "problems in socially useful and participant-relevant or emic ways with whatever theoretical-analytical tools" (p.24). Consequently, given the growing complexity of language-related problems, less frequently used research methodologies and analytical procedures can help researchers address some of those problems. This is so because (a) our knowledge bases are developed, and we can now build on what we already know and address more complex problems, (b) second language learners now have more opportunities for learning beyond the classrooms, (c) technological advances in language teaching and learning, (d) access to more data sources that can help researchers better understand the processes, and (e) advanced analytical procedures that help researchers develop better understandings from the data.

2. A synopsis of the chapters

This volume includes seven less frequently used research methodologies and analytical procedures that match the above discussion, namely:

1. Multiperspectival approach
2. Multimodality: A systemic functional semiotic perspective
3. Conversation analysis
4. Grounded theory
5. Phenomenology
6. Narrative inquiry
7. Repertory grids

Each methodological procedure is discussed in two chapters. The first chapter of each binary discusses theoretical foundations, methodological orientation (principles and affordances, types of research questions that the methodology can address, data collection and analysis procedures, and ethical issues), critiques of the methodology in focus, and responses to those critiques. The second chapter then showcases how the methodological procedure is used to investigate a language-related research problem. As in the case of the first chapters, the showcase chapters also follow an identical structure: They present an overview of the study, the rationale for using the methodology, how the study was implemented, the challenges the researchers faced, how those challenges were addressed, and insights gained utilizing the methodology.

Although the coverage of the less frequently used methodologies is limited (seven methodological orientations), the book covers key methodological approaches. More important, however, is the application of these methodological approaches to a range of research problems in Applied Linguistics. The substantiation of the methodologies with real-life examples of how they were used to address particular research problems helps readers understand the affordances and the challenges of the methodology in focus.

Before moving on to the chapters on each less frequently used methodological approach, a brief overview will help the reader develop a broad insight. As stated earlier, all the chapters follow the same structure. As part of the methodological orientation, the authors discuss ethical issues involved in the methodology. After this introductory chapter, Chapters Two and Three by Jonathan Chrichton and Darryl Hocking discuss the Multi-Perspectival Approach (MPA). The authors explain that MPA brings together five mutually informing perspectives. These five perspectives include those from the researcher, the participants, the semiotic resources, the social practice, and the social-institutional perspective. As Chrichton and Hocking discuss, AL researchers may conventionally focus on one of these perspectives. However, through an MPA, there is the opportunity to address the research phenomenon from different perspectives involved in a research site. The MPA seems to align with King's and Mackey's (2016) proposal for a layered approach to language-related studies. King and Mackey argued "that there are issues and concerns within all areas of second language research that would benefit from examination and analysis from multiple perspectives" (p. 214). The MPA thus responds to this and similar recent methodological discussions in AL. The showcase chapter provides a detailed overview of a program of interprofessional research. The chapter describes and scrutinizes how the MPA was used in a particular research site facilitating the analysis of the student's creative and communicative practices through interdependent and mutually informing perspectives. It shows how the emergent findings from different perspectives were corroborated to produce ecologically grounded responses to the research questions.

Chapters Four and Five by Csilla Weninger, Victor Lim, and Chen Yixiong explain and discuss multimodality from a social semiotic perspective. A growing conception of communication as multimodal has received traction over the last two decades. Speech and writing, which were conventionally conceived as the basis for communication, are now seen as just two semiotic tools and modes. As the authors discuss, other semiotic tools and modes (such as images and videos) and other massive screen-mediated communicative tools can contribute effectively to communication. As we learn from the two chapters on multimodality, it is the orchestration of various semiotic tools that will lead to effective communication. Multimodal researchers like Jewitt and Kress (2003), Kress (2010), and Serafini (2014) are among those who have spawned multimodal theory and empirical investigations within AL. The authors discuss that multimodal turn has explored what it takes to create and interpret meaning from multiple semiotic modes or systems within a variety of contexts, including language teaching and learning. The authors first provide a brief theoretical overview to explicate multimodality as a foundational social semiotics methodology. They then discuss the research concerns and questions that can be investigated through a multimodal approach, highlighting the advantages of multimodal analysis over purely language-based research. Finally, they discuss the extant critiques of the social semiotic approach to multimodality in AL research and potential responses to these critiques by drawing on some empirical studies. The showcase chapter builds on the theoretical tenets of the social semiotic approach to multimodality and how this may translate into empirical research. The authors illustrate how multimodal analysis has been increasingly used as the primary methodology to analyze language textbooks. They then present two studies to showcase the use of multimodal analysis.

Chapters Six and Seven by Numa Markee discuss and showcase conversation analysis (CA). Chapter Six reviews the theoretical underpinnings and contributions of CA to AL. The discussion includes the underlying principles and design procedures of CA. Markee discusses that CA is a crucial offshoot of ethnomethodology, and as he explains, CA originally aimed at investigating language use-related questions concerning how turns are taken, how miscommunication problems are resolved, and how extended sequences of talk are organized in ways that maximize the progressivity of talk. The author explains that CA focuses on using only publicly observable behaviour for analysis. Also, the CA approach has a restricted understanding of context–a point that the author discusses in Chapter Six. The author also discusses that in CA, cognition is understood as a *socially distributed* phenomenon. Along with this discussion, Markee also discusses CA's interest in multimodality (the use of eye gaze, prosody, pointing and other gestures, facial expressions, and the body that complement and, in some cases, replace talk as resources for action) and materiality (how participants contingently talk into the relevance of various objects and cultural artifacts in the environment). In addition to addressing ethical issues when using CA, the author also discusses ethnographic critiques of the narrow view of context adopted by CA and outlines the counter-arguments on these matters. The showcase chapter presents Markee's (2011) article titled "Doing, justifying doing, avoidance". After presenting an overview of the study, the author discusses the rationale behind the choice of CA, how it was implemented, the challenges the researcher faced, how they were addressed, and the insights gained using the methodology.

Chapters Eight and Nine by Gregory Hadley and Hiromi Hadley discuss grounded theory methodology (GTM). The authors argue that while GTM is one of the most widely used approaches for exploring issues in social environments, it is largely neglected in AL research. Chapter Eight discusses the theoretical underpinnings of the GTM and how language teachers and AL scholars may utilize it to develop insightful theoretical explanations of the social interactions taking place in classrooms. Critiques of GTM are addressed, as well as questions related to ethical issues involved in the use of the methodology. Chapter eight is different from other explanations of GTM (e.g., Hadley, 2017, 2019) in that it elaborates in detail on the methodology, purposes, strengths, and weaknesses of GTM. The showcase chapter presents the use of GTM in studying extensive reading in a particular context. The chapter briefly introduces the social processes that learners commonly bring to the extensive reading classroom. After presenting an overview of the study, the authors discuss why they used GTM for researching extensive reading, and how the methodology was implemented. The authors will also discuss the challenges they faced when using GTM, and how they addressed those challenges. Finally, they will share the insights they gained through using GTM that might otherwise have been missed using other methodological orientations.

Chapters Ten and Eleven by Ali Ostovar Nameghi present and discuss phenomenology. In Chapter Ten, the author reviews the philosophical underpinnings of phenomenology to clarify its ontological, epistemological, and axiological assumptions. The author then reviews the different versions of phenomenology, including descriptive and interpretive. After the theoretical discussion of phenomenology, the methodological orientation of phenomenology, including ethical issues, is discussed. Data collection and analysis procedures are then addressed. Finally, the author concludes the chapter by responding to the criticisms that have been leveled against phenomenological studies. More specifically, the author clarifies how the credibility of the findings is established in this qualitative mode of inquiry. The showcase chapter discusses the lived experiences of EFL learners who could maintain their language proficiency in a context where the language they had learned had no social use. After presenting an overview of the study, the author discusses why a phenomenological orientation was chosen to investigate the research problem and how it was implemented. The challenges the researchers faced and how those challenges were addressed are also discussed, along with the insights gained using the methodology.

Chapters Twelve and Thirteen by Sabina Perrino discuss the narrative inquiry. The author discusses the why and how of the narratives as they emerge in interview settings. Drawing on De Fina and Perrion (2011), Perrino (2015), and Perrino and Kohler (2020), the author argues that while the narratives-as-texts have been predominant, the narratives-as-practices approach is neglected while extremely valuable. In particular, the author discusses interviews as "situated speech events" (Mishler, 1986) and the key sites to examine the emerging nature of storytelling practices. In chapter twelve, Perrino discusses the theoretical underpinnings of narrative inquiry, that is, linguistic anthropological and sociolinguistic research. In addition to theoretical underpinnings, the author discusses methodological orientations, critiques, and responses. In chapter thirteen, the author turns to a linguistic anthropological analysis of a set of narrative practices that she collected in Senegal (West Africa) and Northern Italy (Europe) in interview settings. Through an analysis of carefully transcribed interviews, following the insight of linguistic anthropology, the author demonstrates that narratives are not only valued for their content or "denotational text" but also for the emerging dynamics between the interviewer(s) and interviewee(s), or "interactional text" (Silverstein, 1998). After presenting an overview of the study, the researcher author discusses why the methodology was used and how it was implemented. The author also discusses the challenges she faced and how, as a researcher, she addressed those challenges. Finally, she elaborates on the insights gained using the methodology.

Chapters Fourteen and Fifteen by Myles Grogan discuss the repertory grid technique (RGT) to show how people interpret the world around them. As the author discusses, RGT originated from personal construct psychology. The methodological procedure is used to investigate how people construe other people they interact with, the different activities they do, or the objects they use. After discussing the theoretical underpinnings of RGT, the author discusses methodological orientations, including principles and affordances, types of research questions addressed by the methodological approach, procedures of data collection and analysis, and ethical issues involved in using RGT. The showcase chapter presents an RGT investigation of a single setting, focussing on a deeper understanding of classroom teachers' view of grades in a compulsory EFL course in a Japanese university. After presenting an overview of the study, the author discusses the rationale behind using the methodology and how it was implemented. In addition, the author discusses the challenges he faced using the technique and how those challenges were addressed, and the insights gained using the technique.

Finally, in Chapter sixteen, the editor will conclude the book by reflecting on the challenges and contributions of the methodologies included in the volume. In particular, the challenges faced by the researchers and the insights gained using these methodological orientations are discussed. In addition, I provide a synthesis of the main ethical issues raised and discussed in each methodological orientation and discuss their relations to the current discussion of ethics in AL research. Prospective researchers need to know about both the capabilities and challenges of the methodological approaches to make informed decisions. Thus, the final chapter provides a discussion of the methodological procedures included in the volume and how they add to the methodological discussion in AL.

References

Bigelow, M. H. (2014). Blending social and cognitive research traditions in language learning and teaching: A matter of mentoring and modeling. *Studies in Second Language Acquisition, 36*, 402–407.

Byrnes, H. (2013). Notes from the editor. *The Modern Language Journal, 97*, 825–827.

De Fina, A., & Perrino, S. (2011). [Special Issue]. *Language in Society, 40*(1), 1–11.

Douglas Fir Group. (2016). A transdisciplinary framework for SLA in a multilingual world. *The Modern Language Journal, 100*(Suppl. 2016), 19–47.

Firth, A., & Wagner, J. (2007). Second/foreign language learning as a social accomplishment: Elaborations on a reconceptualized SLA. *The Modern Language Journal, 91*, 800–819.

Gao, X. (2019). The Douglas Fir Group framework as a resource map for language teacher education. *The Modern Language Journal, 103*(Suppl. 2019), 161–166.

Hadley, G. (2017). *Grounded theory in applied linguistics research: A practical guide.* Routledge.

Hadley, G. (2019). Grounded theory method. In J. McKinley & H. Rose (Eds.), *The Routledge handbook of research methods in applied linguistics* (pp. 264–275). Routledge.

Hiver, P., Al-Hoorie, A. L., & Murakami, A. (2023). Methodological innovations in studying complex systems in applied linguistics. In S. Li & M. T. Prior (Convenors), *Methodological innovation in applied linguistics research: Perspectives, strategies, and trends.* Invited Colloquium. AAAL, Portland, Oregon. Retrieved on 20 July 2023 from https://www.aaal.org/2023-li-prior-colloquium

Jewitt, C., & Kress, G. (2003). *Multimodal literacy.* Peter Lang.

King, K., & Mackey, A. (2016). Research methodology in second language studies: Trends, concerns, and new directions. *The Modern Language Journal, 100*(Suppl. 2016), 209–227.

Kress, G. (2010). *Multimodality: A social semiotic approach to contemporary communication.* Routledge.

Li, S., & Prior, M. P. (2023, March 18–23). *Methodological innovation in applied linguistics research: Perspectives, strategies, and trends.* Invited Colloquium. AAAL, Portland, Oregon. Retrieved on 20 July 2023 from https://www.aaal.org/2023-li-prior-colloquium

Markee, N. (2011). Doing, and justifying doing, avoidance. *Journal of Pragmatics, 43*(2), 602–615.

Mishler, E. G. (1986). *Research interviewing: Context and narrative.* Harvard University Press.

Ortega, L. (2013). SLA for the 21st century: Disciplinary progress, transdisciplinary relevance, and the bi/multilingual turn. *Language Learning, 63*(Suppl. 1), 1–24.

Perrino, S. (2015). Chronotopes: Time and Space in Oral Narrative. In A. De Fina & A. Georgakopoulou (Eds.), *The Handbook of Narrative Analysis* (pp. 140–159). Wiley-Blackwell.

Perrino, S., & Kohler, G. (2020). Chronotopic Identities: Narrating Made in Italy across Spatiotemporal Scales. *Language & Communication, 70*, 94–106.

Plonsky, L. (2017). Quantitative research methods. In S. Loewen & M. Sato (Eds.), *The Routledge handbook of instructed second language acquisition* (pp. 505–521). Routledge.

Serafini, F. (2014). *Reading the visual: An introduction to teaching multimodality literacy.* Teaching College Press.

Silverstein, M. (1998). Improvisational performance of culture in realtime discursive practice. In K. Sawyer (Ed.), *Creativity in Performance* (pp. 265–312). Ablex Publishing Corp.

CHAPTER 2

The Multiperspectival Approach to Applied Linguistic research
Exploring principles, questions, and orientations

Jonathan Crichton & Darryl Hocking
University of South Australia | Auckland University of Technology

This chapter explores the distinctive features of the Multiperspectival
Approach (MPA) to research: its theoretical and philosophical background,
the questions it addresses, and the research orientations it enables. The
chapter explains how MPA offers researchers a heuristic that addresses
ontological and epistemological challenges to research that are central to the
language-context relationship and consequential for any researcher who
seeks to make claims about the meaning of language in the lives of others at
particular sites. The chapter provides detailed background and guidance on
what MPA involves and its value as a practical ontology that enables
researchers to discover – rather than to search – the worlds of their
participants, iteratively to learn through this process of discovery,
developing warrants and finding themes to bridge these worlds through
multiple, mutually-corroborating perspectives.

1. Introduction

This chapter explores the distinctive features of the Multiperspectival Approach
(MPA) to research: its theoretical and philosophical background, the questions it
addresses, and the research orientations it enables.[1]

The development of MPA was motivated by a challenge that haunts Applied
Linguistic research. The challenge arises because, on the one hand, in order to
investigate how language is used and understood in a particular context, the
researcher needs a principled way of identifying what counts as relevant aspects

---

1. MPA was developed through a twenty-year collaboration between Chris Candlin and the
authors. This chapter and the one that follows are tributes to Chris, our debt to him, and his
vision for Applied Linguistics.

https://doi.org/10.1075/rmal.6.02cri
© 2024 John Benjamins Publishing Company

of that context (Duranti & Goodwin, 1992). Without a means to do this, the context is potentially vast and undifferentiated – a 'lumpen mass' (Brown & Yule, 1983, p. 50). On the other hand, there is a long history in Applied Linguistics of analysing the detailed features of language. The challenge is to integrate language and context in a way which allows the detailed analysis of language in relation to relevant features of context. The danger, as Brown and Yule imply, is that once context is included in the analysis of language, the analysis will become unaccountable, raising the risk that research will be driven by the a priori selection of particular methods or combinations of methods without reference to the characteristics of the particular site of research.

In addressing this challenge, MPA offers a heuristic (Moustakas, 1990; Sultan, 2018), that enables a researcher to 'start with the site' of research (Candlin et al., 2016, p. 3) while leaving methodological options open to selection, combination, and refinement, subject to the evolving nature of the researcher's engagement in and her emerging understanding of the site. In other words, MPA frames Applied Linguistic research as 'the art of the possible.... [after all] one cannot play chess if 16 of the 64 squares are forbidden from the beginning' (Bismarck, 1860, as cited in Steinberg, 2011, p. 133). So what squares do we have on which to play in MPA?

The emphasis in MPA is not so much methodological as conceptual, raising related ontological, epistemological, and methodological questions that transcend those normally associated with Applied Linguistic research. Specifically:

- Ontologically, how to understand the nature of a site, including the potential relationships among researchers, participants, language, and the settings in which it is used;
- Epistemologically, how to understand the worlds of participants, acknowledging the perspectives of researchers and the research participants themselves to establish the relevance of the research in a way accountable to these different perspectives;
- Methodologically, how to translate the responses to these ontological and epistemological questions into a research design and agenda, including methods and techniques of data collection and analysis, to achieve an accountable research program.

In organizing the chapter, we have been mindful that MPA and its responses to these questions have hitherto been presented largely in book-length (Candlin & Crichton, 2011c, 2013b; Crichton, 2010; Crichton et al., 2016; Hocking, 2018). Here, the available space requires a different approach. Mindful of this, we have sought to ease the explanatory gradient using expository devices, such as thought experiments, metaphors, and diagrams, as stepping stones towards a full view of MPA. In setting out this path to common ground, section two explores the theoretical foundations; section three, the methodological orientation; section four, sources of critique and response; and section five discusses ethical issues foregrounded by MPA.

2. Theoretical foundations

Our starting point is a thought experiment. Imagine the following:

> You have just woken up, disoriented and without any memory of how you arrived in this place. When you open your eyes, the darkness is impenetrable, disturbed only by a sharp, chemical smell. The room is silent. When you call out, there's no response. As you reach out, you encounter surfaces, textures, and shapes that feel unfamiliar, almost alien. Gradually, you hear voices –indistinct and distant. It's unclear whether they're in conversation or in what language. As they come closer, you catch fragments: confident, purposeful, tinged with banter. Words surface, yet they're disconnected, and their meaning eludes you. Your memory offers no help. You call out again. Still, no response. Fraught with the need to understand, you strain for answers. What is this place? Where is it? What is it for? Who are they? What are they doing? What are they talking about? For what purposes? How are you involved? Who else is here? What don't you know? What do you do next?

This thought experiment is, as we conceive of it, a fictional story designed to give an intuitive window into the rationale that underlies MPA. The story could have been the start of a science fiction or horror movie. It is, of course, a literary trope across genres in which a character discovers and questions her assumptions when finding herself 'out of her element', and also has affinities with the challenges routinely faced by residents in the aged care (Crichton & Koch, 2007). And this fictive situation in the thought experiment is, in effect, not dissimilar to that of someone starting a research project in which they will seek to make claims about what language means in the lives of others in a context that may be unfamiliar to the researcher. We say 'in effect' because the experiment viscerally dramatises and amplifies uncertainty, vulnerability, urgency, and fear.

We do not deny that the experience of embarking on and conducting research in Applied Linguistics can be existentially challenging. However, our interest for the moment is what we can learn from the experiment as an 'epistemological reset'. That is, a way of simulating the absence of familiar contextual cues, thereby undermining and simultaneously making visible those taken-for-granted assumptions that usually facilitate and justify the interpretation of meaning. The dilemma posed by the structure of the situation is what matters. On the one hand, you are faced with a pressing need to interpret the meaning of the language used by others. On the other hand, your attempts to address this need make it increasingly apparent that the surroundings in which you find yourself are sufficiently unfamiliar to cast doubt on your capacities both to infer meaning and to work out how to do so. Simultaneously, you are faced with the urgent and practical question of what to do next to address the dilemma.

The questions that arise for the participant facing this dilemma are not exhaustive, exclusive, or haphazard. On the contrary, they are principled attempts to find the safe ground of understanding and certainty. Furthermore, the questions are necessarily holistic in scope, whereby collectively, they point to a whole that must be understood before the questioner can find the means to answer the questions individually. We could therefore say that together the questions reveal the 'map' that the participant must – as it were – chart if she is to navigate meaning in this unfamiliar site. So another way of thinking of these questions is by tracing the outline of what we might call, adapting Dallmayr's (1991) term, a 'practical ontology'. In other words, a basal understanding which, if the participant in the experiment could only fill this out for present purposes, might guide and warrant her interpretation of meaning in the situation at hand.

And this notion of a practical ontology brings us to the value of the experiment for us here. MPA is intended to be just such a practical ontology for research in Applied Linguistics. Here and in the following sections, we focus on why this is needed, what it looks like, and how it can be used.

Why MPA is needed becomes evident when Applied Linguistic research moves from its more traditional domains of language teaching and learning to less familiar foci, communities, and institutions. In the latter cases, we are ipso facto obliged to question the relevance of the interpretive and linguistic resources that we bring, throwing us back to questions cognate with those that arise for the participant in the thought experiment. This does not mean that MPA is not relevant to well-trodden domains; only that against the background of the unarguably unfamiliar, its value is more immediately apparent.

So what is being envisaged here? We can see this if we unpack the questions that occurred to the participant in the thought experiment. These questions will be familiar as base questions asked across disciplinary areas in Applied Linguistics that, depending on the area, invoke different analytic perspectives entailing particular methodological and epistemological investments in the analysis of texts, social action, local and broader social-historical contexts, and the perspectives of participants, including those of the researcher. The inclusion of the researcher as a participant is essential. Figure 1 is a schematic representation of the map sought by the participant in the experiment – if she is an Applied Linguist:

Extending this 'map' metaphor a little enables us to model her perspective as a researcher. Thus, in adopting a particular approach to research at a particular site,

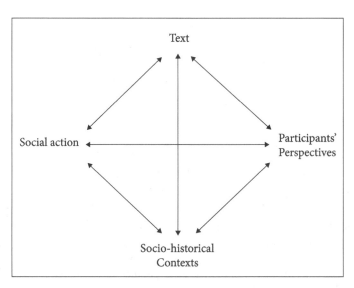

Figure 1. Mapping perspectives (adapted from Candlin et al., 2017, p. 14; Crichton, 2004, p. 25)

a researcher inevitably 'locates' herself somewhere on this map, thereby anticipating what she will find at the site in terms projected by the position she selects on the map. She then enters the site much as one might 'drop' oneself into street view from a particular point on a Google map. From whatever position she adopts, she sees and explores particular analytic vantages points in developing answers to her questions about the site where she finds herself. In other words, in each position, she invokes different ways of seeing the surrounding landscape of language, social action, participants' perspectives, local and broader contextual conditions, and the relationships among these. Of course, this is our understanding of her situation. Whether she is, in fact, mindful of the significance of the different perspectives to where she finds herself is a moot point. The value of the map metaphor here is that it models a potential, what could be relevant to the investigation of language at a site, not that the particular researcher will necessarily be aware of this.

At the same time, and as was clear from the dilemma faced by the participant in the thought experiment, the researcher's understanding of the site will, in any event, be implicated in how she herself interprets and is interpreted at the site. Dropping down into street view, and here our metaphor parts company with Google, she is not only an observer. She is engaged in the site. There is no place to escape – no 'view from nowhere' (Nagel, 1986, p. 57). In other words, with her understanding of where she finds herself only secured through and grounded in mutually interpretive participation at this site, there are no ways of thinking that could enable her to escape the bounds of her engagement in the site without the risk of losing the capacity to warrant claims about it (Crichton, 2018b).

The upshot is that the researcher is now faced with a predicament: her questions may be initiated by her, but the answers will depend at every point on how she engages with the site and on the analytic perspectives that she brings to bear on this engagement. Or, to summarise this in a way that more closely foreshadows MPA, any attempt to find answers to her questions will be necessarily interdependent and reflexive, emerging through the nature of her engagement in the site at the confluence of mutually-imbricated analytic perspectives. It was the challenge of how to address this predicament for Applied Linguistic research in an accountable way that was the impetus to the development of MPA.

The force of this challenge and its implications for ontology and methodology were identified by Candlin (1997), who observed that:

> What emerges is a requirement for a parallel and complex interdiscursivity of analysis, matching the interplay between the macro and the micro, the actual and the historical, the ethnographic and the ethnomethodological, the interactively sociolinguistic and the discoursal and above all acknowledging the need to offer explanations of why rather than merely descriptions of how. (p.xii)

This characterisation of the challenge should be understood in light of Cicourel's (1982, 1996, 2007) call for 'ecological validity' that Cicourel contrasted with the term 'quality control'. The latter refers to ways of safeguarding reliability and validity in data collection and analysis methods. Cicourel used 'ecological validity' to focus on the usually unacknowledged ways in which research processes shape and are shaped by the tacit knowledge of researchers and participants. Again in 1996, he defined it as referring to whether data gathering and analysis methods are 'commensurate with routine problem solving and language use in natural settings' (p.221).

Throughout, Cicourel has emphasised that, in meeting the requirement for ecological validity, researchers need to acknowledge that both researchers' and participants' tacit knowledge necessarily and reflexively shapes how they understand the relevance and coherence of data collection, analysis and findings. To explain how this knowledge shapes peoples' understandings both of the context studied and of the context of the study itself, he (1992) developed the notion of 'interpenetrating contexts' to capture how tacit knowledge and the decisions it informs in one context are developed in and shaped by other contexts. He emphasised that 'context' in this sense is multiple, made up of 'local and more abstract senses of culture or social organization' involving 'multiple ethnographic and/ or organisation settings and informants' (1992, p.305). These types and layers of context may be interrelated in numerous ways. They 'interpenetrate' each other because 'all social interaction and/or speech events presuppose and are informed by analogous prior forms of socially-organized experiences' (1992, p.308). This

Chapter 2. The Multiperspectival Approach to Applied Linguistic research   15

includes the practices associated with research, which are themselves situated within these interpenetrating contexts.

Cicourel's account of the interpenetration of contexts is drawn closer to the predicament our imaginary researcher faces when combined with Fairclough's (1992, 1997) account of 'interdiscursivity'. Drawing on the work of Bakhtin (1986) and Kristeva (1986), Fairclough emphasizes the ways that social practices and their constituent texts are mutually shaping, drawing on, and drawn on by each other. Both Cicourel and Fairclough have emphasised, from their different theoretical orientations, that these relations are central to understanding language-focused research, in which the researcher – her practices and her language – is necessarily implicated in multiple contexts along with the participants. For Fairclough (1997) this implication is an unavoidable consequence of his account of intertextuality because:

> a text is open-ended – we cannot claim to exhaust all possible links between a text and other texts, or genres and discourses, and making these links is manifestly interpretive because it depends on our sociocultural positioning and knowledge.
> (p.10)

Like Cicourel's notion of interpenetrating contexts, interdiscursivity refers to how communicative contexts – in Fairclough's case, and here again relevant to MPA, understood as discursive practices – draw on and enter into each other, and how these interrelations shape and are shaped by other contexts.

In summarising the ontological and methodological challenges represented by the researcher's predicament, Candlin (1997, p.xii), states:

> The issue then immediately arises of how to capture these distinct methodological discourses in a workable program of research, not merely harmonising the different discourses but actively making use of their distinct epistemologies and modes of practice to enrich and expand a grounded analysis.   (p.xii)

To operationalise this 'multi-perspectived' (Candlin, 1997, p.xiv) approach to discourse analysis, Candlin (1997, p.xiii) called for a 'reflexive methodology', in which the research process involves the 'triangulation of the analysed data with the participating sources of that data' requiring that a 'research alliance be forged between the analyst and the [participants]'.

No single methodology will be able to match the demands of such a program. Rather, it requires the engagement of researcher and participant expertise, brought to bear on the integration of multiple methodologies in seeking to make visible and connect the different perspectives that may be relevant. Such an approach will not be limited to particular theoretical positions or methodologies but will be open to and able to bring into play multiple theoretical and methodological orientations depending on relevant and emergent understandings of the research site under scrutiny.

3. Methodological orientation

3.1 Principles and affordances

Figure 2 models MPA. In the Venn diagram, to the left side, the inclusion of the researcher's perspective underscores that the research process emerges through collaborative engagement between the researcher and the participants, shaped by the researcher's decisions around the other perspectives. Each of the overlapping circles represents a distinctive but mutually implicating perspective, all of which are relevant to the investigation of practices at a particular site. The mutuality of these perspectives is indicated by their convergence at the centre of the circles. The different perspectives suggest but do not mandate cognate methodologies – explained below – that may be brought to bear in the investigation. In addition, the overlaps between them highlight the interdiscursive nature of research that seeks to combine these perspectives in the exploration of a particular site.

There is no primacy among the perspectives. What is required is that all the perspectives are – potentially at least – active and interactive, and no perspective is *a priori* subordinate to any others. Also, the ordering of the perspectives in the diagram does not imply a particular chronological sequence but rather the topography of a study, which is open to being iterative and exploratory, not linear.

Where researchers decide to enter MPA will vary in relation to particular sites, to the particular research questions being addressed, and to the emergent understanding of the researcher, but no perspective is prime. Thus, MPA naturally involves a mixing of methodologies and data appropriate to the perspectives in question. What is central is that all of the perspectives need to be 'on the table': available and potentially or actually engaged in an ongoing and mutually-informing way. As Crichton (2010) explains:

> The perspectives are contingently engaged and 'in play'. This means that... the resources drawn on to operationalize the perspectives are held lightly, are responsive to incoming data and analysis, and are open to findings that emerge from the ongoing interplay between the perspectives. (p. 34)

The key point here, as foreshadowed by the overlaps among the circles in Figure 2, is that these methodological selections are not pre-set by or exclusive to particular perspectives. Rather, they are chosen in light of which selection the researcher deems best able to capture particular perspectives and how these choices ecolo-

Chapter 2. The Multiperspectival Approach to Applied Linguistic research

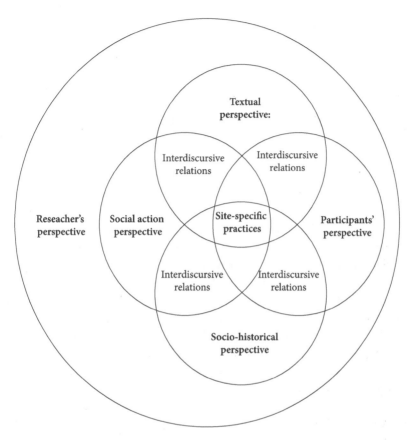

Figure 2. Modelling MPA (adapted from Candlin & Crichton, 2011b, p. 9; Crichton, 2010, p. 34)

gise with her decisions around the other perspectives, given her ongoing engagement with and evolving understanding of the site. In other words, in order to decide on how to operationalise the perspectives as a whole, the researcher needs a sufficient understanding of the site, guided by MPA as a heuristic, to determine how she will set out to prioritise and explore each perspective and in what configuration with the other perspectives. This is a matter of ongoing discovery, the aim being to learn what the research potential of the site will be, the processes that this implies for the research, and the procedures by which it can be realised. This principled flexibility and openness reflect the guiding priority of MPA to 'start with the site' with all options on the table, but to be narrowed through engagement with the site. In effect, MPA provides that table.

We now focus on each of the perspectives in turn, starting with that of the researcher, followed by the participants', textual, social action, and socio-historical perspectives.

3.1.1 The researcher's perspective

The inclusion of the researcher's perspective, at the left of Figure 2, acknowledges the researcher's accountability for the ecological validity (Cicourel, 2007) of the study. This perspective is reflected in the need to explain the researcher's 'motivational relevancies' (Sarangi & Candlin, 2001) and the 'practical relevance' (Roberts & Sarangi, 1999) of the study. Both notions draw attention to the researcher as simultaneously a focus and a shaper of the research. Different researchers with distinct interests, research purposes, understandings of the research context, and research backgrounds will operationalise MPA in different ways, giving different weightings to the perspectives. And this, in turn, will mean that researchers and participants will be brought together in different modes of collaboration depending on their relationship to, and engagement in, the research and practice agenda at the site. Both researchers and participants have motivational relevancies, which will need hermeneutically to be harmonised around how each understands the relevance of the research (Roberts & Sarangi, 1999). The upshot is that the researcher's role in shaping the research is exploratory, site-sensitive, and reflexive: always open and prepared to adjust and refine her assumptions and agenda in light of her developing understanding of the site and its research potential, with a view to bringing into play and mutual engagement all relevant perspectives through the selection, integration, and corroboration of concomitant data and methods.

3.1.2 Participants' perspective

At the right-hand side of Figure 2, the participants' perspective meets the need to develop a shared understanding of the world of the people being studied. The aim here is to account for participants' interpretations of what it is that is going on (Goffman, 1974, p.9), specifically in relation to their interpretations of relevance to the focus of the research (Sarangi & Candlin, 2001). This emphasis meets the need to acknowledge the subjective experience of participants, seeing the world as they see it, understanding its meaning in terms of the meanings it has for them, as 'forged out of what [each participant] perceives, interprets, and judges' (Blumer, 1966, p.542). The perspective is one that needs critical examination because people do not determine the limits of the world that they experience or the conditions that give rise to it, nor are they aware of the contexts outside their own experience; that is, they are unaware of the 'strangeness of an obstinately familiar world' (Garfinkel, 1967, p.38). As mentioned above, the perspective may be explored by means of any number of methodologies, drawing, for example, on journaling, think-aloud, or narrative research and associated methods. In other words, the researchers and participants are 'co-explorers' in this process.

3.1.3 *Textual perspective*

This perspective focuses on accounting for the resources drawn upon by participants to create meaning. The perspective emphasises text as a social semiotic system, potentially including semiotically-oriented (see, for example, Jewitt, 2009; Kress & Van Leeuwen, 2006; Van Leeuwen, 2008), and 'instrumental' (Duranti & Goodwin, 1992) methodologies which emphasise how language is meaningful within the contexts in which it is used. Examples include texts as conventionally understood, such as advertisements, legal documentation, and news articles, as well as transcripts of interactions, interview data, and journal entries. Any of these might, of course, also simultaneously or alternatively be interpreted under the auspices of one or more of the other perspectives, as exemplified in the following chapter. Mindful of the emphasis on discovery in making methodological selections, this perspective may invoke a range of methodologies and associated methods, including but not restricted to narratology, intertextual analysis, text and genre analysis, corpus analysis, functional linguistics, metaphor analysis, and pragmatics.

Here, as with the other perspectives, while the textual perspective may offer itself as a ready home for any of these methodologies, these are only initial, potential options available to a researcher; others may emerge as more suitable and any of them could arise as relevant to operationalising any of the other perspectives.

3.1.4 *The social action perspective*

The social action perspective meets the need to investigate those features of practices at the site which are typically unnoticed by participants because they are routine and taken for granted; in other words, hidden in plain sight. The focus here is on interpreting meaning as it unfolds in interaction, how social action, for example, affirms, reproduces, or disputes the interaction order (Goffman, 1983) at the site. The interpretive onus here is on the researcher because, as Garfinkel (1967, p.37) stresses, a large part of the social resources drawn on in interaction goes unrecognised by participants who may be unaware of the 'obstinately familiar world', with the consequence that 'the limits of the social world are not determined by what the participants perceive them to be' (Carter & Sealey, 2000, p.9). The upshot is that no matter the nature of the collaboration between the researcher and participants, the social significance of social action will not be reported as such by participants but will become apparent to the researcher through her broader engagement with the site. The perspective calls to mind methodologies associated with symbolic interactionism (Blumer, 1969; Goffman, 1959, 1981), ethnomethodology (Garfinkel, 1967), interactional sociolinguistics (Gumperz, 1982, 1992, 2001), membership categorization analysis and conversation analysis (Sacks, 1992). However, as emphasised above, while the work in these areas may be suggestive of potentially relevant resources with which to operationalise the social action perspective, they may or may not find relevance through the researcher's engagement with the particular site. And the nature of this engagement underscores the many-sided role required to enact the researcher's perspective, including here that of the researcher as analyst, while at the same time, she needs to be ever-mindful of the potential, mutual relevance to the research of all the perspectives and their associated data and methods of analysis.

3.1.5 *The socio-historical perspective*

This perspective brings into play the institutional and broader socio-historical conditions – the 'already established character' of social practices and the psycho-social positioning (and also histories) of participants. These conditions cannot be deduced only from how participants experience and engage in the site and associated practices (Layder, 1993). Rather, any such enquiry needs to draw on resources that address how institutions and societies are themselves reproduced over time; in other words, how they have 'an ongoing life that is identifiable apart from specific instances of situated activity' (Layder, 1993, p. 90). As with the other perspectives, guided by the need for ecological validity highlighted under the researcher's perspective, the onus is on the researcher in the selection of data, methods, and analysis in light of her emerging understanding of the site. The socio-historical perspective, then, is suggestive of methodologies including, but as with all the perspectives, not mandated nor restricted to, those associated with document, archival, policy, and historical studies. As with the examples of data identified under the textual and social action perspectives, the data implied here are provisional and interpreted under the auspices of the socio-historical perspective for their potential to evidence features of the social and historical context relevant to a particular site. However, these data could also be interpreted – potentially within the same study – under, for example, the textual perspective for narrative, structural, rhetorical or discourse features. Under the social-historical perspective, the exploration of societal and temporal horizons is open to social-theoretical resources that foreground that 'the meaningful character of human action is given above all by its saturation with language' (Giddens, 1994, p. 3). Ready examples include the work of Geetz (1973, 1983), Giddens (1984, 1991), Bourdieu (1990, 1991), Foucault (1979, 1989, 1980), and Habermas (1984, 1987). Moreover, from different standpoints, their work points to themes that are central to understanding the contemporary world, including potentially the lives of participants and researchers, and therefore to operationalising the socio-historical perspective and, in turn, MPA as a whole (Candlin & Crichton, 2013a; Crichton, 2004, 2010, 2018a).

3.2 Types of research questions addressed by MPA

This thematic connection provides a segue to the next section, in which we explore research agendas and questions that MPA opens up and supports.

The focus in MPA on multiple data sets representing different perspectives, and the requirement that these are approached using different methodological resources, presents a significant challenge for the researcher. This can appear to be a daunting agenda, especially at the outset of the research. In order to identify and warrant research questions and agendas that can initiate and orient such a multi-layered analytical process, Candlin and Crichton (Candlin & Crichton, 2011b, 2013a, 2011c, 2013b; Candlin et al., 2016; Crichton et al., 2016) have recommended a focus on themes of mutual relevance to participants and researchers, along the lines of Roberts and Sarangi's (2005) 'focal themes' and Layder's (1998) notion of the 'orienting concept'. The value of such orientating themes has been previously recognised in both social science and discourse analytical research. As Layder (1998) explains, they can provide a heuristic anchorage point to provide the researcher with theoretical guidance and methodological direction in the preliminary stages of a multi-strategy study.

In MPA research, orienting themes are, as it were, 'lenses' that are tentatively held. As such, they may be differently and emergently understood, invoked, and interrelated in informing a research agenda in different sites of engagement. Moreover, they may become more or less salient as the understandings of researchers and participants coalesce around a particular theme or themes and associated questions. Through this process, further thematic foci and questions may emerge, forming what Candlin and Crichton (2013a), in an extended discussion that takes as an example the theme of 'trust', term a 'conceptual framework', in which 'the concepts within the framework may be potentially referenced to each other and interconnected in different combinations in particular sites of engagement' (p. 10).

As we illustrate in the companion chapter to this, reporting on a study oriented around the theme of 'creativity' (Hocking, 2011, 2018), such themes can not only provide a means for both commencing and configuring the complex, dynamic and explorative process of multiperspectival research, but also a basis for developing the theoretical framework through which the discursive interdependence of the textual, social action, socio-historical, and participant and researcher perspectives can be explained.

The following examples draw on the illustrative themes of 'capacity' and 'risk' to outline issues and questions that such orienting themes may raise for determining and activating a research agenda in so far as these themes are relevant to particular sites of research.

> An orientation to the theme of 'capacity' may invoke questions of measurement and standards against which (in)capacity and (dis)ability are judged. The theme directs attention to the sources of such methods and how they are themselves constructed, implemented and evaluated; how they inform further practices and judgements and for what purposes; what modes of reasoning and argument are drawn upon; whether they are tacit/explicit; how and why they are understood by, and what the consequences may be, for the various participants.
>
> (Candlin & Crichton, 2011b, p.12)

> An orientation to 'risk' foregrounds the ways in which uncertainty is calculated and perceived and the demands this makes on trust and trustworthiness; how risk is variously represented in relation to categories of responsibility and liability, advantage and disadvantage, costs and benefits, profit and loss, threats and security; the types of evidence and modes of argument and explanation in terms of which such risks are evaluated, the implications that are drawn and actions that they justify in relation to individuals and groups, and the institutional, professional and interpersonal discourses associated with the management of risk and the relationships between these at and across particular sites, synchronically and diachronically.
>
> (Candlin & Crichton, 2013a, p.10)

Extended examples of this use of themes to orient individual studies as well as larger scale research agendas include 'risk' (Crichton et al., 2016), 'trust' (Candlin & Crichton, 2013b), 'deficit' (Candlin & Crichton, 2011c), 'commercialization' (Crichton, 2010, 2018a), and 'creativity' (Hocking, 2018)

3.3 Procedures of data collection and analysis

As emphasised above, the data collection and analytic procedures adopted for a particular study will depend on relevant and emergent understandings of the research site under scrutiny. These procedures largely concern ways of operationalising MPA in relation to a given site, in particular *warranting* the integration of the perspectives together with particular methodologies (Crichton, 2018b). Once we begin with a focus on the site, rather than on an *a priori* selection of one or more methodological or analytical models, this question of warrants becomes imperative.

The understanding that guides the answer to the question of warrants will be tentative and lightly held, open to revision in light of incoming data, and dependent on collaborative interpretation among researchers and participants. This approach can be demanding, raising what Sarangi (2007) has identified as 'the analyst's paradox', the problem of how the researcher can align her interpretations with those of participants without either having to become a faux participant or, if not, being irrelevant to their world. Achieving this 'mutuality of perspective' (Sarangi & Candlin, 2001) among researchers and participants is a particular

Chapter 2. The Multiperspectival Approach to Applied Linguistic research 23

challenge because 'achieving a reciprocity of perspectives is not only a matter of mutualising view and stance, it is also a matter of (re)vitalising what is necessarily an ecology' (Candlin, 2002, p.5).

Key to meeting this challenge is an orientation to research central to MPA that starts with the site. This foregrounding of the site of research underscores the need for accountability and sensitivity to the different interpenetrating contexts (Cicourel, 1992) and participant perceptions that localise and situate any particular instance of language use, that is, it acknowledges the need for 'ecological validity' (Cicourel, 2007).

In taking up this orientation, the researcher has, in effect, a license to be playful, in a principled way, engaged on a research pathway that invites constant entertaining of and to-ing and fro-ing between methodologies and perspectives. What transpires on this pathway, what choices are made, and where it ends depend on the character of collaboration the researcher achieves among herself and participants, in turn depending on their relationship to, and engagement in, the research and practice agenda at the particular site. In line with the foregrounding of ecological validity under the researcher's perspective, the data collection and analysis procedures selected for each perspective and their integration, warranting and corroboration will depend of the exigencies of engagement by the researcher at the particular site (see, for example, Candlin & Crichton, 2011a). A detailed explanation and illustration of the potential data collection process and analytical procedures is provided in the following chapter.

3.4 Ethical issues

MPA is not associated with specific ethical issues regarding participants in so far as it does not prescribe in advance particular methodologies or modes of engagement with participants. That said, we take a little time here to underscore the ethical implications of MPA because these bear on the thinking behind MPA and on the role foreshadowed for the researcher. The key point here is that MPA highlights the ethical nature of Applied Linguistic research *per se*. This is because MPA places an ongoing onus on the researcher to keep open, tentative, and mutually engaged and in play multiple perspectives and methodological choices according to her emergent understanding of the particular site. This ongoing need to probe, test, and explore her understanding against that of participants and her experience of the site more broadly is ethically accountable. The issue is that using language with or about others in any context, including practices associated with research, necessarily involves taking decisions and actions based on judgments about those others; and to judge another is *per se* an ethical matter. Lambek (2010) in arguing the implications of this point for research ethics, clearly identifies the issue:

> If practice is rendered possible and meaningful through performative acts, practice also inevitably reveals the inadequacy of such acts and the limits of criteria and descriptions, especially their vulnerability to skepticism, and hence the need to start anew. Ethics, then, is not only about executing acts, establishing criteria, and practicing judgment, but also about confronting their limits, and ours.
>
> (p. 39)

The focus here is less on the ethicality of functions that we may accomplish using language than on that of the language that we use in accomplishing these functions. For example, a question can be raised about the ethicality of a request or the judgements that are implied by the language in which the request is made. It is the latter that we are interested in here. On this, Lambek (2010) explains:

> We may find the wellsprings of ethical insight deeply embedded in the categories and functions of language and ways of speaking, in the common sense ways we distinguish among various kinds of actors or characters, kinds of acts and manners of acting... thus, in the shared criteria we use to make ourselves intelligible to one another.
>
> (p. 2)

As foregrounded in MPA, as researchers, we not only use language with others; the language of others reciprocally constitutes the medium and focus of our collaborations with them. At the same time, we make it our business to make claims about the meaning of language that we use with others. This implies a double accountability for the Applied Linguist, in which we not only make judgements about others, but also make judgements about their judgements. In effect, we are judging judges. As Sarangi (2015), put it:

> If language and discourse are context specific, who owns the description and interpretation of context? In other words, whose categorisation of observed phenomena should prevail?
>
> (p. 32)

What is at stake here? We can distinguish ethical from methodological risks. In both cases, the risks are greater the further our interpretive repertoires diverge from those of our participants. As Sarangi is emphasising, the methodological risk is that without sufficient understanding of our participants' perspectives, we may overreach our interpretive license in, for example, analysing data. In other words, we may risk becoming imposters – or at best faux participants – who judge. But attending to these methodological risks does not, as such, touch the ethical dimension.

What are the implications if we leave ethical considerations out of these judgements? Are we failing to acknowledge an ethical accountability that is particularly acute for Applied Linguistics? Acute because Applied Linguistics' attention to the language of participants and its remit to make claims about meaning in their lives creates quintessentially ethical risks for those involved: for example, trust may be jeopardised, mutual understanding compromised, expertise and experience misrepresented, and identities put on the line.

These ethical concerns are highlighted in MPA, underscoring the importance of the researcher's ongoing mindfulness of her reciprocal relationship with participants, and her accountability to the ecological validity of the study, in warranting her decisions in light of her emerging understanding of the site. As emphasised throughout this chapter and evidenced in the next, how a particular researcher interprets and attends to these ethical accountabilities will depend of how she engages with the exigencies of the particular site of research, while remaining reflexively alert to the ethical consequences of her actions and language for participants, and the ethical complexity that the MPA process brings.

4. Critiques and responses

Though not raised in the literature to date, two questions commonly raised in conferences, research seminars, and supervision are:

- How do you know MPA is exhaustive?
- Isn't MPA just mixed methods research?

The two questions are related. The first reflects a concern that MPA aspires to be all-encompassing: that it seeks to contain all options available to a researcher, the recipe of all recipes. The second question again probes the reach of MPA, but now reflecting a concern that it is more modest than it appears.

On the first question, MPA does not claim fully to encompass or anticipate the conceptual and methodological resources available or set limits on these. As emphasised above, it is best understood as a heuristic: an expansive, site-sensitive, interpretive resource that opens and is open to multiple entry points, to be developed and refined in light of the emergent interests and understandings of particular researchers through their engagement at particular sites.

This leads us to the second question. Clearly, there are affinities between the multi-strategy emphases of MPA and mixed methods research (MMR). Recognising the value of mixing methods as a departure from adherence to traditionally opposing paradigms has significant implications for theory and practice in Applied Linguistics in general. It offers significant opportunities and challenges for both researchers and practitioners.

Current discussion on research principles and methodologies favours a synergistic and pragmatic MMR approach drawing on a range of methods (Riazi & Candlin, 2014). MMR has concentrated on validation – on the use of different methods that can be drawn upon to enrich each other (Riazi & Candlin, 2014) with a focus on what methodologies are deemed appropriate and 'what works' in relation to specific research questions being asked (Tashakkori & Teddlie, 2003).

While fully embracing the premise that mutual enrichment of methods is necessary, from the perspective of MPA, it is not sufficient. Mutual enrichment needs to be located/situated not only in relation to a problem or issue under investigation but in relation to the placement of such issues in relation to the focal site of engagement. This can only be achieved if, from the beginning, we consider the site, which implies that the selection and harmonizing of methodologies and associated data sets reflect the nexus of practice at that site (Candlin et al., 2017).

The starting point is then not the issue of preferring one or another methodologies but how their selection and integration can be warranted and made relevant by consideration of the site. This is not an argument between paradigms. The position of MPA is not so much methodological as conceptual, one not focused on choosing among paradigms but on how to select and harmonise different data sets and their associated methods of analysis into an integrated account.

5.   Conclusions

Bringing multiple perspectives to a research agenda, like any metaphor, essentially engages a conceptual contrast between at least two worlds which has been a central theme of the chapter. We have argued that the visual and orienting metaphors of perspective, mapping and ways of seeing are suited to engage research across the potentially incommensurate worlds of Applied Linguistic researchers and those that are and could be the focus of their research. The device of starting with an unknown world was just to provide a veil of ignorance by which to estrange us from the familiarity of knowing in advance. In this way, we sought to underscore that the worlds of researchers and participants alike can be profoundly and 'obstinately familiar' (Garfinkel, 1967, p. 38) or, of course, unfamiliar or shades between, both to themselves and to each other. It is through this awareness of not knowing, we have argued, that the value of MPA becomes visible, a heuristic that enables researchers to discover – rather than to search – the worlds of their participants, iteratively to learn through this process of discovery, developing warrants and finding themes to bridge these worlds through multiple, mutually-corroborating perspectives.

References

Bakhtin, M. M. (1986). *Speech genres and other late essays* (V. W. McGee, Trans.). Texas University Press.

Blumer, H. (1966). Sociological implications of the thought of G. H. Mead. *American Journal of Sociology, 71*, 535–544.

Blumer, H. (1969). *Symbolic interactionism: Perspective and method.* Prentice-Hall.

Bourdieu, P. (1990). *The logic of practice* (R. Nice, Trans.). Stanford University Press.

Bourdieu, P. (1991). *Language and symbolic power* (G. Raymond & M. Adamson, Trans.). Polity Press.

Brown, G., & Yule, G. (1983). *Discourse analysis.* Cambridge University Press.

Candlin, C. N. (1997). General editor's preface. In B. L. Gunnarsson, P. Linell, & B. Nordberg (Eds.), *The construction of professional discourse* (pp. viii–xiv). Longman.

Candlin, C. N. (2002). Introduction. In C. N. Candlin (Ed.), *Research and practice in professional discourse* (pp. 1–36). City University of Hong Kong Press.

Candlin, C. N., & Crichton, J. (2011a). Emergent themes and research challenges: Reconceptualising LSP. In M. Peterson & J. Engberg (Eds.), *Current trends in LSP research* (pp. 277–316). Peter Lang.

Candlin, C. N., & Crichton, J. (2011b). Introduction. In C. N. Candlin & J. Crichton (Eds.), *Discourses of deficit* (pp. 1–22). Palgrave Macmillan.

Candlin, C. N., & Crichton, J. (2013a). From ontology to methodology: Exploring the discursive landscape of trust. In C. N. Candlin & J. Crichton (Eds.), *Discourses of trust* (pp. 1–18). Palgrave Macmillan.

Candlin, C. N., & Crichton, J. (Eds.). (2011c). *Discourses of deficit.* Palgrave Macmillan.

Candlin, C. N., & Crichton, J. (Eds.). (2013b). *Discourses of trust.* Palgrave Macmillan.

Candlin, C. N., Crichton, J., & Firkins, A. (2016). Crucial sites and research orientations: Exploring the communication of risk. In J. Crichton, C. N. Candlin, & A. Firkins (Eds.), *Communicating risk* (pp. 1–16). Palgrave Macmillan.

Candlin, C. N., Crichton, J., & Moore, S. (2017). *Exploring discourse in context and in action.* Palgrave Macmillan.

Carter, B., & Sealey, A. (2000). Language, structure and agency: What can realist social theory offer to sociolinguistics? *Journal of Sociolinguistics, 4*(1), 3–20.

Cicourel, A. V. (1982). Interviews, surveys, and the problem of ecological validity. *American-Sociologist, 17*(1), 11–20.

Cicourel, A. V. (1992). The interpenetration of communicative contexts: Examples from medical encounters. In A. Duranti & C. Goodwin (Eds.), *Rethinking context: Language as an interactive phenomenon* (pp. 291–310). Cambridge University Press.

Cicourel, A. V. (1996). Ecological validity and 'white room effects': The interaction of cognitive and cultural models in the pragmatic analysis of elicited narratives from children. *Pragmatics & Cognition, 4*(2), 221–264.

Cicourel, A. V. (2007). A personal, retrospective view of ecological validity. *Text & Talk, 27*(5/6), 735–759.

Crichton, J. (2004). Issues of interdiscursivity in the commercialisation of professional practice. (Unpublished doctoral thesis). Macquarie University.

doi Crichton, J. (2010). *The discourse of commercialization: A multiperspectived analysis*. Palgrave Macmillan.

doi Crichton, J. (2018a). Framing a 'community of consumption': Field theory, multiperspectival discourse analysis and the commercialization of teaching. In J. Albright, D. Hartman, & J. Widin (Eds.), *Bourdieu's field theory and the social sciences* (pp. 117–131). Palgrave Macmillan.

doi Crichton, J. (2018b). Transdisciplinary applied linguistics: Issues of perspectivity and transcendence. *International Association of Applied Linguistics Review, 31*(1), 143–148.

doi Crichton, J., Candlin, C. N., & Firkins, A. (Eds.). (2016). *Communicating risk*. Palgrave Macmillan.

doi Crichton, J., & Koch, T. (2007). Living with dementia: Curating self-identity. *Dementia, 6*(3), 365–381.

Dallmayr, F. R. (1991). *Life-world, modernity and critique: Paths between Heidegger and the Frankfurt School*. Polity Press.

Duranti, A., & Goodwin, C. (1992). Rethinking context: An introduction. In A. Duranti & C. Goodwin (Eds.), *Rethinking context: Language as an interactive phenomenon* (pp. 1–42). Cambridge University Press.

Fairclough, N. (1992). *Discourse and social change*. Polity Press.

Fairclough, N. (1997). Discourse across disciplines: Discourse analysis in researching social change. *AILA Review, 12*, 3–17.

Foucault, M. (1979). *Discipline and punish: The birth of the prison*. (A. Sheridan, Trans.). Penguin.

Foucault, M. (1989). *The archeology of knowledge*. Routledge.

Foucault, M. (Ed.) (1980). *Power/knowledge: Selected interviews and other writings 1972–1977*. Pantheon Books.

Garfinkel, H. (1967). *Studies in ethnomethodology*. Prentice-Hall.

Geertz, C. (1973). *The interpretation of culture*. Basic Books.

Geertz, C. (1983). *Local knowledge: Further essays in interpretive anthropology*. Basic Books.

Giddens, A. (1984). *The constitution of society*. Polity Press.

Giddens, A. (1991). *Modernity and self-identity*. Polity Press.

Giddens, A. (1994). Introduction. In A. Giddens, D. Held, D. Hubert, D. Seymour, & J. Thompson (Eds.), *The Polity reader in social theory* (pp. 1–8). Polity Press.

Goffman, E. (1959). *The presentation of self in everyday life*. Doubleday Anchor.

Goffman, E. (1974). *Frame analysis: An essay on the organization of experience*. Harper & Row.

Goffman, E. (1981). *Forms of talk*. Wiley Blackwell.

doi Goffman, E. (1983). The interaction order. *American Sociological Review, 48*, 1–17.

doi Gumperz, J. (1982). *Discourse strategies*. Cambridge University Press.

Gumperz, J. (1992). Contextualisation and understanding. In A. Duranti & C. Goodwin (Eds.), *Rethinking context: Language as an interactive phenomenon* (pp. 229–252). Cambridge University Press.

Gumperz, J. (2001). Interactional sociolinguistics: A personal perspective. In D. Schiffrin, D. Tannen, & H. E. Hamilton (Eds.), *The handbook of discourse analysis* (pp. 215–228). Routledge.

Chapter 2. The Multiperspectival Approach to Applied Linguistic research   29

Habermas, J. (1984). *The theory of communicative actio, Volume one: Reason and the rationalization of society* (T. McCarthy, Trans.). Beacon Press.

Habermas, J. (1987). *The theory of communicative action. Volume two: Lifeworld and system: A critique of functionalist reason* (T. McCarthy, Trans.). Beacon Press.

Hocking, D. (2011). The discursive construction of creativity as work in a tertiary art and design environment. *Journal of Applied Linguistics and Professional Practice, 7*(2), 235–255.

Hocking, D. (2018). *Communicating creativity: The discursive facilitation of creative activity in arts.* Palgrave Macmillan.

Jewitt, C. (Ed.) (2009). *Routledge handbook for multimodal analysis.* Routledge.

Kress, G., & Van Leeuwen, T. (2006). *Reading images. The grammar of visual design.* Routledge.

Kristeva, J. (1986). Word, dialogue and novel. In T. Moi (Ed.), *The Kristeva Reader* (pp. 34–61). Blackwell.

Lambek, M. (2010). Introduction. In M. Lambek (Ed.), *Ordinary ethics: Anthropology, language, and action.* (pp. 1–36). Fordham University Press.

Layder, D. (1993). *New strategies in social research.* Polity Press.

Layder, D. (1998). *Sociological practice: Linking theory and social research.* Sage.

Moustakas, C. E. (1990). *Heuristic research.* Sage.

Nagel, T. (1986). *The view from nowhere.* Oxford University Press.

Riazi, A. M., & Candlin, C. N. (2014). Mixed-methods research in language teaching and learning: Opportunities, issues and challenges. *Language Teaching, 47*(2), 135–173.

Roberts, C., & Sarangi, S. (1999). Hybridity in gatekeeping discourse: Issues of practical relevance for the researcher. In S. Sarangi & C. Roberts (Eds.), *Talk, work and institutional order: Discourse in medical, mediation and management settings* (pp. 473–504). Mouton de Gruyter.

Roberts, C., & Sarangi, S. (2005). Theme-oriented analysis of medical encounters. *Medical Education, 39*, 632–640.

Sacks, H. (1992). *Lectures on conversation, Volumes I and II.* Blackwell.

Sarangi, S. (2007). Editorial. The anatomy of interpretation: Coming to terms with the analyst's paradox in professional discourse studies. *Text & Talk, 27*(5/6), 567–584.

Sarangi, S. (2015). Experts on experts: Sustaining 'communities of interest' in professional discourse studies. In M. Gotti, S. Maci, & M. Sala (Eds.), *Insights into medical communication* (pp. 25–50). Peter Lang.

Sarangi, S., & Candlin, C. N. (2001). 'Motivational relevancies': Some methodological reflections on social theoretical and sociolinguistic practice. In N. Coupland, S. Sarangi, & C. N. Candlin (Eds.), *Sociolinguistics and social theory* (pp. 350–387). Longman.

Steinberg, J. (2011). *Bismarck: A life.* Oxford University Press.

Sultan, N. (2018). *Heuristic inquiry.* Sage.

Tashakkori, A., & Teddlie, C. (2003). *Handbook of mixed methods in social and behavioural research.* Sage.

Van Leeuwen, T. (2008). *Discourse and practice: New tools for critical discourse analysis.* Oxford University Press.

CHAPTER 3

Implementing the Multiperspectival Approach (MPA)

A study of art and design communication

Darryl Hocking & Jonathan Crichton
Auckland University of Technology | University of South Australia

This chapter provides a detailed account of the researcher's journey as they employ the Multiperspectival Approach (MPA) to investigate the interplay between communicative and creative practices within a university art and design studio. The chapter identifies the key reasons that attracted the researcher to MPA, the advantages it offered, its impact on their project, its design and findings, and how MPA was implemented. It concludes by considering the issues and challenges that arose in the researcher's use of MPA and how these were addressed. Ultimately, the chapter serves to illustrate the implementation of MPA as a practical ontology and research heuristic for both traditional Applied Linguistic studies and those that go beyond the focus on language education and acquisition.

1. Introduction

With the aim of exemplifying the Multiperspectival Approach (MPA) in practice, this chapter focuses on a study originally conceived as an ethnographically grounded investigation of the "studio brief" genre and its conditions of production and reception (Hocking, 2014, 2018a). In the art and design education context, the studio brief is a two- or three-page document written by lecturers to provide students with the requirements and stimulus for their creative projects. Each new studio brief is typically presented to the students in a brief launch, which involves the elucidation of its more important points, followed by a question-and-answer session. Once they begin developing their creative work, students regularly engage in one-to-one studio tutorials with their lecturers about their work and also attend 'group crits' with a larger group of students. After a certain period, the students present their completed creative works for assessment.

https://doi.org/10.1075/rmal.6.03hoc
© 2024 John Benjamins Publishing Company

The study was primarily motivated by the researcher's experience of working in a foundation-level art and design programme and the questions that arose about the role that these spoken and written interactions played in shaping the students' particular conceptualisation of their creative practices. In the university context, such preparatory courses are designed to introduce students to a range of artistic media, for example, painting, printmaking, photography, sculpture, and installation, in preparation for subsequent specialisation in their undergraduate degrees. The preparatory year, however, is also often the students' first real engagement with the types of beliefs and values that shape, and are shaped by, the institutions of the art world. As a result, an important underlying function of such courses is the socialisation of students towards these institutional conceptualisations so that they successfully pathway, firstly, into an undergraduate degree, and then ultimately into the professional world of the art or design practitioner. In order to examine the complex relationship between these communicative and creative practices, the researcher turned initially towards the methodological resources of genre analysis (e.g., Swales, 1990) used previously in his explorations of the art and design exegesis (Hocking, 2003) and the visual arts dissertation (Turner & Hocking, 2004).

This chapter will begin by identifying the primary reasons why the researcher was attracted to MPA, the impact that MPA had on the project once adopted, and how MPA was subsequently implemented throughout the project. The chapter concludes by reflecting on issues and challenges that arose in the researcher's use of MPA and how these were addressed. In order to capture the decision-making processes of the researcher, however, and to avoid misrepresenting MPA as a passive or quasi-mechanical undertaking, the remainder of this chapter will be presented in the first person (alluding to the first author of this chapter), notwithstanding that this is an artifice with both authors contributing. It is important to note that the site of the study, a university art, and design studio, represents the type of site-relevant institutional or professional domain that transcends those normally associated with Applied Linguistics research, and whose interactional and discursive complexity MPA is designed to address.

2. An overview of the study: The journey to MPA

The ethnographic approach to the analysis of genre, which first informed the study into the studio brief, arose as many of the leading researchers in the field began to consider genre as a situated, social practice, rather than simply as a text or process (Bhatia, 2004; Johns, 1997, 2003; Swales, 1998). Bhatia (2004), in particular, found that the earlier text-based focus of genre analysis was "weak on the processes and procedures of genre participation, the receptivity of genres, and also the factors that make a particular instance of a genre successful. (p.112), and along with Johns (2003) argued that genre analysis should be focused more on "the contextual elements that influence genres" (p.607). One important result of this development is that interviews with those involved in the contexts of a genre's production and reception became a primary source of data for genre analyses.

Taking into account the recommendations of Bhatia (2004) and Johns (2003), among others, interviews with staff and students about the nature of the studio brief, its component parts (e.g., creative requirements, presentation information), and their perceptions of its impact on studio creative practice, were carried out as a crucial component of the ethnographically grounded investigation into the studio brief genre and its conditions of production and reception. Furthermore, and given the initial focality of the studio brief, a larger corpus of brief texts was also collected from other similar programmes from other universities. The analysis began by looking for connections and patterns between the lexico-grammatical, discoursal, and rhetorical components of the studio brief and the responses from staff and students about its function and their engagement with the genre. The studio brief's relationship to the other genres in the studio context (e.g., the brief writing meeting, the brief launch, and the studio tutorial) was also considered.

With reference to the thought experiment in the previous chapter, however, the results of this preliminary analysis, while of much interest, made few useful explanatory connections between the broad fragments of data collected for the study to date. The voices of the different participants, in particular, although they usefully triangulated interpretations about the generic characteristics of the studio brief, appeared to offer much more than was being realised, and attempts to make warrantable claims about the role and meaning of language in the lives of the participants only raised more uncertainty about what was going on in the context of the study. Drawing upon Bhatia (2004), I also conceded that a greater understanding of the wider social and institutional histories surrounding art and design education and practice would be crucial to the study, yet this raised questions about the extent of this wider context; that is, what social and historical situations might be included or excluded as relevant data. Furthermore, and perhaps overshadowing these concerns, were the challenges of how a correspondence between the potentially increasing number of diverse data sets might be established and questions about the types of methodological strategies that might be enacted to achieve this mutuality. It was at this point that I was introduced to the Multiperspectival Approach (MPA) and its practical ontology.

3. Why was MPA used?

In this section, I identify four key areas of MPA which initially attracted me to the approach.

Firstly, the MPA ontology supported and helped me to think through initial observations about the complexity of the studio brief and its multifaceted relationships, not only to the exigencies of the local and broader institutional contexts and the potentially disparate values of the lecturing staff, but to the wider social histories and discourses of art and design education, practitioner practice, and diverse understandings of creativity. Furthermore, in doing so, MPA provided a way of systematising and harmonising this complexity into an accessible and meaningful whole, helping to confirm the relevance of the information that had already been collected for the study, and at the same time indicating areas where certain pieces of the puzzle were missing. In many respects, this ontological insight was akin to making visible and tractable the array of contextual clues that would help guide a researcher towards answering the types of questions introduced in the thought experiment.

Secondly, by aligning the different sets of data collected for the study with different perspectives, the MPA ontology provided insights as to the types of methodological resources with which they might be explored. This prevented the answers to questions from being constrained or distracted by a focus on those analytical resources already familiar to the researcher (i.e., genre analysis) potentially resulting in only a partial understanding of the phenomena at hand. Instead, I was guided by MPA to firstly entertain those methodologies which were potentially relevant to the questions being asked and the information being examined.

Thirdly, and perhaps more importantly, the ontology foregrounded the interdiscursive relationships among the perspectives. The result is that information collected as representing one particular perspective could also be viewed as representing another perspective, and therefore it could be examined from a different angle, using different, and differently combined methodological resources. Again, referring to the thought experiment in the previous chapter, this methodological interdiscursivity acknowledges the potential of each perspective to provide a response to each of the individual questions. "What is this place?", for example, could be partially answered through the accounts of participants, partially answered by analysing the texts found in the site being investigated, partially answered by observing the interactions of participants in the site, and partially answered by examining the social and institutional histories of the site. As a result, it also follows that the responses from the perspectives, each of which represents a cut into the data from a different angle, contributes to a mutually informed and enriched response to each question.

Fourthly, MPA foregrounds a further shift towards problem-driven studies in which attention is drawn towards the exploration of key orienting themes (Layder, 1993) and their underpinning conceptual constructs that occur within the practices and sites that surround such special purpose texts (Candlin & Crichton, 2011a, 2011b). It does not suggest that specific genres used by participants in the situated context are ignored in the analysis, but that instead, they become one of many areas of investigation and discovery. As Candlin and Crichton (2011a, 2011b), have pointed out, genres, rather than necessarily being the focal point of a study, might instead provide one of many entry points into a problem or thematically driven exploration of a domain-specific practice. This shift in emphasis was particularly resonant, as while I was ostensibly focused on the studio brief in the first instance, my concerns were ultimately on the wider role played by language in the facilitation of creative practice.

It should be noted at this point that MPA's focus on multiple data sets, each of which represents a different perspective and is approached using various analytical resources, presents a considerable challenge for a researcher. The use of orienting themes, however, can address this difficulty and help structure the study by providing a number of distinct and bounded areas of focus to facilitate a coherent examination of the site's textual, social action, social-historical, and participants' perspectives (Candlin & Crichton, 2013). As will be discussed in the next section, the study discussed in this chapter was framed by six distinct orienting themes: work, agency, motivation, exploration, ideas, and identity. While these particular themes emerged through the preliminary examinations of the data, they can be established in other ways, for example, a researcher might be required at the outset to address a particular thematic concern. Candlin and Crichton (2013) also offer a set of pervasive and more general-orienting themes for MPA research that are often, though not exclusively, associated with particular domains. These include characterisation, responsibility, identity, relationships, capacity, recognition, agency, and membership. Some of these more general themes, it will be noted, align with the themes mentioned above that framed the study discussed in this chapter.

Enlarging upon these preliminary discussions, the following sections will explain how I used MPA to carry out an analysis of the tutors' and students' communicative and creative practices through interdependent and mutually informing perspectives, each of which was represented by an array of distinct data sets. These data sets include the micro-level discourse of the written texts found in the studio, the situated and emergent properties of the studio interactions, the macro-level discourses of certain social-historical and institutional events in the art world, and the lived narratives of the students and their tutors. The following sections will also exemplify the iterative and abductive process by which each of

4. How was the MPA implemented?

This section provides an exemplification of how I implemented MPA for the study of communication and the facilitation of creative practice in the university art and design studio. It demonstrates the methodological choices made to operationalise the different perspectives and how this process unfolded in response to my emerging understanding of the site. Due to limitations of space, this section represents only part of a much larger analysis (see Hocking ,2011, 2014, 2015, 2016, 2018a, 2018b for a full account).

The preliminary stages were probing and exploratory, typically beginning with the examination of an individual data set that I believed would provide a potentially useful entry point into the study. For this particular study, these initial stages often focused on the textual perspective, and were carried out using the resources of corpus analysis; notably keyword analysis, which has a capacity for identifying the 'presence of discourses' (Baker, 2006, p.121) or the 'aboutness' (Scott & Tribble, 2006, p.79) of a collection of texts.[1] As indicated in the previous section, an important aim of this initial stage of the study was the identification of orienting themes. If an orienting theme of potential interest emerged, it was used to provoke other points of entry into the data, involving either data sets from the same or different perspectives and deploying relevant methodological tools. This procedure was continually repeated, generating emergent findings which were scrutinised alongside existing findings in order to augment or extend the ongoing analysis. As with all actions in MPA, the researcher's evolving perspective, including their prior theoretical assumptions and knowledge of extant theoretical concepts, shape the recognition and choice of certain themes, as well as decisions regarding methodological choice and application.

---

1. Keywords are words in one corpus whose frequencies are identified as unusually high when referenced with the frequencies of words occurring in another corpus; usually a reference corpus which provides a general benchmark of what is considered normal within the target language community. Reference corpora can be easily located in online corpus tools such as Sketch Engine or downloaded from relevant websites. For this study, a one million word New Zealand reference corpus was used, as was a 37,000 word Professional Brief corpus, developed by the researcher using professional briefs located online. McEnery et al. (2006) provide useful information on using reference corpora and building DIY corpora.

In an example of this process from the study, an initial keyword analysis of a 36,605-word corpus of 33 studio briefs collected from four different universities (see Table 2), drew my attention to the cognates *work* (freq. 333), *works* (freq. 68), and *working* (freq. 96). Since the noun *work* is habitually used to refer to the art or design artifact, the keyness of these cognates was not, in the first instance, considered of particular significance. However, a subsequent concordance analysis of *work, works*, and *working* in their immediate textual context found that they were frequently used in the studio briefs as material processes to construe successful creative practice in the studio as demanding a degree of physical labour. An example of one of the concordance tables produced for this part of the analysis is reproduced in Table 1. The table shows concordance lines from the studio brief corpus containing the gerund *working*.

Table 1. Concordances with working, semantically related to the habit and routine of working

1	will form a regular part of your	working	life formulating a
2	Working in Studio. July 27 – 9am start	working	in studio Wk 3: Aug 1
3	12.30 Lunch Self Directed: Continue	working	10.00 – 12.00 Drawing
4	duration of this project you will be	working	individually on site
5	will need:- appropriate clothing for	working	at the beach. – wet
6	pieces of masking tape Exercise:	working	within the given time
7	the importance of understanding good	working	Habits – to develop an
8	thoughts 4) To simply get everyone	working	on something. After

It became clear from the concordance analysis that the brief constituted art and design production as habitual, routine-based, and occurring in often predesignated and concentrated time periods. Furthermore, and as seen in Table 1, I found that the students were routinely required to be *working* on something, rather than *creating, developing*, or *generating* art and design; that is, it was expected that the process of labour was actively taking place.

In short, from my initial location at the textual perspective the concept of 'work' began to emerge as a potential orienting theme. To expand this preliminary exploration, and due to its close proximity to the textual perspective of the studio brief genre, I then decided to move to the social action perspective. Here, I would be able to venture further into the landscape of the site by looking at the tutors' interactions in the brief writing meeting. The analytical resources of linguistic ethnography (Copland & Creese, 2015; Rampton, 2007) were considered the most appropriate to explore for this data set from this perspective. Linguistic ethnography draws upon the resources of conversation analysis, but includes an ethnographic focus on the socio-cultural contexts and personal experiences that participants bring to, and take from, the communicative encounter. Keeping the initial observations from the textual perspective in play, I found that through the unfolding interaction of the brief writing meeting, the tutors discursively co-constructed successful student creative practice as involving 'a lot of work'. This could be seen in an extract from the study where the students' tutors are discussing the number of individual creative artifacts that students will need to produce to constitute an acceptable output for their final assessment, and how this requirement will be written into the studio brief (Extract (1)).

Extract 1. First brief writing meeting

```
1    Mike: you can you can then judge on their performance
2          [can't you
3    Anna: [mm mm
4    Mike: and, and the amount of engagement
5          that was required
6    Anna: yep
7    Mike: within what they do present↑
8          it might only be two or three pieces in the end
9    Anna: mm mm
10   Mike: but if it involves you know-
11   Anna: a lot of work
```

As I examined the first of two brief writing meetings recorded as data for the study,[2] it became clear that the number of individual creative artifacts that the tutors believed was necessary for the students to complete for their assessment shifted first from 20 to 12, and then to the two or three indicated in Extract (1). However ultimately, as evidenced in line 11, the tutors conceded that the number of works produced by the students was more or less irrelevant, as long as what they produced could be assessed as involving *a lot of work*.

I decided to revisit the textual perspective to see how these discussions might have played out in the studio brief. Here, I was interested in looking at the brief that was presently informing the students work, and in particular the assessment criteria which I believed might provide information regarding the conceptualisation of student creative success. An extract of the first and third assessment criteria can be viewed in Extract (2).

---

2. Each of the periods where students followed a particular studio brief to develop a series of creative works (usually 5–10 weeks) was preceded by a brief writing meeting. In the brief writing meeting, the lecturers collectively developed the brief to be used by the students. Initially, briefs were designed to be used by the entire cohort of students, but as the year progressed, the brief writing meeting involved the development of a separate brief for each of the different student specialisations, e.g., painting, sculpture, design (see Table 2).

Extract 2. Assessment criteria 1 and 3

1 Employs a systematic process of making work, accompanied by processes of visual experimentation and analysis. Uses a variety of media and technical processes appropriate to the work produced. Uses media to explore, develop and communicate ideas/issues being addressed. Produces work that meets the requirement of the brief

3 Develops a good work habit by attending consistently, organising resources (i.e. equipment and materials), and producing work that effectively meets the requirements of the brief. Works cooperatively, with respect for others and observes all Art and Design School protocols.

Drawing upon Systemic Functional Linguistics in order to focus on the structural placement of information, I found that theme of the first clause in the first criterion is *employs*. Although *employs* appears here as a synonym of *use*, the material process has a semantic association with the concept of paid work. This first criterion also concludes with an emphasis on the production of work. The main clause of the third criterion prioritises the view that student creative success occurs through the habitual activity of work. This is defined in the subsequent clause, which foregrounds a requirement for regular studio attendance. As with the verb forms *employs* and *produces work* in the first criterion, *works* is placed in the thematic position of the final sentence of the third criterion. It was clear that these criteria discursively constructed the nature of the students' activity in the studio as work-like, habitual, and orderly.

I then chose to corroborate these emergent findings by moving on to the participant's perspective, where following a qualitative analytical method, salient themes in the interview data were observed. As an example, in the interview with the tutor Anna, our discussion moved to a focus on the nature of creativity. Anna suggested that creativity was very important in arts education, and she initially aligned the concept of creativity with the more conventional discourse of novelty (e.g., Hennessey & Amabile, 1988), which she described as coming from the few students who had something "new to offer". She went on to admit, however, that creativity was a "hard thing to define" and then found it difficult to construct a definition of creativity that was exclusive from the notion of hard work (Extract (3)).

Extract 3. Interview with the tutor Anna

Anna: … some people can be really hard workers and be really good designers, you know, and not necessarily … oh, well, yeah, I suppose you've still got to be sort of quite creative, um, sometimes maybe through the hard work the creativity comes out.

I then returned to the social action perspective and the use of linguistic ethnography, as I wanted to see whether Anna's conceptualisation of creative practice as hard work appeared in her introduction of the new brief to the students in the brief launch (Extract (4)).

Extract 4. Brief launch

1 Anna: um just also wanted to just draw your attention to the fact that umm
2   if you are doing one area: . rather than another
3   it doesn't mean that you've got more or less work to do:
4   the expectations . for each brief . is about the same↑
5   so we expect you guys to be working really hard .hh

In the extract, I observed that Anna emphasised to the students (*draw your attention to the fact that,* line 1) her belief that workload expectations are equivalent across the different art and design disciplinary areas (*it doesn't mean that you've got more or less work to do,* line 3). This utterance, and the emphasis Anna places on it, perhaps reveals a presupposition that students choose their areas according to perceived workload. Anna then reinforced the creativity as hard work discourse through her subsequent utterance in line 5, where she states that the students are expected *to be working really hard* (line 5).

As I increasingly viewed the site being studied from different perspectives, what started out as an orienting theme eventually became manifested as a discursive construct that shaped the practices of the students and the types of artifacts that they would produce. In order to corroborate this emergent understanding, I decided to move to the socio-historical context, where relevant historical literature was examined to identify the possible socio-historical discursive formations of a creativity as work discourse. Analytically, this investigation of wider socio and historical contexts to identify the discursive production of contemporary phenomena drew upon the discourse historical approach. Among other insights, I found that in the 1960s, a number of influential scholars, including the sociologist Pierre Bourdieu and the literary theorist Pierre Macherey, developed a critique of universal taste and the romantic notion of creativity, suggesting instead that the centrality of the creative artifact or the process of making was overlooked in creativity theories. At the same time, artists in the twentieth century began to move away from the traditional skills and materials associated with mimetic representation (Molesworth, 2003), and turned towards other criteria that would be valued by their audiences. This involved, in part, constituting themselves as workers, and a replacement of the traditional skills of art with activities that represented work. A consequence of this reconceptualisation of creativity as work was that artistic culture shifted from its traditional associations as a pleasurable leisure activity of the wealthy, to an act which could be justified by the notion that work was being done (Steinberg, 1972). This creativity as work discourse still motivates the activities of many artists, as well as the views of many critics and creativity scholars. Representing the latter, for example, I found that Jeanes (2006) bemoans the conscious attempt by many contemporary artists to develop creative outcomes which are conceptually innovative, but lack any hardship or prolonged effort. Instead, she argues that creativity should involve 'a process of personal and perpetual crisis', where the artist is persistently '*working* on the continually evolving, unfinished and "unfinishable" project' (p. 131, italics added).

In order to make explicit the multi-perspectival process of exploration and discovery to a reader of MPA research, it is useful to present details about the relationship between the four inner perspectives, the data collected, the methodological orientation and particular analytical tools used in table form. This process can also provide a useful guide for the MPA researcher. As an example, Table 2 provides a description of the component of study motivated by the orienting theme *work*.

Table 2. The data analysed and methodological foci for each of the perspectives relevant to the orienting theme *work* (Hocking, 2018a)

Perspective	Data	Methodological orientation	Resources
Textual perspective	A 36, 605-word corpus of 33 student briefs The text of the current brief, including extracts from the requirements section and the assessment criteria	Corpus analysis Systemic functional analysis	Keyword analysis Concordance analysis Thematic Structure Transitivity
Social action perspective	Audio recording of the first brief writing meeting, where the tutors co-establish the text of the current brief. The tutors Anna and Mike are participants in this meeting	Linguistic ethnography	Micro analysis of the participants' unfolding interactions.
Participants' perspective	Semi-structured interviews with tutors about the student brief and their studio teaching Semi-structured interviews with students about the student brief and their creative work	Ethnographic analysis	Observation of salient themes in the participants' interactions.
Socio-historical perspective	Theoretical and historical literature regarding creativity and art production	Discourse-historical analysis	An account of wider socio-political and historical contexts to identify how these have shaped the phenomena and context under analysis Thematic analysis

The study of communication in the university art and design studio presented above raises a number of further points.

Firstly, and as indicated in the previous chapter, MPA is dependent on the 'motivational relevancies' (Sarangi & Candlin, 2001) of the researcher. Motivational relevancies refer to the ways in which the researcher's motivations, values, experiences, skills, and knowledge shape the resources they draw upon and the particular paths they take, as they examine their data. As Crichton (2010) points out (and as exemplified throughout this chapter), in addressing ecological validity (Cicourel, 1982) a researcher's motivational relevancies and explanations of the decisions they have taken in shaping the research process should always be made explicit in light of their emergent understanding of the site.

Secondly, as evidenced above, an important aspect of MPA research is its iterative and abductive nature (the constant back and forth movement between data and inference making), and the constant to-ing and fro-ing between the different perspectives, methodological resources, and theoretical frameworks that it involves. As was pointed out in the previous chapter, the perspectives, along with the resources through which they are operationalised are held lightly, and continually kept in play (Crichton, 2010). This means that the MPA researcher is provided the freedom to continually reassess the incoming data and emergent findings, and as a result, make methodological decisions to re-enter, and in some cases expand, previously examined data sets in different and opportune ways. While this freedom – informed by the researcher's motivational relevancies – might potentially result in variation between accounts of a particular research site by different researchers, any particular account will be explicitly warranted and corroborated by the researcher with reference to their engagement with and resultant understanding of the site. In this sense, then, findings are not arbitrary or idiosyncratic, but always justified with reference to their ecological validity.

An iterative, non-linear, and exploratory analytical approach can be observed in other discourse and sociological research. Wodak (2001), for example, has indicated that a key tenet of the discourse-historical approach is its abductive nature, while the sociologist Layder's (1993) multi-strategy approach attempts to capture 'the "textured" or interwoven nature of different levels and dimensions of social reality' (p.7). For Layder, this is achieved through the application of a flexible research model which, while grounded in methodological systematicity, encourages discovery and theory construction instead of conventionally rigid processes of data collection, analysis, and presentation.

Thirdly, the implementation of MPA described in this chapter only refers to one of the six orienting themes, work, that emerged from the analysis of communication in the university art and design studio. The other five orienting themes, as indicated, were agency, motivation, exploration, ideas, and identity. These are represented in Figure 1, in a manner that captures their interdependency. Furthermore, and as was discussed with the analysis of *work*, the study concluded that these six orienting themes represent an intersecting network of historically formed discourses that facilitate creative practice and constitute the nature of creativity in the educational context. Although not a focus of this chapter, data collected from the professional context was also included in the study, and I found that these discourses remain present in the practices of creative professionals long after they have completed their studies at the type of institutional context identified above.

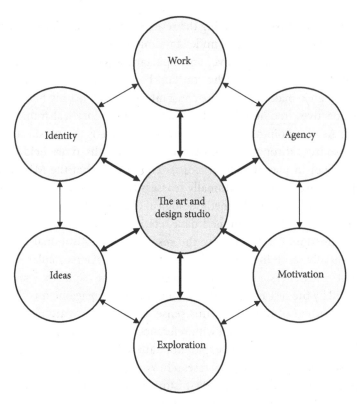

Figure 1. The orienting themes forming the analytical framework for the MPA study of communication in the university art and design studio (Hocking, 2018a)

In order to provide insights into the other components of this study, and the methodological interdiscursivity not specifically captured in this chapter, Table 3 provides a suite of analytical resources used for each of the orienting themes and perspectives (Hocking, 2011, 2015, 2016, 2018a). It can be seen from the table that a particular analytical resource is not necessarily limited to the exploration of a particular perspective.

Finally, and as indicated in the previous chapter, a focus of MPA involves identifying the practical relevance (Roberts & Sarangi, 1999) of the research to the participants, and for the site in question. To address this concern, I would suggest that as an art and design tutor, an awareness of the socio-histories of the creativity as work discourse helped me to understand, at least in part, certain complications that I had observed in the foundation year university art and design course. First of all, the creativity as work discourse, often competed with discourses of a more traditional nature that many of the students had previously encountered and subsequently internalised. This was evident in other data collected for the study,

Table 3. Suite of analytical resources used for each of the orienting themes

Perspectives	Orienting themes					
	Work	Agency	Motivation	Exploration	Ideas	Identity
Textual	Corpus analysis systemic functional analysis	Corpus analysis Pragmatics	Textual analysis Systematic functional analysis	Corpus analysis Metaphor analysis	Corpus analysis Ethnographic analysis	Multimodal (inter)action analysis
Social action	Linguistic ethnography	Linguistic ethnography Pragmatics	Linguistic ethnography Membership categorisation analysis Multimodal (inter)action analysis		Corpus analysis Linguistic ethnography	Linguistic ethnography Membership categorisation analysis Multimodal (inter)action analysis
Participant's	Ethnographic analysis	Ethnographic analysis	Ethnographic analysis	Metaphor analysis	Ethnographic analysis Corpus analysis Genre analysis	Ethnographic approach to discourse analysis
Socio-historical	Discourse historical analysis	Content analysis	Content analysis	Metaphor analysis Discourse historical analysis	Discourse historical analysis	

where I noticed that students displayed anxiety about their drawing abilities, often because they believed that their tutors were looking for displays of a particular artistic quality, rather than evidence of regular studio attendance and adherence to a particular work ethic, which the tutors believed would facilitate a systematic process of creative development and exploration. Arguably, the work discourse also provided insights into the structure of contemporary studio education, where rather than being explicitly taught skills, students are given a brief and a studio space and are expected to begin *working*. Importantly, I also believe it is difficult to constitute a work ethic as underpinning creative activity in students' minds. Because of the abstract nature of creativity as work, the tutors find it difficult to define exactly what working entails in a way that students might understand. Consequently, and as was also found in my data, the students are constructed by the tutors as lacking motivation. In order to motivate students and facilitate creative action in the studio, they then often resort to what was referred to by the participants in my study as 'the numbers game'; an aspect of which is captured in Extract (1).

The outcome of this instance of MPA research has a number of implications for art and design education. These include making transparent to students, the wider discourses which were found to shape art and design practice, their historical origins and how they are realised in the studio. Alternatively, students could be encouraged to examine how the more problematic aspects of these discourses might be transformed or resisted. As an example, the discourse of exploration, mentioned above as another orienting thematic in the study, entails a taken-for-granted belief in the benefits of unrestrained discovery and scientific pursuit. For some design scholars, however (e.g., Findeli, 2001), the modernist aesthetics of novelty associated with this discourse, and the resulting focus on production as the consequence of design practice, is ultimately an unsustainable practice. Consequently, they seek to "end the fetishism of the artifact" (Findeli, 2001, p. 14). From an Applied Linguistics perspective, this discursive shift might be achieved through the deployment of an ecological or sustainability discourse, one that perhaps involves the conscious use of sustainability metaphors in the writing of student brief and in the studio interactions that follow. As has been pointed out by Goatly and Hiradhar (2016), metaphors can be purposefully replaced or modified to challenge common-sense ways of thinking and facilitate social and ideological change.

5. What were the challenges of MPA, how were they addressed, and what insights emerged?

This section reflects on certain issues and challenges that arose in the implementation of this programme of MPA research and how these were, or might be addressed. Their discussion here provides advice to those interested in using MPA for their own future research.

The first challenge involved the demands of collecting the large and diverse range of data necessary to represent the different inner perspectives. I found that this required a detailed planning stage, one which included preparatory meetings with the different participants and a comprehensive examination of the site of engagement in order to establish what data could be collected, and when and where this could occur. Being something of an 'insider' (Hammersley & Atkinson, 2007, p. 86) and having prior knowledge and experience of the site being investigated assisted this process. As pointed out by Sarangi and Candlin (2003), the benefits of being an insider are multiple, and can include increased trust between researcher and informants, greater access to data, and the provision of 'insights otherwise unavailable to the external researcher' (p.279). Nevertheless, insider status also presents challenges for the researcher who may fail to detect the "the strangeness of an obstinately familiar world" (Garfinkel, 1967, p.38). In addressing these concerns, the MPA ontology firstly provided a valuable practical resource for exploring and mapping out the research terrain, and secondly, its emphasis on an analytical engagement with the different perspectives in an ongoing and mutually informing way routinely drew my attention to what were otherwise taken-for-granted aspects of the site.

Once the analysis was underway, another key challenge involved identifying which data set should be first examined, from which perspective, and using which analytical resources. I found that these decisions were best determined by the relevance of a particular data set or perspective to the study and the other data collected. For the reasons stated at the outset of this chapter, the studio brief was viewed as a text around which the other activities of the art and design studio were centred, and hence I often chose to examine data from the textual perspective of the studio brief as the first analytical stage of the research process. Furthermore, and as was also mentioned earlier, I found that for this particular study, the resources of corpus analysis–in particular, keyword analysis–would provide useful preliminary insights into the data, and consequently assist in identifying orienting themes which were able to help structure the subsequent analysis.

Due to the particular interests or prior experiences of the researcher, key methodological decisions are commonly made prior to the commencement of a research project. However, because methodological choice in MPA is not pre-decided, but referenced to the unfolding MPA research process and emergent understanding of the researcher, a further challenge was the need to be familiar with the range of potential methods that could be invoked for both data collection and analysis. To address this issue, I found it necessary to review methodological approaches with which I was less acquainted. This often occurred throughout the research process as new places for exploration and discovery became apparent. Importantly, as indicated in Table 2, I realised that MPA was oriented less to the wholesale and exclusive importation of methodological traditions, such as conversation analysis, ethnography, or action research, and more open to potentially eclectic configurations of analytic resources (e.g., keyword analysis, transitivity analysis, thematic analysis) drawn from diverse methodologies (e.g., corpus analysis, systemic functional analysis, linguistic ethnography), tailored to the researcher's understanding of the insights emerging from their exploration of the perspectives (see Table 2).

Given that the expanse of data collected from the four inner perspectives can be examined in multiple ways to produce a rich array of findings, another challenge encountered involved establishing the limits of any particular stage of MPA research. This was exacerbated by the dynamic nature of MPA, in that the findings emerging from one perspective impacted upon those from the others, thus constantly reshaping and enriching emergent results. The use of orienting themes provided a set of guiding and hence limiting parameters for the ongoing analysis. For the study discussed in this chapter, I deemed a particular analytical stage more or less complete when a substantial degree of corroboration across the perspectives occurred, and together, the findings began to emerge in the form of a 'coherent overarching story' (Corbin & Strauss, 2008, p.104). In most cases, this process also coincided with a sense that data saturation had taken place.

A final challenge involved capturing the dynamic, multifaceted, and explorative process of the study using the linear conventions of research report writing. While I found it useful at a macro-level to structure the written version of the study around the six orienting themes, it was nevertheless challenging to represent the dynamic process of exploration and discovery that occurred within the context of each thematic foci. I initially considered addressing this challenge by discussing the findings from each of the four inner perspectives in turn; however, this approach did not convey the rich interdiscursivity of the multi-perspectival analysis. Instead, I found that the findings were best captured in written form through a coherent toing and fro-ing between the various perspectives, data sets, and methods, in a manner that captured the emerging narrative of the research process. As represented by Table 2, I also realised that this narrative description could be grounded for the reader using a table that outlined the methodological resources used in relation to the data collected from each of the different perspectives.

6. Conclusions

To conclude, this chapter has drawn upon a study that investigated the relationship between communicative and creative practices in a university art and design studio to demonstrate how MPA can be successfully implemented as a practical ontology and research heuristic for site-specific Applied Linguistics research. In doing so, the chapter has shown how MPA can facilitate the exploration and discovery of the participants' worlds, in a manner that makes explicit the emergent interests, backgrounds, and motivations of the researcher. The chapter has also demonstrated the iterative and flexible nature of MPA and how this enables themes to be explored, related questions to be addressed and methodological decisions made, through a principled and reflexive process of discovery. Finally, the chapter illustrates how Applied Linguistics can open its research horizons, as well as the reach and relevance of its applications, thereby expanding beyond its traditional emphasis on language education and acquisition.

References

Baker, P. (2006). *Using corpora in discourse analysis*. Continuum.

Bhatia, V. K. (2004). *Worlds of written discourse: A genre-based view*. Continuum.

Candlin, C. N., & Crichton, J. (2011a). Introduction. In C. N. Candlin & J. Crichton (Eds.), *Discourses of deficit* (pp. 1–22). Palgrave Macmillan.

Candlin, C. N., & Crichton, J. (2011b). Emergent themes and research challenges: Reconceptualising LSP. In M. Petersen & J. Engberg (Eds.), *Current trends in LSP research: Aims and methods* (pp. 277–316). Peter Lang.

Cicourel, A. V. (1982). Interviews, surveys, and the problem of ecological validity. *American-Sociologist, 17*(1), 11–20.

Candlin, C. N., & Crichton, J. (2013). From ontology to methodology: Exploring the discursive landscape of trust. In C. N. Candlin & J. Crichton (Eds.), *Discourses of trust* (pp. 1–18). Palgrave Macmillan.

Copland, F., & Creese, A. (2015). *Linguistic ethnography: Collecting, analysing and presenting data*. Sage.

Corbin, J. M., & Strauss, A. L. (2008). *Basics of qualitative research: Techniques and procedures for developing grounded theory* (3rd ed.). Sage.

Crichton, J. (2010). *The discourse of commercialisation: A multi-perspectived analysis*. Palgrave Macmillan.

Findeli, A. (2001). Rethinking design education for the 21st century: Theoretical, methodological, and ethical discussion. *Design Issues, 17*(1), 5–17.

Garfinkel, H. (1967). *Studies in ethnomethodology*. Polity Press.

Goatly, A., & Hiradhar, P. (2016). *Critical reading and writing in the digital age: An introductory coursebook*. Routledge.

Hammersley, M., & Atkinson, P. (2007). *Ethnography: Principles in practice*. Tavistock.

Hennessey, B. A., & Amabile, T. M. (1988). The conditions of creativity. In R. J. Sternberg (Ed.), *The nature of creativity: Contemporary psychological perspectives* (pp. 11–38). Cambridge University Press.

Hocking, D. (2003). The genre of the postgraduate exegesis in art and design: An ethnographic examination. *Hong Kong Journal of Applied Linguistics, 8*(2), 54–77.

Hocking, D. (2011). The discursive construction of creativity as work in a tertiary art and design environment. *Journal of Applied Linguistics and Professional Practice 7*(2) 235–255.

Hocking, D. (2014). The brief in art and design education: A multi-perspectival and mixed-methodological study (Unpublished doctoral dissertation). Macquarie University.

Hocking, D. (2015). The use of corpus analysis in a multi-perspectival study of creative practice. In P. Baker & T. McEnery (Eds.), *Corpora and discourse studies: Integrating discourse and corpora* (pp. 192–219). Palgrave Macmillan.

Hocking, D. (2016). Motivation in the tertiary art and design studio: A multi-perspectival discourse analysis. *Text & Talk, 36*(2) 155–177.

Hocking, D. (2018a). *Communicating creativity: The discursive facilitation of creative activity in arts*. Palgrave Macmillan.

Hocking, D. (2018b). Conversation words in art and design practice: A corpus-based ethnography. *Journal of Applied Linguistics and Professional Practice, 13*(1–3), 196–220.

Jeanes, E. L. (2006). 'Resisting creativity, creating the new': A Deleuzian perspective on creativity. *Creativity and Innovation Management, 15*(2), 127–134.

Johns, A. M. (1997). *Text, role, and context: Developing academic literacies.* Cambridge University Press.

Johns, A. M. (2003). Genre and ESL/EFL composition instruction. In B. Kroll (Ed.), *Exploring the dynamics of second language writing* (pp. 195–217). Cambridge University Press.

Layder, D. (1993). *New strategies in social research.* Polity Press.

McEnery, T., Xiao, R., & Yukio, T. (2006). *Corpus-based language studies: An advanced resource book.* Routledge.

Molesworth, H. (2003). Work ethic. In H. Molesworth (Ed.), *Work ethic* (pp. 25–51). Pennsylvania State University Press.

Rampton, B. (2007). Neo-Hymesian linguistic ethnography in the United Kingdom. *Journal of Sociolinguistics, 11*(5), 584–607.

Roberts, C., & Sarangi, S. (1999). Hybridity in gatekeeping discourse: Issues of practical relevance for the researcher. In S. Sarangi & C. Roberts (Eds.), *Talk, work and institutional order: Discourse in medical, mediation and management settings* (pp. 473–504). Mouton de Gruyter.

Sarangi, S., & Candlin, C. N. (2001). 'Motivational relevancies': Some methodological reflections on social theoretical and sociolinguistic practice. In N. Coupland, S. Sarangi, & C. N. Candlin (Eds.), *Sociolinguistics and social theory* (pp. 350–387). Longman.

Sarangi, S., & Candlin, C. N. (2003). Introduction. Trading between reflexivity and relevance: New challenges for applied linguistics. *Applied Linguistics, 24*(3), 271–285.

Scott, M., & Tribble, C. (2006). *Textual patterns: Key words and corpus analysis in language education.* John Benjamins.

Steinberg, L. (1972). *Other criteria: Confrontations with twentieth-century art.* Oxford University Press.

Swales, J. M. (1990). *Genre analysis: English in academic and research settings.* Cambridge University Press.

Swales, J. M. (1998). *Other floors, other voices: A textography of a small university building.* Lawrence Erlbaum Associates.

Turner, J., & Hocking, D. (2004). Synergy in art and language: Positioning the language specialist in contemporary fine arts study. *Art, Design and Communication in Higher Education 3*(3), 149–162.

Wodak, R. (2001). The discourse-historical approach. In R. Wodak & M. Meyer (Eds.), *Methods of critical discourse analysis* (pp. 63–94). Sage.

CHAPTER 4

Multimodality

A systemic-functional semiotic perspective

Yixiong Chen, Csilla Weninger & Fei Victor Lim
National Institute of Education

Multimodality examines how language and other resources (e.g., images
and gestures) are integrated to make meaning for communication. This
chapter aims to introduce two approaches to multimodality from a
systemic-functional semiotic perspective, namely social semiotics and
systemic functional multimodal discourse analysis (SF-MDA), and discuss
their applications in applied linguistics. Specifically, this chapter begins with
an overview of the theoretical underpinnings of the two approaches,
focusing on their shared functionalist origins and the origin's theoretical
and methodological implications. Next, the chapter discusses the affordance
of social semiotics and SF-MDA and highlights data collection procedures
and analytical processes in applied linguistic studies informed by the two
approaches. Finally, critiques of the two approaches are addressed with
multimodal research facilitated by eye-tracking technology.

1. Introduction

The term multimodality refers to a central aspect of human communication
whereby texts convey meaning through multiple ways (i.e., modes) of expression
(e.g., words, images, and gestures). As Korhonen (2010) put it, multimodality captures "the interplay between different representational modes, for instance, between images and written/spoken word" (p. 211). While multimodality has always
characterized human communication (for instance, even in speech, we rely on both
aural and visual cues to express and interpret meaning), it has been made particularly salient due to the explosion of digitally-mediated forms of communication in
the last twenty years. As a result, a new field of scholarship has also emerged to theorize and empirically study the multimodal nature of contemporary communication.

Several approaches are discernable in multimodal research, namely, social
semiotics (e.g., Kress & van Leeuwen, 2001, 2006; Kress, 2015), systemic functional multimodal discourse analysis (SF-MDA) (e.g., O'Halloran, 2004; O'Toole,

https://doi.org/10.1075/rmal.6.04che
© 2024 John Benjamins Publishing Company

2011), multimodal interaction analysis (e.g., Norris, 2004) and conversation analytic approaches to multimodality (e.g., Stivers & Sidnell, 2005). Of these approaches, social semiotics and SF-MDA are closely connected by their roots in linguistic functionalism, and specifically in Halliday's systemic functional grammar (SFG; Halliday & Mathiessen, 2004), although social semiotics draws on a broader disciplinary base that includes interactional sociolinguistics, art history and discourse theories, among others (Jewitt, 2009). By contrast, multimodal interaction analysis is developed from mediated discourse analysis and linguistic anthropology, and thus differs from social semiotics and SF-MDA (Jewitt, 2014b).

This chapter focuses on social semiotics and SF-MDA and their applications within the contexts of language learning (Bezemer & Kress, 2016). First, a brief overview is given to discuss the theoretical underpinnings of the two approaches, focusing on their shared functionalist origins and what that means in terms of theory and methods. Second, the chapter will discuss the types of research concerns and questions within Applied Linguistics that have been informed by social semiotics and SF-MDA, highlighting data collection procedures and analytical processes. Finally, extant critiques of the two systemic-functional semiotic approaches to multimodality will be reviewed and addressed specifically with relevance to Applied Linguistics research.

2. Theoretical foundations

2.1 Multimodality as a functionalist social semiotic inquiry

The theoretical underpinnings of social semiotics and SF-MDA can be characterized as linguistic functionalism (Van Leeuwen, 2005) and the idea of "language as social semiotic" (Halliday, 1978). In what follows, we will explain these two concepts and their epistemological implications and, on this basis, demonstrate how they have shaped the theories and methods of social semiotics and SF-MDA.

Linguistic functionalism postulates that linguistic structure is shaped or even determined by its function emerging from specific contexts (Thomas, 2020). A case in point would be the brevity of expression used to warn someone of an imminent danger (e.g., the utterance "Watch out!" directed to someone under a falling tree). The successful fulfillment of the warning function in that context simply does not allow extended linguistic structure. From an ontological stance, linguistic functionalism thus conceptualizes language as "an instrument of social interaction among human beings used with the intention of establishing communicative relationships" (Dik & Hengeveld, 1997, p.3). Epistemologically, this leads to an analytic orientation within functional linguistics to build theoretical models of language that explicate how linguistic structure "conforms to" contextually embedded linguistic functions (Thomas, 2020, p. 11).

The notion of "language as social semiotic" (Halliday, 1978) entails at least two fundamental conceptions of language and its functions. This is evident in the linguistic theory underpinning the approaches to multimodality examined here, that is, systemic functional grammar (SFG). First, the formulation means that language "arises in the life of the individual through an ongoing exchange of meanings with significant others" (Halliday, 1978, p. 1). That is, language functions in communication via the exchange of meaning. Second, "language as social semiotic" also means that language functions "both as expression of and as metaphor for social process" to make "possible all the imaginative modes of meaning" (Halliday, 1978, p. 3). In other words, language is about meaning and meaning-making with symbols, hence the "semiotic" bit in the formation (semiotics has been used to denote the study of meaning long before Halliday).

The two conceptions have informed the multimodal approaches of social semiotics and SF-MDA. First, the conceptions view language and its social settings as semiotic constructs. Significantly, language is a system of meaning-making resources that enable language users to fulfill social purposes via motivated choices and orchestration of the resources. The "functionally motivated" nature of meaning-making (Halliday, 1978, p. 18) also makes theories built on it fundamentally social, because linguistic functions (i.e., what we do with language) emerge from the social process that language users are embedded in. The social semiotic perspective also means that language is just "one symbolic resource" out of many because meaning can be made via non-linguistic resources such as gestures (Halliday, 1978, p. 4). Furthermore, the conceptions also place meaning at the center of SFG and the multimodal approaches that it informed, because meaning made through motivated choices is used to link three major strata in SFG (i.e., semantics, grammar, and phonology), with semantics or sociosemantics being "the key to the whole system" (Halliday, 1978, p. 40). In other words, SFG, like its functionalist precursors, also uses "meaning as an analytic tool" in the sense that meaning is taken as the starting point to understand structural patterns (Thomas, 2020, p. 28). This, as will be explained in the last section, could be problematic when meaning is interpreted solely from the analysts' perspective, and multimodal meaning reception by the viewers is taken for granted.

It is also important to briefly review here how SFG explains the relation between language and social process since these concepts underpin multimodal analyses. SFG posits that the social and the symbolic (i.e., language, gesture, gaze) are linked via an elaborate system and organized along three metafunctions, namely, the ideational, the interpersonal, and the textual metafunction (Halliday & Matthiessen, 2004). In SFG, a metafunction refers to a "kind of meaning" that emerges from the fulfillment of a social purpose in a specific context (Halliday & Matthiessen, 2004, p. 61). Specifically, the ideational metafunction, which encodes meaning underlying the capacity of language to construct human experience, is aligned to the part of the context that describes "what is going on" (i.e., field). Similarly, the interpersonal metafunction, which encodes meaning related to the social dynamics among language users, is linked to the aspect of context that describes "who is taking part" in a speech event (i.e., tenor). Lastly, the textual metafunction, which provides resources to organize meanings encoded in the previous two metafunctions as a coherent text unfolding in its context, is associated with the aspect of context that describes "how meanings are being exchanged between language users" (i.e., mode). In sum, the metafunctions are projected from three constituents of the context of situation, which reflects the analytical orientation resulting from the functional ontology of language explained above.

2.2 Social semiotics and systemic functional multimodal discourse analysis (SF-MDA)

The tenets of systemic-functional semiotics introduced above have been further developed to answer a fundamental question underlying much of current multimodal research, namely, how meanings are made by multiple semiotic resources. Research in this area has yielded two influential approaches to the study of multimodal communication, namely social semiotics (e.g., Kress & van Leeuwen, 2001, 2006; Kress, 2010) and the systemic functional multimodal discourse analysis (e.g., O'Toole, 2011; O'Halloran, 2005, 2008). In this subsection, we will explain how the scope and goals of these two approaches were shaped by the tenets explained above.

Social semiotics can be conceptualized as a theory of communication modelled on SFG. The modelling is realized through several theoretical constructs. First, the notion of "meaning potentials" was introduced and defined as "semiotic resources available to a specific individual in a specific social context" (Kress & van Leeuwen, 2006, p. 9). The use of semiotic resources, such as images in communication, is therefore not arbitrary but motivated, and the motivation should be "formulated in relation to the sign-maker and the context in which the sign is produced" (Kress & van Leeuwen, 2006, p. 8). Second, the concept of "design" was also introduced to link the "determinative power of cultural forms and social structures" to "individual agency" of meaning-making (Kress, 2000, p. 153). Briefly, design refers to sign-making with "sign-makers selecting modes for making signs and signs complexes that they believe are apt for their rhetorical purposes, given the affordances of the modes chosen" (Bezemer & Kress, 2016). The execution of design necessitates an idealized sign-maker who is aware of accepted social semiotic regularities in a domain and the know-how of transforming and orchestrating existing social semiotic resources for a social purpose (Kress & van Leeuwen, 2001). This idealized sign-maker is later formulated as the Rhetor (Kress, 2010). Third, it was also postulated that multimodal meaning-making is different from communication through language – and this was explained via the conceptual tools of "modes" and "affordance" of modes. Briefly, a mode can be understood as a type of social semiotic resource that is socially shaped and culturally given, such as images and words (cf. Kress, 2014 for in-depth discussion), and affordance denotes the meaning potential of a mode (i.e., meanings that can and cannot be made with a particular type of social semiotic resources). For instance, Kress and van Leeuwen (2006) contrast and compare the narrative process in language and image, where language is better at expressing typological meanings (e.g., the literal meaning of the phrase "he's a good guy") and image at topological meanings (e.g., meanings made by two interactors connected with a double-headed arrow), to underscore the affordance of each mode (p.78). Therefore, when social semiotics is used as an integrating theory for research, the research questions that it addresses are always about "meaning and meaning-making" (Kress, 2015, p.55).

SF-MDA can be understood as an expansion of SFG to account for multimodal communication. The expansion is based on several principles directly informed by SFG, including function, system, and intersemiosis (O'Halloran, 2011; O'Halloran & Lim, 2014). First, SF-MDA inherited the conception of function from SFG and sees language and other semiotic systems as communicative tools functioning to create meaning and structure thought and reality. Because of this conception, SF-MDA uses SFG's metafunctions as blueprints in its endeavour to understand multimodal meaning and their functions. Second, SF-MDA also adopted the conceptions of system from SFG and consequently describes semiotic resources as systems of choices that realize the metafunctions. However, the systems of the linguistic mode explicated by SFG are not always applicable for other modes. As a result, SF-MDA needs to develop or discover systems that are specific to multimodal communication. This need gives SF-MDA three distinctive analytical components, including (1) "describing the systems of meanings for different semiotic resources", (2) "specifying the units of analysis", and (3) "analysing the meanings that arise through semiotic interactions according to context" (Jewitt et al., 2016, p.37). Third, SF-MDA also postulates that different modes of social semiotic resources can interact and combine with each other through systemic choices to amplify meaning potentials (i.e., intersemiosis). The postulated process of intersemiosis has inspired many studies, most of which tend to focus on specific conditions that allow intersemiosis to happen (see, e.g., O'Halloran, 2008; Bateman, 2014).

Social semiotics and SF-MDA share fundamental similarities, which is not surprising given the common intellectual foundation of these two approaches. First, the two approaches started from the functionalist premise of meaning-making as a social practice. Second, they share the conception that functionality is central to language and other social semiotic systems. As a result, both approaches use the three metafunctions of SFG as a unifying platform to understand multimodal meanings arising from the orchestration of semiotic resources. Third, both approaches recognise different meaning potentials with each semiotic resource, and in their co-deployment in a text, the meaning is multiplied (Lemke, 1998).

The similarities notwithstanding, social semiotics and SF-MDA also differ in, among others, analytical orientation. SF-MDA concerns with the "grammatics" of semiotic resources (Jewitt et al., 2016, p.30); that is, it seeks to explicate the realization of functions with different semiotic resources and the structural arrangements in this process. By contrast, social semiotics aims to inform "critical disciplines" where power relations of meaning-makers are of interest (Kress & van Leeuwen, 2016, p.14). The differences in analytical orientation bring about different degrees of granularity in analysis. Due to its interest in the grammatics of multimodality, SF-MDA often offers more fine-grained analysis than social semiotics, which concerns more on broader conceptions such as power and ideologies. Furthermore, the differences in analytical orientation also result in different emphases in the two approaches. To study the agency of meaning-makers and the power relations between them, social semiotics foregrounded the *motivated* nature of meaning-making. This emphasis on motivation is admissible but less emphasized by SF-MDA; indeed, SF-MDA often talks about *systemic* choice in meaning-making. The differences in analytical orientation are also translated into different foci in research practices: while studies informed by social semiotics often demonstrate a salient critical inclination (e.g., Weninger & Kiss, 2013), research based on SF-MDA focuses more on describing the systems and processes of multimodal meaning-making (e.g., Lim, 2021a).

3. Methodological orientation

3.1 Principles and affordances

The fundamental tenets of systemic-functional semiotics also lay the foundation for methodological principles for multimodal research in Applied Linguistics. Firstly, the conception of language as a social semiotic facilitated approaching literacy competence from a meaning-making perspective. Second, language is now seen as just a special case of social semiotic systems, so that literacy involves all forms of semiotic activity (*multi*literacies) rather than just meaning-making with linguistic symbols. Furthermore, the notion of design gave literacy an "intentional" dimension (New London Group, 1996, p.73) as a goal-oriented activity. We can see this in the focus of much multimodal Applied Linguistics research as researchers aim to describe teachers and learners as agentive meaning-makers driven by purposes derived from contexts of communication. Finally, an emphasis by the New London Group on teaching literacy as multimodal meaning-making situated within *authentic* social practices. This emphasis on authenticity in teaching and learning resonates with the general preference of contextualized data in multimodal research.

3.2 Types of research questions addressed by social semiotics and SF-MDA

A defining characteristic of multimodal analysis (whether taking a social semiotic or SF-MDA approach) is its fine-grained analytic apparatus which can be deployed to examine and describe the nuanced processes of situated meaning-making. This focus on meaning and contextualized practices of meaning-making, as pointed out by Kress (2015), unites multimodal research within formal and informal sites of literacy and learning. Within Applied Linguistics, three broad strands of empirical research can be identified; namely, multimodal orchestration of teaching and learning; learners' multimodal meaning-making; and representing multimodal meanings in language learning materials.

The first strand of research utilizes multimodal analysis as a methodology to examine joint meaning-making processes in classrooms, asking how teachers and students draw on multimodal social semiotic resources like image, text, and gesture to co-create knowledge and enact social relations within the language classroom. In a seminal work, Kress et al. (2005) showed how complex pedagogic discourses are realised by choices in the layout of the classroom, the visual display, as well as the teacher's movement and positioning in the classroom space. Lim (2021a) conceived teaching and learning as a multimodal experience, during which the teacher as a designer of learning (Kress & Selander, 2012) orchestrates semiotic resources such as gesture, movement, and language during the lesson. Methodologically, studies, mostly from the SF-MDA approach, propose systems to analyse the range of semiotic resources used by the teacher, such as the teachers' gaze (Amundrud, 2018), gestures (Hood, 2011; Lim, 2021b), and use of space (Lim et al., 2012).

Learners' multimodal meaning-making is possibly the most voluminous body of work within multimodal Applied Linguistic research and is closely connected to the first strand. Research under this rubric encompasses empirical studies that have examined how students make meaning through multiple semiotic modes as part of their learning. Theoretically, such work rests on the expansion of traditional language skills, most notably the "productive" skills of speaking and writing, into the notion of multimodal composing (see, e.g., Bezemer & Kress, 2008; Miller & McVee, 2013). Methodologically, studies typically utilize close or micro-analysis of students' (multimodal) texts as well as embodied action to describe and illuminate the complex process of meaning-making. Often, researchers emphasize the creative and expressive dimensions of learners' (digital) multimodal composing to underscore how literacy as skilful design enables students to not only communicate meaning but also to develop their own voice and identities as writers and composers (see, e.g., Darvin, 2020; Jiang, Yang, & Shu, 2020). Going beyond a focus on linguistic output, these studies draw attention to learners' communicative practices as evidencing an orientation to design, audience as well as the semiotic technologies involved in creating multimodal texts.

The third strand of Applied Linguistic research utilizes multimodal analysis to investigate meaning-making in educational materials. Key questions explored by researchers in this strand revolve around how the representational, as well as pedagogic functions of textbooks, are realized through their multimodal design (Weninger, 2021). This multimodal focus seems necessary given that today's textbooks, particularly those produced by large publishers for global audiences, often resemble magazines full of pictures and stories. Many of these studies utilize social semiotics to analyse what values, people, places, and practices are portrayed (i.e., the ideational metafunction of language and images) and have often revealed stereotypical representations (see, e.g., Chapelle, 2016; Joo, Chik & Djonov, 2020). Others have interrogated the intermodal links between textual and other semiotic modes in language learning materials, often focusing on the interactive meanings (i.e., the interpersonal metafunction) that textbooks' multimodal design engenders; for instance, how text and visuals foster reader engagement and communicate values (see, e.g., Feng, 2019; Teo & Zhu, 2018) or whether text-image connections reinforce denotational meaning or open up opportunities for critical reflection (Weninger & Kiss, 2013; Xiong & Peng, 2021). Uniting all these approaches is the social semiotic principle of viewing semiotic resources in textbooks as meaning potential that can be designed to not only realize language learning goals but also to communicate ideological stances about the world.

3.3 Procedures of data collection and analysis

3.3.1 *Data collection*

All multimodal research is empirical, but there is variation in whether researchers examine only the *output* of meaning-making (e.g., a textbook or a multimodal video produced by students) or whether they aim to capture the *process* of meaning-making (e.g., how two students co-construct meaning multimodally as they navigate a task during the lesson) or whether they do both. The case studies of chapter two illustrate this process versus output focus. But broadly, a key difference in terms of data collection concerns whether some form of fieldwork is required (for examining processes of meaning-making) or whether data can be collected without fieldwork, perhaps utilizing existing databases of student work, a collection of multimodal teaching materials, or online/social media multimodal content. Specific considerations of data collection for each type are detailed in the following chapter. It must also be noted that fieldwork may be physical (such as a language classroom) or virtual; especially with the recent expansion in online or digital learning due to the COVID-19 pandemic, there has been much interest in how learners and teachers negotiate meaning in online spaces multimodally (e.g., Wigham & Satar, 2021)

Apart from deciding whether to study multimodal meanings in a semiotic artefact or in unfolding interaction, basic tenets in the theoretical foundation of social semiotics and SF-MDA will also impact research design. First, as explained in Section 2, social semiotics and SF-MDA seek functional explanations for semiotic expressions; as such, all empirical research will be based on authentic multimodal data, gathered in such a way that rich contextual information about the communicative situation. This will minimally include participants' beliefs and histories, the school, classroom, or community culture, broader societal norms and expectations, but there may be other aspects of context relevant to specific studies).

The second theoretical tenet with methodological implications concerns the analytic focus on modes, their different affordances, and how they interact with each other in the meaning-making process. To capture the interplay between meanings made across various modes, the data should be collected at the granularity that allows "fine-grained analysis to support an account of all the modes that are in use" (Jewitt et al., 2016, p. 136). This is especially crucial for research involving fieldwork where the unfolding process of meaning-making is being described and analyzed. As a result, researchers must carefully plan the means of capturing multimodal data in a way that enables them to describe the multi-party, multimodal co-construction of meaning in a communicative event. For classroom-based research, several video cameras will be needed, and their placement (along with other means of data collection such as audio recording and fieldnotes) must be planned in view of the specific research focus (see the study on embodied teaching in the next chapter). When researchers study multimodal textual artifacts, the key consideration is sampling, which will be discussed through the case study in the following chapter.

Finally, as explained previously, social semiotics and SF-MDA inherited from functional linguistics the limited generalization and the accretional strategy in knowledge production. Consequently, while the quantity and representativeness of data are important considerations, they must be balanced with the quality and depth of analysis. In other words, while research scope will shape whether one analyses a series of lessons (e.g., Kress et al. 2005) or the process of a single student's multimodal composing (e.g., Ranker, 2017), the in-depthness of multimodal analysis typically involves smaller datasets.

Fieldwork is essentially about executing the plan, although contingencies often emerge. In addition, researchers could also benefit from understanding the affordances of data collection and storage means. The typical ways of collecting and storing data for multimodal research include audio and/or video recordings of interaction in context and selection and digitalization of multimodal artifacts such as textbooks. For instance, in classroom discourse analysis that focuses on the interactions between the teacher and the students (e.g., Lim, 2021a), video recording is typically the primary tool of data collection. The value of classroom video recording is in preserving "the temporal and sequential structure which is so characteristic of interaction" (Knoblauch et al., 2009, p.19) and in allowing the researcher analyst to review the video sequence "several times, with sound, without sound, in real-time, slow motion and fast forward" (Flewitt, 2006, p.28). Notwithstanding, video recording must be recognised as only offering a partial and restrictive view of the classroom discourse, as it can exclude other perspectives of the classroom interaction. The massive amount of multimodal data retrieved from a video recording of the lesson adds to this challenge. Thus, in practice, the amount of materials should be guided by the research questions, aims, and approach, along with "more practical questions such as how much time and resource are available" (Jewitt et al., 2016, pp.142–143).

3.3.2 *Data analysis*

The procedures for multimodal data analysis arise from the concern within functional social semiotics with meaning. Social semiotics and SF-MDA share the tendency to see data as "semiotic material residue of a sign maker's interests" (Jewitt et al., 2016, p.74) and, consequently, the general goal to examine the social world represented in the data. The analysis orientated to this goal is often guided by rich descriptions of the context in which the artifacts or interactions were situated (Jewitt et al., 2016, p.74); hence the point above about the need to obtain a deep understanding of elements of context. The analytical process has been likened to the work archaeologists in that analyst aims to reconstruct semiotic practices based on records of past events (Jewitt et al., 2016). This type of analytic approach is also known as abduction which can be defined as "reasoning to the best explanation" (Bateman et al., 2017, p.61).

The analytical process facilitated by abduction is often realized in three iterative phases; namely, data preparation, description, and interpretation. First, data preparation often needs to make the trade-off between depth and breadth of analysis; in other words, between observing and taking account of the infinite semiotic complexity of situated meaning-making and being able to say something about the larger social functions of semiotic activity in a given context. A broad scope, while offering a more inclusive and exhaustive perspective of the data, can be overwhelming for the analyst and reveal only superfluous or cursory insights. On the other hand, an in-depth analysis, while helpful in eliciting more profound observations, can likewise be criticised as being too narrow in focus, thus limiting its applicability. A way to address this conundrum, as Jewitt et al. (2016) suggest, is to "sample the data to select instances (fragments or episodes) for detailed analysis" (p.144). It is also helpful to have a theory of contexualisation to situate the instances of detailed analysis within the context of the lesson and the curriculum. For classroom discourse analysis, Christie's (2002) Curriculum Genre Theory and O'Halloran's (2004) proposal of Lesson Microgenre offer a helpful frame to situate specific instances of the lesson within a Lesson Microgenre and its corresponding Lesson Genre, Curriculum Genre, Curriculum Macrogenre and Curriculum Hypergenre.

The preparation stage also involves transcription, which is a fundamental part of the analysis. In this stage, crucial questions on what to transcribe and how to transcribe need to be considered carefully. Furthermore, transcription involves the translation (Kress, 2010) of dynamic video data, often to words and images, which invariably leads to losses in meaning (Bezemer & Mavers, 2011). As such, it can be helpful to preserve the multimedia format of the data as much as it is practicable. This task can be done with the use of video analysis software such as the Multimodal Analysis Video (MMAV) developed by O'Halloran et al. (2012) or the EUDICO Linguistic Annotator (ELAN) developed by Max Planck Institute for Psycholinguistics (Wittenburg et al., 2006). Researchers have also adopted various ways of representing multimodal data in print using for example a table or timeline format (see, e.g., Cowan, 2014), the inclusion of screenshots or drawings of spatial layout and gestures/body language (see., e.g., Bowcher & Zhang, 2020) as well as the use of network graphs (Lim, 2021a).

The next step, after data preparation, is to identify the nature of choices made with the semiotic resources to surface patterns and trends for interpretation systematically and rigorously. The analysis and interpretation are guided by the specific research questions identified for the study. This would involve the annotation of the data using various frameworks that have been and can be, developed. The consistent use of existing frameworks builds on prior knowledge and advances the field by allowing for cross-studies and multi-site comparisons to be made (Bateman et al., 2017). As such, the analyst should first consider selecting and applying existing frameworks to annotate data. Where necessary, adaptations can be made to refine, sharpen, and customise the instrument to specific texts and contexts.

The framework to analyse the multimodal texts should be informed by the existing theoretical understandings and iterated with the empirical data it is applied to, that is, to adopt both a top-down and bottom-up orientation in its development (O'Halloran, 2011). The meanings are typically examined from the perspective of the Hallidayan metafunctions – the ideational, interpersonal, and textual meanings in the discourse. Both SS and SF-MDA studies utilize Halliday's notion of metafunctions as a central heuristic to conceptualise how semiotic activity and the social context within which it unfolds interact and to examine the specific ways in which the semiotic resources interact at the granular level in specific instantiations.

The final step aims to discover patterns emerging from the description and link them to the research questions. It is helpful to identify possible connections between the data, sign makers, their interests, and the choice they made to construct multimodal meaning and then link the connections to the research questions. Notably, too much focus on the description in step two could risk falling into the "description trap" where analytical attention focuses more on the nuances of multimodal data than answering the research questions (Bateman et al., 2017, p. 231).

3.4 Research ethics

The importance of research ethics is increasingly appreciated across disciplines, which is manifested in the quantity of research ethics boards in universities and other research institutes. While there are no ethical guidelines or benchmarks unique to multimodal research, ethical issues in research projects informed by systemic-functional semiotics can be approached from the ethical base of social semiotics, as explicated by Kress (2015). Social semiotics adopts an egalitarian stance to ethical issues embodied in the theory. As Kress (2015) put it, social semiotics is not designed to "advantage certain groups to the detriment of others (p. 69)"; rather, it "assumes a common social participation in the shaping of cultural/semiotic resources (p. 69)". It follows from this ethical stance that researchers of and participants to a social semiotic research project are more or less equal contributors to the semiotic work involved in it. This means that researchers need to uphold the basic rights that the participants enjoy as humans, such as the right to be thoroughly informed about the research project and the right to opt-out the project at any time.

Two ethical considerations may be worth highlighting that are somewhat specific to multimodal research. When analyzing data, researchers often make inferences about small details of participants' semiotic activities; for instance, describing a gesture and what particular social function it fulfilled in the communicative situation. Given the granularity of analysis, researchers must exercise great reflexivity not to overinterpret small details of meaning-making in their efforts to build an analytic apparatus based on data. This can be safeguarded, for instance, by rich contextualization – such as showing how the purported function of that gesture is visible in how others in the interaction took it up. Another possibility is to involve others in the data analysis process. While the notion of interceding rarely applies in multimodal, given the need to describe and account for unfolding meaning-making, it is important that data analytic claims are verified by co-researchers through co-coding.

The second ethical concern relates to the need to show, especially in published work, video screenshots of participants, which often include their bodies and faces. This makes it very difficult to adhere to the confidentiality agreements generally required by ethics boards. One practical solution to this issue may be the blurring of faces and aspects of context that could compromise confidentiality of research location (e.g., school logo visible on the wall). Another solution we find in published work is to hire a graphic artist to recreate a scene in a sketch with non-descript faces; this has the added advantage that images can zoom in on particular details of multimodal meaning-making (e.g., direction of gaze) without compromising participant confidentiality and often resulting in a clearer focalization of semiotic detail (e.g., just the facial expression).

4. Systemic-functional semiotics: Critiques and responses

Despite its increasing popularity in Applied Linguistics, systemic-functional semiotics has also been critiqued for various issues. These critiques range from impressionist interpretation of meaning (Jewitt, 2014a) and the rigidity of analytic categorizations (Mills, 2015), to over-determinativeness in the proposition of affordance (Jewitt et al., 2016). Arguably the most crucial of such critiques concern how meaning and meaning-making are modelled, which resonates with the critique in Jewitt (2014a) and which we wish to discuss here.

Systemic-functional semiotics, as explained previously, aims to offer a theory of contemporary communication (Kress & van Leeuwen, 2001). Given that communication entails *both* meaning-making and meaning-reception (Holsanova, 2014), the theory should aim to model and explain this reciprocal process. However, theoretically as well as empirically, systemic-functional semiotics has primarily concerned itself with the production side of meaning-making through multimodal semiotic resources. As an approach to multimodality, systemic functional semiotics is distinguished from others (notably, multimodal interaction analysis) by its analyst-centered perspective. That is, systemic functional semiotics models multimodal communication on "an ideal model viewer/reader in mind" (Boeriis & Holsanova, 2012, p.261), where the interpretation of multimodal meaning tends to rely solely on researchers who analyse the multimodal texts. Due to this analyst-centered tendency in theorizing, viewer/reader engagement with multimodal artifacts and meanings is often taken for granted. Indeed, the agents of meaning-making, as Pirini et al. (2018, p.650) rightly pointed out, are only "theoretically present" in the sense that the agent's "psychological aspect intersecting with semiotic resources is not addressed" in the analysis of multimodal meaning. This tension can be sensed perhaps more intensely in the interpersonal metafunction, which deals with "the relations between the producer of a (complex) sign and the receiver/reproducer of that sign" (Kress & van Leeuwen, 2006, p.42) and thus logically entails the reception of multimodal meaning. To address the reciprocity of communication, certain assumptions on viewers' engagement with multimodal artifacts and meanings wherein have been taken in systemic functional semiotics. For instance, Kress and van Leeuwen (2006) postulated that semiotic resources deployed in multimodal texts can evoke various viewer responses, ranging from a "sense of empathy" induced by the represented participants in an advertisement (Kress & van Leeuwen, 2006, p.68) to specific "reading paths", or sequences in which the viewers visually register different portions of a multimodal text (Kress & van Leeuwen, 2006, p.204).

The assumptions on viewers' engagement with multimodal texts have aroused concerns among researchers and have been included in methodological debates in theoretical linguistics (Butler, 2006; Newmeyer, 2005) and critical discourse analysis (Bateman, 2018; Ledin & Machin, 2018). Scholars in these debates, despite substantial differences on other issues, agreed that the assumptions are problematic (see e.g., Bateman, 2018; Butler, 2006; Ledin & Machin, 2018; Newmeyer, 2005). One way to address this problem is to conceptualize the assumptions as hypotheses and test them with behavioral data like eye-movement metrics (see, e.g., Holsanova, 2014; Holsanova et al., 2006; Jewitt et al., 2016). Eye tracking is a technology of measuring eye movement events (e.g., gazing) and functions to identify and monitor a person's allocation of visual attention in terms of location, objects, and duration. In other words, eye-tracking technology quantifies human visual perception. Eye tracking is relevant to testing the assumptions because viewers' engagement with multimodal texts often involves visual perception (Conklin, Pellicer-Sánchez, & Carrol, 2018; Godfroid, 2019).

Testing the assumptions on viewers' engagement with multimodal texts with eye-tracking data remains nascent in multimodal research and is far from settling the debates summarised above. Nevertheless, some of the existing studies seem to support some of the assumptions on how viewers interact with multimodal texts. Holsanova et al. (2006), which is a pioneering study in this area, formulated seven hypotheses based on systemic-functional semiotics and tested some of them with eye movement metrics obtained from a free viewing task involving a newspaper spread. Significantly, Holsanova et al. (2006) found that some of the hypothesized viewing behaviors were visible in the eye-tracking data, including viewers' tendency to look for graphically salient elements and paratexts. Similarly, Boeriis and Holsanova (2012) compared visual segmentation suggested by a systemic-functional semiotic framework and found that some aspects of the segmentation were traceable in the behavioral data. More recently, Bateman et al. (2018) reported an eye-tracking experiment exploring the hypothesized guiding effect of multimodal orchestrations related to page composition and correlated variances in page compositions to viewers' gaze behavior measured in fixation durations (p. 138). Similarly, Chen (2022) tested hypotheses of the information value theory in the grammar of visual design (Kress & van Leeuwen, 2006) with a between-group eye tracking experiment on print advertisements. Briefly, information value theory hypothesizes that the information represented in multimodal texts differs in its value to the viewers, and this value is determined by the relative positions of semiotic resources conveying the information. For example, information represented at the top of the semiotic space is assumed to be of "higher" value than information at the bottom. Using a data clustering algorithm to discover the common viewing patterns of a group of viewers, Chen (2022) found supporting evidence for the hypothesis explained above. Specifically, the viewers in the two groups, regardless of the goals of viewing, tended to visually register salient sales copy text positioned at the upper 1/3 of the ads while ignoring almost all the information represented at the bottom.

In sum, there is a growing body of behavioral research geared toward testing the assumptions on viewers' engagement with multimodal texts formulated by systemic-functional semiotics approaches. As such, this line of research offers a new and exciting area pushing systemic-functional semiotics to more fully account for the complexity of human multimodal communication.

5. Conclusions

This chapter set out to provide an overview of the field of multimodality, with a focus on systemic-functional semiotics and its application in the contexts of teaching and learning. We have discussed how "linguistic functionalism" and "language as social semiotic" have conceived communication as a semiotic construct that facilitated the development of multimodal approaches such as SS and SF-MDA. Within Applied Linguistics, multimodal analysis has the potential to yield insights into the orchestration of semiotic resources to realize a communicative purpose embedded in a specific social cultural context. As such, multimodal analysis is well-suited to answer research questions related to the role of social agents and meaning-making in language educational contexts.

References

Amundrud, T. (2018). Applying multimodal research to the tertiary foreign language classroom: Looking at gaze. In H.D.S. Joyce & S. Feez (Eds), *Multimodality across classrooms: Learning about and through different modalities* (pp. 160–177). Routledge.

Bateman, J. (2014). *Text and image: A critical introduction to the visual/verbal divide*. Routledge.

Bateman, J.A. (2018). Towards critical multimodal discourse analysis: A response to Ledin and Machin. *Critical Discourse Studies, 15*(5), 1–9.

Bateman, J.A., Beckmann, A., & Varela, R.I. (2018). From empirical studies to visual narrative organization: Exploring page composition. In A. Dunst, J. Laubrock, & J. Wildfeuer (Eds.), *Empirical comics research: Digital, multimodal, and cognitive methods* (pp.127–153). Routledge.

Bateman, J., Wildfeuer, J., & Hiippala, T. (2017). *Multimodality: Foundations, research and analysis*. Walter de Gruyter.

Bezemer, J., & Kress, G. (2008). Writing in multimodal texts: A social semiotic account of designs for learning. *Written Communication, 25*(2), 166–195.

Bezemer, J., & Kress, G. (2016). *Multimodality, learning and communication: A social semiotic frame*. Routledge.

Bezemer, J., & Mavers, D. (2011). Multimodal transcription as academic practice: A social semiotic perspective. *International Journal of Social Research Methodology, 13*(3), 191–206.

Boeriis, M., & Holsanova, J. (2012). Tracking visual segmentation: Connecting semiotic and cognitive perspectives. *Visual Communication, 11*(3), 259–281.

Bowcher, W.L., & Zhang, Z. (2020). Pointing at words: Gestures, language and pedagogy in elementary literacy classrooms in China. *Linguistics and Education, 55*, 100779.

Butler, C. (2006). On functionalism and formalism: A reply to Newmeyer. *Functions of Language, 13*(2), 97–227.

Chapelle, C.A. (2016). *Teaching culture in introductory foreign language textbooks*. Palgrave Macmillan.

Chen, Y. (2022). Salient visual foci on human faces in viewers' engagement with advertisements: Eye-tracking evidence and theoretical implications. *Multimodality and Society, 2*(1), 3–22.

Christie, F. (2002). *Classroom discourse analysis: A functional perspective*. Continuum.

Conklin, K., Pellicer-Sánchez, A., & Carrol, G. (2018). *Eye-tracking: A guide for applied linguistics research*. Cambridge University Press.

Cowan, K. (2014). Multimodal transcription of video: examining interaction in early years classrooms. *Classroom Discourse, 5*(1), 6–21.

Darvin, R. (2020). Creativity and criticality: Reimagining narratives through translanguaging and transmediation. *Applied Linguistics Review, 11*(4), 581–606.

Dik, S. C., & Hengeveld, K. (Eds.). (1997). *The theory of functional grammar, Part 1: The structure of the clause*. Walter de Gruyter.

Feng, W. D. (2019). Infusing moral education into English language teaching: An ontogenetic analysis of social values in EFL textbooks in Hong Kong. *Discourse: Studies in the Cultural Politics of Education, 40*(4), 458–473.

Flewitt, R. (2006). Using video to investigate preschool classroom interaction: Education research assumptions and methodological practices. *Visual Communication, 5*, 25–50.

Godfroid, A. (2019). *Eye tracking in second language acquisition and bilingualism: A research synthesis and methodological guide* (1st ed.). Routledge.

Halliday, M. A. K. (1978). *Language as social semiotic: The social interpretation of language and meaning*. Hodder Education.

Halliday, M. A. K., & Matthiessen, C. (2004). *An introduction to functional grammar* (3rd ed.). Edward Arnold.

Holsanova, J. (2014). Reception of multimodality: Applying eye tracking methodology in multimodal research. In C. Jewitt (Ed.), *The Routledge handbook of multimodal analysis* (pp. 285–296). Routledge.

Holsanova, J., Rahm, H., & Holmqvist, K. (2006). Entry points and reading paths on newspaper spreads: Comparing a semiotic analysis with eye-tracking measurements. *Visual Communication, 55*(1), 65–93.

Hood, S. E. (2011). Body language in face-to-face teaching: A focus on textual and interpersonal meaning. In E. A. Thompson, M. Stenglin, & S. Dreyfus (Eds), *Semiotic margins: Meaning in multimodalities* (pp. 31–52). Continuum.

Jewitt, C. (2009). Different approaches to multimodality. In C. Jewitt (Ed.). *The Routledge handbook of multimodal analysis* (pp. 28–39). Routledge.

Jewitt, C. (2014a). An introduction to multimodality. In C. Jewitt (Ed.). *The Routledge handbook of multimodal analysis* (pp.15–30). Routledge.

Jewitt, C. (2014b). Different approaches to multimodality. In C. Jewitt (Ed.). *The Routledge handbook of multimodal analysis* (pp. 31–43). Routledge.

Jewitt, C., Bezemer, J., & O'Halloran, K. (2016). *Introducing multimodality*. Routledge.

Jiang, L., Yang, M., & Shu, Y. (2020). Chinese ethnic minority students' investment in English learning empowered by digital multimodal composing. *TESOL Quarterly, 54*(4), 954–979.

Joo, S. J., Chik, A., & Djonov, E. (2020). The construal of English as a global language in Korean EFL textbooks for primary school children. *Asian Englishes, 22*(1), 68–84.

Knoblauch, H., Schnettler, B., Raab, J., & Soeffner, H.-G. (Eds.). (2009). *Video analysis: Methodology and methods; qualitative audiovisual data analysis in sociology* (2nd ed.). Peter Lang.

Korhonen, V. (2010). Dialogic literacy: A sociocultural literacy learning approach. In A. Lloyd & T. Sanna (Eds.), *Practising information literacy* (pp. 211–226). Chandos.

Kress, G. (2000). Design and transformation: New theories of meaning. In B. Cope & M. Kalantzis (Eds.), *Multiliteracies: Literacy learning and the design of social futures* (pp. 149–158). Routledge.

Kress, G. (2010). *Multimodality: A social semiotic approach to contemporary communication.* Routledge.

Kress, G. (2014). What is mode? In C. Jewitt (Ed.), *The Routledge handbook of multimodal analysis* (pp.60–75). Routledge.

Kress, G. (2015). Semiotic work: Applied linguistics and a social semiotic account of multimodality. *AILA Review, 28*(1), 49–71.

Kress, G., Jewitt, C., Bourne, J., Franks, A., Hardcastle, J., Jones, K., & Reid, E. (2005). *English in urban classrooms: A multimodal perspective on teaching and learning.* Falmer.

Kress, G., & Selander, S. (2012). Multimodal design, learning and cultures of recognition. *The Internet and Higher Education, 15*(4), 265–268.

Kress, G., & van Leeuwen, T. (2001). *Multimodal discourse: The modes and media of contemporary communication.* Edward Arnold.

Kress, G., & van Leeuwen, T. (2006). *Reading images: The grammar of visual design* (2nd ed.). Routledge.

Ledin, P., & Machin, D. (2018). Doing critical discourse studies with multimodality: From metafunctions to materiality. *Critical Discourse Studies, 15*(1), 1–17.

Lemke, J. (1998). Multiplying meaning: Visual and verbal semiotics in scientific text. In J. R. Martin & R. Vell (Eds.), *Reading science: Critical and function* (pp. 87–113). Routledge.

Lim, F. V. (2021a). *Designing learning with embodied teaching: Perspectives from multimodality.* Routledge.

Lim, F. V. (2021b). Investigating intersemiosis: A systemic functional multimodal discourse analysis of the relationship between language and gesture in classroom discourse. *Visual Communication, 20*(1), 34–58.

Lim, F. V., O'Halloran, K. L., & Podlasov, A. (2012). Spatial pedagogy: Mapping meanings in the use of classroom space. *Cambridge Journal of Education, 42*(2), 235–251.

Miller, S. M., & McVee, M. B. (Eds.). (2013). *Multimodal composing in classrooms: Learning and teaching for the digital world.* Routledge.

Mills, K. A. (2015). *Literacy theories for the digital age: Social, critical, multimodal, spatial, material and sensory lenses.* Multilingual Matters.

New London Group. (1996). A pedagogy of multiliteracies: Designing social futures. *Harvard Educational Review, 66*(1), 60–92.

Newmeyer, F. J. (2005). Review of Christopher S. Butler Structure and function: A guide to three major structural-functional theories. *Functions of Language, 122*, 275–283.

Norris, S. (2004). *Analyzing multimodal interaction: A methodological framework.* Routledge.

O'Halloran, K.L. (2005). *Mathematical discourse: Language, symbolism and visual images.* Continuum.

O'Halloran, K.L. (2008). Systemic functional-multimodal discourse analysis (SF-MDA): Constructing ideational meaning using language and visual imagery. *Visual Communication, 7*(4), 443–475.

O'Halloran, K.L. (2011). Multimodal discourse analysis. In K. Hyland & B. Paltridge (Eds.), *Companion to discourse* (pp. 120–137). Continuum.

O'Halloran, K.L. (Ed.). (2004). *Multimodal discourse analysis: Systemic-functional perspectives.* Continuum.

O'Halloran, K.L., & Lim, F.V. (2014). Systemic functional multimodal discourse analysis. In S. Norris & C. Maier (Eds.), *Texts, images and interactions: A Reader in multimodality* (pp. 135–154). De Gruyter.

O'Halloran, K.L., Podlasov, A., Chua, A., & Marissa, K.L.E. (2012). Interactive software for multimodal analysis. *Visual Communication, 11*(3), 363–381.

O'Toole, M. (2011). *The language of displayed art* (2nd ed.). Routledge.

Pirini, J., Matelau-Doherty, T., & Norris, S. (2018). Multimodal analysis. In A. Phakiti, P. De Costa, L. Plonsky, & S. Starfield, (Eds.), *The Palgrave handbook of applied linguistics research methodology* (pp. 639–658). Palgrave Macmillan.

Ranker, J. (2017). The role of signifier differences, associations, and combinations in creative digital video composing: Making meaning with gestures, objects, actions, and speech. *Pedagogies: An International Journal, 12*(2), 196–218.

Stivers, T., & Sidnell, J. (2005). Introduction: Multimodal interaction. *Semotica, 156*, 1–20.

Teo, P., & Zhu, J. (2018). A multimodal analysis of affect and attitude education in China's English textbooks. *Multimodal Communication, 7*(1), 20170014.

Thomas, M.A. (2020). *Formalism and functionalism in linguistics: The engineer and the collector.* Routledge.

Van Leeuwen, T. (2005). *Introducing social semiotics.* Routledge.

Weninger, C. (2021). Multimodality in critical language textbook analysis. *Language, Culture & Curriculum, 34*(2), 133–146.

Weninger, C. & Kiss, T. (2013). Culture in English as a Foreign Language (EFL) textbooks: A semiotic approach. *TESOL Quarterly, 47*(4), 694–716.

Wigham, C., & Satar, M. (2021). Multimodal (inter)action analysis of task instructions in language teaching via videoconferencing: A case study. *ReCALL, 33*(3), 195–213.

Wittenburg, P., Brugman, H., Russel, A., Klassmann, A., & Sloetjes, H. (2006, May 24–26). *ELAN: A professional framework for multimodality research* [Conference presentation]. The International Conference on Language Resources and Evaluation, Genoa, Italy. https://aclanthology.org/events/lrec-2006/

Xiong, T. & Peng, Y. (2021). Representing culture in Chinese as a second language textbooks: A critical social semiotic approach. *Language, Culture & Curriculum, 34*(2), 163–182.

CHAPTER 5

Applying multimodal analysis
Embodied teaching and textbook analysis

Csilla Weninger, Fei Victor Lim & Yixiong Chen
National Institute of Education

This chapter builds on Chapter 4 and introduces two main applications within applied linguistics stemming from a systemic-functional semiotic theory of multimodality: embodied teaching and language textbook analysis. The chapter first gives a brief overview of the broader field of research that each of these applications is located in. Then each focal area is elaborated and illustrated via a case study conducted by the authors. Each case study provides a rationale for why multimodal analysis is appropriate given the research focus and questions, demonstrates how multimodal analysis was implemented and conducted, and reflects on the challenges of its implementation in applied linguistic research contexts.

1. Introduction

This chapter builds on the theoretical tenets outlined in the previous chapter and discusses two studies from the systemic-functional semiotic approach to multi-modal analysis. The first study uses the systemic-functional multimodal discourse analysis (SF-MDA) to study teachers' gestures, positioning and movements in the language classroom, or what we call embodied teaching. The second study falls within the research strand of multimodality in educational materials and takes a social semiotic perspective to examine how textbooks' multimodal design can facilitate or impede critical engagement with ideas represented therein. The chapter will situate these two studies within their respective Applied Linguistics research areas and discuss the advantages of this methodology for the study of embodied teaching and language textbooks before delving into each case study and how they applied multimodal analysis. We also reflect on the challenges of using multimodal analysis in Applied Linguistic research contexts and discuss the insights gained through using multimodal analysis as a methodology.

https://doi.org/10.1075/rmal.6.05wen
© 2024 John Benjamins Publishing Company

2. An overview of the research focus and the case studies

2.1 Embodied teaching

Classroom discourse is more than words. Teachers make meaning using speech as well as other embodied resources, such as gestures, positioning and movement during the lesson. While the analysis of speech has been the focus of most classroom discourse analysis studies, casting a multimodal lens on how the teacher orchestrates the range of semiotic resources in communication and interactions with the students can be productive. The teacher's orchestration of embodied resources in the expression of their pedagogy is described as "embodied teaching" (Lim, 2021a). This section turns our analytical focus on the teacher's multimodal meaning-making (Kress, 2010), specifically their use of gestures and positioning and movement during the lesson. While the meanings made with these embodied semiotic resources are often neglected in most classroom discourse analysis studies, we argue that the outcome of teacher's use of embodied meaning-making studies can contribute to the students' learning experience. As Jewitt (2008) explains, "how teachers and students use gaze, body posture, and the distribution of space and resources produces silent discourses in the classroom that affect literacy" (p. 262).

Classroom discourse (Christie, 2002) can be analysed in relation to instructional discourse, a discourse on specialised competencies and disciplinary content, and to regulative discourse, a discourse on the maintenance of order, relations, and identity (Bernstein, 1990). Hasan (2001) describes regulative classroom discourse as comprising visible semiotic mediation, expressed through the explicit instruction, and invisible semiotic mediation, expressed through how the instruction is communicated, with non-verbal resources. The endeavour to make visible these forms of invisible semiotic mediation is a primary motivation in applying multimodal analysis on embodied teaching.

The study we will use to illustrate this methodology was conducted by Lim (2021a), the second author of this chapter, who examined a teacher's embodied teaching in an English Language lesson. The goal of the study was to understand how the teacher's use of embodied resources in the classroom expresses specific pedagogies and contributes to the design of the students' learning experience.

2.2 Language textbook analysis

Language textbooks have been a subject of applied linguistic research for some time, given the central role they continue to play as teaching materials, especially in foreign or second language classrooms. Some researchers (e.g., Tomlinson, 2011) investigate and assess the suitability of textbooks for particular groups of learners or particular language learning goals. However, a broader tradition of scholarship has also developed which sees textbooks primarily as repositories of meaning about the world (e.g., Weninger & Williams, 2005). Given textbooks' focal place as instruments of language socialization (Curdt-Christiansen, 2017), especially in classroom contexts, this line of research aims to critically examine what kinds of meanings textbooks communicate through the stories, characters, and activities they contain. Underpinning such investigations is the assumption that language learning is not simply about being linguistically competent in a new code; rather, it entails becoming familiar with new cultural practices and values and assuming a new identity (Kramsch, 2006) through meaning-making. The social semiotic lens on learning involves students actively designing meaning through "the very process of engagement, transformations and sign making to explore the world and take part and communicate with others in a certain context" (Kress & Selander, 2012, p.267). Language textbooks provide a window to these more symbolic aspects through how they present information to learners.

If we look at language textbooks as repositories of meanings, it is easy to see how a multimodal approach lends itself very well to their analysis. As emphasized in the previous chapter, social semiotics is fundamentally concerned with describing the design of meaning; how sign makers (Kress, 2010) choose semiotic resources of diverse modes to express meanings that best fit their communicative needs. However, Kress (2010) also stressed that design as a semiotic activity is different from rhetoric as the politics of communication. As he observed,

> *Rhetor* and *designer* share similar interests, while their tasks differ. The *rhetor* assesses the social environment for communication as a whole. Then, they need to shape their *message* so that the audience will engage with it and, ideally, *assent* to it. That is a political task. The *designer* assesses what semiotic – representational – resources are available, with a full understanding of the *rhetor's* needs and aims, in such a way that the *rhetor's* interests, needs, and requirements, are met and make the best possible match with the interests of the audience".
>
> (p. 49, italics in original)

Multimodal research on language textbooks can thus illuminate both the processes of design and rhetoric; that is, how textbook writers use textual, visual, and spatial resources to convey different types of meaning (design), and how such representations reflect broader ideological positions and values (rhetoric).

The research that serves as a case study to illustrate the multimodal textbook analysis was also motivated by similar questions. It is a study that Weninger, the first author of this chapter, and Kiss (Weninger & Kiss, 2013) conducted to examine cultural representations in Hungarian EFL textbooks. Broadly, we wanted to find out how multimodal resources in these textbooks worked together to communicate ideas about the world and positioned the writer and reader within the textual world. Specifically, we wanted to zoom in on the pedagogic elements in language textbooks and to examine how the pedagogic tasks mitigate or anchor the meaning potential of text and visuals. In this way, we wanted to foreground the didactic nature of language textbooks and the role of pedagogic mediation as an ideological process in language learning.

3. Why multimodal analysis?

3.1 Multimodality in embodied teaching

During Lim's attachment to a specialised Singapore secondary school for low-progress students preparing for post-secondary vocational training, the researcher was invited to observe Xi's lesson. Xi was a teacher with more than ten years' experience, who started her career teaching in a school for children with special needs and had joined this school about five years. It was an English language lesson for twenty 14-year-old students. As it was one of the first few lessons of the academic year, the teacher and the students were still getting to know each other. Moreover, the lesson was just after the recess time for the students, and sitting in class on a hot afternoon was getting some of them restless and distracted. The lesson's topic was grammar, and Xi wanted the students to identify the correct and incorrect sentence constructions derived from the students' earlier writing assignment. She led the class to examine these sentences using her prepared presentation slides and sought student's collective and individual responses to her questions.

What was more interesting than the instructional discourse was Xi's use of embodied resources in several instances when the students were showing signs of inattentiveness. Xi would pause and direct her gaze at the disengaged student. It was enough for the student to sit up and pay attention. The silent communication was well understood by the students, who responded to the teacher's silence and gaze accordingly. Her pregnant pauses brought the class to a hush. Her gaze and gesticulation to a distracted student were reciprocated with a quick nod from the student. Her movement towards the students who were disengaged led them to look at her and smile. It could have been a potentially disruptive lesson, but because Xi spoke not a single negative word to regulate the disruptions, the classroom atmosphere was pleasant and positive. Xi used language to express the instructional discourse, but the regulative discourse was mostly expressed through silences, gazes, gestures, and positioning and movement in the classroom. It was a fascinating example of embodied teaching. The recognition of Xi's expression of regulative discourse would perhaps have been missed in a classroom discourse analysis that focuses solely on language.

Many effective teachers teaching classes prone to disciplinary issues have developed such competencies through experience. Some, like Xi, might be surprised when this 'orchestration skill' was pointed out to them and might self-deprecatingly brush it off as nothing significant. However, a multimodal analysis rooted in systemic functional semiotics can shed light on how a teacher uses semiotic resources differently to express the instructional and regulative discourses during the lesson. A range of research questions can be explored from this perspective. For example, descriptive questions could include how the teacher uses language, gestures, positioning, and movement to express specific meanings during the lesson and design different pedagogies. Comparative questions could include examining how teachers with contrasting experiences or teaching different subjects differ in their embodied teaching. Comparative questions could also engage with gains and losses (Kress, 2005) in embodied teaching in the physical classroom and the online context. Finally, evaluative questions could involve reflecting on how the orchestration of the teacher's embodied resources contributes to designing a practical lesson experience and examining the students' perspectives and responses to the teacher. Specifically, in the case study reported in this chapter, descriptive questions were asked to understand the teachers' embodied teaching during the lesson.

3.2 Multimodality in analyzing language textbooks

Early critical research on language textbooks often analysed only the textual material presented in textbooks (e.g., Hellinger, 1980; Liu, 2005). The reason for that choice was likely twofold: Language textbooks were more dominated by monochrome, textual content, and also because social semiotics and the multimodal turn within linguistics did not gain momentum until the mid-to-late 2000s. As such, early work often utilized critical discourse analysis (Fairclough, 2001), which continues to be a fundamental theoretical approach within textbook evaluation studies. Often, when studies included visual analysis, it primarily entailed content analysis. Researchers coded images in textbooks based on a particular research focus; for example, men vs. women in a study on gender representation (Lee, 2014) or country of origin in a study on cultural diversity in Hong Kong English textbooks (Yuen, 2011). Subsequently, researchers compared the frequency of occurrence of the different categories to argue for the representation balance (or lack thereof).

However, when we look at language textbooks today, especially those for major world languages produced for the global market, they are thoroughly multimodal, with photos, charts, and graphs interspersed with written text and often supplemented with web resources and audio material. If we only examine the textual components of textbooks, we are missing half the story, so to speak. In other words, we would miss the meanings non-linguistic modes convey and the role they play in the language learning and socialization process. How does the multimodal design of these textbooks, understood as the choice and arrangement of various semiotic elements in diverse modes, facilitate different types of meaning? And how are those meanings linked to broader social-ideological interests that shape not only what goes or should go into textbooks but, even more fundamentally, what counts as legitimate knowledge about the world (cf. Apple, 1990)? Multimodal analyses of language textbooks are motivated by finding answers to these questions using the analytic tools of social semiotics.

For the case study on Hungarian language textbooks, a multimodal anaysis was closely motivated by the research purpose to understand how the textbooks' various elements, including visuals and pedagogic task, interacted to steer the learning process. Specifically, we were interested in finding out what types of meaning the interaction of task-visual-text fostered in the textbooks under scrutiny. Our point of departure was the recognition from within applied linguistics scholarship that language learning should not merely encompass the acquisition of linguistic knowledge. Rather, language must be understood and used in context, and English is increasingly being used in intercultural communication. As such, the goal of the analysis was to find out, using the conceptual tools of multimodality, to what extent textbooks fostered cultural learning through the types of meanings learners were asked to focus on and engage with.

4. Implementing the studies using multimodal analysis

4.1 Case study 1: Systemic-functional multimodal discourse analysis (SF-MDA) of embodied teaching

The previous chapter detailed the key methodological steps and considerations for studies wishing to adopt multimodal analysis from a systemic-functional semiotic perspective. In the case study of embodied teaching in Xi's English language classroom using the SF-MDA approach, these included consideration of (a) the level of granularity of data needed to answer the research question, which in turn shaped (b) the type and amount of data to be captured; (c) tools of capturing to ensure high-quality data; (d) method for transcribing and analysing the data; and (e) ways of visualizing the findings for the interpretation of the data.

In Lim's study, six video cameras were placed in the classroom to capture the teacher's use of embodied resources during the lesson. The teacher's semiotic choices in gestures, positioning, and movement were annotated with the other semiotic resources at the one-second interval. The framework for gestures was based on Martinec's (2000, 2001) system of actions, which Lim (2019, 2021b) extended as a taxonomy for the classification of gestures concerning their communicative intent and relationship with language. Gestures can be performative or communicative. Performative gestures serve a practical function, such as folding of arms to keep warm. Communicative gestures can operate independently, dependently, or correspondent with language.

The meanings in communicative gestures were described with the way they expressed ideas (ideational meanings), enacted social relations (interpersonal meanings), and organised the multimodal discourse (textual meaning). For example, the ideational meanings in communicative gestures were described in terms of the functional semantic categorisation (Hood, 2007) as congruent entities, which could denote objects, and metaphorical concepts which could connote abstract ideas. Ideational meanings in communicative gestures could also be expressed with hands out and open palms to signify receptivity.

Interpersonal meanings in communicative gestures could encompass the nature of attitude, engagement, and graduation. For example, an open palm gesture could express engagement by signifying an expansion of "heteroglossic space, inviting student voices into the discourse" (Hood, 2011, p.46). Likewise, graduation could be expressed through the speed of the gesture. Slow moves could connote emphasis and deliberateness. Fast moves could convey a sense of urgency, energy, and dynamism. Textual meanings in communicative gestures could be expressed through the act of pointing. Directionality and specificity could be communicated with pointing, with specificity at its highest degree when conveyed by the "smallest body part... the little finger" (Hood, 2011, p.38). The teacher could relate speech with visuals on the whiteboard or direct her words to a specific student. The act of pointing could also function interpersonally as an imperative as well as ideationally to demand engagement.

The framework developed for gestures offered a way for analysts to examine the teacher's use of gestures in the classroom. By applying the metafunctional perspective on the meanings made with gestures, the analyst could identify the semiotic choices made in specific instances and patterns and trends of the teacher's use. It also enabled comparisons across the teacher's use of different semiotic resources. For example, the analyst was able to explore how the nature of interpersonal meanings expressed in gestures converged or diverged with the nature of interpersonal meanings made with language or through positioning and movement.

In relation to the teacher's positioning and movement in the classroom, four types of classroom space were situated within Hall's (1966) Social-Consultative Space and described as Authoritative Space, (2) Supervisory Space, (3) Interactional Space, and (4) Personal Space (Lim et al., 2012). The Authoritative Space was often expressed when the teacher is standing before the classroom, usually in the front centre. The Supervisory Space was expressed through the teacher's pacing amongst the students and standing at the back of the classroom to monitor the students' work. Both spaces could signify authority, power, and formality in interpersonal meanings.

Interpersonal meanings of rapport and solidarity could be expressed when the teacher used the Interactional Space. This was when the teacher stood next to the student to offer personal guidance. During frontal teaching, the teacher would also move into the interactional space to mitigate the power differential and relate with the students. The Personal Space was where the teacher retreated behind an imaginary wall, usually behind the teacher's desk, to rest or organise her materials. Typically, there would be no interaction with the students. While functional meanings have been inscribed to the use of these spaces, the meanings are remade in context and statically through the stationary position of the teacher in a specific location and dynamically through the teacher's movement and pacing. The meanings must also be interpreted concerning the teacher's use of other semiotic resources in each instantiation.

As discussed in the earlier chapter, we can visualise the data using network graphs to model the patterns of meanings made. In Lim's study, the teacher's temporal use of classroom space during the lesson is visualised with network graphs in Cytoscape, a free, open-source software (Figure 1). The nodes reflect the teacher's positioning and movement through shapes, positioning duration, and frequency of movement with sizes. Other attributes, such as the directionality of the teacher's movement from one space to the next, are represented with arrows and the use of colours and thickness to indicate frequency.

The findings from Lim's study showed how the teacher designed for 'structured informality' through her semiotic choices to reduce hierarchical distance with the adolescent students in the learning, while maintaining a didactic structure in her lesson. She used gestures and language to express a sense of relatability and informality to encourage the students' response and participation in her lesson. However, a sense of structure and authority were expressed through her use of space and her organisation of the instructional discourse. The insights revealed from the multimodal analysis prompted further interest on how teachers can design different learning experiences for students through their embodied teaching.

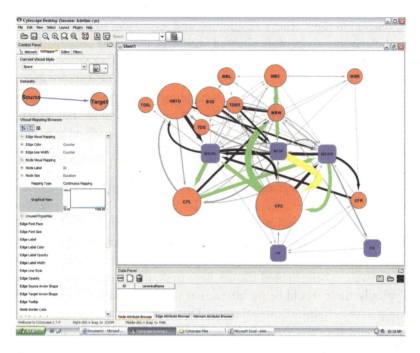

Legend:

	Space		Movement
BTD	Behind Teacher's Desk	MFW	Move Forward
HBTD	Half Behind Teacher's Desk	MBW	Move Backward
TDSL	Teacher's Desk Side Left	MSWL	Move Sideway Left
TDSR	Teacher's Desk Side Right	MSWR	Move Sideway Right
CFL	Classroom Front Left	PL	Pace Left
CFR	Classroom Front Right	PR	Pace Right
CFC	Classroom Front Centre	PF	Pace Front
WBL	Whiteboard Left		
WBC	Whiteboard Centre		
WBR	Whiteboard Right		

Figure 1. Visualisation of the teacher's positioning and movement using Cytoscape

4.2 Case study 2: Conducting multimodal language textbook analysis

Multimodal analyses of textbooks in the tradition of social semiotics overwhelmingly orient to a qualitative and interpretivist (hermeneutic) paradigm. That means the goal of the research is primarily to describe and understand a phenomenon in its contextual complexity; in this case, to describe and interpret how meaning potentials are embedded within the visual-textual-spatial makeup of language textbooks. Such an approach acknowledges the analyst's subjectivity and is characterized by the in-depth description and contextual interpretation of semiotic resources and processes. Within this general epistemological orientation, several key aspects of methodology must be considered for multimodal textbook analysis. Unlike the first case study, and in fact most applied linguistics research that examines language learning as teachers' and learners' situated multimodal meaning-making, textbook analysis entails the investigation of semiotic artefacts and as such, issues of data collection such as video recording or transcription do not apply. However, others that do include (a) data (including type and sampling); and (b) framework or method for data analysis. In what follows, we will elaborate on these two methodological questions and describe how they were answered for the case study featured here.

While the focus of the research delineates its object and research data (i.e., language textbooks), there are further questions to contemplate. For instance, what type of textbooks are we interested in? Those produced for the global market by big commercial publishers (e.g., Oxford, MacMillan) or rather textbooks written locally for a specific country, often in consultation with local educational authorities? The choice depends on access as well as research interest. However, it is important because if we consider the design and the broader context of communication (rhetoric, in Kress' terms), then the choice will shape whether our analysis and critique will be situated within a more specific or a more global context. Additionally, information about a textbook's circulation is a common principle for selecting data whereby textbooks that are used frequently and by many teachers or schools are generally preferred as data.

The selection of data in Weninger and Kiss (2013) was guided by our overall intention to offer a typology or model for how the textual and visual resources of the textbooks were linked to the accompanying task, and thus to what extent links facilitated meanings that went beyond a linguistic focus. In short, we characterized the relationship across image-text-task as either converging denotationally or being linked connotationally. In other words, whether there is a connection based on a shared linguistic focus (e.g., a text about food will have images of food accompanying it and a labelling task), or whether images are also used to prompt more critical engagement with what was represented visually. In light of this research interest in cultural learning, we chose textbooks specifically written for Hungarian learners by local writers because it could be assumed that most of these learners had a shared cultural background (unlike for global textbooks) which could be productively exploited and drawn upon in the activities by the textbook designers. In addition, it was important that the chosen textbooks were written for learners at the same level of language competence so that adequate comparisons can be made. In our case, this was the introductory level. Finally, it was decided that we would focus on two textbooks which were being used widely in Hungarian secondary schools based on information from professional networks, in the absence of publicly available statistics in this regard.

Perhaps a more difficult question to answer in connection with data is: how much data to analyse? This question is closely connected to the notion of sampling: provided we have selected a textbook or series of textbooks (our sampling frame), we will need to take a sample of data to analyse. As mentioned in the previous chapter, given the close and detailed analysis required for a social semiotic account of meaning-making, for most projects, it is not feasible to analyse textbooks in their entirety, let alone a whole series. Rather, sampling generally hinges on the particular focus of one's study. For the case study of Hungarian textbooks, sampling of the textbooks was aligned with the study's overall goal to describe how multimodal resources in these textbooks interacted with the pedagogic discourse present in tasks. As such, the unit of analysis was the composition of text-image and pedagogic tasks, rather than individual images and texts, as in other studies. Again, this is because we aimed to examine how the links across the three facilitated particular cultural meanings as a critical aspect of intercultural learning. The process of sampling thus entailed going through each textbook and identifying sections where a visual was included as part of a task.

We should add that when analyzing textbooks multimodally, it is also possible to utilize the existing segmentation of language textbooks to aid the process of sampling. In other words, most language textbooks are divided into units that are often thematically organized. Within each unit, textbooks tend to follow a recurrent structure such that each unit, for instance, may have a longer reading passage, contain a 'culture corner', or a section devoted to grammar or project work. Depending on the research and focus, this pre-existing segmentation can provide a principled way of sampling data across a set of textbooks and ensure systematicity in data selection.

One important distinction we must make, which is not consistently discussed in published work, is whether one is interested in analysing the ideational or the interpersonal meanings in textbooks (see Weninger, 2021). As briefly explained in the previous chapter, ideational meaning in systemic-functional semiotics deals with representing aspects of the physical, social or mental world through semiotic means. In contrast, interpersonal meaning (referred to as interactive meaning in Kress & van Leeuwen, 2006) has to do with how we utilize language and other symbolic modes to enact social relations (Halliday & Matthiessen, 2004, p.30). When examining textbooks, a focus on either one will engender different questions to be answered through analysis. When we analyse ideational meanings, we often ask: *how do textbooks, through their textual or visual features, represent X*, where X can be any aspect of reality that we are interested in, such as a language, a social group (e.g., women, young people) or values. When we aim to analyse interpersonal meanings, we may ask: *How do textual and visual elements position the writer and reader/viewer? How do textbooks engage readers or viewers?* The two metafunctions operate in discourse simultaneously; nevertheless, it is helpful to distinguish them analytically. It enables us to ask the right questions and choose the right tools to analyse the text.

A third option, and one that was taken in the case study, is to explore how ideational and interactive meanings are made to relate to each other through the multimodal design of the textbook; what Kress and van Leeuwen (2006, p.175) called composition and others intermodal or intersemiotic (Royce, 2007) relations. In other words, the question here becomes: how do the different semiotic modes interact with one another to communicate ideational meaning and position the reader/viewer? Not every study that analyses language textbooks from a social semiotic perspective looks at intermodal relations; it is not uncommon that researchers examine text and visuals separately (e.g., Joo, Chik, & Djonov, 2019; Puspitasari et al., 2021) within an overall social semiotic theoretical frame.

For the analysis of the Hungarian textbooks, we did not use an existing analytic framework to analyze the intermodal connections. And that is because models of intersemiosis were not explicitly developed with textbooks in mind (e.g., Royce, 2007; Van Leeuwen, 2005) or those that were (e.g., Chan, 2011) did not seem to take account of the fact that textbooks are a unique, didactic genre where the meaning potentials of text and visuals are anchored (Barthes, 1977) to a large extent through their pedagogical nature. Yet what our analysis required was analytic tools to capture this process of 'anchoring'. So instead of using an existing framework, once all possible units were identified, we utilized semiotic principles to establish how the meaning of the text and visual were brought together (or not) within the pedagogic task. That is, whether the multimodal composition of each image-text-activity unit facilitated linguistic-denotational meaning or was designed to explicitly prompt learners to look for cultural-connotative meanings. The findings revealed that in practically all the units we analysed, image-text relations were primarily denotational and reinforced linguistic knowledge, particularly vocabulary. In other words, the image's meaning was 'fixed' by the text and was further constrained by the focus of the task on linguistic competence rather than cultural competence. The case study also highlighted the importance of not relying on existing frameworks when they do not fit the data or research questions. When one aims to map out the orchestration of semiotic modes and resources in shaping meaning in language textbooks or other contextualized instances of communication, an element of emergence is inherent in the analysis.

5. Conclusions

As we have argued throughout Chapters 4 and 5, multimodal analysis is well-positioned to answer questions about the nature of meaning and meaning-making in a large variety of genres and technologies of multimodal communicative practice. In contrast to other methodological approaches that analyse only linguistic or textual aspects of meaning-making, multimodal analysis is better positioned to unearth the complex interplay of linguistic and other semiotic modes to represent ideas and enact identities and relationships. In short, the goal is to realize the myriad social functions which human communication systems have evolved to fulfil. Given Applied Linguistics' concern with the application of linguistic theories to contexts of teaching and learning (particularly of language and literacy), multimodal analysis offers a way forward to analyse classroom discourse, be it within the context of teaching a lesson or the material dimensions of learning such as textbooks.

References

Apple, M. (1990). The text and cultural politics. *The Journal of Educational Thought, 24*(3A), 17–33.

Barthes, R. (1977). *Image–music–text* (S. Heath, Trans.). Hill and Wang.

Bernstein, B. (1990). *Class, codes and contro, Volume IV: The structuring of pedagogic discourse*. Routledge.

Chan, E. (2011). Integrating visual and verbal meaning in multimodal text comprehension: Towards a model of intermodal relations. In S. Dreyfus, S. Hood, & M. Stenglin (Eds.), *Semiotic margins: Meaning in multimodalities* (pp. 144–167). Continuum.

Christie, F. (2002). *Classroom discourse analysis: A functional perspective*. Continuum.

Curdt-Christiansen, X. L. (2017). Multilingual socialization through (language) textbooks. In P. Duff & S. May (Eds.), *Language socialization* (pp. 195–210). Springer.

Fairclough, N. (2001). *Language and power* (2nd ed). Pearson Education.

Hall, E. (1966). *The hidden dimension*. Doubleday.

Halliday, M. A. K., & Matthiessen, C. M. I. M. (2004). *An introduction to functional grammar* (3rd ed.) Arnold.

Hasan, R. (2001). The ontogenesis of decontextualised language: Some achievements of classification and framing. In A. Morais, I. Neves, B. Davis, & H. Daniels (Eds.), *Towards a sociology of pedagogy: The contributions of Basil Bernstein to research* (pp. 47–80). Peter Lang.

Hellinger, M. (1980). 'For men must work, and women must weep': Sexism in English language textbooks used in German schools. *Women's Studies International Quarterly, 3*(2–3), 267–275.

Hood, S. (2007, December 10–12). *Gesture and meaning-making in face-to-face teaching* [paper presentation]. Semiotic Margins Conference, University of Sydney, Australia.

Hood, S. (2011). Body language in face-to-face teaching: A focus on textual and interpersonal meaning. In S. Dreyfus, S. Hood, & M. Stenglin (Eds.), *Semiotic margins: Meaning in multimodalities* (pp. 31–52). Continuum.

Jewitt, C. (2008). *Technology, literacy, learning: A multimodality approach.* Routledge.

Joo, S. J., Chik, A., & Djonov, E. (2019). The construal of English as a global language in Korean EFL textbooks for primary school children. *Asian Englishes, 22*(1), 68–84.

Kramsch, C. (2006). From communicative competence to symbolic competence. *The Modern Language Journal, 90*(2), 249–252.

Kress, G. (2005). Gains and losses: New forms of texts, knowledge, and learning. *Computers and Composition, 22*(1), 5–22.

Kress, G. (2010). *Multimodality – A social semiotic approach to contemporary communication.* Routledge.

Kress, G., & Selander, S. (2012). Multimodal design, learning and cultures of recognition. *The Internet and Higher Education, 15*(4), 265–268.

Kress, G., & van Leeuwen, T. (2006). *Reading Images: The grammar of visual design* (2nd ed.). Routledge.

Lee, J. F. K. (2014). A hidden curriculum in Japanese EFL textbooks: Gender representation. *Linguistics & Education 27*, 39–53.

Lim, F. V. (2019). Analysing the teachers' use of gestures in the classroom: A systemic functional multimodal discourse analysis. *Social Semiotics, 29*(1), 83–111.

Lim, F. V. (2021a). *Designing learning with embodied teaching: Perspectives from multimodality.* Routledge.

Lim, F. V. (2021b). Investigating intersemiosis: A systemic functional multimodal discourse analysis of the relationship between language and gesture in classroom discourse. *Visual Communication, 20*(1), 34–58.

Lim, F. V., O'Halloran, K. L., & Podlasov, A. (2012). Spatial pedagogy: Mapping meanings in the use of classroom space. *Cambridge Journal of Education 42*(2), 235–251.

Liu, Y. (2005). The construction of cultural values and beliefs in Chinese language textbooks: A critical discourse analysis. *Discourse: Studies in the Cultural Politics of Education, 26*(1), 15–30.

Martinec, R. (2000). Construction of identity in Michael Jackson's 'Jam'. *Social Semiotics 10*(3), 313–329.

Martinec, R. (2001). Interpersonal resources in action. *Semiotica 135–1*(4), 117–145.

Puspitasari, D., Widodo, H. P., Widyaningrum, L., Allamnakhrah, A., Lestariyana, R. P. D. (2021). How do primary school English textbooks teach moral values? A critical discourse analysis. *Studies in Educational Evaluation, 70*, 101044.

Royce, T. D. (2007). Intersemiotic complementarity: A framework for multimodal discourse analysis. In T. D. Royce & W. L. Bowcher (Eds.), *New directions in the analysis of multimodal discourse* (pp. 63–110). Lawrence Erlbaum Associates.

Tomlinson, B. (2011). *Materials development in language teaching* (2nd ed.). Cambridge University Press.

Van Leeuwen, T. (2005). *Introducing social semiotics.* Routledge.

Weninger, C. (2021). Multimodality in critical language textbook analysis. *Language, Culture and Curriculum, 34*(2), 133–146.

Weninger, C., & Kiss, T. (2013). Culture in English as a Foreign Language (EFL) textbooks: A semiotic approach. *TESOL Quarterly, 47*(4), 694–716.

Weninger, C., & Williams, P. (2005). Cultural representations of minorities in Hungarian textbooks. *Pedagogy, Culture & Society, 13*(2), 159–180.

Yuen, K. M. (2011). The representation of foreign cultures in English textbooks. *ELT Journal, 65*(4), 458–466.

CHAPTER 6

Conversation analysis

Numa Markee
University of Illinois at Urbana-Champaign

This chapter introduces conversation analysis to researchers who are not familiar with this methodology for analyzing naturalistic language use and how it has been applied to develop behavioral alternatives to cognitive approaches to second language acquisition. Specifically, I: (1) review what CA is; (2) discuss typical research questions in CA and how these questions are generated; (3) outline how CA data are gathered, transcribed and analyzed; (4) review turn-taking, repair, sequence, and preference organization; (5) discuss ethical issues in CA; (6) outline important critiques of CA and how CA researchers have rebutted these criticisms; and (7) summarize the arguments presented in this chapter with a view to promoting a constructive, critical dialog between cognitive and socially-oriented SLA researchers.

1. Introduction

Although conversation analysis (CA) has been used in Applied Linguistics (AL) for over 30 years or more, it is still an unfamiliar methodology for all kinds of researchers who are interested in cognitive second language acquisition (SLA) studies. For example, generative linguists rely on their native speaker intuitions to make judgments about what constitutes a grammatical sentence. Others embrace experimental research and its reliance on sometimes exotic statistical methods that are widely used in all the social sciences to develop and validate their theories about SLA. Lastly, a third group of researchers use a variety of qualitative techniques that were first developed in anthropology and ethnography to understand how second language learning works. As we will see, CA sort of belongs in this anthropological tradition. In this Chapter, I particularly invite non-specialists in ethnomethodological CA to discover what this discipline is about.

I therefore: (1) review the ontological and epistemological foundations of ethnomethodology and CA; (2) discuss the types of research questions that we conversation analysts ask ourselves and how we generate these questions; (3) outline the procedures that we use to gather, transcribe and analyze our talking/

https://doi.org/10.1075/rmal.6.06mar
© 2024 John Benjamins Publishing Company

gesticulating data; (4) consider how we treat the foundational practices of turn-taking, repair, sequence, and preference organization to do – or achieve – different social actions and agendas, including socially distributed cognition; (5) discuss the ethical issues to which we must pay attention; (6) outline how our critics have reacted to our ideas and how we typically respond to such criticisms; and (7) summarize what I say here and, more importantly, invite readers to critically evaluate what contributions CA's social approach to understanding language learning might make to modern SLA studies.

2. The ontological and epistemological foundations of ethnomethodology and CA

Let us now begin by discussing the ontological and epistemological foundations of ethnomethodology and CA.

2.1 Ethnomethodology

Harold Garfinkel, the founder of ethnomethodology, originally developed this qualitative sociological sub-discipline to create emic (or participant-oriented) accounts of how members[1] understand their own mundane social actions (Garfinkel, 1967). This perspective is behavioral, though not behaviorist, meaning that while CA focuses on conversational behavior, it does not subscribe to Behaviorist psychology. As I already noted, this ethnographically inspired perspective differs considerably from the etic (or researcher-oriented) epistemologies to which all other SLA researchers subscribe. Ethnomethodology first emerged at Harvard, where Garfinkel (1952) wrote his dissertation. This work was a phenomenologically based critique of Parsons (1937) – who was his dissertation adviser. Parsons was a major figure in developing an etic theory of social action, but Garfinkel countered his work by appropriating the notion of the "natural attitude" that was first championed by phenomenological philosophers Edmund Husserl and his student Alfred Schütz (see Husserl, 1983, 1989, 2001; and Schütz, 1967, 1973, 1975, respectively). Briefly, phenomenology focuses on how ordinary people experience the world about them in common sense terms.

Garfinkel also respecified Husserl's and Schütz empirically untestable ideas regarding the nature of "(inter)subjectivity" or, in plain English, how speakers ensure that they are on the same page as their conversational partners. He achieved this by redefining this construct in sociological terms by showing how

---

1. The terms "participants" and "members" are interchangeable in ethnomethodology and CA.

competent members of society use the empirically observed microdetails of conversation to understand their mundane lives and actions in real-time. This research agenda is grounded in ethnomethodology's distinctively agnostic "indifference to a priori theory." As Garfinkel and Sacks explain:

> Ethnomethodological studies of formal structures are directed to the study of such phenomena, seeking to describe members' accounts of formal structures wherever and by whomever they are done, while abstaining from all judgements of their adequacy, value, importance, necessity, practicality, success or consequentiality. (Garfinkel & Sacks, 1986, p.166)

I now address the ontological and epistemological implications of this stance in the following section.

2.2 Conversation analysis (CA)

CA is the most important offshoot of ethnomethodology. It emerged in the late 1960s and early 1970s at the University of California, Los Angeles, and other West Coast universities as a synthesis of Garfinkel's ethnomethodological ideas and Erving Goffman's more ethnographic, sociolinguistic interests in interaction ritual and face (Goffman, 1967), and speaker's footing and participation frameworks (Goffman, 1981). Schegloff's article (1968), which summarizes the empirical results of his dissertation (which was directed by Goffman), is the first recognizably CA paper to be published.

CA soon influenced other disciplines such as philosophy of mind, psychology, medicine, anthropology, communications, education, (applied) linguistics, and SLA studies. Here, I am concerned with how conversation analysts do socially oriented research in AL and SLA studies. This socially-oriented approach to SLA is known as CA-for-SLA (Markee & Kasper, 2004) or, following Kasper and Wagner (2011), as an approach to second language acquisition (CA-SLA). These terms are synonymous; I use this more up-to-date term from now on.

As conversation analysts, we have no interest in language per se (Sacks, 1984) nor, indeed, in what people say during talk either. Rather, we treat naturally occurring conversational materials as convenient empirical resources for locating and understanding how social order emerges in and through real-time "talk-in-interaction" (Schegloff, 1987a, p.207). This superordinate term subsumes "ordinary conversation" and "institutional talk" (Sacks, Schegloff, & Jefferson, 1974; Schegloff, Jefferson, & Sacks, 1977). Ordinary conversation – the everyday chit-chat that routinely occurs between friends or acquaintances – is treated as the default speech exchange system in CA. Institutional talk – such as classroom talk, which is my principal interest – adapts the norms of ordinary conversation to talk into being institutional identities and agendas (Drew & Heritage, 1992).

Schegloff (1968) and other members of the "first generation" of conversation analysts in the 1970s and 80s (Lerner, 2004) first focused on analyzing ordinary conversation. However, by the early 1990s, Schegloff (1992) and others (especially Goodwin, 1979, 1994, 1995, 2000, 2013, 2017, who was heavily influenced by the anthropologist Hutchins, 1995) began to consider how to educate cognitive psychologists about the post-cognitive insights that CA might usefully contribute to their discipline. Specifically, while cognitive psychologists assume(d) that mind resides in the head of individuals and thus shapes behavior, conversation analysts argue that cognition is distributed among interacting participants and is enacted as collaborative behavior. Thus, the body shapes the mind just as much as the mind shapes behavior. The best example of this idea in action is Goodwin's extensive research on how his aphasic father Chil, whose vocabulary was limited to the words "yes," "no," and "and" after he had a massive stroke, was nonetheless able to get his co-participants to verbalize complex actions on his behalf through a broad range of embodied actions.

As a first pass at understanding how we might conceptualize this concept, Figure 1 shows that artifacts in the general environment, the physical organization of (institutional) work (specifically, nursing, in this case), and the information flow that naturally occurs in real-time talk all contribute to doing socially distributed cognition. I discuss these ideas in more detail shortly by reviewing Hutchin's, Goodwin's, and Schegloff's ideas referenced above. Note that this last account of socially distributed cognition applies to all forms of talk-in-interaction, not just institutional talk.

In 2006, the editor of Discourse Processes asked contributors from various disciplines to reflect on whether discourse/conversation and cognitive analysis could be combined in fruitful ways (see Van Dijk, 2006). Schegloff (2006a, 2006b)[2] compellingly shows that CA is indeed well-suited to address cognitive issues, if analysts take care to develop a rigorously procedural methodology that is native to CA to demonstrate how interlocutors achieve real-time understandings and knowledge through talk. So, for example, at the level of turn-taking, first speakers observably plan the "recipient – or individually tailored – design" of turns-at-talk (Schegloff, 1979) in particular ways. That is, they observably orient to (or, to use the cognitive equivalent of this terminology, "pay attention to") the amount of knowledge (or lack thereof) which, based on information that they have already exchanged in prior talk, they may reasonably assume second speakers to know already. If second speakers are indeed knowledgeable about the cur-

---

2. See also, Schegloff (1991).

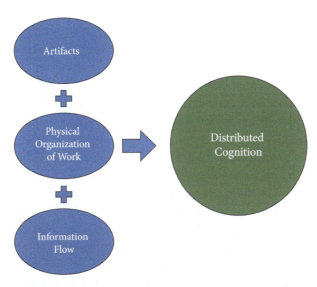

Figure 1. Principles of distributed cognition
(Agency for Healthcare Research and Quality, Rockville, MD)[3]

rent topic, they are said to be K+ speakers; if they are not, they are said to be K- speakers (Heritage, 2013). If/when these assumptions turn out to be wrong, both speakers repair their talk to re-establish and maintain intersubjectivity as quickly as possible.

Moreover, Edwin Hutchins' seminal work on "cognition in the wild" (i.e., cognition that is not studied under laboratory conditions) posits that mind is "embodied," "embedded" in social contexts, and "extended" among participants (Hutchins, 1995). He rejects Descartes' position that the mind and body are separate entities and, as I noted previously, argues that while the mind certainly shapes the body, the body also shapes the mind (see also Gallagher, 2005). On this view, members use various kinds of embodiment (eye gaze, pointing, and other gestures, etc.) to achieve socially distributed cognition. Finally, Hutchins argues that mind is also embedded in social contexts that participants make interactionally relevant to each other during talk. I discuss these matters in more detail in Section 5.2.

---

3. https://www.ahrq.gov/patient-safety/reports/issue-briefs/distributed-cognition-er-nurses2.html

2.2.1 Context in CA

How do conversation analysts understand context, and how is/are our position(s) from those of ethnographers? Briefly, following Goodwin and Duranti (1992), there is no widely accepted definition of this construct. This assertion remains as valid today as it was in the early 1990s, not least because Faulkner, Baldwin, Lindsley, and Hecht (2006, pp. 29–30) have identified at least 313 different definitions of this construct.

However, we can generally say that while modern ethnographers typically treat context as a broad phenomenon, conversation analysts tend to view context more narrowly. So, an ethnographic analysis of gendered talk in classroom interaction might "invoke a broad range of macro-and micro-sociocultural factors (which, in descending order, might include the economic, political, social, educational, institutional, and classroom context(s) of [such talk]) ..." (Markee, 2012).[4] In contrast, the purist, Schegloffian position is that talk provides its own microcontext. Specifically, a current turn is not only shaped by talk that occurs in the immediately preceding turn but also by talk that occurs in the next turn. So, an answer "counts" as an answer because the previous speaker has asked a question in the previous turn. And the last turn in our hypothetical three-turn sequence counts as an agreement or disagreement depending on the personal beliefs and opinions of the interlocutor who speaks in the third turn. Thus, talk is simultaneously (and without contradiction) both context-shaped and context-renewing (Heritage, 1989).

Anthropologists have often criticized this narrow view of context. For example, Moerman (1988, p. 57), the ethnographic originator of the contextual critique of CA, argues that "sequential analysis delineates the structure of social interaction and thus provides the loci of actions. Ethnography can provide the meanings and material conditions of the scenes in which the actions occur." However, as Markee (2012) further points out, how practitioners in these two disciplines view context is not a black-and-white matter. For example, Charles Goodwin and Alessandro Duranti, whose chapter I cited previously, are conversation analysts and anthropologists, respectively. But Goodwin is a leading exponent of so-called anthropological CA and therefore does not necessarily subscribe to the purist CA position on context.[5]

---

4. However, following Schegloff (1987a), empirically demonstrating how these different levels of context meaningfully articulate with each other is a non-trivial problem.

5. In the last 15 years or so of his career, Goodwin no longer called himself a conversation analyst. My own suggestion, which Candy Goodwin thinks is interesting, is to describe him as a very *sui generis* sort of ethnomethodologist. See also Goodwin and Salomon (2019), which provides some support for this idea.

Things get even more complicated when we note that even Schegloff (1987b, 1991) argues that it is permissible for conversation analysts to invoke ethnographic context in institutional talk provided that: (1) participants themselves orient to such information as they talk, and: (2) analysts can convincingly demonstrate the procedural consequences that such information has for their analyses. Relatedly, Maynard (2003) became a certified AIDS counsellor in the early part of his career so that he could competently understand what the AIDS patients and their therapists that he was studying were saying to each other. And finally, he suggests that post hoc ethnographic information may be used to explain "curious sequential patterns" that sequential analysis has revealed but cannot fully explain. Finally, Pomerantz (2005) makes the similar claim that conversation analysts may use ethnographic stimulus recall interviews post hoc to complement their conversation analyses of (in this case) doctor-patient communication.

In conclusion, to rephrase Heritage's (1989) contention that talk is both context-shaped and context-renewing, context in CA is a highly fluid and dynamic construct that emerges in real time talk. It is, in fact an endogenous (or talk-internal) matter which members collaboratively build on the fly by orienting to the sequential position of a turn in relation to the turns that precede it and follow it. Thus, the Initiation-Response-Evaluation sequences (see Long, 2015; Mehan, 1979), that are still prevalent in so many classrooms all over the world today are a prototypical example of how participants do "narrow" context in CA terms.

3. An overview of how conversation analysts set about doing emic research

Let me now outline how we do CA research. I begin by focusing on various aspects of the epistemology of CA.

3.1 What types of research questions do conversation analysts address, and how do we generate them?

Unlike experimental researchers, who use etic theories such as markedness, phonological, or chaos/emergentist theories, and so on to inform their work, conversation analysts engage in emic explorations of themes that occur naturalistically in the data. Specifically, research questions emerge as ex post facto members' conversational objects that arise in specific conversations between specific speakers (Schegloff, 1997). Thus, trying to impose a priori research questions on raw CA data is likely to become a futile exercise in frustration simply because the phenomena that we want to examine may not occur in our recordings.

3.2 Procedures of data collection, transcription, and analysis

Informed by the principle of ethnomethodological indifference to a priori theory, conversation analysts use the technique of "unmotivated looking" (Sacks, 1984) to allow research questions to emerge organically from the primary and secondary data. In CA, audio and/or (preferably) video recordings constitute the primary data for subsequent analysis. Transcripts constitute secondary data, which are a necessary intermediate resource that allows researchers to examine and re-examine complex phenomena at their leisure. They also function as preliminary analyses of talk in that, like all discourse analysts, CA researchers are constantly making decisions about what features of interaction they need to transcribe (or not) and how to transcribe features they consider to be important. The final, explicitly analytic phase of research starts in earnest when analysts have a good idea of what the phenomenon under study looks and sounds like and how it works.

Two forms of analysis characterize CA work: (1) "single case analyses," and: (2) "collections-based analyses" (see Schegloff, 1987b). In single-case analyses, we analyze a single case of a phenomenon (for example, how participants do telephone openings and closings) in depth to develop a deep understanding of how, in principle, this phenomenon works. In collections-based analyses, we analyze many cases of the same phenomenon to verify initial findings and to account for it in terms of a single overarching principle. The prototypical example of this approach is Schegloff (1968), who formulated an initial distribution rule for first utterances in telephone talk – answerers speak first – that was based on a collection of 500 empirical cases. His preliminary analysis of the data set accounted for 499/500 cases. However, emic analyses of talk-in-interaction attempt, in principle, to re-produce participants' behaviors in their terms, not researchers' terms. Consequently, Schegloff decided to develop an analysis that accounted for all 500 cases satisfactorily. He finally solved this problem when he noticed that the ring of the telephone was the first observable event in what he now called "summons-answer sequences." And it was this post hoc, analytically derived reformulation of the problem that eventually enabled Schegloff to account for all 500 cases in his collection. So, to conclude, this is why conversation analysts cannot arbitrarily set aside members' odd but still locally rational actions based on exogenous or a priori theory. We are thus obligated to unpack how these emic behaviors work in their own terms.

An interesting – and unexpected – implication of this tour de force[6] is that there may be less divergence between qualitative and experimental researchers' epistemologies on this matter than we might at first think. Specifically, what qual-

---

6. To be clear, few, if any, other researchers have been able to live up to this ideal result.

itative researchers call the "trustworthiness" of their analyses and the potential broader utility of this kind of research in other contexts (I am not using this word in a CA technical sense here) closely resembles quantitative researchers' concerns with reliability, validity, and generalizability Over time, qualitative CA findings inevitably accumulate as insights from potentially hundreds of studies ultimately converge on observed commonalities. We may therefore compellingly argue that these cumulative results amount to much more than anecdotal accounts of human behavior. And as even Schegloff (1993) notes at the end of his article that fiercely critiques the then heretical claims that were beginning to emerge that CA data could and should be quantified, he does acknowledge that in the case of a well-understood phenomenon such as repair, there is not, in principle, any reason why experimental research in the laboratory may not complement prior qualitative research. This position is now widely accepted (see, for example, Heritage, 1999; Kendrick, 2017; and Kronman et al., 2020).

4. The formal structure of talk: Turn-taking, repair, sequence, and preference organizations

Before I discuss how the formal structures that underlie all talk-in-interaction work, let me make three preliminary observations. First, I use Fragment 1 below to give practical examples that demonstrate how participants achieve turn-taking, etc., on the fly. Second, we should understand that these normative rules inter-penetrate each other massively. This technical term allows conversation analysts to talk about how frequently various practices occur without using the exogenous terminology of statistics. And third, the symbol "[" shown in lines 1 and 2 of the fragment represents an overlap that occurs naturally during the flow of talk-in-interaction (Appendix 1 provides a complete glossary of CA conventions used in this paper).

Fragment 1. What is your last name Loraine

```
1   Desk:  What is your last name [Loraine
2   Caller:                        [Dinnis
3   Desk:  What?
4   Caller: Dinnis
```

(Sacks, Schegloff, & Jefferson, 1974, p. 702, Note 12)

4.1 Turn-taking

This section is based on Sacks, Schegloff, and Jefferson (1974). They identify four underlying normative rules or practices to which participants observably orient as they achieve speaker change.

1. Rule 1a specifies that if a 'current speaker selects next' technique is not used, then self-selection for the next speakership may, but need not continue unless another speaker self-selects.
2. Next, Rule 1b states that if a 'current speaker selects next' technique is used, then the person selected by this rule has the right and indeed must take the next turn to speak; no others have such rights and obligations, and transfer occurs at that place.
3. Furthermore, Rule 1c says that if a 'current speaker selects next' technique is again not used, then the current speaker may, but need not continue unless another speaker self-selects.
4. Finally, Rule 2 proposes that if neither Rule 1a nor 1b has been triggered, and, following the provision of Rule 1c, the current speaker has continued, then the rules 1a-c re-apply at the next transition relevant place until transfer is successfully achieved.

I now unpack in more detail how some of these rules are instantiated in Fragment 1. Speaker change occurs at a "transition relevant place" at the end of an initial "turn-constructional unit." A transition-relevant place occurs when the second speaker projects that the first speaker's turn has ended. Meanwhile, a turn-constructional unit represents the first projectable, grammatically appropriate opportunity for speaker change to occur. These units are the building blocks of turns and include lexical, phrasal, clausal, or sentential units. The turn-constructional unit to which Loraine orients in line 1 is the sentence "What is your last name".

However, as line 2 of Fragment 1 demonstrates, second speakers sometimes come in early and overlap the first speaker's talk. Thus, when Caller/Loraine "projects" (or predicts) that Desk has finished her turn in line 1, this misfire results in a "collaborative" overlap. Collaborative overlaps happen when second speakers jump in before a first speaker's turn actually comes to an end. Overlaps may also count as "interruptions" when, for example, second speakers disagree with what first speakers have just said. It is the analyst's job to show empirically how interlocutors orient to each instance of this phenomenon to determine what actions they are performing.

4.2 Repair

This section is based on Schegloff, Jefferson, and Sacks (1977). Specifically, repair is the self-righting mechanism that participants use to fix breakdowns in inter-subjectivity between speakers as these occur in real-time talk. Such breakdowns include any sort of trouble that occurs during talk, such as problems in speaking, hearing, or understanding what has just been said. It also covers potential dis-agreements between speakers. Examples of repairs include emerging indications of trouble, such as:

1. intra-turn pauses that are realized as beats of silence that typically last 0.1 of a second, and longer inter-turn silences that typically last 0.3 of a second or longer. Jefferson (1989) considers that any silence that lasts 1.0 second or longer is a noticeably long silence;
2. words like "well" and "what," vocalizations like "huh," "uh," "uhm," and clauses like "I mean;"
3. elongations or cut-offs (usually of vowels) in such words and vocalizations;
4. overlaps, run-ons, and changes in the relative speed with which a speaker does a turn constructional unit in relationship to the speed of the immediately surrounding talk.

These perturbations often cluster together massively. When this happens, the more confident we can be as analysts that some sort of repair is underway. The most important effect of these indications of trouble is that they interrupt the ongoing progressivity of talk, an observation to which I return at the end of the next paragraph. Specifically, repair involves members orienting to a trouble source that occurs in one interlocutor's talk and which either the current speaker (known as Self) or another speaker (identified as Other) attends to as the next item of business to be addressed in the unfolding talk. Analysts use these terms to distinguish between who "initiates" and who "completes" repair sequences.

There are technically three, possibly four, kinds of repair,[7] which result in dif-ferent sequential trajectories. "First-position repairs" are initiated and completed by Self, either in the middle of their own turn or at the end of it. In the latter case, such a repair is classified as a "transition space repair." Neither kind of repair results in further sequential development. In "second-position repairs," trouble occurs in the first turn of a repair sequence but is not repaired by Self. Conse-quently, in the second turn of the sequence, Other initiates a repair on the trouble source that occurred in the first turn. This kind of repair does result in sequen-

---

7. I do not discuss fourth position repairs here because it is unclear how they differ from third position repairs and are also extremely rare.

tial development. Finally, "third-position repairs" happen when Other does not comment in the second turn on a trouble that occurred in the preceding first turn. However, the trouble in the first turn – which is owned by Self – is resolved when Self repairs this trouble in the third turn. Specifically, Self chooses to publicly notice the trouble source in their first turn and to deal with it before continuing to talk about the current topic. Consequently, this kind of repair does result in sequential development. Finally, anything, including repair itself, is potentially repairable. Consequently, a repair of a repair just becomes nested into a chain of repairs. If we now look at Fragment 1 again, we have already observed that when Loraine incorrectly projects in line 2 that Desk's turn is over at the end of line 1, Desk immediately says "What?" in line 3. This lexical turn construction unit constitutes a second-position repair. Finally, first-position repairs are the least dispreferred form of repair, while third-position repairs are the most dispreferred.

4.3 Sequence organization

This section is based on Schegloff (2007). Sequence organization has to do with how participants build up extended sequences of talk. Adjacency pairs – such as question and answer sequences – are the building blocks of sequence organization. Specifically, adjacency pairs consist of a so-called "first pair part." Typical objects that we often find in such objects include questions, greetings, or invitations (among many other actions). Prototypically, these first actions are immediately followed by a "second pair part" such as an answer, a return greeting, or an acceptance/declination of the invitation. Under certain circumstances, second pair parts are separated from their first pair parts by intervening material called "insertion sequences."

In Fragment 1, we can see that Caller and Desk use question-and-answer sequences to do three adjacency pairs in this fragment. Specifically, the first question and answer sequence occurs in lines 1 and 2. The second question-and-answer sequence is observable in lines 3 and 4. Moreover, Caller's last turn in line 4 also functions as the delayed second pair part answer to Desk's first pair part question in line 1.

4.4 Preference

This section is based on Pomerantz and Heritage (2013). Preference has nothing to do with an individual's psychological motivation to do or not do something. It is a technical term that refers to how members routinely prioritize doing simple actions rather than complex ones. The former favor the progressivity of talk, while the latter complicate sequential development. For example, as Schegloff (2007) notes, invitees who decline invitations not only repair their talk but also routinely offer excuses that attempt to justify their behavior. Consequently, the way that the talk in Fragment 1 runs off is dispreferred in at least three senses. First, Loraine's faulty projection in line 2 of when Desk's turn in line 1 is coming to an end forces Desk to initiate the second position repair that occurs in line 3. Second, this action results in the insertion of the repair sequence, which Desk initiates in line 3 and which Loraine completes in line 4. And third, this action has the further dispreferred effect of delaying Loraine's answer in line 4 to Caller's initial question in line 1. Thus, Desk and Caller's competent performance in this seemingly unremarkable fragment reveals a great deal of unexpected interactional complexity.

5. Transcription conventions: From words to multimodality and materiality

I first discuss how CA transcription conventions have evolved over the years and then discuss the analytical affordances that these different approaches to transcription offer to analysts. I concentrate on the work of Gail Jefferson, Charles Goodwin and Lorenza Mondada, as I consider that these writers have made the most important contributions to this literature.

5.1 Jeffersonian transcription conventions

Most approaches to transcription in AL and cognitive SLA studies have historically focused on producing "words only" transcripts that only record what subjects/participants say, not how they say it. Jeffersonian transcripts are notably different because they focus on how people produce talk. The transcription conventions developed by Jefferson (2004) constitute the default transcription system in our discipline. Jefferson first developed these conventions in the early 1970s to capture the details of ordinary conversation. Early CA work often used telephone conversations as sources of data (see, for example, the Two Girls transcript in Sacks, Schegloff & Jefferson, 1974). Since participants who are speaking on the telephone do not have access to their interlocutors' embodied actions, Jeffersonian transcripts of such interactions necessarily focus on verbal behaviors only. The perturbations associated with repair (see Sub-section 4.2) exemplify how granular these conventions are.

5.2 Multimodal transcription

The data gathered by Goodwin (1979) were based on video recordings. This innovation opened affordances for novel forms of analysis that expand on those that are available to analysts who only focus on verbal behavior. Indeed, it eventually led to the current programmatic interest in how members orient to: (1) "logographic" (verbal) and "visuocentric" (i.e., embodied) actions (Mondada, 2016); and (2) the cultural artifacts and material objects that members orient to or manipulate in the immediate "exogenous" (or talk-external) environment. Thus, members routinely – and skillfully – weave many kinds of resources together into a multi-semiotic tapestry of behavior. In so doing, they accomplish mundane – but complex – social actions which constitute the analytical bread and butter of multimodal CA.

Following Nevile (2015), it seems that a majority of the papers published in the prestigious journal Research on Language and Social Interaction now uses multimodal transcription as the default mode of transcription. However, unlike the default status enjoyed by Jeffersonian transcription conventions in the logocentric literature, no such agreement exists in the visuocentric literature. For example, even in my own practice, the transcript that I analyze later in this Chapter differs significantly from the one that I analyze in the next chapter.

As I suggested previously, Charles Goodwin and Lorenza Mondada are, for me, at least, the two most important researchers in the multimodal CA literature. The transcription conventions that they use in their work are available in Goodwin (2017) and Mondada (2013). In a personal communication that Mondada sent me by email on 9/6/2016, she commented as follows on how her transcripts differ from those of Goodwin:

> I think there is a slight difference in the way I consider transcripts and the way Chuck does it. He works much more on the images. Images are not just referring to what happened in the video but they superimpose analyses and schematic indications. My transcripts are much more based on temporal precision. The two are very complementary.

I would first like to add a comment that piggybacks on Mondada's observation about the complementarity of these two approaches and then illustrate what one author's transcripts (mine) currently look like. First, Jeffersonian and multimodal transcripts imperceptibly morph into each other; they are not incommensurate with each other. Given Jefferson's seminal role in developing the transcription conventions for the eye gaze behaviors that Goodwin (1979) studies, she is perhaps the covert founder of multimodal transcription. Indeed, this position finds support in Goodwin and Salomon (2019). And second, my own transcripts constitute a hybrid synthesis of "Goodwinian" and "Mondadan" approaches to transcription. This is because I appreciate both the graphic richness of Goodwin's transcripts and the temporal precision that characterize Mondada's. I illustrate what this synthesis looks like in Fragment 2 to flesh out this position.

However, before I analyze this fragment, I first need to briefly discuss a version of communicative language teaching known as "task-based language teaching" (TBLT) and how TBLT uses "information gap" tasks. I then use CA to analyze how I used such a task in a demonstration English as a second language class for MATESL students enrolled in a practicum at an American university that I taught circa 1993. The ESL students that I taught in this demonstration of TBLT came from the local community. They received free instruction in exchange for agreeing to being videotaped so that the MATESL students could subsequently reflect on their own teaching or observe the innovative teaching practices of guest lecturers such as myself. My brief was to demonstrate what the methodology of TBLT à la Mike Long looked and sounded like.

Communicative language teaching emerged as a reaction to the teacher-centered classroom talk that was a legacy of the Behaviorist methods that were still used throughout the 1970s and mid 1980s (which, indeed, are still popular today). This kind of talk is massively dominated by Initiation-Response-Evaluation sequences, which give students few opportunities to engage in anything that approximates how participants do ordinary conversation. Task-based Language Teaching (TBLT) is one of many interpretations of communicative language teaching that emerged in the mid 1980s. Furthermore, the kind of TBLT that influenced me in the 1980s was based on the work of Long (2015) and Pica, Kanagy, and Falodun (1993), among many other researchers.[8] This version of TBLT relies on various kinds of small group work-mediated tasks that are designed to give learners the opportunity to produce talk that, in CA terminology, supposedly simulates the norms of ordinary conversation. Tasks operate on the principle that if information is distributed unequally among participants, the resulting "information gap" provides an incentive for learners to bridge this gap and to complete the task successfully with whatever linguistic resources they might currently possess, irrespective of their proficiency level.

The non-interventionist methodology that I used involved not pre-teaching any grammar or vocabulary to the students, thus forcing the participants to rely on their currently available linguistic resources to complete the task. All I did during the first phase of instruction (which lasted for approximately 25 minutes) was

---

8. This discussion therefore excludes any discussion of the important work of Prabhu (1987), who pioneered the first version of TBLT during the implementation of the Bangalore Project in southern India.

to act as a timekeeper who ensured that students remained reasonably on-task. I only adopted a more conventional teacher's role during the second phase of instruction (not shown here), when I gave feedback on errors that I had observed in the previous phase. These were mostly lexical in nature.

The information gap task that I used is exhibited in Figure 2:

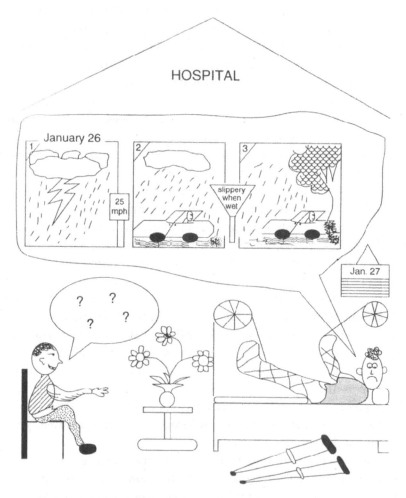

Figure 2. The Hospital Task (Markee, 1997, p. 36)

The multimodal transcript of the interaction which the Hospital Task generated is shown in Fragment 2. This fragment shows concurrent views from Cameras 1 and 2. The first view in the upper part of the graphic captured activity at the blackboard, while the second view recorded the actions of the remaining students in the class. The students recorded by Camera 2 all had copies of the drawing shown in Figure 2 and were, therefore, the K+ participants in this task. Student C, who was recorded by Camera 1, did not have access to this drawing and was thus the K- party in this task.

Fragment 2. A hybrid multimodal transcription of the Hospital Task (Majlesi & Markee, 2018, p. 253)

1   C: u::hm?
2   I: hh you↑can't↓ u:h.(.)draw↑again.
3   (1.0) **you::**? (0.7) drawing (ze)
4   one two three (0.*8) and (.) a:(h)ll hh*
                          * ....I draws a bubble in the air=*
5   *(0.1)*
         * ....=A draws a bubble in the air*

Frame Grab 1

Student I draws a bubble in the air. This is followed by Student A who does the same.

5.2.1 *Analysis*

Fragment 2 combines the graphic richness and analytic commentary that characterizes Goodwinian transcripts with the temporal precision of Mondadan transcripts. But what does this hybrid multimodal transcript afford us analytically that earlier Jeffersonian transcripts (such as the one that I exhibited in Fragment 1) cannot? The answer to this question is complicated. Student I was a true beginner who had few pre-existing linguistic resources at his disposal. Consequently, he had hardly participated at all in the previous 25 minutes or so of interaction. Yet, his multi-semiotic actions in lines 2–5 of Fragment 2 eventually led to the successful completion of this task. Specifically, note how he exquisitely choreographs his talk with his large gesture in line 4. Then observe the perfect orchestration between the 0.1 second pause that occurs in line 5 that co-occurs with Student A's similar, though smaller, gesture. After another 19 lines of interaction (not shown here), Student C finally understood that the disconnected pictures in the top right part of her picture on the blackboard were part of the story being told by the stick figure lying in bed in Figure 2. Interestingly, she just drew a big speech bubble around these objects and linked them to the face of the injured man lying in bed. But she did not say anything to demonstrate that she had understood the instructions initiated by Student I.

A preliminary analysis of this fragment that we had transcribed to Jeffersonian standards of granularity in Majlesi and Markee (2018) had considerable power and yielded undeniably impressive results. However, the analytic affordances of a Jeffersonian transcript are limited in comparison with those of the multimodal transcript exhibited here. For example, the Jeffersonian transcript did not allow us to capture the full complexity of the participation framework that is empirically observable in Fragment 2. Specifically, this kind of transcript could not tell us that, although she was silent, Student A was nonetheless actively participating in giving instructions to Student C by replicating Student I's circular gesture. When compared to the multimodal analysis discussed above, the analysis based on a Jeffersonian transcript was, therefore, incomplete, not to say misleading.

This apparently small observation has at least three important implications for CA. First, the fact that Student I starts the breakthrough moment that ultimately leads Student C to successfully complete the task is a remarkable achievement of socially distributed cognition by Students I, A and C (among others). Second, Student I's gesture is more important than the halting talk that he concurrently produces as a resource for achieving task success. Third, remember that both Student C and A's embodied actions are completely silent response turns to previous turns that are done in-and-through-talk. So, turn-taking is observably not an exclusively verbal activity. It can also be a multi-semiotic action. It remains to be seen how frequently this situation obtains. This is a research question that quantitative, experimental research would be well-placed to answer.

6. Critiques and responses

CA has always been a polemical discipline. There are at least three major controversies that illustrate how CA practitioners and their critics (some of whom are other CA practitioners) have debated how talk should be analyzed. Chronologically speaking, the first involves Moerman's (1988) contextual critique of CA, in which he charges that CA analyses that are not embedded in a larger ethnographic context are too "dry." The second, known as the Schegloff/Wetherell/Billig debates, was initiated by Schegloff (1998). His argument focuses on whether critical discourse analysts should use CA as a preliminary resource to ground in a "properly" non-ethnographic fashion their a priori contention that talk is a product of political and other factors. And the third concerns epistemics, a line of research that was pioneered by John Heritage and colleagues (for example, Heritage, 2012; Heritage & Raymond, 2005). Here, I concentrate particularly on the Schegloff/Wetherell/Billig debates, as these exchanges are more accessible to non-specialists in terms of showing how CA researchers typically respond to external criticism. I, therefore, first discuss Moerman's and then Lynch and Douglas' critiques of CA quite briefly. Finally, I look at the polemic between Schegloff on the one hand and Wetherell and Billig on the other in more detail.

6.1 Moerman's contextual critique of conversation analysis

As I showed in Section 2.2.1, trying to understand context in CA is a byzantine undertaking. Furthermore, the ongoing controversy between disciples of Schegloff's narrow, purist perspective on context and followers of Charles and Marjorie Goodwins' broader anthropological point of view on this matter remains unresolved. I therefore think that while both sides have good arguments to support their positions, there is little more that I can usefully say about this matter.

6.2 The epistemics debate

Lynch and Wong (2016, p. 526) argue that "the [epistemic program] is cognitivist in the way that it emphasizes information exchange as an underlying, extra situational 'driver' in social interaction." These and other critiques contained in the 2016 Discourse Studies special issue on epistemics boil down to five criticisms, which Heritage (2018) attempts to debunk in a rebuttal issue of the same journal. Specifically, he pushes back against claims that his work: (1) is cognitivist; (2) flouts basic methodological principles in CA; (3) introduces certain analyses of something called 'oh' prefacing, an important early research topic in Heritage's career, that are unwarranted; (4) is marred by the introduction of extraneous "hidden orders" imported from sociology and psychology; and (5) unduly emphasizes the importance of a so-called "informationist" stance at the expense of exploring other potentially more viable native CA explanations of conversational behavior. In other words, the main takeaway that I want to emphasize about these criticisms is that they violate several aspects of CA's foundational principle of ethnomethodological indifference to a priori theory.

6.3 The Schegloff/Wetherell/Billig debates

I now discuss the concerns about the ontological and epistemic assumptions of critical discourse analysis expressed by Schegloff (1998), the paper which initiated exchanges with Whetherell (1998) and then Billig (1999a, 1999b). He argues, contra Whetherell, that invoking ethnographic context "too early" unwittingly leads critical discourse analysts to swim in treacherous waters. He forcefully argues against this practice and backs up his position empirically by doing a conversation analysis of two fragments of gendered talk. As Schegloff points out, critical discourse analysts frequently focus on gender issues in their work. Briefly, he first uses the results of a study by West and Zimmerman (2015), which statistically shows that men interrupt women more frequently than women interrupt men. He then demonstrates that if we focus instead on how interruption behaviors unfold in real-time, women ultimately "win" many more of these interruptions than we had previously thought.

In her response, Whetherell (1999) counters that while CA can be a valuable tool for critical discourse analysts, the practical effect of Schegloff's position is that it imposes an external standard of analytical validity on critical discourse analysts, which they cannot be compelled to accept. She then adds on page 388 that CA "does not offer an adequate answer to its own classic question about some piece of discourse – why this utterance here?" (see Schegloff, 1997). She also argues, à la Moerman, that a more synthetic approach that marries CA and ethnographic understandings of context is desirable. Finally, she buttresses her arguments with a well-argued empirical demonstration that shows how ethnographic insights can usefully illuminate how male school students construct their masculine identities.

The exchanges between Schegloff and Wetherell were civil enough, but those between Billig and Schegloff were not so pleasant. Specifically, in two papers, Billig (1999a, 1999b) argued that CA is just as ideological as any other approach to discourse analysis. He points out in the first paper that despite conversation analysts' claims that CA is radically emic, CA's ultra-technical terminology (what he calls "CA talk") could not be more different than the plain language that members routinely use in mundane talk. He then contends that the use of terms such as "members" or "conversation" etc. "conveys a participatory view of the world, in which equal rights are often assumed" (p. 543). He maintains that this assumption cannot be true, particularly when sexist talk leads to rape. Schegloff's (1999a) response to this argument is characteristically vigorous and, depending on our epistemological predispositions, possibly quite compelling. Billig (1999b) then tries to tone down his previous criticisms by identifying where common ground might exist between Schegloff and himself. Grudgingly, Schegloff (1999b) tries to respond in kind by offering an olive branch of his own. But frankly, even though I am a die-hard conversation analyst myself, I can't say that I find either attempt particularly convincing.

7. Ethical issues

Universities' institutional review board guidelines properly require that all researchers strictly adhere to regulations that specify how research should be conducted. Like all other researchers, my own human subjects-based research projects have been subject to review and approval by my university's institutional review board. In one instance, obtaining participants' informed consent meant translating and explaining the original English language version of the permission forms that I had developed into Italian. Fortunately, I have native-like competence in this language, but I also took the precaution of enlisting the help of a doctoral student who was a "real" native speaker of Italian to check my translations. I was, therefore, able to: (1) provide oral explanations to potential participants without any problems that explained in general terms what my research questions were; (2) explain that the worst thing that was likely to happen to volunteers who chose to participate in my research project was mild embarrassment caused by an unintended interactional faux pas;[9] (3) offer the option to anybody who remained unconvinced by such clarifications to decline to participate in my project; and (3) allow anybody to back out at any time of any previous commitments that they might have agreed to previously. In conclusion, note that these safeguards are an inescapable part of doing good research and that doctoral students and other researchers who are beginning their academic careers need to understand how important these ethical issues are.

8. Conclusions

My principal audience for this Chapter has been non-CA specialists. I have therefore prioritized making the difficult ideas and complex technical language of CA as accessible as possible to such readers. Now, as I indicated in Section 5.3, CA has always been a polemical discipline, so it should come as no surprise that my concluding remarks are too. Recall that conversation analysts' interest in socially distributed cognition perhaps depends on the use of multimodal transcription techniques such as the ones I used in this Chapter. Now this is obviously not true of cognitive SLA research that uses transcripts as empirical data. But more importantly, I want to point out that the work of Hutchins (1995) – and indeed, earlier writers who were writing about socially distributed cognition at least ten

---

9. Thus – unlike subjects in medical research who might die by participating in an experiment that is designed to test whether a treatment that is not available to the general population is safe – CA research involves minimal risk to participants.

years earlier – has been consistently ignored by psycholinguistic researchers in the mold of Long and Doughty (2003). This is disappointing because the notion that cognition is a phenomenon that resides inside the individual mind was somewhat passé even when these two authors wrote this chapter.

So, I now want to ask experimental researchers three questions:

1. how compelling (or not) do you find the arguments that I have sketched out here?
2. are these arguments too radical for you to accept? If so, what is/are the main stumbling block(s) that cause you to have this reaction?
3. However, if you do agree with some of these arguments, where do your current ideas converge with those that I have sketched out here and why?

And now, I repeat a question that I first raised in Markee (2015) and add a follow-up question that I first asked colleagues in sociocultural theory, which they have yet to answer. To update what I said then, I argue that doing "hybrid" CA (Markee, 2019)[10] inevitably means accepting that a priori theory frames subsequent empirical work. So, on this matter at least, sociocultural researchers' ontology is isomorphic with that of experimental researchers regarding how research should be done. I therefore respectfully ask you:

1. even if violating the principle of ethnomethodological indifference to a priori theory is methodologically unimportant to you, does this ontological similarity with the etic assumptions of experimental research not seriously undermine your claims to be doing emic research?
2. If you accept this position, how might this be reflected in the way you do your research in the future?
3. If you do not accept this position, can you please explain why?

References

Agency for Healthcare Research and Quality, Rockville, MD. The theory of distributed cognition. Content last reviewed August 2022. Agency for Healthcare Research and Quality, Rockville, MD. Retrieved on 21 July 2023 from https://www.ahrq.gov/patient-safety/reports/issue-briefs/distributed-cognition-er-nurses2.html

Billig, M. (1987). *Arguing and thinking: A rhetorical approach to social psychology.* Cambridge University Press.

---

10. That is, unproblematically using the methodology of CA as a tool for doing sociocultural theory.

Billig, M. (1999a). Whose terms? Whose ordinariness? Rhetoric and ideology in conversation analysis. *Discourse & Society*, 10, 543–557.

Billig, M. (1999b). Conversation Analysis and the claims of naivety. *Discourse & Society*, 10, 572–576.

Drew, P., & Heritage, J. (1992). *Talk at work*. Cambridge University Press.

Gallagher, S. (2005). *How the body shapes the mind*. Oxford University Press.

Garfinkel, H. (1952). *The perception of the other: A study in social order*. Harvard University Press.

Garfinkel, H. (1967). Studies in ethnomethodology. *Prentice Hall*.

Garfinkel, H. (1984). *Studies in ethnomethodology*. Polity Press.

Garfinkel, H. (2002). *Ethnomethodology's program: Working out Durkheim's aphorism*. Rowman & Littlefield.

Garfinkel, H., & Sacks, H. (1986). On formal structures of practical actions. In H. Garfinkel (Ed.), *Ethnomethodological studies of work* (pp. 160–193), Routledge & Kegan Paul.

Goffman, E. (1967). *Interaction ritual: Essays on face-to-face interaction*. Doubleday.

Goffman, E. (1981). Footing. In E. Goffman (Ed.), *Forms of talk* (pp. 124–159). Oxford University Press.

Goodwin, C. (1979). The interactive construction of a sentence in natural conversation. In G. Psathas (Ed.), *Everyday language: Studies in ethnomethodology* (pp. 97–121). Irvington.

Goodwin, C. (1994). Professional vision. *American Anthropologist*, 96, 606–633.

Goodwin, C. (1995). Co-constructing meaning in conversations with an aphasic man. *Research on Language and Social Interaction*, 28, 233–260.

Goodwin, C. (2000). Practices of color classification. *Mind, Culture, and Activity*, 7, 1–2, 19–36.

Goodwin, C. (2013). The co-operative, transformative organization of human action and knowledge. *Journal of Pragmatics*, 46, 8–23.

Goodwin, C. (2017). *Co-operative action*. Cambridge University Press.

Goodwin, C., & Duranti, A. (1992). Rethinking context: An introduction. In A. Duranti & C. Goodwin (Eds.), *Language as an interactive phenomenon* (pp. 1–42). Cambridge University Press.

Goodwin, C., & Salomon, R. (2019). Not being bound by what you can see now: Charles Goodwin in conversation with René Salomon. *Forum Qualitative Sozialforschung/Forum: Qualitative Social Research*, 20(2), Art. 11.

Heritage, J. (1989). Current developments in CA. In D. Roger & P. Bull (Eds.), *Conversation* (pp. 21–47). Multilingual Matters.

Heritage, J. (1999). Conversation analysis at century's end: Practices of talk-in-interaction, their distributions, and their outcomes. *Research on Language and Social Interaction*, 32, 69–76.

Heritage, J. (2013). Action formation and its epistemic (and other) backgrounds. *Discourse Studies*, 15, 551–578.

Heritage, J. (2018). Epistemics, CA, and 'post-analytic' ethnomethodology: A rebuttal. *Discourse Studies*, 20, 14–56.

Heritage, J., & Raymond, S. (2005). The terms of agreement: Indexing epistemic authority and subordination in talk-in-nteraction. *Social Psychology Quarterly*, 68, 15–38.

Heritage, J., & Sefi, S. (1992). Dilemmas of advice: aspects of the delivery and reception of advice between health visitors and first-time mothers. In P. Drew & J. Heritage (Eds.), *Talk at work* (pp. 359–417). Cambridge University Press.

Husserl, E. (1969). Formal and transcendental logic (D. Cairns, Trans.). Martinus Nijhoff. (Original work published in 1929).

Husserl, E. (1983). Ideas pertaining to a pure phenomenology and to a phenomenological philosophy. *First book: General introduction to a pure phenomenology* (F. Kersten, Trans.). Martinus Nijhoff.

Husserl, E. (1989). Ideas pertaining to a pure phenomenology and to a phenomenological philosophy. In *Second book: Studies on the phenomenology of constitution* (R. Rojcevicz & A. Schuwer, Trans.). Kluwer. (Original work published in 1952).

Husserl, E. (2001). *Logical investigation* (Vol. 2). Routledge. (Original work published in 1900–1901).

Hutchins, E. (1995). *Cognition in the wild.* The MIT Press.

Jefferson, G. (2004). Glossary of transcription conventions with an introduction. In P. J. Glenn, C. D. LeBaron, & J. Mandelbaum (Eds.), *Studies in language and social interaction* (pp. 221–240). Lawrence Erlbaum Associates.

Kasper, G., & Wagner, J. (2011). A conversation-analytic approach to second language acquisition. In D. Atkinson (Ed.), *Alternative approaches to second language acquisition* (pp. 117–142). Routledge.

Kendrick, K. H. (2017). Experimental and laboratory approaches to conversation analysis: Using conversation analysis in the lab. *Research on Language and Social Interaction, 50,* 1–11.

Kendrick, K. H., & Torreira, F. (2015). The timing and construction of preference: A quantitative study. *Discourse Processes, 52,* 255–289.

Kronman, M. P., Gerber, J. S., Grundmeier, R. W., Zhou, C., Robinson, J. D., Heritage, J., Stout, J., Burges, D., Hedrick, B., Warren, L., Shalowitz, M., Shone, L. P., Steffes, J., Wright, M., Fiks, A. G., & Mangione-Smith, R. (2020). Reducing antibiotic prescribing in primary care for respiratory illness. *Pediatrics, 146*(3), e20200038.

Lerner, G. (2004). *Conversation analysis: Studies from the first generation.* John Benjamins.

Long, M. H. (2015). *Second language acquisition and task-based language teaching.* Wiley Blackwell.

Long, M. H., & Doughty, C. J. (2003). SLA and cognitive science. In C. J. Doughty & M. H. Long (Eds.), *Handbook of second language acquisition* (pp. 866–870). Wiley Blackwell.

Lynch, M., & Wong, J. (2016). Reverting to a hidden interactional order: Epistemics, informationism, and CA. *Discourse Studies, 18,* 526–549.

Majlesi, A. R., & Markee, N. (2018). Multimodality in second language talk: The impact of video analysis on second language acquisition studies research. In D. Favareau (Ed.), *Co-operative engagements in intertwined Semiosis: Essays in honour of Charles Goodwin* (247–260). University of Tartu Press.

Markee, N. (1997). *Managing curricular innovation.* Cambridge University Press.

Markee, N. (2012). Emic and etic in qualitative research. In C. A. Chapelle (Ed.), *The Encyclopedia of applied linguistics* (pp. 1–4). Wiley Blackwell.

Markee, N. (2015). Where does research on classroom discourse and interaction go from here? In N. Markee (Ed.), *The handbook of classroom discourse and interaction* (pp. 509–526). Wiley Blackwell.

Markee, N. (2019). Some theoretical reflections on the construct of interactional competence. In M. R. Salaberry & S. Kunitz (Eds.), *Teaching and testing L2 interactional competence: Bridging theory and practice* (pp. 60–76). Routledge.

Markee, N., & Kasper, G. (2004). Classroom talks: An introduction. *Modern Language Journal, 88*, 491–500.

Maynard, D. (2003). *Bad news, good news: Conversational order in everyday talk and clinical settings*. The Chicago University Press.

Mehan, H. (1979). *Learning lessons: Social organization in the classroom*. Harvard University Press.

Moerman, M. (1988). *Talking culture: Ethnography and CA*. University of Pennsylvania Press.

Mondada, L. (2013). The conversation analytic approach to data collection. In Jack Sidnell and Tanya Stivers (Eds.), *The handbook of Conversation Analysis* (pp.32–56). Blackwell.

Mondada, L. (2016). Challenges of multimodality: Language and the body in social interaction. *Journal of Sociolinguistics, 20*, 2–32.

Mondada, L. (2021). *Sensing in social interaction*. Cambridge University Press.

Nevile, M. (2015). The embodied turn in research on language and social interaction. *Research on Language and Social Interaction, 48*, 121–151.

Nevile, M., Haddington, P., Heinemann, T., & Rauniomaa, M. (Eds.). (2015). *Interacting with objects: Language, materiality, and social activity*. John Benjamins.

Parsons, T. (1937). *The structure of social action*. McGraw-Hill

Pica, T., Kanagy, R., & Falodun, J. (1993). Choosing and using communication tasks for second language instruction. In G. Crookes & S. M. Gass (Eds.), *Tasks and language learning: Integrating theory and practice* (pp. 9–34). Multilingual Matters.

Pomerantz, A. (1984). Agreeing and disagreeing with assessments: Some features of preferred/dispreferred turn shapes. In J. M. Atkinson & J. Heritage (Eds), *Structures of social action: Studies in CA* (pp. 152–163). Cambridge University Press.

Pomerantz, A. (2005). Using participants' video stimulated comments to complement analyses of interactional practices. In H. Te Molder & J. Potter (Eds.), *Conversation and cognition* (pp. 93–113). Cambridge University Press.

Pomerantz, A., & Heritage, J. (2013). Preference. In J. Sidnell & T. Stivers (Eds.), *The handbook of CA* (pp. 211–228). Wiley Blackwell.

Prabhu, N. S. (1987). *Second language pedagogy*. Oxford University Press.

Sacks, H. (1984). Notes on methodology. In J. M. Atkinson & J. Heritage (Eds.), *Structures of social action: Studies in CA*, (pp. 21–27). Cambridge University Press.

Sacks, H., Schegloff, E. A., & Jefferson, G. (1974). A simplest systematics for the organization of turn-taking for conversation. *Language, 50*, 696–735.

Schegloff, E. A. (1968). Sequencing in conversational openings. *American Anthropologist, 70*, 1075–1095.

Schegloff, E. A. (1979). The relevance of repair to syntax-for-conversation. In T. Givon (Ed.), *Syntax and semantics* (pp. 261–286). Academic Press.

Schegloff, E.A. (1987a). Between macro and micro: Contexts and other connections. In J. Alexander, B. Giesen, R. Munch, & N. Smelser (Eds.), *The micro–macro link* (pp. 207–234). University of California Press.

Schegloff, E.A. (1987b). Analyzing single episodes of interaction: An exercise in CA. *Social Psychology Quarterly, 50*, 101–114.

Schegloff, E.A. (1991). CA and socially shared cognition. In L.R. Resnick, J.M. Levine, & S.D. Teasley (Eds.), *Socially shared cognition* (pp. 150–171). American Psychological Association.

Schegloff, E.A. (1991). Conversation analysis and socially shared cognition. In Lauren B. Resnick, John M. Levine and Stephanie D. Teasley (Eds.), *Perspectives on socially shared cognition*, (pp. 150–171). American Psychological Association.

Schegloff, E.A. (1993). Reflections on quantification. *Research on Language and Social Interaction, 26*, 99–128.

Schegloff, E.A. (1997). Whose text? Whose context? *Discourse and Society 8*, 165–87.

Schegloff, E.A. (1998). Reply to Wetherell. *Discourse & Society, 9*, 457–460.

Schegloff, E.A. (1999a). Schegloff's Texts' as Billig's Data: A Critical Reply. *Discourse & Society*, 10, 558–572.

Schegloff, E.A. (1999b). Naivete vs sophistication or discipline vs self-indulgence: A rejoinder to Billig. *Discourse Society*, 10, 577–582.

Schegloff, E.A. (2006a). Interaction: The infrastructure for social institutions, the natural ecological niche for language, and the arena in which culture is enacted. In N. Enfield & S.C. Levinson (Eds.), *Roots of human sociality* (pp. 70–96). Oxford University Press.

Schegloff, E.A. (2006b). On possibles. *Discourse Studies 8*, 141–157.

Schegloff, E.A. (2007). *Sequence organization in conversation.* Cambridge University Press.

Schegloff, E.A., Jefferson, G., & Sacks, H. (1977). The preference for self-correction in the organization of repair in conversation. *Language, 53*, 361–82.

Schütz, A. (1967). *The phenomenology of the social world.* Northwestern University Press. (Original published in 1932).

Schütz, A. (1973). *Collected papers I. The problem of social reality.* Martinus Nijhoff.

Schütz, A. (1975). *Collected papers III. Studies in phenomenological philosophy.* Martinus Nijhoff.

Van Dijk, T.A. (2006). Introduction: Discourse, interaction and cognition. *Discourse Studies, 8*, 5–7.

West, C., & Zimmerman, D.H. (2015). Small insults: A study of interruptions in cross-sex conversations between unacquainted persons. In V. Burr (Ed.), *Gender and psychology* (pp. 59–75). Routledge.

Whetherell, M. (1998). Positioning and interpretative repertoires: CA and post-structuralism in dialogue. *Discourse and Society, 9*, 387–412.

Chapter 6. Conversation analysis **109**

Appendix 1. Jeffersonian transcription conventions (based on Markee, 2015)

Note: Jeffersonian transcripts use a Courier font.

Identity of speakers

Dan:	pseudonym of an identified participant.
?:	unidentified participant.
He Hua?:	probably the participant He Hua.
PP:	several or all participants talking simultaneously.

Simultaneous utterances

Dan:	[yes	
He Hua:	[yeh	simultaneous, overlapping talk by two speakers.
Dan:	[huh? [oh] I see]	
He Hua:	[what]	
Feng Gang:	[I don't get it]	simultaneous, overlapping talk by three (or more) speakers.

Contiguous utterances

=	indicates that there is no gap between two contiguous turns.

Intervals within and between turns

(0.3)	a pause of 0.3 second
(1.0)	a silence of one second.

Characteristics of speech delivery

?	rising intonation, not necessarily a question.
!	strong emphasis, with falling intonation.
yes.	a period indicates (final) falling intonation.
so,	a comma indicates low-rising intonation.
descr↑iption↓	an upward arrow denotes a marked rising shift in intonation, while a downward arrow denotes a marked falling shift in intonation.
go:::d	one or more colons indicate a lengthening of the preceding sound, usually a vowel; each additional colon represents a lengthening of the original vowel or consonant.
no-	a hyphen indicates an abrupt cut-off, with level pitch.
because	underlined letters indicate marked stress.
SYLVIA	capitals indicate increased volume.
°sylvia°	degree sign indicates decreased volume, often realized as a whisper.
·hhh	a superscripted period indicates an in-drawn breath
hhh	laughter tokens.
>the next thing<	>...< indicates speeded up delivery relative to the surrounding talk
<the next thing>	<...> indicates slowed down delivery relative to the surrounding talk

Commentary in the transcript

((coughs))	((xxxx) are verbal descriptions of actions noted in the transcript, including non-verbal actions.
((unintelligible))	indicates a stretch of talk that is unintelligible to the analyst.
... (radio)	single parentheses indicate an unclear or probable item.

Other transcription symbols

co/l/al	slashes indicate phonetic transcription.
→	an arrow in transcript draws attention to a particular phenomenon the analyst wishes to discuss.

Minor variations (see Goodwin, 2017, p. 18)

Note: Goodwinian transcripts use a Myriad Pro font. In addition, bold italics represent some sort of emphasis which involves changes in pitch or amplitude. And superscripted asterisks before an *h are used instead of the superscripted periods that are used in Jeffersonian transcripts to indicate an in-drawn breath: ˙hhh

CHAPTER 7

Doing conversation analysis
Investigating Avoidance Strategy

Numa Markee
University of Illinois at Urbana-Champaign

Avoidance is one of the oldest strategies identified in cognitive second language acquisition. Since participants are hiding that they are avoiding using a particular item of language, behavioral methodologies that normally do not use introspection might seem ill-equipped to identify dissimulation. However (based on Markee, 2011), I show here how avoidance can be respecified and productively re-analyzed by using a longitudinal CA methodology (see Markee, 2008) to trace how: (1) ethnographic data that are "talked into relevance" by participants can be used to demonstrate how avoidance is verbally achieved in real time over time; and (2) based on feedback from an anonymous reviewer, how CA methods can also identify how different participants can simultaneously pursue conflicting agendas.

1. Introduction

This Chapter showcases my article 'Doing, and justifying doing, avoidance' (Markee, 2011). Avoidance is one of the oldest strategies identified in cognitive second language acquisition. I specifically chose the topic of doing avoidance because of its inherent difficulty for conversation analysis (CA) to handle. Since participants who do avoidance are deliberately hiding the fact that they are avoiding using a particular item of language, behavioral methodologies that do not use introspection methodologies and only use publicly observable behavior might seem ill-equipped to identify dissimulation. Nonetheless, by using a classroom PowerPoint presentation combined with a self-assessment form from a subsequent office hour as empirical data, it was possible to make the case that avoidance had, in fact, occurred. An interesting issue that emerged during the review process was how I used ethnographic context in the original analysis. One reviewer argued that it was not sufficient to demonstrate that the student had avoided the use of a particular vocabulary item based on ethnographic evidence, even if it had been "talked into relevance" by the student – a key condition for the use of such information in CA. Instead, s/he urged me to rely on publicly observable behavior

https://doi.org/10.1075/rmal.6.07mar
© 2024 John Benjamins Publishing Company

to unpack what the concurrent but different agendas of the teacher and student were as they discussed the student's classroom performance. This critique resulted in a more detailed analysis of the data that provided a more satisfying demonstration of the power of CA methods.

2. An overview of the present study

In the previous Chapter, I introduced readers who are not specialists in CA to the main themes of contemporary work in this discipline. Specifically, I: reviewed the ontological and epistemological foundations of ethnomethodology and CA; (2) discussed the types of research questions that we conversation analysts ask ourselves and how we generate these questions; (3) outlined the procedures that we use to gather, transcribe and analyze our talking data; (4) considered how we treat the foundational practices of turn-taking, repair, sequence and preference organization; (5) discussed the ethical issues to which we must pay attention; (6) outlined how our critics have reacted to our ideas and how we typically respond to such criticisms; and (7) critically summarized what I said in this Chapter and invited readers to explore new methodological ideas.

In the present Chapter, I first briefly review how the individual mental construct of communication strategies was respecified in social terms. I then outline how a longitudinal methodology first developed by Markee (2008) was used to trace how the avoidance work achieved by participants evolved over time in this study.

2.1 Communication strategies

In two influential papers, Tarone (1978, p. 195) originally suggested that communication strategies are "used by an individual to overcome the crisis which occurs when language structures are inadequate to convey the individual thought" and identified paraphrase, transfer and avoidance as key types of communication strategies. However, she later adopted a more interactional perspective and argued that:

> ... the term communication strategies relates to a mutual attempt of two interlocutors to agree on a meaning in situations where requisite meaning structures do not seem to be shared (meaning structures here would include both linguistic structures and sociolinguistic rule structures). Communication strategies, viewed from this perspective, may be seen as attempts to bridge the gap between the linguistic knowledge of the second-language learner and the linguistic knowledge of the target language interlocutor in real communication situations. Approximation, mime, and circumlocution may be used to bridge this gap. Message abandonment and avoidance may be used where the gap is perceived as unbridgeable.
>
> (Tarone, 1981, p. 288)

These two definitions of communication strategies illustrate how language learning was conceptualized in the early days of second language acquisition. Specifically, Tarone views communication strategies as individual, cognitive phenomena. That is, Speaker 1 first linguistically encodes message X in *her* mind and then transfers it to the mind of Speaker 2 through speech. Through a process of reverse engineering Speaker 1's intent, Speaker 2 then decodes the message in *his* mind, thus achieving final understanding of what Speaker 1 said. Thus, Tarone's first definition of communication strategies is based on a psycholinguistic model of mind in which communication is understood as a telementational phenomenon.

Under the influence of Hatch (1978), Tarone's second definition of communication strategies added a discoursal dimension to the initial definition of this construct, which represents an important theoretical step forward in terms of understanding the complexity of these phenomena. However, she retains the individual, psycholinguistic understanding of how mind is theorized and carries this over into the second definition. As we will see shortly, multimodal CA offers an alternative, empirically-based respecification that shows how speakers observably achieve mind, knowledge, and cognition as real-time socially distributed behaviors.

2.2 Learning behavior tracking

In Markee (2008), I developed a multimodal methodology to trace how language learning processes respecified in behavioral terms might be observed over time. Specifically, learning behavior tracking subsumes two more detailed levels of analysis: learning process tracking and learning object tracking. Specifically, "[Learning object tracking] involves documenting every time a learning object or practice identifiably occurs in different speech events, while learning process tracking uses CA methods to analyze how participants observably co-construct these objects or practices in each speech event (Markee, 2011, p. 605). In the context of the data analyzed in this chapter, I use this learning behavior tracking methodology to "show how a learner and her instructor actively orient to such issues as they manage the learner's oral avoidance of the word *prerequisites* during an episode of classroom talk ([Speech event 1], and then in office hour talk [(Speech event 2)] that occurred 11 days later" (Markee, 2011, p. 605). Finally, this analysis also shows how two exogenous written cultural artifacts, in this case the Power Point slide shown in Fragment 1 and the self-evaluation form shown in Hand out 1, are contingently talked, pointed, and gazed into relevance by the two participants.

2.3 Participants

Dan is an English native speaking English as a Second Language teacher and English for Specific Purposes curriculum designer who worked at an intensive English institute that is part of a university in the United States. He Hua is a male mathematician, and Huang Ling is a female computer science lecturer. They come from different universities in the Chinese Peoples' Republic of China and were enrolled in a special program to upgrade their science teaching skills through the medium of English. The names of all participants are pseudonyms, and the research project from which the data analyzed here are drawn was approved by the host university's institutional review board.

2.4 Data and analysis

Table 1 exhibits a simplified learning object tracking matrix which shows when the word *prerequisites* was used by Dan, He Hua and Huang Ling over an 18-day period of instruction.

Table 1. Learning object tracking matrix for the word *prerequisites*

	1/26/04	1/28/04	1/30/04	2/02/04	2/10/04	2/11/04	2/13/04
Dan (T)	X						
He Hua		X					
Huang Ling			X	X			X

For present purposes, we are mostly interested in the talk involving Dan and Huang Ling. Specifically, on 1/26/04, Dan contingently introduces this word during a teacher-fronted lecture on how to organize academic course descriptions. On 1/28/04, He Hua engages in thematically related talk with Dan, during which he attempts to recycle this word, although with mixed success (see Markee, 2008 for details). On 1/30/2004, this word first appears in written form in the mock-up of a Power Point presentation that was developed during some small group work involving Huang Ling and some of her peers. However, none of the participants verbally produced this word during this talk. On 2/2/2004, which constitutes Speech Event 1, Huang Ling then orally presents her Power Point presentation on the topics that will be discussed during a course on Visual Basic programming that she teaches in the Peoples' Republic of China. Eleven days later (i.e., on 2/13/2004), Speech Event 2 occurs, during which Huang Ling and Dan discuss how successful her presentation on 2/2/2004 had been. During this second Speech Event, the two participants orient to a written self-evaluation form that Dan had distributed to all students so they could evaluate their previous performances.

Following Maynard (2003), the ways in which Dan and Huang Ling use this form show how ethnographic evidence may legitimately be used in the context of institutional talk (see Section 2.2.1 in Chapter 1) to demonstrate that Huang Ling had indeed avoided the word *prerequisites* during Speech Event 1. At the same time, the conversation analysis of the talk that occurred during Speech Event 2 also shows how the two participants also pursued different agendas, a level of analytical complexity that could not be captured by a purely ethnographic analysis of these data. Let us now see how these data unfolded in real time.

2.4.1 *Analysis*

Before I begin my analysis of Fragment 1, note that Power Point presentations are written-documents-that-are-designed-to-be-talked-through-by-the-presenter. Specifically, we can see that in the *Other Information slide* of her presentation shown in Fragment 1, Huang Ling provides information about what the prerequisites for taking her course are. These prerequisites include background knowledge of how the Windows interface works, and basic knowledge of calculus and algebra. In addition, she also covers the topics of what textbooks will be used in the course and how students will be assessed. These written data specifically demonstrate that Huang Ling knows: (1) what prerequisites are, and: (2) how they should be presented in the discoursal context of a course description. However, if we now look at lines 7–17, which exhibit the speech that is concurrently produced as she talks her way through the slide, it becomes apparent that, although Huang Ling observably knows what the word *prerequisites* means, she is nonetheless experiencing some sort of trouble as she attempts to explain what this term means to her audience.

Fragment 1. Power Point Presentation, 2/2/04

```
1    HL:   last uh:: at the end↑ of the::
2          semester↓ we will introduce some
3          principle of the: (h)u-
4    ?:    ((sneeze))
5    HL:   user
6    ?:    ((sneeze))
7    HL:   (interfacity) design (.) this uh-
8          [(0.6)
9          [
```

Other Information

- Prerequisites
  - A background of Windows User Interface
  - A basic knowledge of calculus and algebra
- Textbooks
  - Visual Basic Programming (required)
    - By Huang Runfa, Qiang Shasha
    - China Textile University Press
  - Visual Basic Programming 6.0 (recommended)
    - By Gong Peizeng, Lu Weimin
    - High Education Press
- Grading
  - Grades will be determined on the basis of homework (10%), lab activities (20%), a midterm (30%) and a final (40%).

```
10    a::ll information about the
11    courses uh (1.0)  and uh:::  (.)
12    the restuh is uh:: (.)some
13    knowledge uh you've (.) you'll
14    will (.) (prepare) attention to:
15    (.) about uh: (.) before this
16    class/e/ you you'll have some uhm
17    (.) background/e:/and uh::
18    textbooks and uh grading and-  (.)
19 ?: that's a: ll. (0.3) thank you.
20    huh huh
      ((Clapping from the audience.))
```

Specifically, in the course of an extended, multi-Turn Constructional Unit description that begins at line 7, she glosses the meaning of *prerequisites* as "this uh- (0.6) the restuh is uh:: (.) some knowledge uh you've (.) you'll will (.) (prepare) attention to: (.) about uh: (.) before this class/e/you you'll have some uhm (.) background/e:/". This gloss is potentially an example of a "curious sequential pattern" (Maynard, 2003; see also Section 2.2.1 in Chapter 1), which may need to be explicated by ethnographic data to supplement the interactional data shown in this fragment. However, before we accept this conclusion too readily, let us see what a CA-based interpretation of this fragment can buy us. First, note that the talk in lines 7–17 is marked by a massive number of perturbations of various kinds (specifically, pauses, cut offs, sound stretches and vocalizations such as "uh" and "uhm"). These signs of trouble are indicative of extensive first position repairs (see Scheglof, Jefferson, & Sacks, 1977).[1] Furthermore, it is noticeable that Huang Ling never orally produces the word *prerequisites* during this extended spate of talk. Instead, she finally produces the word "background/e" as a generic synonym for this word in line 17. In contrast, the way she talks about textbooks and grading policies is short and trouble free, possibly suggesting that Huang Ling is observably doing avoidance on the fly because she may be having some sort of trouble pronouncing the word *prerequisites*. Let us now see whether this analysis holds up by looking at Handout 1 (the self-evaluation form) and Fragment 2 (the office hour talk that occurred on 2/13/2004 during Speech Event 2). For analytical convenience, I subdivide Fragment 2 i into Fragments 2a–2d.

---

1. See the related discussion of repair in Section 3.5 of my previous Chapter.

Handout 1. (the self-evaluation form)

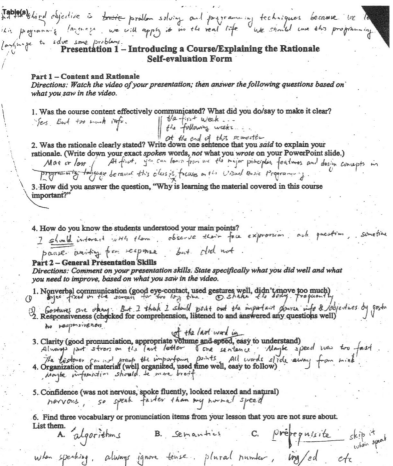

What is the epistemological status of this form in the current analysis? If we now focus specifically on Huang Ling's answers to Question 6 on this form, we can see that she explicitly identifies the word *prerequisites* as a vocabulary or pronunciation item that she was unsure about during her classroom presentation. In addition, she further annotates her response to this question with the written observation "skip it when speak."

Let us now analyze how Huang Ling confesses to Dan that she could not pronounce this word by producing a set of simultaneous and exquisitely choreographed embodied and verbal behaviors.

Fragment 2a. Office hour, 2/13/04, lines 1–6

```
1   HL:  and
2        [thi- this word uh-
```

```
3        I ·hh couldn't (0.3) I can't uh
4        speak it u::h pronounce it uh
5        correctly so I skippeduh this
6        word [ahhah]
```

Huang Ling first points to the approximate spot on the self-evaluation form where the word *prerequisites* is located (see Handout 1) as she simultaneously verbally admits to Dan in lines 3–6 that she could not pronounce this word and that she had therefore contingently skipped producing it during her presentation. This fragment is methodologically interesting on several different levels. First, these data illustrate how Huang Ling observably uses Handout 1 in Fragment 2 as an exogenous aide-memoire, thus engaging in *extended* socially distributed cognition[2] that transcends what goes on in the individual mind. In addition, Fragment 2a also shows how the activity that occurs in this fragment of talk functions as an example of socially distributed cognition that is not only *embodied* but also *embedded* in the institutional context of classroom talk. Second, they show how triangulated, ethnographic self-report data that are gazed, pointed, and talked into relevance by Huang Ling and Dan in real time may be used to confirm the emerging analysis that Huang Ling had indeed engaged in avoidance behavior in Fragment 1. Finally, note that Huang Ling does not produce the word *prerequisites* in this (or indeed any) subsequent sub-fragments of Fragment 2 that we have yet to analyze. Thus, Huang Ling continues to engage in avoidance behavior *in the very moment(s)* that she is simultaneously discussing with Dan why she engaged in this behavior in the first place.

As they continue to talk, it becomes increasingly obvious that Dan and Huang Ling are orienting to different institutionally relevant roles, responsibilities, and agendas. As a student, Huang Ling is obligated to use the form as a resource for providing Dan with a verbal account that evaluates what went well and what went badly in her presentation. At the same time, she also tries to establish herself as a good, conscientious student. In contrast, Dan does being a teacher by using this form as a resource which gives him professional opportunities to provide Huang

---

2. See also Section 2.2 in my previous Chapter.

Ling with pedagogical feedback on her work. As we will now see, these different agendas require Dan and Huang Ling to engage in some delicate negotiation work.

Fragment 2b. lines 5–14

```
5    HL:    … so I skippeduh this word
6           [ahhah]
7    Dan:   [yeah ] right well that's
8           probably strategic
9    HL:    u[hu::h, ]
10   Dan:   [I think] almost everybody
11          who [used ] that word
12   HL:        [ºuhuhº]
13   Dan:   had [a hard] t(h)i(h)i:me
14   HL:        [ºuhº ]
```

Specifically, in line 6 of Fragment 2b, Huang Ling incrementally adds a laughter token to her previous admission in line 5 that she had skipped using "this word." This action solicits an affiliative response from Dan in next turn. The laughter in line 6 is the first of many pieces of evidence that Huang Ling is orienting to the fact that her admission of avoidance is a delicate matter, as this action might open her up to the charge of being a bad student. For his part, in lines 7–8, 10–11 and 13, Dan provides a relatively positive assessment of Huang Ling's actions in two phases. During the first phase, Dan overlaps Huang Ling's laughter in line 6 with the word "yeah." In lines 7 and 8, he then proceeds to characterize her action as "probably strategic".[3] In the second phase, which occurs in lines 10–11 and 13, Dan continues by saying "I think almost everybody who used that word had a hard t(h)i(h)i:me". Note that, in phase 1, the hedge "probably" withholds complete approval of Huang Ling's action. Similarly, the word "well" in line 7 – which is frequently used as a preface to repair – and the clause "I think" in line 10 all work to dilute the strength of Dan's validation. Finally, further reinforcing this emerging impression of mitigated approval, the continuation of the unfolding assessment during the second phase of Dan's talk represents a shift away from commenting specifically on Huang Ling's action to a more generalized assessment of the class' problems with this word in general. Again, this lukewarm response – which does not significantly upgrade Dan's first assessment – is probably not what Huang Ling is looking for. Thus, Dan's laughter tokens and sound stretch that mark the word "t(h)i(h)i:me" in line 13 suggest that Dan is also orienting to the delicate nature of the talk in this fragment.

Meanwhile, in lines 9, 12 and 14, we can also see that Huang Ling is carefully monitoring how Dan's talk is unfolding on a moment-by-moment basis. This

---

3. In so doing, Dan unconsciously reveals that he agrees with Tarone's individual, psycholinguistic perspective on communication strategies.

behavior is consistent with the on-going analysis that Huang Ling and Dan are engaged in doing socially distributed cognition. Specifically, she displays her active listening by producing two precisely placed passing turns in lines 9 and 12. Furthermore, the whispered "°uh°" token in line 14 suggests that Huang Ling: (1) has picked up on the tentative nature of Dan's assessment; (2) may already be projecting when Dan's turn is coming to a close; and (3) is planning when to make a preliminary bid for next turn (see Sacks, Schegloff, & Jefferson, 1974), presumably to strengthen her justification for avoiding the word "prerequisites" in the first place. Thus, it is at about this point in the interaction that Huang Ling and Dan's competitive agendas begin to emerge.

Fragment 2c. lines 15–30

```
15   Dan:    .hhh I think the easiest thing
16           to do is
17           [ [break]  it apart
18   HL:     [ [°uh° ]
             [
             [
             [
             [
             [
             [
             [
             [
19   Dan:    in fact in our pronunciation↓ we
20           break it apart. .hh
21           [h      be]cause uh-
22   HL :    [°yea:h° ]
23   Dan:    we figure-
24   HL:     °uhm°
25   Dan :   it's like pre:::  is one wo:rd
26           [and]
27   HL:     [°uh°]
28   Dan:    then re[qui  ] site
29   HL:            [yea:h.]
30   Dan:    is the next.
```

Specifically, in Fragment 2c, we can now see how Dan proceeds with his own pedagogical agenda instead of further orienting to Huang Ling's validation agenda by providing feedback on how this word is pronounced. If we now focus on how this pronunciation work is organized in lines 17–30, we can see from the frame grab in this fragment that both Dan and Huang Ling are gazing intently at Handout 1. Simultaneously, in another display of socially distributed cognition, Dan choreographs his talk with multiple verbal and graphic behaviors that collectively break the word *prerequisite* down into its constituent parts. Specifically, the primary video data show that as Dan says "break it apart" in line 17, he simultaneously inscribes a slash into the word "prerequisite", thus: pre\requisite (see also Handout 1). In addition to these various granular, multi-layered, and multi-semiotic courses of action,[4] Dan then proceeds in lines 21, 23, 25–26, 28 and 30 to construct a detailed verbal explanation of what he is doing by including more information about how this word is stressed (see how Dan emphasizes the first syllable of "requisite" in line 28). Meanwhile, as we already saw in Fragment 2b, Huang Ling again responds with several short, place holding turns in lines 18, 22, 24, 27 and 29, all in overlap, that further demonstrate that she is actively listening to how Dan's talk is unfolding moment-by-moment. Furthermore, by line 29 (if not earlier), she also seems to be projecting when Dan's pedagogical agenda is likely to come to an end so that she can then jump in to reinstate her still incomplete agenda of justifying her avoidance of the word "prerequisites."

So, to summarize the analysis-so-far: (1) Fragment 2b illustrates how Dan asserts his pedagogical agenda at the expense of Huang Ling's competing justification agenda; (2) It also shows how Huang Ling prepares herself to assert her own agenda; (3) Furthermore, the multimodal aspects of the analysis demonstrate how Dan skillfully and contingently appropriates and alters Handout 1 on the fly as a resource for enacting his institutional agenda of doing pronunciation teaching. And finally, this fragment also shows how Handout 1 shapes the unfolding interactional organization of Dan's explanation of how to pronounce the word "prerequisites." I return to this point in the conclusion of this chapter.

Finally, let us now see how Huang Ling finally gets to assert her counter-agenda of justifying why she avoided saying the word "prerequisites" in Fragment 2d, and how successful she is in achieving this aim.

Fragment 2d. lines 28–45

```
28   Dan:   then re[qui   ]site
29   HL:         [yea:h.]
30   Dan:   [is the next.]
31   HL:    [I pra/x/c   ]iced pra/x/ci-
32          [it ]
33   Dan:   [si-]
34   HL:             in my do:rm ·hh fo:r (.) several
35          times the butuh when I stand
36          i:n the:: ·hh bui- in
37          front of the Power Point I forgot
38          it [hhh ]
39   Dan:      [huhh]
40   HL:    [so I skipuh this word huh  ]
41   Dan:   [↑heh ↑huh ↓hah ↓huh huh huh]
42          huh huh
43   HL:    I just- I justuh use another
44          worduh backgroundu:h hhh [huh]
45   Dan:                            [huh]
```

---

4. See also the multimodal analyses by Goodwin (2003a, 2003b) which document how an experienced archeology professor uses a trowel to highlight for a neophyte graduate student the presence of physical evidence in the dirt of an archeological dig to teach this student to see – and thus understand in a professional sense – what she is looking at in the soil that she is excavating.

```
46        huh °ih° that makes that works?
47        that works? that's a
48        perfect>ly:::< (.) goo:d
49        stra:tegy.
```

In line 29 of this fragment, observe how Huang Ling: (1) overlaps the first syllable of the partial lexical item "r̲e̲quisite" in Dan's turn in line 28; and (2) is finally able to expand her previous self-reported account of what she was doing in Fragment 2b. She achieves this goal by by saying in lines 31–32 and 34–38 "[I pra/ x/c]iced pra/x/ci- it in my do:rm ˙hh fo:r (.) several times the butuh when I stand i:n the:: ˙hh bui- in front of the Power Point I forgot [hhh] [so I skipuh this word huh] I just- I justuh use another worduh backgroundu:h hhh [huh]".

What is again noticeable about this extended turn is that it is heavily repaired: note the multiple cut offs, sound stretches, intra-turn pauses, in-breaths and the multiple overlaps with Dan's talk in lines 30, 33, 39, and 41–42, which are all characteristic of a repair-in-progress. Collectively, these various repair-relevant behaviors all support the analysis that Huang Ling is competing with Dan for the floor during this spate of talk. On the other hand, the laughter tokens that Huang Ling appends to the end of her turns in lines 38, 40 and 44 simultaneously ask Dan for validation of her claims that she is in fact a conscientious, not to say resourceful, student who had done her best to prepare adequately for her Power Point presentation. Finally, for his part, Dan reciprocates Huang Ling's laughter with: (1) his own multiple, affiliative – and therefore preferred – laughter tokens in lines 41–42 and 45; (2) follows up with the relatively favorable verbal assessment "that works?" twice (see lines 46–47), and (3) again praises Huang Ling for using a "perfect>ly:::< (.) goo:d stra:tegy." in lines 48–49. In the talk that follows, the participants then abandon this topic and move on to address other matters, so that the word "prerequisites" disappears from the conversation.

3. Why was Conversation Analysis (CA) used? And how was it implemented?

As I noted in the introduction, I chose the topic of avoidance because of its inherent difficulty for CA methods to handle. CA's exclusive reliance on using observable behavior enacted by participants might therefore seem ill-suited to identifying dissimulation. However, by using a multimodal learning behavior tracking methodology, I was able to show that avoidance had, in fact, occurred. The empirical analysis that I offered in the previous section is thus an example of purist CA as practiced by Schegloff and others, which only uses ethnographic context when it is observably talked into relevance by members.

4. What challenges did the researchers face? How were the challenges addressed?

Apart from the difficulties discussed in the previous section, the most important challenge that I encountered was how to make the micro-longitudinal learning behavior tracking methodology that I had first developed and used (somewhat unsuccessfully) in Markee (2008) yield meaningful results. In this last paper, I was forced to use unwarranted ethnographic data to show how this methodology *should* have worked. However, I *was* able to demonstrate that the job of respecifying the cognitive construct of learning as *language learning behavior* (see Markee, 2008, pp.408–409) was not only a *useful* but also a *viable* project. The present paper successfully builds on these foundations by using purist CA methods to track Huang Ling's language learning behaviors over an 18-day period (see Table 1).

5. Insights gained using the conversation analysis

In the introduction to this chapter, I noted that the original draft of this piece that I had submitted to the *Journal of Pragmatics* had emphasized the importance of showing how ethnographic notions of context could legitimately be used to supplement a conversation analysis of Fragments 2a–2d as the main empirical finding of the paper. However, one of the journal's anonymous reviewers encouraged me not to rest on my laurels on this matter. S/he suggested instead that I should develop a more granular analysis that showed how the participants observably oriented to the practices of turn taking, repair, sequence and preference organizations as they produced the talk in Fragments 2a–2d on a moment-by-moment basis. This suggestion proved to be good advice. The augmented analysis outlined in this chapter made me realize that Dan and Huang Ling were in fact pursuing different agendas during this talk. In this context, it is also worth remembering that ethnomethodological CA has little interest in analyzing the *content* of talk (Sacks, 1984).[5] Thus, there is also a natively ethnomethodological reason to move away from a concern with the relative truth value of Huang Ling's claims in Fragments 2a–2d and to focus instead on developing a granular analysis of how Dan and Huang Ling actually developed their competing agendas on a moment-by-moment basis.

---

5. See also the related discussion in Section 2.2 in my previous Chapter.

6. Conclusions

In summary, I have shown how the theoretical/methodological issues regarding CA that I discussed in my previous Chapter play out in observable, empirical terms in this second chapter. Now, Elaine Tarone's early work on communication strategies in general and avoidance in particular was seminal, as was her use of the ethnographic, retrospective recall methods that she used to do research on communication strategies.[6] However, neither the cognitive orientation of her work nor her use of ethnography are by any means the only way to develop a deep, qualitative understanding of how avoidance works in second language acquisition. Specifically, I argue that by *combining the naturally occurring ethnographic information volunteered by Huang Ling with* CA's post-cognitive, micro-analytic procedures, I have provided a compelling case *that she had indeed engaged in avoidance.* Emically speaking, these findings entail developing a post-cognitive, behavioral respecification of avoidance as a locally contingent practice that participants co-construct in real time. To this end, this analysis uses the longitudinal learning object tracking methodology first developed in Markee (2008). Beginning with learning behavior tracking, we can pinpoint *when* Huang Ling publicly avoids using this word (most importantly, on 2/2/04, and 2/13/04). And by using CA methods during the learning process tracking phase of the analysis, we can show *how* Huang Ling and Dan design their talk in order to achieve their divergent agendas.

In conclusion, what were the most important lessons that I learned from this project? First, recall that in Section 3 of this chapter, I noted that I was encouraged by an anonymous reviewer to go beyond an analysis that concentrated primarily on demonstrating how ethnographic context could legitimately be invoked by CA practitioners in the context of institutional talk and to develop the more granular sequential analysis of the talk exhibited in Fragments 2a–2d. As I have just suggested, this feedback resulted in the richer analysis of *how* and *when* Dan's and Huang Ling's divergent agendas-as-topics-of-talk ran off on a moment-by-moment basis.

Second, in retrospect, I now realize that, although I was familiar – at least in theory – with Maynard's (2003) warnings against relying on ethnographic data too quickly, I did not pay enough attention to his warnings. Specifically, by not fully taking into account the *procedural consequences* of the ethnographically grounded behaviors that I had documented in my first round of analysis, I had

---

6. Typically, these procedures involve researchers sitting down with participants in a post hoc interview to review interesting or puzzling behaviors that are instantiated in the data.

lost important dimensions of the data that I was studying.[7] This realization attests to the fact that when we analysts attempt to include ethnographic information in conversation analyses of talk, we must always carefully evaluate whether we are inadvertently putting on methodological blinders that potentially prevent us from engaging with other, more interesting substantive issues.

Finally, in terms of what further research this paper might generate, I originally suggested in Markee (2011) that the empirical findings in this paper might serve as a catalyst for further discussion between advocates of cognitive and social approaches to second language acquisition.[8] In addition, I also speculated that this paper might lead to more empirical work in the same vein that shows how cognition works as socially situated activity (see Eskildsen & Markee, 2018). And last, in the specific context of institutional language learning behavior, I also predicted that it might lead to research on how participants orient to, and use, a broad range of exogenous pedagogical materials.

With the benefit of hindsight, it also turns out that Markee (2011) was an unintended pre-cursor to the research program initiated by Guerrettaz and Johnston (2013) on how pedagogical materials shape interaction and vice versa. This program proved productive, and was further developed by Guerrettaz, Engman, and Matsumoto (Eds.) (2021), and Mathieu, Marcos Miguel, and Jakonen (2021). I would like to conclude this chapter by suggesting that the research documented in Markee (2011) might in future also prove to be a useful contribution to this emerging literature, especially in terms of how to conduct longitudinal CA research on language learning behavior and socially distributed cognition.

References

Eskildsen, S., & Markee, N. (2018). L2 talk as social accomplishment. In R. Alonso Alonso (Ed.), *Speaking in a second language*, (pp. 69–10). John Benjamins.

Garfinkel, H., & Sacks, H. (1986). On formal structures of practical actions. In H. Garfinkel (Ed.), *Ethnomethodological studies of work*, (pp. 160–193). Routledge & Kegan Paul.

Goodwin, C. (2003a). Pointing as situated practice. In S. Kita (Ed.), *Pointing: Where language, culture and cognition meet*, (pp. 217–241). Lawrence Erlbaum Associates.

Goodwin, C. (2003b). The body in action. In J. Coupland & R. Gwyn (Eds.), *Discourse, the body, and identity*, (pp. 19–42). Lawrence Erlbaum Associates.

Guerrettaz, A-M., & Johnston, B. (2013). Materials in the classroom ecology. *The Modern Language Journal, 97*, 779–796.

---

7. See Section 2.2.1 in my previous Chapter.

8. In this context, see the productive exchange of ideas between Markee and Kunitz (2013) and Shintani and Ellis (2014).

Guerrettaz, A-M., Engman, M. M., & Matsumoto, Y. (2021). Introduction: Classroom discourse at the intersection of language education and materiality. *Classroom Discourse, 105*(S1), 3–20.

Hatch, E. (1978). Apply with caution. *Studies in Second Language Acquisition, 2*, 123–143.

Markee, N. (2008). Toward a learning behavior tracking methodology for CA-for-second language acquisition. *Applied Linguistics, 29*, 404–427.

Markee, N. (2011). Doing, and justifying doing, avoidance. *Journal of Pragmatics, 43*, 602–615.

Markee, N., & Kunitz, S. (2013). Doing planning and task performance in second language acquisition: An ethnomethodological respecification. *Language Learning, 63*, 629–664.

Mathieu, C. S., Miguel, N. M., & Jakonen, T. (2021). Introduction: Classroom discourse at the intersection of language education and materiality. *Classroom Discourse, 12*, 1–14.

Maynard, D. (2003). *Bad news, good news: Conversational order in everyday talk and clinical settings*. The Chicago University Press.

Sacks, H. (1984). Notes on methodology. In J. M. Atkinson & J. Heritage (Eds), *Structures of social action: Studies in conversation analysis* (pp. 21–27). Cambridge University Press.

Sacks, H., Schegloff, E. A., & Jefferson, G. (1974). A simplest systematics for the organization of turn-taking for conversation. *Language, 50*, 696–735.

Schegloff, E. A., Jefferson, G., & Sacks, H. (1977). The preference for self-correction in the organization of repair in conversation. *Language, 53*, 361–382.

Shintani, N., & Ellis, R. (2014). Tracking 'learning behaviours' in the incidental acquisition of two dimensional adjectives by Japanese beginner learners of L2 English. *Language Teaching Research, 18*, 521–542.

Tarone, E. (1978). Conscious communication strategies in interlanguage: A progress report. In H. D. Brown, C. A. Yorio, & R. C. Crymes (Eds.), *On TESOL '77: Teaching and learning English as a second language: Trends in research and practice* (pp. 194–203). TESOL.

Tarone, E. (1981). Some thoughts on the notion of communication strategy. *TESOL Quarterly, 15*, 285–295.

CHAPTER 8

Grounded Theory

Gregory Hadley & Hiromi Hadley
Niigata University

This chapter explores the underutilized Grounded Theory Methodology
(GTM) in applied linguistics, detailing its procedures, objectives, benefits,
and limitations from a post-positivist perspective. It suggests ways for
educators and scholars to apply GTM to generate insightful social
interaction theories within classrooms and discusses the role of technology
in data collection. The text addresses critiques and ethical questions
associated with GTM. When implemented rigorously, GTM can enhance
not only teaching practices within applied linguistics but also offer fresh
insights to scholarly communities beyond this field.

1. Introduction

When viewed in light of the interest shown in Applied Linguistics (AL) to quantitative research methodologies or better-known qualitative or mixed methodologies such as ethnography, action research, or narrative inquiry, the Grounded
Theory Methodology (GTM) has been something of a minority interest. Certainly, one can search online to find a myriad of papers in AL claiming to have
taken a grounded theory approach, but many of these tend to be either narrative
analyses (e.g., Benson, 2018; Griffiths et al., 2014) or descriptive forms of thematic
analysis (Akcan et al., 2017; Kalan, 2016; Tarp, 2006). Empirical evidence for this
view is admittedly in short supply, but a SCOPUS search on major articles, books,
and book chapters in AL over the past fifteen years using GTM as a significant feature of their content found that only a little over two hundred works catalogued,
with the majority of these being only in the past few years. SCOPUS does not cat-
alogue the myriad of conference presentations, student theses, and reports in the
lesser-known journals, but these findings resonate with our experience over the
years concerning the attention given to GTM in AL.

When mentioned in the methodological literature of AL, descriptions have
often tended to be inaccurate. GTM has been mistakenly associated with ethnography (Harklau, 2005) or as a way of describing any form of empirically-based

https://doi.org/10.1075/rmal.6.08had
© 2024 John Benjamins Publishing Company

qualitative or mixed methods research (Canagarajah, 1999, p. 5; Nunan, 1992, p. 4). Burns (1999) conflates action research with GTM, explaining that it "parallels the directions and approaches of qualitative research, such as 'grounded theory'" (p. 25). Misunderstanding at the top leads to misrepresentation further down the line, and within graduate AL programs, egregious cases of "methodological malpractice" (Hadley, 2019b, p. 264) involving the misuse of GTM happen regularly. This is sometimes the result of poorly-informed student decisions, which may come from graduate supervisors and ethics committee members. These colleagues are often oblivious to the exploratory nature of the GTM and attempt to shift the methodology towards the strictures of theory verification, bureaucratic processes derived from biomedical practices, or methods customarily associated with post-positivist studies. The perplexity experienced by students, graduate supervisors, scholarly journal editors, and reviewers has led many to view Grounded Theory as a methodology of questionable quality, or as Silva (2005) writes, something that requires "a whole lot of effort for very little gain" (p. 5).

However, what many AL researchers may not know is that by the turn of the century, GTM was already one of the most widely used interpretive research methodologies in the world (Denzin & Lincoln, 1998). Some indication can be seen in another SCOPUS survey of journal papers, book chapters, and monographs on research publications developed from using grounded theory methodology, which found that they have continued to increase every year. In 2000, SCOPUS catalogued five-hundred works claiming to use GTM for that year. In 2010, the yearly rate had risen to almost two thousand. By 2019, nearly thirty-five hundred had been published in that year alone, with a representation ranging from Psychology, Management Studies to Nursing. Researchers in these and related fields recognize GTM as extremely useful for making new discoveries. In AL, the relatively low number of papers using this methodology suggests to us that its under-utilization stems from a misunderstanding about its procedures and purposes.

In this chapter, we will reappraise the potential of the Grounded Theory Method for AL research. When used appropriately, we will argue that GTM provides researchers with a set of iterative procedures for developing valid theories about the social and communicative interactions taking place in our second language classrooms.

We will begin with a discussion of the theoretical foundations of GTM, which will help in unpacking what is meant by "grounded" and "theory". The methodological orientation of GTM will then be discussed, together with suggestions for dissemination. This will help clarify the purposes of GTM and distinguish it from other qualitative research methodologies and quantitative methodologies of verification. Other concerns, such as the role of technology in data collection and analysis, ethical issues, and critiques of GTM, will also be discussed in subsequent sections. Finally, some of GTM's potential applications for AL research will be considered in the conclusion.

2. Theoretical foundations

Somewhat like a metaphorical sausage, most research methodologies are created from the scraps of earlier practices and scholarly sources. Some sausages are admittedly better than others, and while Saxe's Aphorism warns that one should never see how such they are made (Nagle, 2011), there is little to fear of taking a peek at what has gone into the making of Grounded Theory. The main ingredients of GTM, as we will see in this section, are those of American Pragmatism, empirical sociology, and the methodological perspective of Symbolic Interactionism.

2.1 American pragmatism

Grounded Theory was created by a school of sociology deeply influenced by the philosophy of American Pragmatism (Annells, 1996, 1997; Clarke, 2005; Locke, 2005). American Pragmatists view the social world as a multidimensional maelstrom of ideas, perspectives, and activities. Social systems are provisionally imposed upon the multidimensional cognitive and behavioral worlds. We cannot understand these social worlds without participating in them. Social reality is created and maintained by language. We agree upon mental symbols and use these to make sense of the social and empirical world. This social reality is then maintained through constant interactive discourse. Truth is an empirical experience that draws upon ideas, actions, and practices that are useful to society. That which is false does not endure because it fails to satisfy society's long-term and best interests. In order to find out this truth, American pragmatism requires one to study what people are doing. It is a constant interplay of "investigation, interpretation, and action" (Ruhe & Nahser, 2001, p. 319). However, early forms of American Pragmatism lacked clarity on how to look for social actions, symbols, and ways that reality was being maintained through interactive discourse. This necessitated further development in the form of Symbolic Interactionism.

2.2 Symbolic interactionism

The sociological perspective of Herbert Blumer from the University of Chicago is an important methodological ingredient of GTM. Blumer had greatly developed the ideas of his mentor, the American Pragmatist George Herbert Mead, and coined his version of Mead's concepts as Symbolic Interactionism (Blumer, 1969/1998). Symbolic Interactionism conceived human cognition as based on social exchanges. People learn symbols for communicating and maintaining a social life, while the symbols change meaning based on context. Social groups emerge out of constant reciprocal action and discourse. Based on these notions, Blumer encouraged graduate students, such as Anselm Strauss, one of the founders of Grounded Theory, to get out into the field and collect qualitative data on how people used symbols and discourse to maintain their lives in social groups (Gerhardt, 2000).

These key elements penetrated Barney Glaser and Anselm Strauss's intellectual and methodological perspectives, which later would take shape as GTM. However, in addition to these intellectual influences, it is essential to remember that Glaser and Strauss were developing GTM in the 1960s. This was a time of nonconformity, undercutting authority, and of giving power to the people. Glaser especially was one to thrive in the rarified air of the 1960s, and Holton's (2011) study of Glaser's life reveals him to be a personable free spirit with an artistic temperament, one who is more than willing to challenge authority while brilliantly innovating in line with his own vision. For Strauss, it was important to find new and innovative ways for uncovering unseen social dynamics taking place in the field (Legewie & Sherivier-Legewie, 2004). Instead of relying on abstract sociological theories handed down from revered scholars, Glaser and Strauss sought to develop sociological theories from what was happening in the field. That is, to construct them from the ground up.

2.3 Empirical sociology

Empirical sociology is another essential feature of GTM, especially the work of Robert Merton (Merton, 1949, 1967) and Paul Lazarsfeld (Lazarsfeld, 1962). During the middle of the 20th century at Columbia University, these two founding fathers of modern sociology developed research methods that utilized both quantitative and qualitative data and analysis. They applied these methods to study social trends and the behaviors of large populations. One of the future originators of GTM, Barney Glaser, was their student. Glaser developed many of his coding ideas from his interaction with these sociologists. He also developed relevant concepts to describe social activities and integrated qualitative and quantitative data to develop sociological theories (e.g., Glaser, 1998; Holton, 2011).

Glaser (1998) has written about how Merton would create lists of descriptive terms – sociological codes – that were developed from his published theories. According to Glaser, Merton would arm his graduate students with these codes and send them marching out into the field with orders to validate his preconceived theory. Some students could do it, but many more could not find ways to shoehorn Merton's theories into what they were encountering in the field. Figuratively, the academic futures of these students died on the battlefield because, as Glaser (1998) explained, they could never finish their Ph.D. work. Seeing the academic lives of good students being wasted on a scholar's incompatible theory left a mark on Glaser's life, which influenced the development of GTM's emphasis on creating codes from only the data collected from the field. This will be discussed in more detail later.

2.4 Emergence of the grounded theory methodology

The origins of GTM begin with Glaser and Strauss teaching sociology and research methodology in the Nursing Department at the University of California San Francisco. Both sociologists had parents who were sick and dying in hospitals at this time. They documented their experiences and wrote a landmark book on the experience of death and dying in hospitals (Glaser & Strauss, 1965/2007). None of the two sociologists had medical experience or previous insight into hospital life. However, they were able to craft such insightful work. In order to explain their work, Glaser and Strauss wrote another book to the sociological world about their methodology, which they called the Grounded Theory (Glaser & Strauss, 1967/1999). For Glaser and Strauss, *grounded* meant that findings were rooted in firsthand evidence – the problems, actions, symbols, and aspirations of the people being studied. They also used *theory* to refer to an explanatory model that "fits empirical situations. It should be understandable to sociologists and laymen alike. Most important it works – it provides us with relevant predictions, explanations, interpretations and applications" (Glaser & Strauss, 1967/1999, p.1). As a method of inquiry, GTM seeks to:

> encourage researchers to use their intellectual imagination and creativity to develop theories relating to their areas of inquiry; to suggest methods for doing so; to offer criteria to evaluate the worth of discovered theory; and to propose an alternative rhetoric, that of generation, to balance out the rhetoric of justification featured in journal articles and monographs. (Locke, 2005, p.33)

A popular view of theory of it being is extensive and all-encompassing, like Einstein's Theory of Relativity. For sociologists, there are various levels of theory. Some are known as Grand Theories; these theories attempt to transcend specific times and cultures to describe dynamics that happen in one form or another in all human systems. The work of Weber, Marx, or Durkheim would fit within these categories. Middle-range theories (Merton, 1949) are less abstract than Grand Theories and study specific people and places to make general conclusions about distinct social worlds. Micro, or substantive theories, are those developed about specific groups' actions and social processes within specific social arenas. Grounded theories typically address the level of substantive theory, so they apply to the specific empirical social circumstances for which they were made (e.g., extensive reading classes, British presessional EAP programs, etc.). However, Glaser and Strauss (1967/1999) state that substantive grounded theories can be raised to middle-range sociological theories if the social processes of the specific area of study are convincingly applied to a wider variety of situations.

It should be noted for the sake of clarity that when using the term Grounded Theory, Glaser and Strauss (1967/1999) were often unclear as to whether they were referring to the process (methodological procedure) or the product (theory created from the methodology). In recent years, more theorists (Bryant, 2017; Hadley, 2017b) use GTM and/or GT to refer to the method and the product as *a* or *the* grounded theory.

Today, there are several versions of GTM. This development began after Glaser and Strauss had an unfortunate parting of ways later in their careers. First came the emergence of Glaserian (Glaser, 1978, 1992) and Straussian (Strauss, 1987; Strauss & Corbin, 1990) versions of GTM. Later came Constructivist (Charmaz, 2006), Post-modern (Clarke, 2005), and Critical versions (Hadley, 2019a). The variety in GTM represents different philosophical perspectives affecting how one approaches and interprets qualitative research data. While differences exist, GTM is viewed today as a family of closely-related methodologies (Bryant & Charmaz, 2007). Like most families, the different forms of GTM have more in common than differences. Some of these main commonalities are:

- Exploration over verification. While GTM might eventually develop links with the findings of other research and of theories developed by people who have also been studying the same substantive area, at the onset, grounded the-orists do not begin by seeking to validate another pre-existing theory
- Simultaneous data collection and analysis. Each piece of data (i.e., a written observation log of an event, interpretation of statistical analysis, interview transcript of an interview or online chat, etc.) is coded and then further unpacked through memos and notes. Only after one is finished with each piece of data do they search for more

- Multiple levels of coding are generated from field data and scholarly sources. These procedures break the data down into more manageable bits for analysis and prepare them for theoretical reconstruction
- Constant comparison of data, codes, memos, and incidents in the field to discover not only patterns of similarity but also situations where important exceptions occur
- A trajectory of empirical description moving steadily towards more abstract levels of theorization.

Let us now consider the methodological orientation of GTM in light of the discussion offered up to this point.

3. Methodological orientation

3.1 Principles and affordances

From the beginning, grounded theory was designed to be an exploratory research methodology. It was not intended to be used as a verification methodology, though later methodologists (Creamer, 2021; Strauss & Corbin, 1990) have added verification processes to the basic methodology. As mentioned earlier, GTM is distinct from other more popular methodologies used in applied linguistics, such as action research (AR). While both GTM and AR attend to problems that arise in the social arena, (and in the case of applied linguistics, that would be the classroom), the principles of grounded theory lead to the discovery of problems as understood by the research participants, and to learn about the solutions they find for resolving their quandary. Also, Grounded Theory is, in principle, different from ethnography as the focus is not upon a "thick description" (Geertz, 1973) of a social group, but instead, more upon "thick theorization" about what and why people do things in certain social situations (Hadley, 2017b).

GTM affords researchers ways of learning more about human action and interaction in areas or situations that have been either overlooked or under-researched. For applied linguists, this might be an attempt to better understand the ways that students negotiate tasks in second-language learning, to understand the strategies used by language teachers when creating supplemental learning materials, or, as will be seen in the next chapter, uncovering some of the conditions and processes used by students in extensive reading classes.

3.2 Types of research questions addressed by the GTM

The exploratory nature of GTM means that research questions focus on discovering human actions and interactions in general terms during the beginning of the investigation. The primary disposition of a grounded theorist is to stay open and not jump to conclusions. The main research question expressed at the beginning is *What is going on here?* Due to the influence of Symbolic Interactionism, grounded theorists seek answers by studying observable behavior and symbolic interactions. This leads to further questions seeking to learn more about the significance of what people are doing and saying. The theorist will watch for activities and take note of discourse that people in the social arena might be taking for granted but would be inexplicable to those outside the group. Grounded theorists are also interested in questions about the typical problems experienced by people in the specific social environment and any solutions that are being worked out.

Questions, therefore, become more specific later as more data comes in and after one has proceeded with data analysis. Along the lines of GTM's principles and affordances, research questions do not seek verification of the past work of scholars. Instead, the questions should provide the starting point for developing new perspectives. For example, if a second language teacher were to use GTM to investigate Extensive Reading (ER), the question would not be, "To what degree are current theories of motivation a predictor of success in ER classes?" Instead, a grounded theory question might be, "What are some of the main processes used by second-language learners in Extensive Reading?" With more research through interviews and observations, these answers will become more apparent. Then more focused questions about the properties, conditions, trajectories, problems, and solutions surrounding these processes are investigated through GT. Let us now consider how this is undertaken.

3.3 Procedures of data collection and analysis

After a period of primary initialization – that moment when the researcher's curiosity is first aroused – GTM is used to engage in three stages of data collection, which run concurrently with analysis. These are Open Exploration, Focused Investigation, and Theory Construction.

The impetus for open exploration starts with a moment of interest around something the teacher-researcher encounters in their classes, or something affecting the quality of second language learning (e.g., language curriculum committees, interaction with textbook publishers, English language speech contests, and so on). This seminal moment is when the researcher questions why people interact in certain ways. Open exploration begins with observation. The theorist takes notes of what they see and hear from the social group they are studying. The focus is empirical, so for example, if a group of students constantly falls asleep in class, the researcher would record this descriptively rather than interpreting it as an indication of student demotivation. The right margin of the observation notes should be kept open for the researcher to write short codes – which in GTM at this stage are called initial codes or open codes. More will be discussed about coding shortly, but these codes will summarize any actions or interactions recorded in the observation log. Codes will be used later in subsequent interview transcripts to describe what is happening in the data. Grounded Theorists engage in observation at this stage for a limited period since memo-writing and coding will help in the rapid development of questions that find their answers through initial interviews.

When interviewing informants during open exploration, the initial sampling of informants is open-ended and based on both a combination of curiosity and convenience sampling (Bryant, 2017). Theorists speak with anyone in the social arena willing to share their thoughts and insights. They can be conducted either in-person, online via Skype or Zoom, or as a text chat through one of the many platforms available. The added advantage of conducting an interview via text is finishing with a ready-made transcript later for analysis. The disadvantage is that sometimes it is more difficult to convey an emotion or explain things that may be complicated. Regardless of one's choice, GTM is flexibly able to accommodate one's means for conducting an interview.

For language teachers using GTM, interviews would naturally occur with students. However, they could also be carried out with curriculum designers, administrative managers, and support personnel such as frontline office workers or cleaning staff. New and surprising perspectives can be discovered because the theorist is not limiting their search to the validation of someone else's published work.

Interviews during open exploration seek for a better lay of the social landscape. Questions formulated from earlier observations will undoubtedly be asked, and more general questions about the social environment. Informants are asked to describe what a good day or a bad day looks like for them. Questions about good days help identify social processes and typical routines people use to maintain their specific social circle. Asking about bad days helps uncover problems and strategies used as possible solutions. The study of social interaction around routines, problems, solutions, and the maintenance of social reality, is the bread and butter of Grounded Theory research.

In addition to interviews, in the beginning, we also advocate the use of repertory grids (Hadley, 2019a; see Grogan, this volume). This method of inquiry does much to lessen the imposition of the researcher's inferences and constructs by allowing informants greater latitude in expressing their worldview and concerns on the research issue. Moreover, the data elicited by repertory grids often lend themselves to becoming useful informant-generated codes. In GTM literature, these are called "in-vivo codes" (Corbin & Strauss, 2015, p.216), which is another type of open code used at this stage.

Turning our attention now to coding, Charmaz (1983) describes it as "simply the process of categorizing and sorting data" in order to "summarize, synthesize, and sort many observations made out of the data" (pp.111–112). Codes in GTM are generated from the data. In response to Merton's tendency of giving graduate students prepackaged codes and then requiring them to find data for verification, GTM goes in the other direction, in that *the analyst must do his own coding.* (Glaser, 1978, p.58, emphasis in original).

To understand coding, we find it helpful to think about some ancient manuscripts one might find in a great library. Later copies of these writings will often have titles and subtitles that have been written later by those trying to interpret the texts. Thinking about an old book or manuscript with those titles and subtitles can serve as an excellent mental picture of what we mean when talking about open codes. In addition, many today follow Charmaz's (2014) advice of writing initial codes in the form of gerunds. This gerunding process "sticks closely to the data" (Charmaz, 2014, p.112) by helping researchers avoid premature interpretations and to focus on empirical actions. This will set the stage later for uncovering "implicit meaning and actions" (Charmaz, 2014, p.124).

At the same time that grounded theorists are coding an observation log or an interview, they also will write memos when any good ideas or questions come to mind. A memo allows the researcher to define and thoroughly explain what it means, especially when one has created a code that seems to faithfully encapsulate some meaningful range of human activity. Memo-writing is vital to GTM. It is an activity for brainstorming, developing new working hypothetical explanations, formulating questions, and deciding who should be interviewed for the following data collection event.

After writing a memo, the researcher will return to coding. They use any codes and ideas made from the earlier data collection event(s) that fits for dataset they are currently analyzing. However, new open codes will be added when additional information emerges from the data. This will be followed by the writing of new memos. This process repeats, perhaps with no more than six to eight informants. We are often asked as to how many people are typically interviewed throughout the process of doing grounded theory research. Methodologists report that between 20 to 40 interviews are usually sufficient for developing a robust grounded theory (Creswell, 1998; Hadley, 2017b; Stern & Porr, 2011). Interviews during open exploration are only the beginning of a process that will become more and more focused on specific topics over time. This is why grounded theorists do not stay in open exploration for a long time. Otherwise, they would make hundreds of open codes that would be extremely difficult to focus on for later stages of the investigation.

Throughout this and later stages, theorists engage in Constant Comparison (Glaser & Strauss, 1967/1999). This entails thinking about the activities, words, beliefs, and other social symbols that are similar from interview to interview and from situation to situation. It also entails noticing when, where, and why human activities differ in certain situations. Constant Comparison helps theorists to avoid developing a confirmation bias that, similar in some ways to a conspiracy theory, one begins seeing patterns everywhere. Instead, they actively search for times, places, and situations where the developing theory does NOT work, because this further delineates the limitations of the developing grounded theory.

A controversial feature of GTM is that theorists should not seek out scholarly literature they believe might apply to their study during open exploration. This aspect of GTM is often misunderstood, and we will discuss this point later. At this point, it is sufficient to note that consulting the scholarly literature is avoided only during open exploration. However, the literature study becomes a vital part of the next stage of the focused investigation.

The focused investigation starts after a few cycles of interviewing, open coding, and memo writing. By this time, the theorist will have started to get some indication about the key concerns and social interactions taking place in the data. Therefore, It is important to temporarily stop data collection and engage in a focused coding (Charmaz, 2014). This is essentially a coding of the open codes. The researcher studies the open codes and organizes them into small groups that seem to share some element of commonality. These main groupings of open codes are then given summative coding labels. Ideally, these should highlight action in the form of a gerund. These focused codes will be more interpretive since they have been created from open codes instead of directly from the empirical data from the field. The open codes are still inside these focused codes, and the researcher will write memos that define the focused codes and should build that definition from a discussion of the open codes contained within each focused code. Any open codes that do not seem to fit anywhere or seem otherwise peripheral to the main group of other open codes are stored away for safekeeping and removed from future analysis. The researcher should have no more than ten to fifteen focused codes. From this point onward, the researcher uses only these action-oriented focused codes (e.g., *encountering push-back, managing study challenges, steeping oneself in English*) for future data collection and analysis.

As focused investigation commences, the researcher theorist uses the focused codes to inform the theoretical sampling (Charmaz, 2006). Theoretical sampling is the practice of seeking out people, materials, and places that reveal more *about the focused codes*. The researcher is not sampling people per se but instead wants to learn more about the activities represented within the focused codes. In addition to searching for whoever and whatever helps explain the behavior, they also search for pertinent research literature. These are published materials that fit with the emerging social interactions. Grounded theorists do not use this literature to validate their work (or their research to validate scholarly sources). Instead, as Glaser (1978, p.138) explains, they treat the literature like another research informant. Instead of using literature to legitimate their developing theory, they enter into a dialog with other scholars who were working with similar ideas.

In the same manner as if one were conducting an interview, focused codes are attached to the pertinent parts of scholarly literature that one accesses at this stage. Memo-writing is very important since the researcher needs to both explain and justify the interpretive choices for applying the code to certain material and will explain other insights, such as the additional conditions affecting the code, trajectory of specific strategies or behaviors, problems encountered, additional dimensions of the code, and times when the social processes are diverted or disrupted in some way.

There may be times, however, when the theorist uncovers something new and significant, which up to this point, has not been represented by their set of focused codes. In this case, they may need to go back to open exploration and look at other open codes that had been put aside to see if they have any bearing on the new discovery. However, the grounded theorist needs to return to focused coding as soon as possible, not to become mired in constant open exploration. If this happens, the flow of theory development can become short-circuited.

When does the researcher then shift towards theoretical construction? Ian Dey (1999), a qualitative researcher at the University of Edinburgh, developed a helpful notion called 'theoretical sufficiency'. This means that once the researcher has enough material to create a convincing and well-documented theory, it is unnecessary to discover every possible contingency. A good rule of thumb is that if one is spending more and more time and energy to find less and less that is new or unexpected, then one has probably approached theoretical sufficiency. From this point, the focus is on theory construction.

Theory construction takes all the material that the grounded theorist has broken down and reconstructs everything into a conceptual map of social interactions. The way this is carried out is similar to the start of the focused investigation. First, focused codes are grouped together and given more abstract categorical titles. To find out more about how these higher, more abstract categories work, the researcher continues to interview, conduct field observations, and study scholarly material to find more about the dimensions and external conditions that might affect how a particular category relates with other theoretical categories. Next, the theorist connects them with lines and describes the nature of their interactive links with short descriptive phrases. These descriptions are called theoretical codes. Over time, one category may emerge that seems to be more interconnected than the rest. This is often called the core category of the grounded theory. Other times, however, again, similar to how focused codes and other theoretical categories were formed, another higher-order category that captures the features of the other theoretical categories will be created. This overarching category expressed sometimes in a manner similar to the title of a book, will poignantly reveal the social phenomenon that is the heart of the grounded theory. It is the sum of what the researcher has been studying. However, getting to this point is rarely easy and straightforward, and the researcher typically must go back and forth between focused investigation and theory generation. Throughout the process, the researcher continues with constant comparison analysis and persists in looking for as many ways to break as they do to make the theory. By finding places where the theory does not work, one discovers the limits of its explanatory power. This facilitates the construction of a more well-defined and plausible theory of what is going on in the studied social settings.

It can be seen that the analysis of data runs concurrently with its collection throughout the process of GTM. This can be done by maintaining a system of notes and of ordering transcripts in a word processing program, where one can affix codes using the insert comments function. Specialist software tools also exist for facilitating the analysis of qualitative data. Known as Computer Assisted Qualitative Data Analysis Software (CAQDAS), these programs are designed to facilitate the storing, coding, searching, and graphing qualitative data and can be used for grounded theory projects. Some of the more well-known CAQDAS are NVIVO (QSR International, 2018), MAXQDA (VERBI Software, 2019) , and ATLAS.ti (Scientific Software Development, 2020). Such programs are very helpful in organizing qualitative data, because they keep everything in one place and make the coding of transcripts and memos fast and easy. Some programs, such as MAXQDA, have robust statistics packages, which would be of great help to theorists. As useful as these programs are, however, all are extremely expensive, difficult to use, and researchers may find themselves limiting their theorization to what is accommodated by the programs. In addition, none of the programs are vital. The engine of analysis is the grounded theorist, not the software. From a grounded theory perspective, research papers mentioning the name of a CAQDAS package should not necessarily impress readers any more than informing readers about the word processing software used to write the research paper.

With a bit of organization using a program such as Microsoft Excel or Word, or even with notebooks and a note card system, researchers can develop a grounded theory without CAQDAS. GTM is a methodology that continues to be

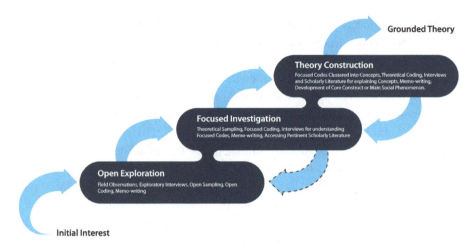

Figure 1. Grounded Theory Process

available to all interested researchers, regardless of their access to funding to purchase technology.

Wrapping up our discussion on data collection and analysis, as seen in Figure 1, the steps and stages move recursively and methodically from descriptive open exploration to focused interpretative investigation and then towards a creative theoretical explanation. When finished, one will have constructed an explanatory theory about how and why people do things in specific social environments (such as a second language classrooms, for example). The grounded theory will enable second language educators to develop new insight when they hear others making certain statements or seeing them engaged in certain activities.

The theory equips second language educators with a new set of vocabulary – conceptual tools for relating to a social situation. This is empowering because those aware of the theory can decide how to act to improve a particular setting and recognize when it might be best to make a strategic exit. The ability to make informed decisions will allow them to interact more intentionally within specific social circumstances.

3.4 Ethical issues

Ethical review of the qualitative research project proposals has been the source of much controversy over the past several years. The creep of governmental and bureaucratic bodies within educational institutions, such as university institutional review boards (IRBs), have placed increasing demands on qualitative researchers to ensure that their research is ethical. The intellectual freedom to engage in exploratory research, such as that found in grounded theory, often depends upon the particular institution and the personalities sitting on IRBs. Hammersley and Traianou (2012) have documented egregious cases of what they have called "ethicism" – a situation where the term *ethics* becomes a proxy for intellectual censorship and enforced conformity to post-positivist beliefs about what constitutes proper research. In such institutions where ethicism is rampant, research not engaging in hypothesis verification can become the object of suspicion, leading it to be stigmatized as potentially unethical (Cheek, 2005; Lincoln, 2005). This is because hypotheses cannot be clearly stated beforehand, and research questions tend to be very general and open-ended until later, when the investigation begins to progress. Sometimes, an IRB may come across as being tasked more with protecting their institution from possible lawsuits resulting from an informant claiming harm due to unpleasant questions. In such cases, it may be difficult to gain permission to conduct a study using a method such as grounded theory.

Cases like the above scenario, however, are often the most extreme. More enlightened IRBs will understand that mixed methods and qualitative research methodologies, such as GTM, are not in and of themselves unethical simply because they may not conform to predetermined bureaucratic processes. Rose et al. (2019, p. 121) state that so long as "researchers have taken necessary precautions: to avoid coercing participants, to protect their privacy and identity, to prepare participants by letting them know what is expected of them, and to be respectful always", then one can use GTM and avoid the pitfalls of being accused of engaging in unethical behavior. To remain ethical, grounded theorists must strive to design questions and lines of inquiry that consider the research informants. They should not pry if their participants seem uncomfortable with one's line of questioning. An ethical focus for the grounded theorist is on seeking to understand with compassion. This stance entails working together with research informants to develop an explanatory theory that empowers them with deeper insight into their situation and the reasons for specific problems and ideas for possible solutions. It is not the unethical approach of one seeking to mine people for data simply in order to construct a theory.

4. Critiques and responses

Even though GTM, as Miller and Fredericks (1999) have noted, "…has become a paradigm of choice in much of the qualitatively oriented research in nursing, education, and other disciplines" (p. 538), questions remain regarding the nature of the methodology. In this section, we will address some of the most common concerns – those of confusing terminology, a lack of critical awareness of issues in the field, the potential for bias confirmation, the apparent lack of verification procedures, and the role of scholarly literature during the beginning stage of the investigation.

Critics of GTM have pointed to what they see as confusing terminology (Backman & Kyngas, 1999; Bell, 2005), an overemphasis on inductive reasoning (Harry et al., 2005; Schenk et al., 2007), theoretically strengthening an oppressive status quo (Burawoy, 1991; Layder, 1982), and the risks of bias (Allan, 2003).

Charmaz (2006, p. 134) has responded to critiques regarding confusing terminology first by noting that many critiques are based upon a limited reading of Glaser and Strauss's (1967) original work. In addition, she notes that most critics have neither used GTM nor followed how it has matured and evolved over the years. Grounded Theory developers (Charmaz, 2009; Strauss & Corbin, 1994) argue that most critics are unaware that Glaser and Strauss moderated many of their initial claims and that later books on GTM have sought both to clarify terminology and to encourage transparency in methodological practices (Bryant, 2017; Charmaz, 2006; Corbin & Strauss, 2008). The charge of Grounded Theory as over-relying on induction, a result of Glaser's excessive polemics (Glaser, 1992; Glaser & Holton, 2004), has also moderated by the later work of other grounded theorists (e.g., Gibson & Hartman, 2014).

A more serious critique is on the focus GTM has traditionally placed on the informant's specific social environment. Burawoy (1991) argues that 'in focusing on variables that can be manipulated within the immediate situation, [Grounded Theory] represses the broader macro forces that both limit change and create domination in the micro sphere' (p. 282). Layder (1993) agrees and calls for GTM to give more attention to oppressive social influences that affect the informants. Charmaz (2006) admits that early grounded theorists were uninterested in problems related to power and inequality. However, she argues this as a shortcoming of the *theorists*, not the *methodology*. Grounded Theory is eminently capable of addressing social justice issues, as we have demonstrated over the past several years (Hadley, 2015, 2017a, 2019a).

The objections to GTM we most frequently encounter at AL conferences or from reviewers of scholarly journals relate to questions of mistrust. This is expressed as concern about the potential of researcher bias and the apparent lack of verification procedures for strengthening the theory's process and product reliability and validity. Both Glaser (2002) and Charmaz (2009) acknowledge that bias will always be a challenge when viewed from a post-positivistic perspective. We are all limited by our experiences, perspectives, and degree of theoretical sensitivity. Together with Allan (2003), they inveigh theorists to maintain an awareness of their potential for bias and make concrete efforts at checking with others to challenge any assumptions. This works in conjunction with constant comparison. As we saw earlier, a theorist must actively debunk any emerging patterns early on and critically assess evidence when negative cases are uncovered. Grounded theorists may be limited, but the good ones constantly challenge their bias to construct a fair and unfettered account.

Concerns about reliability and validity are post-positivist standards more appropriate for quantitative research. Qualitative researchers, such as Sikolia et al. (2013), have suggested that other standards, such as credibility, transferability, dependability, and confirmability, are better ways to judge the quality of a grounded theory. While some AL researchers may balk at such alternative standards on philosophical grounds, such objections on their own do not necessarily invalidate the quality of a grounded theory study.

Especially when one considers the spread of GTM over the years, there is considerable concern about how it might be damaging to graduate students, especially with the stipulation of avoiding the scholarly literature during the early stages of exploration. This has led some to believe that one can construct a grounded theory without reading academic literature (McCallin, 2003). To dispel these assumptions, three points need to be made. The first is that Glaser and Strauss (1967/1999) were writing primarily to sociologists with theoretical perspectives developed from their years of study and field research (Glaser & Strauss, 1967/1999). These insights and perspectives are called 'theoretical sensitivity' (Glaser & Strauss, 1967/1999, p. 46). They explained that theoretical sensitivity would guide experienced researchers, who, while well-informed, nevertheless had chosen to stay open to other possibilities about what might be taking place in their area of study. This point cannot be understated because, with respect to AL, the current problem of GTM methodological malpractice stems from those who want to use the methodology but lack qualitative research experience and/or require more time to better understand the basic texts in our field. GTM is an advanced methodology better suited for Ph.D. students and classroom practitioners who have already carried out a few qualitative research projects. The theory is only as good as the theorist, so a good grounding in the scholarly discussions within our academic community is necessary. This will develop one's sensitivity, even as the theorist is careful to curb any proclivity towards bias.

According to Glaser (1998), the second point is that consulting the scholarly literature in the early stages of GTM risks limiting the theorist to verifying concepts gleaned from their readings. This concern very likely comes from Glaser's experience of Merton as a Ph.D. student, as mentioned earlier in this paper (Glaser, 1998, pp. 30–31). Glaser's intention is for grounded theorists to enter the field free from other people's ideas, because the focus is on exploration rather than verification. Reading other material that seems pertinent to the field's concerns at this stage might cause a researcher to overlook clues that could lead to new insights or discoveries. Glaser did not want grounded theorists to risk getting 'stuck' from not being about to fit pre-packaged ideas with data emerging from the field, or to resorting to forcing the data to fit with the scholarly concepts in ways that were inappropriate.

Finally, Birks and Mills (2011) have noted that even though Glaser and Strauss went in different directions later regarding the role and timing of scholarly literature, neither they nor any other reputable grounded theorist has ever advocated for one to completely neglect the reading pertinent academic sources. Instead, as seen earlier in our discussion of the methodology, it is more a case of putting off the consultation of the literature until specific problems, processes, and issues – as expressed by the informants – get noticed by the investigator. Hallberg (2010) admits this to be a tricky balance to maintain – one of being well-informed, purposefully open to new ideas, and allowing the data to guide the literature review. Nevertheless, accessing the data in this way, which occurs later during the focused investigation stage of GTM, often yields dividends later in the form of insightful interdisciplinary studies. This means that GTM encourages the formation of links with pertinent scholarly literature and with what is happening in the field and results in interdisciplinary studies with the potential of reaching academic fields beyond the confines of AL. We believe this is one of the most significant potential contributions of GTM. Too long as a scholarly community, we, as applied linguists, have been reliant on other disciplines to feed us with new ideas and insights. And yet, many applied linguists are multilingual, endowed with insight into different cultures. Many of us interact daily with people in places far beyond researchers' access from other fields. We have much that we can offer to the world, and GTM has excellent potential as a vehicle for making that happen.

5. Conclusions

Although largely neglected in applied linguistics research, the Grounded Theory Methodology is one the most widely used set of procedures for exploring issues in social environments. This chapter has elaborated on the methodology, purposes, strengths, and weaknesses of GTM (for those more comfortable with quantitative methods used from a post-positivist perspective). We have argued that language teachers and scholars can utilize GTM to develop insightful theories on social interactions in our classrooms and beyond. Critiques of GTM have been addressed, as well as questions related to ethics. GTM, when carried out in an informed and rigorous manner, can contribute not only to better practices within our own areas of teaching but also aid in providing new insights to scholarly communities beyond the field of applied linguistics.

Funding

This work was supported in part by a JSPS Grant-in-Aid for Scientific Research (Grant Number 19K00846). We have no conflicts of interest to disclose.

References

Akcan, S., Aydin, B., Karaman, C., Seferoğlu, G., Korkmazgil, S., Özbilgin, A., & Selvi, A. (2017). Qualities and qualifications of EFL professionals: What do intensive english program administrators think? *TESOL Journal, 8*(3), 675–699.

Allan, G. (2003). A critique of using grounded theory as a research method. *Electronic Journal of Business Research Methods, 2*(1), 1–10. Retrieved 18 March 2021 from https://academic-publishing.org/index.php/ejbrm/article/view/1168/1131

Annells, M. (1996). Grounded theory method: Philosophical perspectives, paradigm of inquiry, and postmodernism. *Qualitative Health Research, 6*(3), 379–393.

Annells, M. (1997). Grounded theory method, part 1: Within the five moments of qualitative research. *Nursing Inquiry, 4*(2), 120–129.

Backman, K., & Kyngas, H. (1999). Challenges of the grounded theory approach to a novice researcher. *Nursing and Health Sciences, 1,* 147–153.

Bell, J. (2005). *Doing your research project: A guide for first-time researchers in education, health and social science* (4th ed.). Open University Press & McGraw-Hill Education.

Benson, P. (2018). Narrative analysis. In A. Phakiti, P. De Costa, L. Plonsky, & S. Starfield (Eds.), *The palgrave handbook of applied linguistics research methodology* (pp. 595–613). Palgrave Macmillan.

Birks, M., & Mills, J. (2011). *Grounded theory: A practical guide.* Sage.

Blumer, H. (1969/1998). *Symbolic interactionism: Perspective and method.* University of California Press.

Bryant, A. (2017). *Grounded theory and grounded theorizing: Pragmatism in research practice.* Oxford University Press.

Bryant, A., & Charmaz, K. (2007). Grounded theory research: Methods and practices. In A. Bryant & K. Charmaz (Eds.), *The SAGE handbook of grounded theory* (pp. 1–28). Sage.

Burawoy, M. (1991). The extended case method. In M. Burawoy, A. Burton, A. Ferguson, K. Fox, J. Gamson, N. Gartrell, L. Hurst, C. Kurzman, L. Salzinger, J. Schiffman, & S. Ui (Eds.), *Ethnography unbound: Power and resistance in the modern metropolis* (pp. 271–287). The University of California Press.

Burns, A. (1999). *Collaborative action research for english language teachers.* Cambridge University Press.

Canagarajah, A. (1999). *Resisting linguistic imperialism in english teaching.* Oxford University Press.

Charmaz, K. (1983). The grounded theory method: An explication and interpretation. In R. Emerson (Ed.), *Contemporary field research* (pp. 109–126). Little, Brown, and Company.

Charmaz, K. (2006). *Constructing grounded theory.* Sage.

Charmaz, K. (2009). Shifting the grounds: Constructivist grounded theory methods. In J. Morse, P. Stern, J. Corbin, B. Bowers, K. Charmaz, & A. Clarke (Eds.), *Developing grounded theory: The second generation* (pp. 127–154). Left Coast Press.

Charmaz, K. (2014). *Constructing grounded theory: A practical guide through qualitative analysis* (2nd ed.). Sage.

Cheek, J. (2005). The practice and politics of funded qualitative research. In N. Denzin & Y. Lincoln (Eds.), *The SAGE handbook of qualitative research* (3rd ed., pp. 381–409). Sage.

Clarke, A. (2005). *Situational analysis: Grounded theory after the postmodern turn.* Sage.

Corbin, J., & Strauss, A. (2008). *Basics of qualitative research: Techniques and procedures for developing grounded theory* (3rd ed.). Sage.

Corbin, J., & Strauss, A. (2015). *Basics of qualitative research: Techniques and procedures for developing grounded theory* (4th ed.). Sage.

Creamer, E. (2021). *Advancing grounded theory with mixed methods.* Routledge.

Creswell, J. (1998). *Qualitative inquiry and research design: Choosing among the five traditions.* Sage.

Denzin, N., & Lincoln, Y. (1998). Introduction: Entering the field of qualitative research. In N. Denzin & Y. Lincoln (Eds.), *The landscape of qualitative research: Theories and issues* (pp. 1–34). Sage.

Dey, I. (1999). *Grounding grounded theory: Guidelines for qualitative inquiry.* Academic Press.

Geertz, C. (1973). Thick description: Toward an interpretive history of culture. In C. Geertz (Ed.), *The interpretation of cultures* (pp. 3–30). Basic Books.

Gerhardt, U. (2000). Ambivalent interactionist: Anselm Strauss and the "schools" of Chicago sociology. *The American Sociologist, 31*(4), 34–64.

Gibson, B., & Hartman, J. (2014). *Rediscovering grounded theory.* Sage.

Glaser, B. (1978). *Theoretical sensitivity: Advances in the methodology of grounded theory.* Sociology Press.

Glaser, B. (1992). *Basics of grounded theory analysis.* Sociology Press.

Glaser, B. (1998). *Doing grounded theory: Issues and discussions.* Sociology Press.

Glaser, B. (2002). Constructivist grounded theory? *Forum Qualitative Social Research, 3*(3). Retrieved 22 October 2006 from http://www.qualitative-research.net/fqs-texte/3-02/3-02glaser-e.htm

Glaser, B., & Holton, J. (2004). Remodeling grounded theory. *Forum Qualitative Social Research, 5*(2). Retrieved 9 October 2006 from http://www.qualitative-research.net/fqs-texte/2-04/2-04glaser-e.pdf

Glaser, B., & Strauss, A. (1965/2007). *Awareness of dying.* AladineTransaction.

Glaser, B., & Strauss, A. (1967/1999). *The discovery of grounded theory: Strategies for qualitative research.* Aldine de Gruyter.

Griffiths, C., Oxford, R., Kawai, Y., Kawai, C., Park, Y.Y., Ma, X., Meng, Y., & Yang, N.-D. (2014). Focus on context: Narratives from east asia. *System, 43*, 50–63.

Hadley, G. (2015). *English for academic purposes in neoliberal universities: A critical grounded theory.* Springer.

Chapter 8. Grounded Theory 147

Hadley, G. (2017a). The games people play: A critical study of 'resource leeching' among 'blended' english for academic purpose professionals in neoliberal universities. In M. Flubacher & A. Del Percio (Eds.), *Language, education, and neoliberalism: Critical studies in sociolinguistics* (pp. 184–203). Multilingual Matters.

Hadley, G. (2017b). *Grounded theory in applied linguistics research: A practical guide.* Routledge.

Hadley, G. (2019a). Critical grounded theory. In A. Bryant & K. Charmaz (Eds.), *The SAGE handbook of current developments in grounded theory* (pp. 564–592). Sage.

Hadley, G. (2019b). Grounded theory method. In J. McKinley & H. Rose (Eds.), *The Routledge handbook of research methods in applied linguistics* (pp. 264–275). Routledge.

Hallberg, L. (2010). Some thoughts about the literature review in grounded theory studies. *International Journal of Qualitative Studies on Health and Well-Being, 5*(3).

Hammersley, M., & Traianou, A. (2012). *Ethics in qualitative research: Controversies and contexts.* Sage.

Harklau, L. (2005). Ethnography and ethnographic research on second language teaching and learning In E. Hinkel (Ed.), *Handbook of research in second language teaching and learning* (pp. 179–194). Lawrence Erlbaum Associates.

Harry, B., Sturges, K., & Klingner, J. (2005). Mapping the process: An exemplar of process and challenge in grounded theory analysis. *Educational Researcher, 34*(2), 3–13.

Holton, J. (2011). The autonomous creativity of Barney Glaser: Early influences in the emergence of classic grounded theory methodology. In V. G. Martin, A. (Ed.), *Grounded theory: The philosophy, method and work of barney glaser* (pp. 201–223). BrownWalker Press.

QSR International Pty Ltd. (2018). *NVIVO qualitative data analysis software 12.0.* QSR International.

Kalan, A. (2016). Teaching anglo-american academic writing and intercultural rhetoric: A grounded theory study of practice in ontario secondary schools. *Current Studies in Comparative Education, Science and Technology, 3,* 57–75.

Layder, D. (1982). Grounded theory: A constructive critique. *Journal for the Theory of Social Behaviour, 12*(1), 103–122.

Layder, D. (1993). *New strategies in social research: An introduction and guide.* Polity Press.

Lazarsfeld, P. (1962). The sociology of empirical social research. *American Sociological Review, 27*(6), 757–767.

Legewie, H., & Sherivier-Legewie, B. (2004). "Research is hard work, it's always a bit suffering. Therefore on the other side it should be fun." Anselm Strauss in conversation with Heiner Legewie and Barbara Schervier-Legewie. *Forum Qualitative Sozialforschung / Forum: Qualitative Social Research, 53*(22). Retrieved 17 January 2021 from https://www .qualitative-research.net/index.php/fqs/article/view/562/1219

Lincoln, Y. (2005). Institutional review boards and methodological conservatism: The challenge to and from phenomenological paradigms. In N. Denzin & Y. Lincoln (Eds.), *The SAGE handbook of qualitative research* (3rd ed., pp. 165–181). Sage.

Locke, K. (2005). *Grounded theory in management research.* Sage.

McCallin, A. (2003). Grappling with the literature in a grounded theory study. *Contemporary Nurse, 15*(1–2), 61–69.

Merton, R. (1949). *Social theory and social structure*. The Free Press.

Merton, R. (1967). *Social theory and social structure*. The Free Press.

Miller, S., & Fredericks, M. (1999). How does grounded theory explain? *Qualitative Health Research, 9*(4), 538–551.

Nagle, J. (2011). Saxe's aphorism (book review of legislation and regulation by John F. Manning and Matthew C. Stephenson. Foundation press 2010). *George Washington Law Review, 79*, 1505.

Nunan, D. (1992). *Research methods in language learning*. Cambridge University Press.

Rose, H., McKinley, J., & Briggs Baffoe-Djan, J. (2019). *Data collection research methods in applied linguistics*. Bloombury.

Ruhe, J., & Nahser, F. B. (2001). Putting American pragmatism to work in the classroom. *Journal of Business Ethics, 34*(3), 317–330.

Schenk, A., Hunziker, M., & Kienast, F. (2007). Factors influencing the acceptance of nature conservation measures--a qualitative study in Switzerland. *Journal of Environmental Management, 83*(1), 66–79.

Scientific Software Development, GmbH. (2020). *Atlas.Ti 9.0*. (Version 9.0) Scientific Software Development.

Sikolia, D., Biros, D., Mason, M., & Weiser, M. (2013). *Trustworthiness of grounded theory methodology research in information systems* The 8th Annual MWAIS Conference, Normal, IL (USA). Retrieved on 24 July 2023 from http://aisel.aisnet.org/mwais2013/16

Silva, T. (2005). On the philosophical bases of inquiry in second language writing: Metaphysics, inquiry paradigms, and the intellectual zeitgeist. In P. Matsuda (Ed.), *Second language writing research: Perspectives on the process of knowledge construction* (pp. 3–16). Lawrence Erlbaum Associates.

Stern, P., & Porr, C. (2011). *Essentials of accessible grounded theory*. Left Coast Press.

Strauss, A. (1987). *Qualitative analysis for social scientists*. Cambridge University Press.

Strauss, A., & Corbin, J. (1990). *Basics of qualitative research*. Sage.

Strauss, A., & Corbin, J. (1994). Grounded theory methodology: An overview. In N. Denzin & Y. Lincoln (Eds.), *Handbook of qualitative research* (pp. 273–285). Sage.

Tarp, G. (2006). *Student perspectives in short-term study programmes abroad: A grounded theory study*. Multilingual Matters.

VERBI Software. (2019). *MAXQDA 2020*. VERBI Software. Retrieved on 24 July 2023 from www.maxqda.com

CHAPTER 9

Applications of Grounded Theory in the field of Extensive Reading

Gregory Hadley & Hiromi Hadley
Niigata University

This chapter discusses the application of Extensive Reading (ER), an English language teaching method encouraging learners to consume large amounts of proficiency-level content, and its spread to second language classrooms globally since the 1990s. Studies show that ER significantly enhances learners' vocabulary, reading speeds, and language comprehension. Despite challenges of passive resistance and apathy from learners, teachers from Japan, Italy, and Southeast Asia are seeking ways to integrate ER into their Academic English curricula. The chapter introduces a grounded theory about learners' social processes in the ER classroom, explaining why the Grounded Theory Methodology (GTM) was selected for this study, its implementation, the faced challenges, addressed solutions, and unique insights gleaned through GTM.

1. Introduction

In this chapter, we will provide a methodological account of a funded grounded theory project that explored social processes related to Extensive Reading (ER) in second-language learning environments. Following an overview of ER and challenges faced by teachers in studying this area of second language education, the reasons for why and how the grounded theory methodology was implemented will then be detailed. This will be followed by considering the challenges encountered in the field and our responses. Finally, an overview of the theoretical insights gained will be offered, which might have otherwise been missed. We will then conclude with a discussion of the possible implications of this theory for second-language educators engaged in classroom research.

https://doi.org/10.1075/rmal.6.09had
© 2024 John Benjamins Publishing Company

2. Overview of the study

Extensive Reading (ER), a student-centered form of English language learning, requires reading large amounts of interesting yet understandable materials without using dictionaries or receiving explicit grammar lessons. Through this immersion in comprehensible English, correct grammatical structures and new vocabulary are learned inductively. Topics from readings are shared in class during focused conversations, presentations, and written reports. In addition, ER requires students to be accountable by regularly reporting new vocabulary they have learned and keeping track of the books (called Graded Readers) that they have read. Over twenty years of ER research (Dao, 2014; Iwahori, 2008; Nakanishi, 2015), there is compelling evidence that English study through ER results in better vocabulary knowledge, improved reading comprehension, faster reading speeds, superior grammatical competence, enhanced oral communication, and that after formal instruction, many learners become lifelong readers.

However, even as these findings are impressive, certain problems also exist. Most of the evidence for ER efficacy is based on studies of small groups of successful learners participating in elective courses. Data on those who have dropped out or failed such classes are rarely available for analysis. ER research has tended to focus more on issues such as student reading motivation (Huang, 2015; King & Herder, 2012; Mikami, 2020), the success or failure of ER implementation (He & Green, 2012; Susser & Robb, 1990; Waring & Hoai, 2020), various language proficiency gains through ER (Aka, 2019; Bourtorwick & Macalister, 2019; Iqbal, 2017; Song, 2020), and a constellation of studies regarding the affective aspects of ER (Eidswick et al., 2011; Kusunagi et al., 2020; Mikami, 2017; Ro, 2016; Schmidt-Fajlik, 2020).

If we were to step back and offer an overview of the focus given to ER among teachers and researchers, the majority of the studies are dedicated to the technique and mechanics of doing Extensive Reading. The concern has been on vocabulary acquisition, reading speeds, and affective issues – anything outside observers might construe as evidence of student (and teacher) success. At the same time, there has been very little research on the 'how' and 'why' of learner success in ER. The few studies that have delved into ER learner strategies (e.g., Mikami, 2017) have tended to be brief, survey-based, descriptive, and limited in terms of practical classroom applications. Some attention has been given to the reading histories students bring from their first language experience (e.g., Judge, 2011; Milliner, 2021). We believe more attention needs to be given to this, as it may significantly influence how our learners approach reading in the second language. Another long-running issue among teachers and researchers of ER and reading in second language learning is that few are drawing sufficiently from reading research findings in fields such as psychology and education. Such research can show how cognitive, social, developmental, and emotional dynamics contribute to whether or not a person becomes an avid reader in their first language are studied (Agler et al., 2021; Hoetker, 1982).

3. Why was the GTM used? How was it implemented?

The reasons discussed thus far worked synergistically towards a grounded theory approach. Our interest began as simply an interest in learning more about the core strategies of second-language learners that contribute to their success in ER. We were also curious about the practices that put others on a trajectory towards failure. We hope to provide language teachers with insight that could aid them in encouraging their students to become better extensive readers. Grounded theory seemed appropriate to potentially look outside the box of the traditional focus of ER research and explore whether we could develop new perspectives and insights that would link ER research with the ongoing efforts taking place in other fields. As the investigation progressed, more salient issues of the type discussed in our overview above began to inform and further validate our choice of grounded theory. This section discusses the implementation of the Grounded Theory Methodology (GTM), with attention to the initial venue, research participants, and research procedures.

3.1 Initial venue

By "initial venue", we mean that while grounded theory research begins in a specific place, it rarely stays there once theoretical concepts and social processes emerge. This shift will be seen at various places throughout our discussion. The beginning exploratory phase of this grounded theory project took place at a Japanese national university from mid-2019 to the beginning of 2021 in an undergraduate English language course featuring Extensive Reading as the primary form of instruction. The minimum requirement was to read 200,000 words over the semester, or approximately (depending on the book level) four to five graded readers a week. Student progress was tracked using the MReader site administered by Kyoto Sangyo University and the Extensive Reading Foundation (https://mreader.org/index.php). This platform contains brief online quizzes on the books that students had read. The number of words within each graded reader has been tallied on this platform, so when a student passes a quiz, the total number of words from the book would be credited towards their 200,000-word reading goal. Each 90-minute class was organized into two parts. First, it began with 30 minutes devoted to interactive games and activities designed to encourage students to share or act out aspects of the stories and books they had read during the previous week. Second, there were 45 minutes of silent in-class reading followed by expansion and discussion activities. Three classes, ranging from twelve to as few as four, participated in the study. There was one class per week for a total of sixteen weeks. The first author was the classroom teacher, and the second author worked in a supporting role.

3.2 Research participants

Twenty-six students gave informed content to participate in the first phase of exploration. The breakdown of gender and nationality can be found in Table 1. The prevalence of female students who joined the classes supports the widely-held view of reading as something which has a gendered preference. However, studies that acknowledge this trend also note that males often read as much as their female counterparts but read differently, choose less challenging readings, and have different motivations than females (Loh et al., 2020; Merisuo-Storm, 2006; Simpson, 1996).

Table 1. Initial stage research participants

Gender		Nationality				
Male	Female	Japanese	Chinese	French	Russian	Korean
4	22	11	9	3	2	1

As noted in the earlier chapter, given the depth of analysis entailed with an interview, between 20 to 40 interviews are sufficient for developing a well-grounded theory (Creswell, 1998; Hadley, 2017, p.130; Stern & Porr, 2011, p.52). During the course of successive interviews, regular social practices, concepts, and theoretical ideas emerged. Later interviews took us to interview many others, such as mothers (two American and one Japanese), Native English speakers (five males and one female), and two online discussions via public social media forums for teachers of Extensive Reading (twenty-three anonymized participants). We realize the conversation here is shifting prematurely to issues of methodology. However, the program used to store and aid in analyzing the collected qualitative data, MAXQDA (VERBI, 2019), contains a feature for data-mining Twitter for discussions related to keyword searches from recurring issues in our interviews. Each search yields 1000 tweets that have taken place over the following week. Twitter is considered public discourse, and any identifying information in the tweets was anonymized. More importantly, this step added the anecdotes and statements of

Chapter 9. Applications of Grounded Theory in the field of Extensive Reading   153

hundreds of people, and further filled in the cracks of what we were learning during the initial and subsequent stages of exploration. This process, however, of research informants becoming increasingly invisible within the study of more general human social processes and interactions, is part of the process of doing grounded theory. Charmaz (1995, pp. 60–62) maintains that the grounded theorist's focus on processes, together with the steady shift away from individual accounts (who may not want their stories to be told in all their fullness), contributes to GTM as a form of research inquiry that encourages ethical practices aimed at protecting the privacy of research informants. We agree with this view, though we acknowledge that ethicists who seek to force the qualitative researcher to conform to their quantitative biomedical norms may feel a sense of quiet unease with these established practices.

3.3 Research procedures in the field

The way in which we carried out the grounded theory methodology followed the manner described in our earlier chapter, and more specifically, as seen in Figure 1 below. During the first six months of our investigation, we conducted open exploratory interviews with students who gave informed consent. Our questions centered on their extensive reading experiences in the class. We asked about their memories of good days and bad days during the class and any aspects of extensive reading that they particularly liked or disliked. We also encouraged sharing any frequent problems encountered with ER and any solutions they may have formulated in response.

The first author interviewed some of the learners, especially the international students, in English. After their first languages, English tended to be their second language. Others, especially Japanese learners with less overseas experience and lower levels of English-language proficiency, were interviewed by the second author in their native language. All interviews were recorded, transcribed, and then open coded. The data was archived, maintained, and further analyzed using the qualitative and mixed methods qualitative software package MAXQDA (VERBI, 2019). During open coding, memos about new ideas, insights, and possible future avenues of inquiry were written and attached to the relevant open codes. In addition to the traditional interview format, twelve of the first wave of research participants offered their thoughts and insights using repertory grids, a form of an interview where informants have, in effect, an internal conversation with themselves around the specific domain of interest. The results of the repertory grid process are expressed in the form of bipolar constructs (see Grogan, this volume). These constructs served as informant-generated codes – also known by grounded

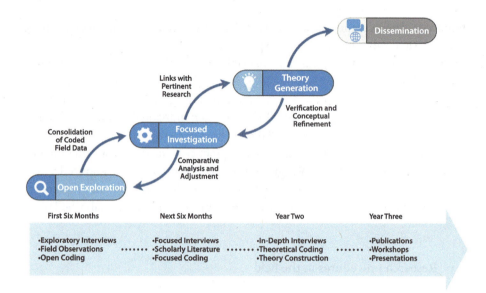

Figure 1. Research procedures and timeline

theorists as *in-vivo codes* (Glaser, 1992), and this data further expanded our developing ideas and theoretical musings.

When we generated nearly 100 open codes from the interviews, these were consolidated into focused codes. We continued to write memos that would further explain the more abstract nature of these codes. Subsequent interviews sought to discover more about these focused codes and better understand the social interactions supporting them. This led us to interview a wider range of informants because our emerging theory of social processes for extensive reading students seems to validate Wallace (1992) and Alderson and Urquhart (1984). Their study of research on the subject led them to conclude that differences in the process of becoming a reader of the first language from that of learning to read a second language are nuanced to the point of being – when viewed from the pragmatic perspective of the classroom – virtually indistinguishable. We followed the breadcrumbs as they appeared in our data towards understanding social processes in reading more generally and theorizing about reading as it happened in our informants' first or second language if they had one.

As we gained a clearer sense of how people became readers, the types of reading strategies used, and problems and contingencies within the trajectory toward avid reading, we found greater insight into these features from scholarly literature in education, psychology, and neuroscience. In addition, during the second year, we began consolidating focused codes into more significant, more theoretical categories and continued to search for research papers that featured studies from researchers who were also engaged in studying the same dynamics found in our categories. Finally, more in-depth interviews, which were held online due to lockdown restrictions resulting from the COIVD-19 world pandemic, were conducted to further investigate these theoretical categories' features.

Admittedly, the process described above was not always as straightforward as it seems. There were seasons of "unknowing" and puzzlement, followed by the reconsideration of earlier codes. Sometimes we needed to go back and rewrite open or focused codes and reconsider some of the conclusions we made during earlier interviews. However, this back-and-forth movement helped us develop a theory that better fit the data, because the theory was constantly being adjusted to accommodate new data and insights. Following the construction of many of the main pillars of our grounded theory, we moved towards disseminating what we had learned in online workshops and scholarly forums. Eventually, we hope to publish a monograph that will comprehensively present our theory.

4. What challenges were faced? How were the challenges addressed?

As many readers may know from their own experiences of conducting qualitative field research, the unexpected is to be expected. This is especially the case when one is located within the social maelstrom of educational environments. The two main challenges that we faced during the open and focused stages of our investigation related to unforeseen effects of changes in our university's curriculum and the effects that the COVID-19 world pandemic had on data gathering.

The first challenge occurred when, due to changes in the second language curriculum at our university, the number of students attending our ER classes began to decline. As a result, late in the second year of the investigation, the course was closed to ensure adjunct faculty would get enough students for their classes. Fortunately, we had conducted enough student interviews from the classes we had taught up to that point. Also, the repertory grid interviews, which had informed an earlier ER study (Hadley & Charles, 2017), served as a vital and helpful supplement. Charmaz (1983, p.111; 2006, pp.39–40) has long argued for the inclusion of this sort of earlier archival research material as a valid and rich source of data for developing grounded theories. Glaser (1978, p.162) also supports the use of such material so long as it is used in context. Because our collected repertory grid data dealt specifically with student reflections of their ER learning experience, we had little doubt as to its suitability, and as mentioned earlier, this data proved to be a helpfully enlightening resource.

The other challenge relates to the limitations placed on us by the COVID-19 pandemic. For example, we had planned on traveling to various venues where

ER was being taught so that we could interview not only a wider selection of participants about their reading experiences, but also interview teachers about their views on ER. However, our university did not permit physical travel outside of the prefecture, and face-to-face interaction within the prefecture was strongly discouraged. In such situations where limits are put upon researchers to access potential participants, Cohen et al. (2007, p.176) suggest that "convenience sampling", that is, "selecting from whoever happens to be available", is acceptable because it "saves time and money and spares the researcher the effort of finding less amenable participants." Therefore, we reached out to potential research participants via social media, and for those who gave informed consent, we interviewed them using the direct messaging function. For a smaller number, interviews were conducted through a series of email exchanges. The advantage of carrying out interviews through the medium of text was that we ended the interview with a transcription already in hand for analysis. The disadvantage was that many of the other social and interactive features of the face-to-face interviews were lost.

In the end, however, our challenges were easy to address. We did not face any ethical dilemmas, as the risk of harm from sharing reflections on one's reading experience was relatively low. We also had good access to online library resources, which further helped us during the later stages of our investigation. With all of this at our disposal, we were able to move forward. The only other impediments were those typical to academics who face the demands of teaching and administrative tasks.

5. Insights gained using the grounded theory method

While this is not the venue for a full discussion of our resulting grounded theory, we think it would be helpful to share some of what we learned in broad impressionistic brushstroke, especially since our theory differs significantly from much of what is discussed among ER educators in scholarly journals and online public forums.

One aspect that we appreciate about GTM is how it encourages informed creativity that complements one's degree of theoretical sensitivity and sociological imagination. A theorist is free to create new theoretical terminology to get a better handle on describing and identifying the social interactions emerging from the study. One example of this for us was coining a new term, "avidization", to describe the various trajectories towards becoming a more intentional extensive reader. We define avidization as the processes by which a certain activity becomes meaningfully integrated within one's professional, social, or personal life. While some might see this as another word for motivation, we purposefully avoided referring to the processes in the theory in this way, because motivation as a conceptual term has become so overanalyzed, problematized, and so rife with contested definitions, that we feel that much of its practical utility has been lost to educators and second-language teachers. We repeatedly witnessed features from many of the competing theories on motivation in second language learning (Deci & Ryan, 1985; Dörnyei & Ushioda, 2013; Gardner, 1985, 2010) having their place among students engaged in different strategic trajectories. Avidization allowed us to pragmatically identify different features of human activity from different theories on motivation, without having to ascribe to one or the other.

Another feature that emerged both for those students who were avidized as well as for those who stayed within the stasis of simply "grazing" on information whenever they had to, was that the stories they shared in interviews about the experience they had with reading in the first language were vital for understanding how they approached ER. This resonated with the findings of other researchers in Second Language Acquisition, who have also identified important links between first and second language reading (Artieda, 2017; Garrison-Fletcher et al., 2022; Granena et al., 2015).

With avidization as a placeholder concept, we created an interconnected framework linking earlier motivational studies with our novel descriptions of social processes in extensive reading. We will briefly discuss three distinct social processes that students are likely to use in extensive reading classes, labeled as Infograzing, Bookmining, and Storyhunting.[1]

5.1 Infograzing

Infograzing as a reading process is affected by some social and neurological factors. Infograzing occurs when a student, capable of reading well enough at a certain level of second language proficiency, does not read until either pressured to do so from the demands of the ER course or until there is some immediate pressing need to read. Even in the latter case, the student will still only read enough to get by. Infograzing is not specific to ER and can be seen during those times when people, in their first language, read to complete immediate mundane tasks or are exposed to reading material during life in our multi-mediated world. Picture a person reading the back of a cereal box while eating breakfast or skimming a commercial inside a subway on the way to work, and one grasps the nature of infograzing. In ER classes offered as a required language course, it is common to

---

1. A fourth process, known as Data Grinding, is still being developed at the time of this writing, and will be revealed in another venue at a later date.

have an inordinate number of infograzers. Moving them towards the trajectory of avidization requires persistent personal interaction to find out what might spark their reading interest. It is also necessary to encourage them to form positive relationships with other students in the class who have already successfully engaged in other reading processes because the path towards avid reading begins with relationships that spark a desire to read.

5.2 Bookmining

As a reading strategy, bookmining is used by goal-oriented readers who wish to acquire something of personal value. Even though bookminers are avid readers, most do not identify themselves being so, and it is not uncommon to find them speaking in guilty tones about how they need to read more. Bookminers tend to focus on biographies, self-help books, and specialist material related to their careers, academic goals, or hobbies. In ER classes, students engaged in bookmaking may read a lot, but the purpose is less one of reading for enjoyment and more one of reading to improve one's English language proficiency. Because they do not thrive in ambiguous learning environments, they need achievable targets, such as word reading amounts, vocabulary goals, and some system that will measure their progress and show them signs of improvement over time. When they are satisfied that they have achieved their personal goals, or when the class ends, few who engage in bookmining will continue to read until something else sparks their interest or need to achieve.

5.3 Storyhunting

Readers who use primarily the storyhunting strategy exhibit the features most observers would label as being an avid reader. Storyhunters, in turn, also self-identify as readers and often have specific tastes, such as a preference for a specific genre or liking the works of a particular author. They describe their life of reading often as feeling something like hunger or an addiction, and that their reading satisfies deep emotional or spiritual needs. If allowed to share in-depth, those who hunt stories will share how earlier experiences of loss or abandonment were instrumental in becoming avid readers and how reading allows them to slip out of the tedium and pain of their daily internal lives to enter a better place. While targets, goals, and vocabulary lists are helpful for those engaged in bookmining, these have the opposite effect on those traveling on the trajectory of storyhunting. Storyhunters tend to know what they want, and within the context of ER, they dislike having anything placed over or between them and their reading. When working with those dedicated to storyhunting, ER teachers may find that one of

Chapter 9. Applications of Grounded Theory in the field of Extensive Reading 159

their major challenges will be in providing enough material for them to read since they can quickly go through large amounts of graded readers in a short period of time.

Again, the discussion of our grounded theory here is only a brief summary. However, we think GTM is better, perhaps, than other methodologies focused on verifying preconceived hypotheses. We feel grounded theory helped us gain fresh insights and gave us the chance to develop new terms for describing the dynamics taking place in our ER classes. By having novel ways of seeing and naming ER strategies, we were then inspired to develop teaching methods and activities to encourage students to read more and do it in ways that best suited their tendency towards personal avidization strategies, goals, and particular needs.

6. Conclusions

In this chapter, we have considered the grounded theory methodology as used in the field during an investigation of social processes in extensive reading. The challenges that we faced and our responses were discussed. A brief discussion of the main features of the resulting grounded theory was also provided. We hope that this chapter will encourage teacher-researchers to reflect on the possibilities of using a grounded theory approach for investigating issues in their classes and within their educational environments. The insights gained from an informed use of the grounded theory methodology are often transformative – not only for the theorist and their students, but also for the wider academic community as well.

Funding

This work was supported in part by a JSPS Grant-in-Aid for Scientific Research (Grant Number 19K00846). We have no conflicts of interest to disclose.

References

Agler, L.-M., Noguchi, K., & Alfsen, L. (2021). Personality traits as predictors of reading comprehension and metacomprehension accuracy. *Current Psychology, 40*(10), 5054–5063.

Aka, N. (2019). Reading performance of Japanese high school learners following a one-year extensive reading program. *Reading in a Foreign Langauge, 31*(1), 1–18.

Alderson, J., & Urquhart, A. (Eds.). (1984). *Reading in a foreign language.* Longman.

Artieda, G. (2017). The role of L1 literacy and reading habits on the l2 achievement of adult learners of english as a foreign language. *System*, *66*, 168–176.

Bourtorwick, T., & Macalister, J. (2019). Two approaches to extensive reading and their effects on L2 vocabulary development. *Reading in a Foreign Langauge*, *32*(2), 150–172.

Charmaz, K. (1983). The grounded theory method: An explication and interpretation. In R. Emerson (Ed.), *Contemporary field research* (pp. 109–126). Little, Brown, and Company.

Charmaz, K. (1995). Between positivism and postmodernism: Implications for methods. *Studies in Symbolic Interaction*, *17*, 43–72.

Charmaz, K. (2006). *Constructing grounded theory*. Sage.

Cohen, L., Manion, L., & Morrison, K. (2007). *Research methods in education* (5th ed.). Routledge.

Creswell, J. (1998). *Qualitative inquiry and research design: Choosing among the five traditions.* Sage.

Dao, T. N. (2014). Using internet resources for extensive reading in an EFL context. *Hawaii Pacific University TESOL Working Paper Series*, *12*, 72–95.

Deci, E., & Ryan, R. (1985). *Intrinsic motivation and self-determination in human behavior.* Plenum Press.

Dörnyei, Z., & Ushioda, E. (2013). *Teaching and researching motivation* (2nd ed.). Routledge.

Eidswick, J., Rouault, G., & Praver, M. (2011). Judging books by their covers and more: Components of interest in graded readers. *The Language Teacher*, *35*(3), 11–19.

Gardner, R. (1985). *Social psychology and second language learning: The role of attitudes and motivation.* Edward Arnold.

Gardner, R. (2010). *Motivation and second language acquisition: The socio-educational model.* Peter Lang.

Garrison-Fletcher, L., Martohardjono, G., & Chodorow, M. (2022). Impact of home language reading skills' on L2 reading comprehension: A study of newcomer emergent bilinguals. *International Journal of Bilingual Education and Bilingualism*, *25*(1), 287–300.

Glaser, B. (1978). *Theoretical sensitivity: Advances in the methodology of grounded theory.* Sociology Press.

Glaser, B. (1992). *Basics of grounded theory analysis.* Sociology Press.

Granena, G., Muñoz, C., & Tragant, E. (2015). L1 reading factors in extensive L2 reading-while-listening instruction. *System*, *55*, 86–99.

Hadley, G. (2017). *Grounded theory in applied linguistics research: A practical guide.* Routledge.

Hadley, G., & Charles, M. (2017). Enhancing extensive reading with data-driven learning. *Language Learning & Technology*, *21*(3), 131–152.

He, M., & Green, C. (2012). Challenges in implementing extensive reading in shanghai senior high schools. *Extensive Reading World Congress* 2011, Kyoto, Japan.

Hoetker, J. (1982). A theory of talking about theories of reading. *College English*, *44*(2), 175–181.

Huang, Y.-C. (2015). Why don't they do it? A study on the implementation of extensive reading in Taiwan. *Cogent Education*, *2*(1), 1099187.

Iqbal, S. (2017). The impact of extensive reading on learning and increasing vocabulary at elementary level. *Studies in English Language and Teaching*, *5*, 481–495.

Iwahori, Y. (2008). Developing reading fluency: A study of extensive reading in EFL. *Reading in a Foreign Language, 20*, 70–91. https://files.eric.ed.gov/fulltext/EJ791535.pdf

Judge, P. (2011). Driven to read: Enthusiastic readers in a Japanese high school's extensive reading program. *Reading in a Foreign Langauge, 23*(2), 161–186. http://hdl.handle.net /10125/66850

King, R., & Herder, S. (2012). Extensive reading: After the honeymoon is over. *Extensive Reading World Congress*, Kyoto, Japan.

Kusunagi, Y., Kobayashi, M., & Fukaya, M. (2020). An effective approach to inspire readers: Introduction to stimulating picture books in extensive reading. *Extensive Reading World Congress 2019*, Taichung, Taiwan.

Loh, C.-E., Sun, B.-Q., & Majid, S. (2020). Do girls read differently from boys? Adolescents and their gendered reading habits and preferences. *English in Education, 54*(2), 174–190.

Merisuo-Storm, T. (2006). Girls and boys like to read and write different texts. *Scandinavian Journal of Educational Research, 50*(2), 111–125.

Mikami, A. (2017). Students' attitudes toward extensive reading in the Japanese EFL context. *TESOL Journal, 8*(2), 471–488.

Mikami, Y. (2020). Goal setting and learners' motivation for extensive reading: Forming a virtuous cycle. *Reading in a Foreign Language, 32*(1), 29–48. http://hdl.handle.net/10125 /66575

Milliner, B. (2021). Stories of avid extensive readers in a university-level EFL course. *Journal of Extensive Reading, 8*(1), 1–16. https://jalt-publications.org/content/index.php/jer/issue /view/10

Nakanishi, T. (2015). A meta-analysis of extensive reading research. *TESOL Quarterly, 49*(1), 6–37.

Ro, E. (2016). Exploring teachers' practices and students' perceptions of the extensive reading approach in EAP reading classes. *Journal of English for Academic Purposes, 22*, 32–41.

Schmidt-Fajlik, R. (2020). Foreign language reading anxiety and mindfulness. *The Language Teacher, 44*(4), 3–11.

Simpson, A. (1996). Fictions and facts: An investigation of the reading practices of girls and boys. *English Education, 28*(4), 268–279. http://www.jstor.org/stable/40172905

Song, M. (2020). The impacts of extensive reading on efl primary school students' vocabulary acquisition and reading comprehension. *Extensive Reading World Congress 2019*, Taichung, Taiwan.

Stern, P., & Porr, C. (2011). *Essentials of accessible grounded theory*. Left Coast Press.

Susser, B., & Robb, R. (1990). EFL extensive reading instruction: Research and procedures. *JALT Journal, 12*(2), 161–185.

VERBI Software. (2019). *MAXQDA 2020*. VERBI Software. Retrieved on 24 July 2023 from www.maxqda.com

Wallace, C. (1992). *Reading*. Oxford University Press.

Waring, R., & Hoai, V. (2020). Challenges of setting up extensive reading programs in Vietnam. *World Conference on Extensive Reading 2019*, Taichung, Taiwan.

CHAPTER 10

Phenomenology

Seyyed Ali Ostovar-Namaghi
Shahrood University of Technology

This chapter aims to explore Phenomenology as a research methodology. To this end, it will first present its epistemological, ontological, and axiological underpinnings. It will then briefly explain its theoretical foundations by explaining the similarities and differences between transcendental and interpretative Phenomenology. This is followed by the principles and properties that differentiate Phenomenology from other modes of qualitative research. Subsequently, the purpose of this mode of research is clarified by explaining and exemplifying the types of research questions it tackles. More practical aspects of this methodology will then be explored by illustrating how the data are collected and analysed and how ethical issues are addressed in the research process and product. Finally, it will present responses to the critiques levelled against this research methodology before concluding the chapter.

1. Introduction

This chapter discusses Phenomenology to help researchers develop a deeper understanding of the theoretical underpinnings of phenomenological research. Although the term Phenomenology is used to refer to both a philosophical tradition and a research methodology, scholars have found it hard to come up with "a consensual, univocal interpretation of phenomenology" (Giorgi & Giorgi, 2003, p. 23). Even in practice, novice researchers find it hard to understand and conduct phenomenological research because (1) a deep understanding of the philosophical underpinnings of Phenomenology is needed (Dowling & Cooney, 2012); (2) even in some phenomenological studies, there is a lack of clarity on philosophical underpinnings (Norlyk & Harder, 2010); and (3) many researchers do not articulate which of the two approaches, i.e., descriptive phenomenology or hermeneutic phenomenology, guides their study (Lopez & Willis, 2004). As such, understanding and using Phenomenology as a research methodology highly depends on understanding the philosophical underpinnings of the interpretivist paradigm, which is a reaction against the positivist paradigm.

https://doi.org/10.1075/rmal.6.10ost
© 2024 John Benjamins Publishing Company

Epistemologically, one major concern in research is to decide what knowledge is and how it should be acquired. Another concern is the relationship between the researcher and what is being researched or the object of research (Allison & Pomeroy, 2000; Lincoln & Guba, 1994). In other words, epistemology concerns the nature of knowledge and its source. Two polar paradigms are addressing this issue in drastically different ways. Advocates of interpretivism believe that knowledge is subjective. Researchers who work within the interpretivist camp try to develop a deep understanding of reality from the participants' perspectives through open-ended interviews and present the reader with a thick description of reality from the participants' perspective. Conversely, positivists hold that knowledge is objective and value-free and is obtained through the application of the scientific method. Researchers who work within a positivist paradigm try to collect numerical data under tight experimental conditions to produce universal laws or generalizable findings (Breen & Darlaston-Jones, 2008).

From an axiological point of view, research should specify the place of values in the research process (West & Turner, 2000). Once again, positivists and interpretivists have opposite views. For the former, values have no place in research, and as such, attempts are made to assure the internal and external validity of the findings. For the latter (the interpretivists), research reports are value-laden because, in this paradigm, researcher reflexivity is a part and parcel of the research process. In phenomenology, which is conducted within the interpretive paradigm, the researcher works with the assumption that the final research report is value-laden, and despite the applied safeguards such as epoche or bracketing, the results may reflect some shades of etic or researcher subjectivity.

2. Theoretical foundations

There are two dominant phenomenological research approaches in educational research: transcendental and interpretive Phenomenology. Although they share some concepts such as description, reduction, imaginative variation, and essences (Moustakas, 1994), they are different in some philosophical assumptions. For instance, while for Husserl (1970), reality is internal to the knower, and the researcher should bracket his own subjectivity in the process of data collection, for Heidegger (1962), it is situated in the lifeworld of the individual, and the researcher is expected to reflect not only on the participants' experience but also reflects on his own experience of the phenomenon. Thus, which one to choose depends on the philosophical assumptions the researcher embraces. What follows aims to explain these two approaches and then summarize the similarities and differences between them to help the reader choose the phenomenological approach, which conforms with the philosophical assumptions they bring to the research process.

Husserl (1970) believed that methods of natural science cannot and should not be applied to psychology because he believed humans respond to their perceptions or what the stimuli mean rather than to the stimuli directly. In other words, he rejected the belief that objects in the external world exist independently of our consciousness since humans attach meaning to external stimuli and therefore do not respond automatically (Moustakas, 1994). In short, he believed that access to the material world was through consciousness and that all knowledge is inductively driven by experience. Rejecting the notion of objective observations of external reality, he argued that the focus of research should be the study of the phenomena as subjectively perceived by consciousness. He further rejected any preconception of the phenomenon under study, including scientific theories, logical deductions, or any psychological speculations that may direct the study. In contrast with scientific naturalism, which considers the person as an object, phenomenologists postulate that consciousness cannot be studied objectively.

According to Husserl (1989), Phenomenology aims to explain the nature of things, capture the essence of a phenomenon, and understand lived experience by sticking to the slogan, 'Back to the things themselves!' (Moustakas, 1994, p. 26). Hence, instead of collecting objective data and coming up with universal laws, this approach to research aims to present a thick description of the phenomenon from the perspective of the people who experienced it. The validity of the description depends on refraining from any preconception of the phenomenon under study and remaining true to the facts. In short, not only did Husserl specify the realm of Phenomenology as the study of lived experience (Greene, 1997), but he also conceptualized the word experience as anything a person is conscious of. Therefore, for Husserl, the word experience refers not only to the tangible concrete objects which are external to the person but also to abstract concepts and the mood state, which are internal to the person (Stewart & Mickunas, 1974).

Martin Heidegger is the original contributor to Hermeneutic or interpretive Phenomenology. It is both a philosophical tradition and a research methodology. Phenomenology studies how humans experience a phenomenon (Laverty, 2003). Hermeneutics is the process of determining the meaning of experience (Moustakas, 1994). In other words, while Phenomenology has an ontological focus – what it means to be or to exist, hermeneutics has an epistemological focus. In other words, hermeneutics focuses on how we assign meaning to an experience or how we acquire knowledge. Heidegger, who was Husserl's student, expanded pure or transcendental Phenomenology. Therefore, there should be common threads and points of divergence between the two as the founding fathers of phenomenology.

A pivotal point of divergence in Heidegger's (1962) thought was that any real phenomenological inquiry should focus on the relationship between the individual and his lifeworld, the reason being that the person's reality is constantly affected by the world in which he inhabits. Another point of divergence from Husserl is that the researchers' prior understanding of the phenomenon is valuable in exploring the phenomenon and, as such, should not be bracketed. What is more, Heidegger (1962) reiterates that it is not possible to separate the researcher from the knowledge that drives him to the research problem (Koch, 1995). Advocates of interpretive Phenomenology further believe that the meanings the researcher derives from the research process are a mixture of meanings contributed by both the researcher and the participants. Gadamer (1976) used the phrase "fusion of horizons" to explain the process of intersubjective understanding.

Just like Husserl, Heidegger reiterates the importance of bracketing or a reflexive awareness of prior knowledge and assumptions. But they disagree on the role of prior knowledge in describing the phenomenon. Husserl (2003) believes in pure Phenomenology. In other words, he believes that the researcher should set his knowledge of the phenomenon aside as irrelevant to our description and base his or her description on the collected and analyzed data. In short, for Husserl, Phenomenology is a purely descriptive process since it aims at capturing the essence of experience (Kvale, 1996; Osborne, 1994). On the other hand, Heidegger believes that Phenomenology is an interpretive process since it aims to bring to the essence of experience an interpretive element. Therefore, the hermeneutic researcher is equally concerned with the participants' descriptions of the phenomenon, as well as the interpretation or meaning of the experience (Barclay, 1992). In Heidegger's conception, there is a shift from the transcendental approach whereby the researcher takes on the detached observer position to the purposeful recognition of both the researcher's and participants' perceptions. In short, a researcher who works within Heidegger's theoretical framework should use the data he or she collects and analyzes to constantly revise his initial understanding of the phenomenon through a hermeneutic circle of interpretation. As such, the final description reflects how the researcher's understanding and the data-driven understating constantly interact to produce the final description.

Husserl and Heidegger are also different in their objectives. For Husserl, Phenomenology has an ontological focus because, with its focus on pure descriptive Phenomenology, it aims to explore what a phenomenon is. Conversely, for Heidegger, Phenomenology has a methodological focus since he believes Phenomenology aims at exploring how humans assign meaning to a phenomenon or what a phenomenon means to a person. In other words, Husserl was interested in the nature of knowledge. On the contrary, Heidegger was interested in the nature of being. Moreover, Heidegger believes that consciousness is not separate from the world because of his emphasis on the historicity of understanding (Koch, 1996). More specifically, what the person determines as real depends on his background knowledge, or what a specific culture gives the person as he lives in that culture. Heidegger went as far as to claim that nothing can be encountered without reference to a person's background understanding. Therefore, Heidegger has a view of the person and the world as entities interconnected in cultural, social, and in historical contexts. This can be described as the inseparability of the world and the person or the unity between the person and the world (Koch, 1996). This is because we construct the world based on our understanding, and the world constructs our undertaking based on our encounters with the world. In short, there seems to be a constant interaction between the person and the world as they constitute and are constituted by each other (Munhall, 1989).

Transcendental and hermeneutic Phenomenology are also different in their final description. A transcendental description reflects an objective description of the essence of the phenomenon as experienced by the participants because the researcher brackets or withdraws his subjective understanding of the phenomenon. Conversely, in a hermeneutic description, the researcher does not bracket his understanding of the phenomenon but rather constantly revises his understanding of the phenomenon in light of the participants' shared understanding of the phenomenon. Moreover, an important assumption underlying descriptive Phenomenology is that there are features to any lived experience that are common to all persons who have experienced the same phenomenon. These are known as essences, or eidetic structures (Natanson, 1973). In less technical terms, within the participants' varied and unique experiences, descriptive phenomenologists try to capture invariant themes which account for the essence of the phenomenon. Moustakas (1994) believes that the emerged essence is transitional in that it reflects the researchers' understanding of the phenomenon at a particular time in the research process.

3. Methodological orientation

3.1 Principles and affordances

Phenomenological studies collect soft verbal data in natural settings and analyze them to present a thick description of the phenomenon and then address issues such as trustworthiness, credibility, and authenticity (Beck, 1993) to ensure that the description truly reflects the essence of the phenomena in focus. Nonetheless, they also acknowledge that the research findings are value-laden. That is, no matter how rigorous the data are collected and analyzed, the findings partially reflect researcher bias because they are colored by the researcher's world views, experiences, and upbringings; hence, as an underlying principle, it is acknowledged that the final research report cannot guarantee the truth-value of what the phenomenon is from a descriptive or transcendental perspective and what it means from an interpretive perspective in an absolute sense.

Another quality that delimits the scope of Phenomenology is intentionality. The use of Phenomenology in philosophy and methodology is traced back to intentionality, which refers to the representational nature of consciousness. Much of the content of our consciousness, including our thoughts and perceptions, are representational in that they are of or about something which is different from the thing itself (Crane, 2001). For instance, when we see a tree, it is a perception of a tree, not the tree itself, or when I express concern about a possible nuclear war in the future, my concern is about a possible future state (McIntyre & Smith, 1989). Therefore, each of these mental states is a representation of something, not the thing itself. This representational character of consciousness is what Husserl calls intentionality. A logical corollary of this thesis is that there are two forms of existence: intentionality and reality. The former is a conscious psychical form, while the latter is a combination of form and matter existing in the real world (Cilesiz, 2010). There may be things in mind with no natural equivalence. For example, God exists in our mind not because it is a tangible entity external to us but because we can think about it. Since we can think about it, it is part of our consciousness; hence, it exists in the realm of intentionality, not reality.

Taking the distinction between intentionality and reality into account, phenomenologists categorize phenomena into natural in the sense that they appear to the person from without and mental as those which appear to the person from within. Husserl expanded this notion by differentiating between external perception and inner perception. He believed that the former is shaped by sense organs while the latter is the result of reflection. These distinctions paved the way for rejecting naturalism which claims that all beings and events are natural and, as such, can be studied objectively through scientific methods of inquiry. While scientific methods can be used to study natural phenomena, Phenomenology can be used to study intentionality or the process whereby the mind consciously directs its thoughts to an object (Holloway & Wheeler, 1996).

Another property that separates phenomenological inquiries from other modes of qualitative research is what is described by Husserl as the natural attitude. The task of a phenomenologist is to shift away from a natural attitude or the common-sense views and assumptions about what we encounter in nature towards a phenomenological attitude. In other words, when the researcher adopts a phenomenological attitude, s/he automatically transcends the natural attitude or straightforward acceptance of experience and knowledge (Hemberg, 2006). With a natural attitude, we see and accept what we experience through our senses at its face value. To deepen our knowledge of the phenomena as they appear to us, Husserl believes that we should adopt a phenomenological attitude and not accept the world as it discloses itself to us. More specifically, we should liberate ourselves from natural attitudes to determine the meaning of what presents itself to us.

Adopting a phenomenological attitude is contingent upon bracketing. Terms such as bracketing, eidetic reduction, and epoché, which are used interchangeably by phenomenological researchers, are descriptive of the researchers' phenomenological attitude (Stewart & Mickunas, 1974). Epoché reflects the moment when the researcher deliberately suspends any prior knowledge or presuppositions and directs his attention solely to the experience of the phenomenon and the data he receives in the context of experiencing the phenomenon (Patton, 1990). The epoché refers to "the elimination of everything that limits us from perceiving things as such, since the natural attitude, due to its objective nature, prevents us from doing so" (Villanueva, 2014, p. 220). In less technical terms, it helps the researcher to explore and understand the phenomenon under study by setting aside previous understandings, including previous explanations and theories, and relying solely on the description of a phenomenon as experienced by the participants. In a nutshell, in descriptive Phenomenology, the researcher purposefully sets aside personal and common-sense prejudices and beliefs and does not allow his perspectives, perceptions, and presuppositions to enter the unique world of the participant (Creswell, 2007). In a similar vein, interpretive phenomenologists move away from the natural attitude towards a phenomenological attitude by letting their prior understanding mature and change in the research process.

Transcendence from a natural to a phenomenological attitude can be achieved through 'imaginative variation' (Giorgi, 1985). An imaginative variation involves removing unnecessary and redundant features and exploring all possible meanings of the data by asking questions about the phenomenon under study (Beech, 1999). This process of phenomenological reduction should characterize the entire research process so that the researcher can achieve the purest form of description (Streubert & Carpenter, 1995). In this process, the researcher clarifies and opens up the meaning of experience through intuition and reflection (Holloway & Wheeler, 1996). This process of intuiting continues until the researchers reach a deep understanding of the phenomenon (Streubert & Carpenter, 1995). Moustakas (1994) explains:

The task of imaginative variation is to seek possible meaning through the utilization of imagination, varying the frames of reference, employing polarities and reversals' and approaching the phenomenon from divergent perspectives, different positions, roles, or functions. The aim is to arrive at structural descriptions of an experience, the underlying and precipitating factors that account for what is being experienced; in other words, the "how" that speaks to conditions that illuminate the "what" of experience.   (p. 85)

3.2   Types of research questions addressed

Phenomenological studies purposively sample a range of participants who have experienced a phenomenon and then inductively explore their perceptions of their lived experience through qualitative interviews. In this process, the researcher tries to gain a deep understanding of the meanings ascribed to experiences. In other words, it tries to understand experience by exploring the perspectives of those who have direct experience (Breaden, 1997). To ensure that the participants express their experience of the phenomenon under study rather than their perspectives, the research questions are phrased by asking, "What is it like to..." (Vagle, 2018, p. 218). Therefore, phenomenological researchers value subjectivity since they consider the participants' perspectives and narratives as a form of knowledge. Moreover, interpretive phenomenologists go beyond subjectivity by embracing intersubjectivity (Heidegger, 2000). In other words, through open-ended qualitative interviews, phenomenological researchers first try to uncover each participant's construction of reality, and then they try to find common threads in a wide range of experiences. Intersubjectivity also entails a joint effort on the part of the researcher and the participants in that they try to co-construct the essence of experience. In a nutshell, phenomenological studies do not explore participants' perceptions of a phenomenon. Rather, they explore the perceptions and perspectives of the participants who have experienced a phenomenon. Phenomenological studies start and stop with lived experience of the phenomenon under study (Creswell, 2007).

The following research questions exemplify how phenomenological researchers try to understand a phenomenon from the perspective of the participants who have experienced it:

–   How do pre-service teachers experience practicum in an EFL context?
–   What is the nature of the teacher-student relationship in the context of teacher education?
–   How do students experience university teachers' justice in the classroom?
–   What are students' lived experiences of the blended learning program in private language schools?

- What is EFL teachers' experience of praxis shock in public high schools in Iran?
- What are language teachers' lived experiences of online assessment in private language schools in Iran?

In short, the phenomenological research question should clearly specify the participants of interest, their experience, and the context in which it happened. In other words, the research question should specify whose and what lived experience is being explored in what context. For instance, the research question, 'What is EFL teachers' (whose) experience of praxis shock (What) in public high schools in Iran (where)" is well formulated because it answers the 'whose, what, and where' questions.

3.3 Data collection and analysis procedure

Prior to exploring the participants' experience of the phenomenon under study, the researcher should specify the sampling procedure. In Phenomenology, participants can be selected in different ways, but one of the most suitable procedures is purposive sampling. In this sampling strategy, the researcher should focus on selecting information-rich cases for an in-depth study (Patton, 2015). In Phenomenology, having a shared experience of the phenomenon and a willingness to share one's experience are the most important criteria. Another strategy is snowball sampling. In this strategy, the sample is expanded by asking each participant who took part in the study to introduce other participants (Miles & Huberman, 1994). Sampling and exploring the participants' experience of the phenomenon continues until the recurrent themes and the common threads that reflect the essence of the phenomenon reach a point of theoretical saturation. According to Hennink et al. (2017), saturation refers to the point where no additional codes emerge, and no further insights can be gained from interview data. Apart from theoretical saturation, a sample consisting of 10 to 15 is sufficient, providing that those selected present a rich description of how they experienced the phenomenon (Speziale & Carpenter, 2007).

The interview process starts with a broad grand tour question that encourages the participants to freely describe their experience of the phenomenon. In face-to-face interviews, the researcher should ask clarification questions not only to encourage the participants to clarify their perspectives but also to deepen their own understanding of the participants' experience of the phenomenon (Speziale & Carpenter, 2007). In studies that are conducted within the transcendental framework, the researcher should set aside his prior biases and schematic knowledge throughout the data collection process by keeping reflective diaries (Wall et al., 2004). Individual interviews elicit the essence of the phenomenon as experienced by the participant. The researcher enriches the data through theoretical sampling. In theoretical sampling, the researcher does not sample the participants. Rather, he samples perspectives that help develop the emerged patterns. Charmaz (2006) explains theoretical sampling as "seeking and collecting pertinent data to elaborate and refine categories in your emerging theory"(p. 192).

When it comes to analysis, descriptive and interpretive phenomenologists follow different procedures. Working within the transcendental framework, Hycner (1985) presents the most elaborate data analysis procedure. Following Hyncer, analysis involves bracketing one's prior knowledge, biases, and preconceptions of the phenomenon to assure openness to the data, designating units of general meaning or giving equal weights to all meaning units, specifying meaningful chunks that are pertinent to the research question, verifying the specified units by trained judges, leaving out the redundant units for abstraction, categorizing meaning units and assigning meaning to each category; verifying the emerged categories through member checking, modifying the categories and themes based on the feedback received from the participants, diving the themes into general and specific, and capturing the essence of the experience by wringing a composite summary of the common threads.

While in transcendental phenomenology, the researcher's prior knowledge and pre-understanding are weeded out as irrelevant, in interpretive phenomenology, the researcher's prior knowledge of the phenomenon is taken as a springboard in the hermeneutic circle. In other words, the researcher cycles from his or her prior understanding of the phenomenon as reflected in the early writings to new understandings, which are to be integrated with later understandings of the phenomenon in the process of data analysis, and this process continues until a fusion of horizons occurs (Rodgers, 2005).

In effect, the credibility of the findings is established in slightly different ways in descriptive and interpretive Phenomenology. In the former, the researcher brackets his prior understanding and, by doing so, makes sure that his final description reflects nothing but an abstraction of the participants' perspectives. In the latter, the researcher establishes the credibility of the description through a 'subjectivity statement' (Merriam, 2009). That is, by adding his horizon of experience, as made transparent in the researchers' reflective journal. In other words, the manuscript should include documentation of not only what motivated the study but also how the researcher's horizon of significance came to the surface in the research process. This helps the reader to see clearly "how researchers' conception of the phenomenon interacted with research questions, approach, methods, results, and/or transferability" (O'Brien et al., 2014). Rigor can also be established through an intersubjective agreement among judges (VanKaam, 1966).

That is, the final description can be verified by trained judges who apply the description to a random sample of cases.

In short, conducting phenomenological research involves four essential steps. The first step is phenomenological reduction or epoché, whereby the researcher verbalizes or writes down his prior understanding of the phenomenon to ensure that his prior knowledge and biases do not contaminate his/her pure description of the phenomenon. In line with the transcendental phenomenological framework, the researcher weeds out his or her prior knowledge as irrelevant to the exploration of the phenomenon. In interpretive phenomenology, the researcher writes down his/her prior knowledge and then critically checks how it evolves in the research process.

The second step is intuiting or being open to the phenomenon given to us in sensory awareness. At this stage, the researcher not only focuses on the topic freshly and naively but also uses the data to establish a basis for what to look for next (Moustakas, 1994). The third step is analyzing the collected data not only to understand each participant's experience of the phenomenon but also to find the common threads or the essential invariant aspects of the phenomenon or the essence of the phenomenon.

The last step is presenting a thick description of the phenomenon organized around the common threads or the recurrent themes and patterns, reflecting the participants' intersubjective understanding of the phenomenon. At this last stage, the researcher tries to integrate textural and structural descriptions from the essence of what is known individually to the essence of what is known by all (Moerer-Urdahl & Creswell, 2004).

3.4   Ethical considerations

Neuman (2011) believes that ethics starts and ends with the researcher. The reason is that the participants may not be aware of ethical considerations; hence, the researcher should have the participants sign an informed consent form being well aware of the potential harms and benefits of the research process for the participants. The consent form clarifies the participants' rights, including the right to have adequate information about the project, the right to decide to participate voluntarily, and the right to be able to choose to withdraw at his or her discretion at any point in the research process (Capron, 1989).

The consent letter should include (1) a clear description of the research purpose; (2) a statement that participants can withdraw at any stage of the study; (3) a notification that the interview data will be audio-taped; and (4) an assurance that the participants' identity and their perspectives will not be revealed to third parties. Moreover, it should disclose any possible harms and benefits of the research project for the participants (Punch, 1998). To prevent harm, it is recommended that the researcher not only replace the participants' names with pseudonyms or fictional names but also keep all the information that may possibly identify the participants confidential.

In addition to having the participants sign an informed consent form and discussing the potential benefits and losses of taking part in the research process, the researcher should:

– avoid "fake relationships" (Kondowe & Booyens, 2014) and ensure quality data by establishing trusting and mutually beneficial relationships with the participants. The researcher must also keep the participants' identity from being identified or discovered by others (Kang & Hwang, 2021)
– ensure that the research process benefits the participants and promotes their welfare (Piper & Thompson, 2016)

4. Critiques and responses

Many criticisms have been leveled against both descriptive and interpretive Phenomenology. To start with, critics who assess descriptive Phenomenology from a positivist perspective argue that it does not meet the psychometric properties of objectivity and reliability through what is called "phenomenological skepticism" (Roy, 2007). Along these lines, Dennett (1991) claims that Phenomenology lacks a rigorous method for describing reality as experienced by the participants, and neither does it have any mechanism to establish the credibility of its findings. In short, he argues that Phenomenology "has failed to find a single, settled method that everyone could agree upon" (Dennett, 1991, p. 44). He believes that Phenomenology is unscientific because its findings reflect separate individual's understanding of reality rather than an inter-subjective understanding of reality and relies on the participants' subjective account of reality rather than reliable observation.

Conversely, phenomenologists who work within the interpretivist paradigm criticize quantitative research by arguing that they approach reality based on preconceived notions and pre-defined categories. They claim that natural attitude imposes a procedure that theorizes about reality prior to observing or studying it. This critique suggests that adopting a phenomenological attitude, which entails precluding any preconceived notion of reality, enables phenomenologists to return to 'the things themselves', to the 'phenomena'. Hence, they argue that research should explore how people experience social reality rather than test whether it fits our preconceptions and previous theories. Moreover, phenomenologists argue that seemingly objective measures used in quantitative studies are inherently subjective in each and every aspect except for scoring. Therefore, the reliability criticism, which presupposes the objectivity of quantitative measures, is too shaky to be leveled against Phenomenology.

Another criticism that has been leveled against Phenomenology is the scientific legitimacy of the phenomenological findings. Critics argue that adopting a phenomenological attitude, relying on the daily experience of reality, and insisting on common-sense knowledge of social phenomena is nothing but claiming that common-sense knowledge is as legitimate as scientific knowledge. Husserl (1960) responds to this criticism by arguing that "we should not accept or adhere to any assertion that is not derived from evidence" (p.13). Husserl takes the evidence-based approach to research as a strength of Phenomenology and rejects theory-driven studies because they all hypothesize something about reality prior to data collection and analysis.

Other critics dismiss Phenomenology as insignificant because they claim it is conservative. A phenomenological study may, for instance, aim at understanding illiteracy from the participants' perspectives. Although their thick description of this phenomenon is verifiable through member checking, their findings have nothing to do with changing the status quo. Critics argue that research should go beyond understanding an unwanted social phenomenon to changing it for the better. The mission of understanding a phenomenon from the perspective of people who have experienced it subconsciously legitimizes the status quo. The phenomenological study that aims to present a thick description of reality should also help change this unwanted phenomenon by empowering the participants to read and write. Phenomenologists respond by arguing that a thick description of reality from the participants' perspective is not synonymous with legitimizing it. Conversely, a deep understanding of the status quo is a prerequisite to realizing what ought to be changed about the status quo.

Other critics argue that phenomenological studies ignore the mediating role of language (Willing, 2008). The final phenomenological report reflects two things: (1) an intersubjective understanding of reality as perceived by the participants; and (2) the participants and the researcher's communicative skills. The problem with phenomenological studies is that the researcher and the participants have the required communication skills; therefore, bracketing, which is one of the foundation stones of Phenomenology, is violated since the participants' and the researcher's communicative skills are taken for granted. Critics argue that the participants and the researcher may not have the required communicative skills. It is also argued that Phenomenology better suits eloquent participants and researchers (Willing, 2008). Fortunately, this criticism does not pose a threat to Phenomenology since, through the purposive sampling procedure, the researcher can choose the participants who have the required communication skills.

To sum up, critics argue that phenomenological findings are subjective, unreliable, and invalid. These scholars would not dismiss Phenomenology and other modes of qualitative inquiry as unscientific if they broadened their perspectives beyond classical measurement theory. They confine the concept validity to quantitative measurement and, as such, consider qualitative research as invalid. In a broader sense, a research method is valid if it investigates what it intends to investigate. In light of this broader definition, Phenomenology can be considered as being valid (Kvale, 1989) since it investigates what it intends to investigate, i.e., a thick description of reality as experienced by the participants. Validity is a major concern both in quantitative and qualitative research. In quantitative research, the findings should have internal and external validity. Internal validity is established through random assignment because it is believed that through random assignment, the effect of confounding variables is evenly distributed. External validity is established through random selection because it is believed that this mechanism enables the researcher to generalize what they find in the sample to the target population.

In qualitative research, validity is equally important though it is established through other theoretically justified mechanisms. Adopting a phenomenological attitude or bracketing is the first phenomenological tool used to ensure that the description of the phenomenon reflects the participants' understanding rather than the researcher's preconception. The validity of the phenomenological findings is also established by exploring the horizontal and vertical consistency of the descriptions (Karlson, 1995). The description meets the horizontal consistency criterion if it fits well with the participants' perspectives or interview transcripts. Likewise, it meets the vertical consistency criterion if it fits in well with higher-order levels of description or with the emerged themes and categories. When the description fits in well with the original data and the emerging themes, the phenomenological findings are valid. But as mentioned before, a research method is valid if it investigates what it intends to investigate. Phenomenology aims at investigating reality from the perspectives of the participants who have experienced it; hence, it is easy to assess the validity of the final description through member checking. This mechanism clearly shows whether the final desecration reflects the participants' understanding of reality or the researcher's preconception.

5. Conclusions

In a nutshell, there are two approaches to Phenomenology: transcendental or descriptive (Husserl, 1970) and hermeneutic (Heidegger, 2000). Both transcendental and hermeneutic Phenomenology are concerned with the life world or how meaning is assigned to experience. Both of them aim at presenting a deep description of the phenomenon and achieving a sense of understanding (Wilson & Hutchinson, 1991). In other words, both approaches aim at presenting a thick description and a deep understanding of a phenomenological experience. They both attempt to unfold meanings as they are lived in everyday existence (Laverty, 2003). A distinctive feature of hermeneutic Phenomenology is that this approach embraces bridling rather than bracketing (Gadamer, 1998; Laverty, 2003). As a methodological consideration, bridling is concerned with setting aside pre-understandings only if they limit one's openness to the data. While bracketing focuses backward on pre-understandings, bridling has a forward focus in that it shows the researcher's openness to the data as the phenomenon appears to our consciousness (Dahlberg, Dahlberg, & Nystrom, 2008).

What distinguishes phenomenological texts and talks from the rest of qualitative rhetoric is what is described by Husserl as the natural attitude. The task of a phenomenologist is to shift away from a natural attitude or the common-sense views and assumptions about what we encounter in nature towards a phenomenological attitude. In other words, when the researcher adopts a phenomenological attitude, s/he automatically transcends the natural attitude or straightforward acceptance of experience and knowledge (Hemberg, 2006). With a natural attitude, we see and accept what we experience through our senses at its face value. Husserl believes that we should adopt a phenomenological attitude and not accept the world as it discloses itself to us to deepen our knowledge of the phenomena as it appears to us. More specifically, we should liberate ourselves from natural attitudes to determine the meaning of what presents itself to us.

Phenomenological studies purposively sample a range of participants who have experienced a phenomenon and then inductively explore their lived experience through qualitative interviews. In this process, the researcher tries to gain a deep understanding of the meanings ascribed to experiences. In other words, it tries to understand experience by exploring the perspectives of those who have direct experience (Breaden, 1997). To ensure that the participants express their experience of the phenomenon under study rather than their perspectives, the research questions are phrased by asking, "What is it like to..." (Vagle, 2018, p. 218). Therefore, phenomenological researchers value subjectivity since they consider the participants' perspectives and narratives as a form of knowledge. Moreover, interpretive phenomenologists go beyond subjectivity by embracing intersubjectivity (Heidegger, 2000). In other words, through open-ended qualitative interviews, phenomenological researchers first try to uncover each participant's construction of reality, and then they try to find common threads in a wide range of experiences. Intersubjectivity also entails a joint effect on the part of the researcher and the participants in that they try to co-construct the meaning of the essence of experience. In a nutshell, phenomenological studies start and stop with lived experience of the phenomenon under study (Creswell, 2007).

References

Allison, P., & Pomeroy, E. (2000). How shall we know? Epistemological concerns in research in experiential education. *Journal of Experiential Education, 23*(2), 91–98.

Barclay, M.W. (1992). The utility of hermeneutic interpretation in psychotherapy. *Theoretical and Philosophical Psychology, 12*(2), 103–118.

Beck, C. (1993). Qualitative research: The evaluation of its credibility, fittingness, and auditability. *Western Journal of Nursing Research, 15*(2), 263–266.

Beech, I. (1999). Bracketing in phenomenological research. *Nurse Researcher, 6*(3), 35–50.

Breaden, K. (1997). Cancer and beyond: The question of survivorship. *Journal of Advanced Nursing, 26*, 978–84.

Breen, L., & Darlaston-Jones, D. (2008). Moving beyond the enduring dominance of positivism in psychological research: An Australian perspective. Paper presented at the 43rd Australian Psychological Society Annual Conference.

Capron, A.M. (1989). Human experimentation. In R.M. Veatch (Ed.), *Medical ethics* (pp. 125–172). Jones & Bartlett.

Cilesiz, S. (2010). A phenomenological approach to experiences with technology: Current state, promise, and future directions for research. *Educational Technology Research and Development, 59*, 487–510. https://www.jstor.org/stable/41414955

Crane, T. (2001). *Elements of mind.* Oxford University Press.

Dahlberg, K., Dahlberg, H., & Nyström, M. (2008). *Reflective lifeworld research* (2nd ed.). Studentlitteratur.

Dennett, D.C. (1991). *Consciousness explained.* Back Bay Books.

Dowling, M., & Cooney, A. (2012). Research approaches related to phenomenology: Negotiating a complex landscape. *Nurse Researcher, 20*(2), 21–27.

Gadamer, H.G. (1976). *Philosophical hermeneutics.* University of California Press.

Gadamer, H.G. (1998). The hermeneutic circle: The elevation of the historicity of understanding to the status of a hermeneutic principle. In L. Alcoff (ed.), *Epistemology: The Big Questions* (pp. 232–249). Blackwell.

Giorgi, A. (Ed.). (1985). *Phenomenology and psychological research.* Duquesne University Press.

Giorgi, A., & Giorgi, B. (2003). The descriptive phenomenological psychological method. In P. Camic, J. Rhodes, & L. Yardley (Eds). *Qualitative research in psychology: Expanding perspectives in methodology and design* (pp. 243–273). American Philosophical Association.

Greene, M. (1997). The lived world, literature and education. In D. Vandenberg (ed.), *Phenomenology and education discourse* (pp. 169–190). Heinemann.

Heidegger, M. (1962). *Being and time* (J. Macquarrie & E. Robinson, Trans.). Harper and Row.

Heidegger, M. (2000). *Sein und Zeit* (J. Macquarrie & E. Robinson, Trans). Wiley Blackwell.

Hemberg, H. (2006). *Husserl's phenomenology: Knowledge, objectivity and others.* Continuum

Hennink, M.M., Kaiser, B.N., & Marconi, V.C. (2017). Code saturation versus meaning saturation: How many interviews are enough? *Qualitative Health Research, 27*(4), 591–608.

Husserl, E. (1960). Ideas: General introduction to pure phenomenology. *MacMillan.*

Husserl, E. (1989). *Ideas pertaining to a pure phenomenology and to a phenomenological philosophy-Second Book: Studies in the Phenomenology of Constitution.* Kluwer Academic Publishers.

Holloway, I., & Wheeler, S. (1996). *Qualitative research for nurses.* Wiley Blackwell.

Husserl, E. (1970). *The crisis of European sciences and transcendental phenomenology* (D. Carr, Trans). Northwestern University Press.

Husserl, E. (1989). *Ideas pertaining to a pure phenomenology and to a phenomenological philosophy.* Kluwer.

Husserl, E. (2003). *Ideas: General introduction to pure phenomenology.* Translated by W. R. Boyce Gibson. Routledge.

Hycner, R. H. (1985). Some guidelines for the phenomenological analysis of interview data. *Human Studies*, 8, 279–303.

Kang, E., & Kwang, H. (2021). Ethical conducts in qualitative research methodology: Participant observation and interview process. *Journal of Research and Publication Ethics*, 2(2021), 5–10.

Koch, T. (1995). Interpretive approaches in nursing research: The influence of Husserl and Heidegger. *Journal of Advanced Nursing*, 21(5), 827–836.

Koch, T. (1996). Implementation of a hermeneutic inquiry in nursing: Philosophy, rigor and representation. *Journal of Advanced Nursing*, 24, 174–184.

Kvale, S. (1996). *InterViews: An introduction to qualitative research.* Sage.

Kondowe, C., & Booyens, M. (2014). A student's experience of gaining access for qualitative research. *Social Work*, 50(1), 146–152.

Kvale, S. (1989). To validate is to question. In S. Kvale (Ed.), *Issues of validity in qualitative research* (pp. 73–92). Student litteratur.

Laverty, S. M. (2003). Hermeneutic phenomenology and phenomenology: A comparison of historical and methodical considerations. *International Journal of Qualitative Methods*, 2(3), Article 3.

Lincoln, Y. S., & Guba, E. G. (1994). *Naturalistic inquiry.* Sage.

Lopez, K. A., & Willis, D. G. (2004). Descriptive versus interpretive phenomenology: Their contributions to nursing knowledge. *Qualitative Health Research*, 14(5), 726–735.

McIntyre, R., & Smith, D. W. (1989). Theory of intentionality. In William R. McKenna & J. N. Mohanty (eds.), *Husserl's Phenomenology: A Textbook.* University Press of America.

Merriam, S. B. (2009). *Qualitative research: A guide to design and implementation.* Jossey-Bass.

Miles, M. B., & Huberman, A. M. (1994). *Qualitative data analysis: An expanded sourcebook.* Sage.

Moerer-Urdahl, T., & Creswell, J. (2004). Using transcendental phenomenology to explore the "ripple effect" in a leadership mentoring program. *International Journal of Qualitative Methods*, 3(2), 1–28.

Moustakas, C. (1994). *Phenomenological research methods.* Sage.

Munhall, P. L. (1989). Philosophical pondering on qualitative research methods in nursing. *Nursing Science Quarterly*, 2(1), 20–28.

Natanson, M. (1973). *Edmund Husserl: Philosophy of infinite tasks.* Northwestern University Press.

Neuman, W. L. (2011). *Social research methods: Qualitative and quantitative approaches* (D. Musslewhite (Ed.), 7th ed.). Allyn and Bacon.

Norlyk, A., & Harder, I. (2010). What makes a phenomenological study phenomenological? An analysis of peer-reviewed empirical nursing. *Qualitative Health Research, 20*(3), 420–431.

O'Brien, B. C., Harris, I. B., Beckman, T. J., Reed, D. A., Cook, D. A. (2014). Standards for reporting qualitative research: A synthesis of recommendations. *Academic Medicine, 89*(9), 1245–1251.

Osborne, J. (1994). Some similarities and differences among phenomenological and other methods of psychological qualitative research. *Canadian Psychology, 35*(2), 167–189.

Patton, M. Q. (1990). *Qualitative evaluation and research methods* (2nd ed.). Sage.

Patton, M. Q. (2015). *Qualitative research & evaluation methods: Integrating theory and practice* (4th ed.). Sage.

Pieper, I., & Thomson, C. J. (2016). Beneficence as a principle in human research. *Monash Bioethics Review, 34*(2), 117–135.

Punch, K. F. (1998). *Introduction to social research: Quantitative and qualitative approaches* (1st ed.). Sage.

Rodgers, B. L. (2005). Interpretive inquiry: The mirror cracked. In B. L. Rodgers (Ed.), *Developing nursing knowledge: Philosophical traditions and influences* (pp. 145–159). Williams & Wilkins.

Roy, J.-M. (2007). Heterophenomenology and phenomenological skepticism. *Phenomenology and the Cognitive Sciences, 6*, 1–20.

Speziale, H. J. S., & Carpenter, D. R. (2007). *Qualitative research in nursing: Advancing the humanistic imperative* (4th ed.). Williams & Wilkins.

Stewart, D., & Mickunas, A. (1974). *Exploring phenomenology. A guide to the field and its literature.* American Library Association.

Streubert, H., & Carpenter, D. (1995). *Qualitative research in nursing: Advancing the humanistic imperative.* Lippincott.

Vagle, M. D. (2018). *Crafting phenomenological research* (2nd ed.). Routledge.

VanKaam, A. (1966). *Existential foundations of psychology.* Duquesne University Press.

Villanueva, J. (2014). *La fenomenología como afirmación de un nuevo humanismo.* Universidad Nacional Mayor de San Marcos.

Wall, C., Glenn, S., Mitchinson, S., & Poole, H. (2004). Using a reflective diary to develop bracketing skills during a phenomenological investigation. *Nurse Researcher, 11*(4), 20–29.

West, R., & Turner, L. H. (2000). *Introducing communication theory: Analysis and application. Mountain View.* Mayfield.

Willig, C. (2008). *Introducing qualitative research in psychology* (2nd ed.). McGraw Hill Open University Press.

Wilson, H. S., & Hutchinson, S. (1991). Triangulation of qualitative methods: Heideggerian hermeneutics and ground theory. *Qualitative Health Research, 1*, 263–276.

CHAPTER 11

Phenomenology

A showcase of EFL learners' experience of foreign language proficiency maintenance

Seyyed Ali Ostovar-Namaghi
Shahrood University of Technology

This chapter aims to showcase Phenomenology as a research methodology by presenting EFL learners' experience of proficiency maintenance in a context where English has no social function. The study started with a participant who was able to maintain her proficiency and then sampled other participants who shared the same experience through snowball sampling. Transcendental phenomenology was chosen to explore the participants' subjective experience of the phenomenon under study in an objective manner. To achieve this objective, a reflexive account of the researcher's preconceptions of proficiency maintenance was written and bracketed as irrelevant to the participants' account of their experience. To present a clear synopsis of the study, the chapter will explain why the mode of inquiry was chosen, how it was implemented, and how the challenges were addressed.

1. Introduction

Phenomenological research aims at understanding a phenomenon from the perspectives of participants who experienced it. This chapter discusses a study to illustrate the procedural knowledge pertinent to conducting a phenomenological study. More specifically, it aims at showcasing the process which was followed to understand lived experiences of EFL learners who could maintain their language proficiency in a context where the language they had learned had no social use. To this end, the chapter will first present an overview of the study and explain the rationale for adopting the methodology. That is, taking the bifurcation in phenomenological research into account, it will succinctly present the rationale for choosing Husserlian or transcendental Phenomenology as the methodological procedure and will then explain how the study was implemented. Having explained how the methodology was implemented, we will then explain the chal-

https://doi.org/10.1075/rmal.6.11ost
© 2024 John Benjamins Publishing Company

lenges we faced and how we I addressed them. Finally, prior to concluding the chapter, we I will briefly explain the insight I gained in the research process.

2. An overview of the study

Creswell (1994) cogently states that irrespective of the research paradigm, research starts with a topic and problem of interest. Although we agree that studies usually begin with the choice of research topic, this study began with problem sensing. As a practitioner in the field of language education, I was fascinated by how teenagers in Iran enthusiastically develop their language skills with the hope of continuing their studies in an English-speaking country. The problem is that these enthusiastic learners do not have a chance to use English outside the classroom, the reason being that English has no social use in Iran.

Sensing this problem, I wondered whether these EFL learners lost their language proficiency over the years or whether they found some ways to maintain their proficiency. I contacted several learners who had an acceptable language proficiency when they were my students. Although most of them said that they had lost their language proficiency, I found one learner who had maintained her language proficiency. I clearly explained the purpose and focus of the study, and she agreed to share her experience of proficiency maintenance. Moreover, she also offered to introduce similar cases and, as such, helped me find participants with similar experiences through snowball sampling. Since I needed assistance in the research process, I introduced my research concerns and the topic to one of my MA students who was doing her master's program at Shahrood University of Technology, and she agreed to help in collecting the data, preparing preliminary reports, and co-authoring a paper entitled 'Exploring EFL Learners' Experience of Foreign Language Proficiency Maintenance.' The paper was published in the *International Journal of Applied Linguistics and English Literature.* Since the paper is co-authored, in what follows, the pronoun 'we' will be used to acknowledge the co-author's contribution.

3. Why was phenomenology chosen, and how was it implemented?

Many phenomenological studies lack in clarity on philosophical underpinnings (Norlyk & Harder, 2010). To avoid this problem, in what follows, we will elaborate on the paradigm within which this study was conducted and the philosophical assumptions which we brought to the research endeavor. Knowing the limitations of methods of science in establishing cause and effect relationships and valuing and respecting subjective data, we conducted this study within an interpretivist rather than a positivist paradigm. Like any other researchers, we explored EFL learners' experience of proficiency maintenance with some philosophical assumptions. Ontologically, we believe that reality is internal to the person, and each person has his or her own construction of reality. Epistemologically, we took an emic approach. In other words, we did our best to develop an insider's view of proficiency maintenance by taking the participants' subjective expression of their experience as knowledge. As for our axiological stance, we believe that values and data are interwoven. Methodologically, we found Phenomenology an ideal methodological procedure for exploring the subjective meanings the participants attach to their experience of maintaining their proficiency.

Since Phenomenology experienced a bifurcation in the process of development, it is essential that the researcher clearly state whether the study is conducted in line with transcendental or hermeneutic Phenomenology. It is sometimes hard for the reader to understand phenomenological research findings and evaluate their rigor and credibility since many researchers do not articulate which approach, i.e., descriptive or hermeneutic, guides the study (Lopez & Willis, 2004). We believe that the subjective understanding of people who have experienced a phenomenon is worth investigating, but this exploration of subjectivity can be conducted in an objective manner; hence, following Husserl (1998), this study was conducted with a transcendental approach, as discussed in the previous chapter.

In order to ensure the study is conducted within a transcendental framework, we wrote a reflexive account of our prior understanding of the phenomenon under study, i.e., proficiency maintenance in an EFL context, and bracketed it as irrelevant to the description of the participants' account of their experience. In other words, in line with Husserl (1989), we intended to capture the essence of a phenomenon and understand lived experience by sticking to the slogan, 'Back to the things themselves!' (Moustakas, 1994, p.26). Moreover, we did our best to explore both inner and external perceptions since, for Husserl, the word experience refers not only to the tangible concrete objects which are external to the person but also to abstract concepts and the mood state, which are internal to the person (Stewart & Mickunas, 1974).

Regarding the implementation phase of the study, we followed both a purposive and snowball sampling procedure with a focus on cases, which could provide rich information concerning the phenomenon under study (Patton, 2015). Along these lines, we selected only 15 EFL learners from among 45 eligible cases. The criteria for inclusion were: (1) having a successful experience of proficiency maintenance; (2) willingness to share the experience; (3) openness and fluency in describing the experience; and (4) meeting a minimum of the four-year time interval between the interview session and their last experience as a language learner.

The sampling process started with a participant who met the foregoing criteria and was completed through snowball sampling, which is a method of expanding the sample by asking one informant or participant to recommend others for interviewing (Babbie, 1995). In addition to sampling information-rich cases, we sampled perspectives that helped develop the themes emerging through theoretical sampling. The theoretical sampling of perceptions, which were pertinent to the development of emerged concepts and themes, continued until theoretical saturation was achieved (Corbin & Strauss, 2008).

Prior to the first interview, which aimed at contextualizing the phenomenon, we explicitly stated the purpose of the study and the research questions. Furthermore, we assured the participants that they could decide to withdraw from the research process whenever they decided to do so. We also observed participants' confidentiality by assuring them that their identities would not be revealed to the reader or any third parties. This was done by de-identifying the data in the research report. Finally, following Lincoln, Lynham, and Guba (2011), the participants filled out an informed consent form, which showed that they were fully aware of the research objective, research questions, and their rights, including the right to withdraw and the right to remain anonymous throughout the research process and in the final report of the findings.

The briefing session was followed by exploring the participants' experience of proficiency maintenance through open-ended qualitative interviews (Giorgi, 1997). Following Moustakas (1994), however, through reflection on our past knowledge and experience, we tried to bring our taken-for-granted assumptions and knowledge about proficiency maintenance to the conscious level. This was done in line with Husserlian transcendental Phenomenology, which requires that the researcher become aware of his natural attitude through bracketing (Merleau-Ponty, 1962). Interviews were conducted in Persian, i.e., the participants' native language, so as to ensure participants' free expression of their thoughts and feelings concerning the phenomenon under study. Moreover, during the interviews, we listened actively and asked clarification questions when we felt the information presented by the participants was cursory and insufficient.

Having adopted a phenomenological attitude through bracketing, we interviewed each participant three times (Seidman, 2006). The first interview, which focused on each participant's life history, aimed at providing context. We believe this first stage of contextualization is necessary because the experience of the life-world stands out against the participants' personal biography (Husserl, 1970). In other words, to understand the participants' experience, we first examined the context which gives meaning to the experience. Therefore, the first interview started with the general question, 'Can you describe your experience of language learning and when you stopped your language learning experience?'

The second interview aimed at understanding the phenomenon by encouraging the participants to present a rich description of their foreign language proficiency maintenance. In other words, we elicited the participants' experience of the phenomenon under study through the general question, 'What did you do to maintain your language proficiency without taking any language classes or without any potential chances to use language for communication in society?' Having asked the general question, we listened more actively to identify areas that needed clarification and to ensure that we had a deep understanding of the participants' descriptions of their experiences. Moreover, in view of the fact that different people have different perceptions of the same phenomenon and each experience has different modes of appearance (Sokolowski, 2000), we explored many experiences and, with a focus on common threads, we tried to capture the essence of the participants' experience.

The third or final interview aimed at clarifying the phenomenon. To achieve this goal, in the final interview, we encouraged the participants to reflect on their descriptions and the meaning of their experiences. Although many researchers consider imaginative variation in the analysis section of phenomenological inquiry, we used it in the data collection section not only to increase the breadth and depth of the participants' deceptions but also to deepen our understanding of the participants' perspectives. Although we were aware of the main elements of experience, we tried to unearth the invariant elements and clarify the structure of experience through imaginative variation (Husserl, 1960).

Although we used imaginative variation to uncover the invariant elements, we did not leave out or ignore the variant parts because we believed they represented each participant's unique experience of the phenomenon. One of the biggest merits of applying imaginative variation at this stage is that clarifications and modifications are grounded in the context of interviews. By involving the participants in the imaginative variation of their experience, we encouraged the participants both in the description of their experience and in the clarification of the structure of the experience.

To analyze and explicate the participants' perspectives, we followed a five-stage process. The first stage was moving away from our natural attitude towards a phenomenological attitude through phenomenological reduction or bracketing. More specifically, we deliberately opened up ourselves to the phenomenon under study in an effort to see the phenomenon "in its own right with its own meaning" (Hycner, 1999). To ensure our openness to the participants' experience of proficiency maintenance, we tried to reflect on our prior knowledge and conception of proficiency maintenance.

In a nutshell, we believed that what EFL learners experience after terminating their language learning experience is language proficiency loss until we encountered a participant who had been able to maintain her language proficiency despite contextual constraints. The basis for this presupposition was that lack of use leads to atrophy. In other words, we believed that language learners lose their proficiency over time because, in EFL contexts such as Iran, English has no social use; hence, we wrote this preconception down and considered it irrelevant to our understanding of the phenomenon. This was done to remind ourselves that the phenomenon of 'language proficiency maintenance' is not what we already knew or what previous theories hypothesized. Rather, it is implicit in the experience of language learners who could maintain their proficiency in a context where English had no social use.

The second stage was specifying units of meaning in the transcripts of the participants' perceptions. To this end, we first read through the transcripts many times over to develop an overall understanding of the phenomenon as experienced by each participant. Then following Cresswell (1998), we isolated those segments of interview transcripts that were indicative of proficiency maintenance. For us, bracketing was not limited to a prior reflection and verbalization of the phenomenon. Rather, it was an ongoing process; hence, in this second stage, we tried to remain open to the participants' perspectives so as to avoid biased interpretations shaped by our prior conception. Having extracted pertinent units of meaning, we read through them critically to eliminate any possible redundancies (Moustakas, 1994). We were careful not to leave out seemingly similar units which might convey different shades of meaning.

The next stage involved categorizing units of meaning to develop transient themes (Creswell, 1998). Even at this stage, we made sure that the emerging themes reflected units of meaning extracted from the participants' descriptions of the phenomenon rather than our prior knowledge. We also tried to develop units of significance (Sadala & Adorno, 2001) by constantly comparing units of meaning with the original interview transcripts. Finally, with a focus on the meaning of categories, we tried to capture the essence of the categories by specifying and briefly describing recurrent themes.

In the fourth stage, we tied to abstract each interview. We made sure that the summary reflects the emerged themes rather than a preconceived notion of the phenomenon. We also made sure that the summary makes sense in light of our contextualization of the phenomenon. Having abstracted each participant's experience of the phenomenon into a summary that incorporated the emerged units of meaning and the recurrent themes, we tried to establish the validity of the summary. This was done by returning the summary to the participants for verification or possible modification. This was done in the light of feedback received from the participants.

Finally, we tried to find the common threads or the recurrent themes and units of meaning in all the interviews. In other words, by taking recurrent themes in different interviews into account, we tried to write the final report. While many phenomenological studies write the final report based on both individual summaries and the composite summary, in this study, we tried to organize the summary around common threads or themes which recurred in different summaries. We also tried to validate the final summary by grounding our final understanding of the phenomenon in excerpts from the participants' perceptions. To ensure that the summary reflects both the common threads and each participant's unique experience of the phenomenon, we selected those excerpts which conveyed both the essence of the phenomenon and the individual's varied experience. For instance, one of the common threads, which portrays the participants' experience of proficiency maintenance, was 'reading for pleasure'.

Although our final report does not present a summary of our prior understandings of the phenomenon, it is suggested that the final report cover both a brief and written documentation of the researcher's pre-understanding of the phenomenon and a summary that is rooted in the participants' experience of the phenomenon. This percussion ensures that the final report of the results reflects an abstraction of the participants' experience rather than the researcher's biases and prior schematic knowledge. What follows aims to illustrate how we abstracted the participants' experience of English language proficiency maintenance around the emerged themes by presenting one of the emerged strategies the participants used to maintain their proficiency. One of the emerging themes was 'reading for pleasure', which clearly describes one of the strategies the participants followed to maintain their proficiency in a context where English has no social use.

Participants found reading for pleasure more fun than reading expository texts, which aimed at testing learners' proficiency. Moreover, they believed that language courses were very stressful since in language classes, their level of performance was consistently compared with each other. It was even more stressful because they had to read to meet the demands of tests. Elaborating on the merits of reading for pleasure, one of the participants states:

> Here, I decide on what to read what not to read. Moreover, I read at my personal pace. Previously, the texts we read were either irrelevant to our interest or too difficult to understand. Now, however, whenever I am free I choose a story from among graded readers, and read it at my own pace without any stress. Since, there are no final exams or comprehension checks, I keep reading without fretting over unknown words.

Participants favored pleasure reading on another ground. They believed reading for pleasure gives them a chance to follow their interests and read what they actually read in their native language. In this mode of reading, participants actively use their background knowledge to derive meaning from words and sentences. Reiterating the importance of background knowledge, one of the participants argues:

> In language courses, I had to read a pre-determined text for which I had no background knowledge. Presently, I follow my own interests. I am very interested in the news; hence, I listen to the news on a daily basis. Reading the news in English is not challenging at all because my understanding of the texts depends mainly on my background knowledge. This gives me a good chance to guess the meaning of unknown words more smoothly and get the meaning of the text more fluently.

Ashworth (1997b) argues that researchers can improve the credibility of their phenomenological findings by making an explicit statement of their pre-understandings of the phenomenon. We assured the credibility of the description by writing a transparent statement of our prior knowledge and biases in a reflective journal. This reflective journal was used as a guide to ensure that our prior undertakings did not affect the nature and direction of data collection and analysis. In short, bracketing our previous experiential and schematic knowledge of the phenomenon, helped us ground our understanding of the phenomenon in the perspectives of the participants who experienced the phenomenon and, as such, gain an insider's view of the phenomenon (Mouton & Marais, 1990, p.70). We used member checking as an additional safeguard against researcher bias (Doyle, 2007; Lincoln & Guba,1985). To this end, first, we summarized each participant's perspectives, and then returned the summary to the participant for verification and any possible modifications. The composite summary, which was organized around recurrent themes and grounded in excerpts from the participants' perspectives, was also verified by the participants, and subsequent modifications were made to accommodate the participants' suggestions.

4. Challenges faced and how they were addressed

Having embarked on conducting this phenomenological study, we faced several challenges. The first challenge was that unlike other qualitative research methods, such as grounded theory, the philosophical underpinnings of phenomenological research were rather complicated and difficult to grasp; hence, we did our best to understand Phenomenology both as a philosophical line of thought and as a research method. This enabled us to better understand variations of Phenomenology as a research method.

The second challenge we faced was the notion of phenomenological attitude. Although we knew understanding the essence of the participants' experience is contingent on adopting a phenomenological attitude, we were also well aware of the fact that we should approach the phenomenon under study from an educational perspective rather than a philosophical one; therefore, as educators, we tried to move beyond the natural attitude towards an educational attitude by bringing the educational implications of this phenomenological study to the foreground. In other words, at the very outset of the study, we reminded ourselves that this is not a philosophical analysis aiming at understanding a phenomenon. Rather, it's an educational study that should benefit language learners and other stakeholders. Our educational attitude created the theoretical sensitivity which is required in the process of data collection and analysis.

Another confusing and challenging issue we faced in conducting this study was the irreconcilable variations of phenomenological research methods. Although phenomenological studies tend to agree on the philosophical assumptions that govern Phenomenology, they seem to diverge when it comes to research methods, i.e., some phenomenological studies follow the transcendental tradition while others follow an interpretive one. Therefore, it was imperative for us to stick to transcendental phenomenology and set aside interpretative phenomenology, not because the latter was not a legitimate mode of inquiry but because we believed that our prior understandings of proficiency maintenance should not affect the process and the product of the study. In short, we chose transcendental Phenomenology over interpretive Phenomenology because it enabled us to explore the participants' subjective experience of proficiency maintenance in an objective and unobtrusive manner.

The last challenge we faced was in the verification stage. At first, we decided to hire three independent judges. Then we decided that such a procedure seems to be misconceived and misguided from a phenomenological perspective; hence, we did our best to bring our prior understanding and assumptions of the phenomenon under study to a conscious level, list them and bracket them to ensure that the final report of the findings reflects an objective analysis of the participants' subjective and intersubjective understanding of the phenomenon. Along these lines, hiring judges to review and verify the final description of the phenomenon seems to be antithetical, the reason being that the judges' decisions are shaped by their prior understanding of the phenomenon; hence, we decided not to hire judges and instead have the final description reviewed and verified by the participants themselves because at its best independent judges can be no better than the participants themselves.

5.   Insights gained using phenomenology

In implementing this study, we gained many insights. Prior to this study, we saw phenomenology as a unified research method, and it was in the implementation phase that we realized we should align the study with either transcendental or interpretive Phenomenology. As another equally important insight, we learned that we are not alone in misinterpreting Phenomenology because we found that many of the published papers have described the adopted research methodology as Phenomenology without specifying whether the study was conducted in line with descriptive or interpretive Phenomenology. Last but not least, we realized that the philosophical underpinnings of phenomenology make the strongest and most solid case for a shift away from theory-driven studies, which are based on a preconceived notion of reality, towards data-driven studies because, as Husserl (1973) states, they help researchers develop a transcendental attitude and "avoid being imprisoned by one's everyday awareness and judgments of the world."

6. Conclusions

The phenomenological study discussed in this chapter aimed at presenting an emic view of how language learners maintained their proficiency in a context where English serves no social functions. To ensure that the final description reflects the participants' experience of proficiency maintenance rather than our prior understanding, we adopted the transcendental or descriptive Phenomenology though we faced many challenges both in the conception and implementation of Phenomenology as a research method. Overcoming the challenges helped us develop a deeper understanding of Phenomenology both as a philosophical line of thought and as a research method; hence, in discussing the phenomenological study, we did our best to avoid declarative knowledge and stick to procedural knowledge and present down-to-earth insights, which reflect our experience of exploring this phenomenon. Taking variations of Phenomenology as a research method into account, it is essential that researchers show their alliance with one variation and make sure that the procedures followed are consistent with the adopted variation.

References

Ashworth, P.D. (1997b). *The variety of qualitative research: Non-positivist approaches. Nurse Education Today, 17*, 219–224.

Babbie, E. (1995). *The practice of social research* (7th ed.). Wadsworth.

Corbin, J., & Strauss, A. (2008). *Basics of qualitative research* (3rd ed.). Sage.

Creswell, J.W. (1998). *Qualitative inquiry and research design: Choosing among five traditions.* Sage.

Doyle, S. (2007). Member checking with older women: A framework for negotiating meaning. *Health Care for Women International, 8*, 888–908.

Giorgi, A. (1997). The theory, practice, and evaluation of the phenomenological method as a qualitative research procedure. *Journal of Phenomenological Psychology, 28*, 236–60.

doi Husserl, E. (1960). *Cartesian meditations: An introduction to phenomenology* (D. Cairns, Trans.). Martinus Nijhoff.

Husserl, E. (1970). *The crisis of European sciences and transcendental phenomenology: An introduction to phenomenological philosophy* (D. Carr, Trans.). Northwestern University Press

Husserl, E. (1973). *Experience and judgment: Investigations in a genealogy of logic.* Routledge and Kegan Paul.

Husserl, E. (1989). *Ideas pertaining to a pure phenomenology and to a phenomenological philosophy-Second Book: Studies in the Phenomenology of Constitution.* Kluwer Academic Publishers.

Hycner, R.H. (1999). Some guidelines for the phenomenological analysis of interview data. In A. Bryman & R.G. Burgess (Eds.), *Qualitative research* (Vol. 3, pp. 143–164). Sage.

Lincoln, Y.S., & Guba, E.G. (1985). *Naturalistic enquiry.* Sage.

Lincoln, Y.S., Lynham, S.A., & Guba, E.G. (2011). Paradigmatic controversies, contradictions, and emerging confluences revisited. In N.K. Denzin & Y.S. Lincoln (Eds.), *The Sage handbook of qualitative research* (4nd ed., pp. 97–128). Sage.

doi Lopez, K.A., & Willis, D.G. (2004). Descriptive versus interpretive phenomenology: Their contributions to nursing knowledge. *Qualitative Health Research, 14*(5), 726–735.

Merleau-Ponty, M. (1962). *Phenomenology of perception.* (Colin Smith, Trans.). Routledge.

doi Moustakas, C. (1994). *Phenomenological research methods.* Sage.

doi Moustakas, C. (1994). *Phenomenological research methods.* Sage.

Mouton, J., & Marais, H.C. (1990). *Basic concepts in the methodology of the social sciences* (Revised ed.). Human Sciences Research Council.

doi Norlyk, A., & Harder, I. (2010). What makes a phenomenological study phenomenological? An analysis of peer-reviewed empirical nursing. *Qualitative Health Research, 20*(3), 420–431.

Patton, M.Q. (2015). *Qualitative research and evaluation methods: Integrating theory and practice* (4th ed.). Sage.

doi Sadala, M.L.A., & Adorno, R.F. (2001). Phenomenology as a method to investigate the experiences lived: A perspective from Husserl and Merleau-Ponty's thought. *Journal of Advanced Nursing, 37*(3), 282–293.

Seidman, I. (2006). *Interviewing as qualitative research: A guide for researchers in education and the social sciences* (3d ed.). Teachers College Press.

Sokolowski, R. (2000). *Introduction to phenomenology.* Cambridge University Press.

Stewart, D., & Mickunas, A. (1974). *Exploring phenomenology. A guide to the field and its literature.* American Library Association.

CHAPTER 12

Narrative inquiry

Sabina M. Perrino
Binghamton University

This chapter examines the key role that narratives have in human communication and engagement across cultures and as fertile analytical and methodological tools. Storytelling practices allow researchers to study speech participants' visible and veiled interactional dynamics. Besides analyzing narratives for their content ("denotational text"), scholars have studied narratives also for their pragmatic effects in the here-and-now of speech participants' interactions, or their "interactional text," and across various spatiotemporal configurations. During their tellings, narrators can assume and reverse roles, for example. Moreover, narratives simultaneously shape and are shaped by their surrounding context. In this light, storytelling practices are actual speech events that are (co)created, and developed, and thus need to be studied as such because of their interactional nature.

1. Introduction

Why and how are narratives key theoretical, analytical, and methodological tools in the social sciences and beyond? This chapter will answer this question by emphasizing the key role that narratives have in human communication and engagement across cultures and as fertile analytical and methodological tools. As research on this topic has demonstrated, storytelling practices are key sites for studying speech participants' visible and veiled interactional dynamics. More specifically, linguistic anthropologists and sociolinguists have studied narratives also for their pragmatic effects in the here-and-now of speech participants' interactions, or their "interactional text" (Silverstein, 1998), and across various spatiotemporal configurations. During these speech events, participants can indeed assume and reverse speech roles while they deliver their stories.

As has been demonstrated in linguistic and ethnographic research, narratives commonly emerge in various sociocultural settings, including interviews, as ways to convey some of the information that researchers seek. In the process, however, other significant interactional dynamics, such as sudden laughter, eye movements, and so forth, often happen in these speech events, depending also on the sociocul-

https://doi.org/10.1075/rmal.6.12per
© 2024 John Benjamins Publishing Company

tural context of occurrence. In this respect, narratives are key methodological and analytical tools and not just *data* since they can function as measures to study not only their content but also participants' concealed and more discernable interactional moves. Within this perspective, narratives need to be studied as *situated speech events* in which the interactional text is as important as the denotational text (Perrino, 2020a, 2022a, 2021). Researchers have collected narratives for various ends. They have appreciated their *referential function*, such as the collected information, for their linguistic analysis (1972), but they have also valued them for their *interactional, discursive nature*, or the emerging dynamics between the speech participants (De Fina & Perrino, 2011; Fontana & Frei, 2004; Wortham et al., 2011). In this light, storytelling practices are actual speech events that are (co)created and developed by the speech participants and thus need to be studied as such because of their *interactional nature*.

Thus, we might ask: What kind of interactional dynamics can develop between researcher and consultants(s) while the stories are told in various sociocultural settings? Why do scholars need to consider narratives as key methodological and analytical tools in their research? In this and the following chapter, I examine two key aspects in which various interactional stances emerge in and through narrative practices: (1) the fundamental and dynamic role played by storytelling practices in the (co)construction of participants' interactional moves; and (2) how speech participants navigate through various spatiotemporal scales and thus enact their chronotopic (in Bakhtin's, 1981 terms) and intimate stances while they narrate their stories. How to collect narratives is thus one methodological skill that researchers need to develop to add more nuanced layers to their studies (Perrino, 2007, 2021, 2022a). Furthermore, since many narratives emerge in research interview settings, it is important to also consider this context of occurrence. As Briggs (1986) has argued, for example, interviews are interactional speech events, and researchers need to learn "how to ask" their questions to research consultants in diverse sociocultural settings. The narratives that emerge from these settings are thus interactional events too. Thus, methodologically, ethical awareness of diverse contexts where narratives might emerge is crucial and necessary before, during, and after these speech events, as I describe in my two chapters. Many of my narratives have indeed been collected during interviewing practices. In this respect, the narratives that emerge over the course of interviews cannot be decontextualized from their interactional surroundings. In the following sections, I first review some of the literature on narratives as interactional speech events from a linguistic anthropological and sociolinguistic perspective before turning to my methodological orientation.

2. Theoretical foundations

Narratives need to be part of researchers' methodologies as they are part of our human nature. Individuals tell stories in many communicative practices while also (co)creating ideologies related to what is considered "good" or "bad" stories. Several scholars have developed this important point in various directions, such as how speakers' different positionalities influence their stories, especially "mock stories" (Depperman, 2013); how the discursive management of social identification is negotiated in interviews with female former colonials of the Belgian Congo (Van De Mieroop & Clifton, 2014); and how Ghanaian migrants' narratives of dis/emplacement are co-constructed, and thus altered, in interviews (Sabaté-Dalmau, 2016). These are just a few examples of a new line of inquiry that has been developing since the early 2000s. Crucially, these and other studies have shown that narratives emerge naturally in conversations or in interview settings.

In this light, in linguistic anthropology, from a methodological perspective, the emerging relations between narrators, what happens interactionally between them, and the sociocultural context are as important as the content of their stories. As I mentioned earlier, narratives are indeed interactional events in which their sociocultural surrounding is always fluid and can influence the story in unpredictable ways as it unfolds (De Fina & Perrino, 2011; Perrino, 2011; Veronesi, 2019; Wortham, 2001; Wortham et al., 2011). As De Fina and Georgakopoulou (2012, p. 61) contend, "[a] significant consequence of the fact that stories are not told in a vacuum but by tellers to audiences in specific settings and for specific purposes is that the mechanisms through which performers contextualize meanings for their audience come to the forefront." Storytelling events are thus intricate and varied since audience members not only can become part of the story, but they also often influence and change it in the process – even silent audience members do.

Along these lines, as Goodwin (1986) argued, in a storytelling event, the structure of the ongoing conversation both molds and is molded by the audience. In this perspective, the content of the stories that are told is in a continuous relationship with their storytelling event in which they are created and solidified across spatiotemporal scales. In my research on Senegalese and northern Italian narratives (Perrino, 2007, 2011, 2015a, 2020b; Perrino & Kohler, 2020), I have been profoundly inspired by the Russian philosopher and literary theorist Mikhail M. Bakhtin's writings (1981). More specifically, I have applied his concept of chronotope, which literally means "time-space," as a way to analyze the entwined temporal and spatial dimensions in narrative practices, as I describe in the next chapter. It is precisely this theoretical and methodological orientation of narrative studies that I extend to the narrative practices that I collected in Senegal and in Northern Italy.

3. Methodological orientations

3.1 Principles and affordances

To better appreciate narratives as methodological tools, it is important to consider how narrative analysis has developed from a text-oriented paradigm to a practice-oriented perspective. While defining a narrative has been a daunting task in narratological studies and across other disciplines, it is worthwhile to note that only since the narrative turn in the 1980s, have narratives been appreciated not only for their content, or "denotational text," but also for their pragmatic effects in the here-and-now of speech participants' interactions, or their "interactional text" (Perrino, 2015c; Silverstein, 1998; Wortham, 2000, 2001). Thus, narratives are always situated speech events that need to be studied within their context of occurrence. The dynamics and content of storytelling practices are always shifting and depend on speech participants' various interactional moves as well as the surrounding sociocultural context. As I mentioned earlier, narratives should thus be studied not just for their content and the information that is collected, but also for their shifting, interactional nature (De Fina, 2020; Perrino, 2007, 2015b, 2020a, 2021, 2022b). Even the referential information, the content, of the story usually changes with the progress of the interaction, and it can (or not) be in concert with the speech participants' interactional moves. Methodologically, it is thus key to incorporate narrative practices in one's research and consider them through these lenses.

While conducting fieldwork in Senegal, for instance, a research consultant of mine started to tell me a story about a disease he had suffered from when he was younger. From the transcript of this storytelling event, which was video recorded, it clearly emerged that this participant was trying to catch my attention using some discursive strategies (Gumperz, 1982), since, interactionally, I was not paying enough attention to his stories. I noted, for instance, that I was not offering minimal responses, engaging in small conversations, asking follow-up questions, smiling, and so forth. I was silent while he was telling me his traumatic stories. In brief, as Tannen (2007) would put it, I was not offering enough interactional "involvement." That is probably why Boubacar not only changed his interactional moves at particular moments of the story, but he also changed the content of his narrative, the *denotational text*. Through these interactional and denotational moves, he not only reclaimed my full attention in his story, but he also took control and authority over our interaction, showing, once again, how fluid the roles inhabited by the researcher(s) and participant(s) can be. Thus, in storytelling practices, speech participants continuously align and misalign with the various topics of the story and with each other. In this way, they engage in interactional positionings, thus demonstrating how narratives simultaneously shape and are shaped by their context (Duranti & Goodwin, 1992).

To better appreciate the interactional nature of narratives, which is an important affordance, methodologically and analytically, it is important to follow linguistic anthropological insights in differentiating the "denotational text" (originally called "narrated event" by Jakobson (1957), from the "interactional text" of speech events (Perrino, 2015c; Silverstein, 1998; Wortham, 2000, 2001). The interactional text includes the many emerging qualities of the various enactments in interaction. More specifically, while the "denotational text" refers to the coherence that the story has in terms of reference and predication about "states of affairs," the "interactional text" refers to the quality of the coherence that the interaction itself has – what the roles of the speech participants are, what actions are being performed, how these actions are enacted, and so forth – and not necessarily the coherence of "what" interactants say (Perrino, 2015c, 2019a, 2020a; Silverstein, 1998; Wortham, 2000, 2001).

Thus, researchers need to analyze narratives not only for their content but also for their interactional text, that is, the various moves that speech participants make during their storytelling practices. For example, variations in speakers' prosody (tone, rhythm, pitch), laughter, pauses, and other discursive maneuvers (Gumperz, 1982), such as gestures, gaze, and movements (Goodwin, 2015) are key interactional details that need to be considered in data analysis. Naturally, these discursive strategies would remain unveiled by just looking at the content of the stories. Methodologically, it is thus crucial to keep in mind that speech participants co-construct their storytelling events while their interactions unfold through the various questions that are asked and answered and the various emerging conversations between them.

3.2 Types of RQs addressed by narrative inquiry

Considering narratives as methodological resources allows researchers to collect data on a wide range of research questions that they wish to study. In my work, for example, I have been exploring issues of intimacy as it emerges in interactional settings, including narrative practices, and as it coalesces among participants and beyond. Furthermore, the interactional nature of storytelling practices allows researchers to study participants' identity (co)construction as it is connected with their interactional dynamics (De Fina, 2013, 2020; Perrino, 2021 Perrino & Wortham, 2022). This is possible, for example, when speech participants engage in long conversations in which several personal narratives emerge, as shown in the two case studies in the next chapter. When speech participants assume certain positionings vis-à-vis each other to assert their points during their stories, for instance, they often also enact their individual and collective identities. At times, their entire interaction can be suddenly reoriented, and some of their participant roles can be reversed too. This is the case when they share similar life experiences or when they need to ask and/or answer sensitive questions.

3.3 Procedures of data collection and analysis

The data collection and analysis through narratives require certain key steps. First, researchers need to audio- or video-record the interactions with the appropriate technological devices (Kohler & Murphy, 2022). Second, they need to carefully transcribe the collected data (Shohet & Loyd, 2022), identifying, counting, and analyzing the narratives produced by the speech participants. Once the transcription is finalized, researchers usually perform their analysis by looking at the various discursive strategies (Gumperz, 1982) that speech participants enact during their storytelling practices. Importantly, in my research, I use linguistic anthropological methods for my transcription and analysis tasks (Shohet & Loyd, 2022). In the summer of 2002, for example, I interviewed a man in his thirties, Boubacar, in Thiès, a small town in inner Senegal, since I wanted to learn more about Senegalese ethnomedical practices. Upon careful transcription and a fine-grained analysis, I discovered that there were several narratives in which participants shifted their interactional roles at particular moments (Perrino, 2005, 2007).

Furthermore, it is important to emphasize that narratives have often been analyzed through the notions of stance and stance-taking, which typically emerge in interaction (Jaffe, 2009c, 2015; Perrino, 2018). Speech participants usually align or disalign (Goffman, 1981) with a certain topic or claim and thus take various fluid stances during the entire interaction. They might agree or disagree with a narrative move, for example, and thus position themselves in favor or against it. Jaffe (2009a, p.2) defines stance as "taking up a position with respect to the form or the content of one's utterance," and this notion has been widely applied in linguistic anthropology and sociolinguistics (Du Bois, 2007; Jaffe, 2009b; Lempert, 2008; Perrino, 2019b; Walton & Jaffe, 2011). For Jaffe (2009a, p.4), moreover, stance is *performative* in the sense that it is "an emergent property of interaction" which is not transparent and thus needs to be studied in empirical material within a sociocultural and historical context. As she writes,

> Speaker stances are thus performances through which speakers may align or disalign themselves with and/or ironize stereotypical associations with particular linguistic forms; stances may thus express multiple or ambiguous meanings. This makes stance a crucial point of entry in analyses that focus on the complex ways in which speakers manage multiple identities (or multiple aspects of identity). The focus on process also foregrounds multiplicities in the audiences indexed by particular linguistic practices, and on the social dynamics and consequences of audience reception, uptake, and interpretation. (Jaffe, 2009a, p.4)

In my analysis, stance is thus a useful notion to study speech participants' various moves during their storytelling practices. As I demonstrate through the analysis of my two case studies in the next chapter, these analytical frameworks are essential to unveil the interactional dynamics between speech participants. It is indeed important to accurately analyze participants' interactional moves in their storytelling practices to be able to appreciate their significance and the value of the collected data.

3.4 Ethical issues

Ethical concerns should always be primary in every research methodology, including the collection of narratives. Some linguistic anthropologists (Black, 2017; Black & Conley Riner, 2022; Briggs, 1986) have variously emphasized ethical issues in their research projects. Before embarking on their research, scholars need to make sure that their projects follow some key ethical guidelines. First, their overall projects need to be approved by the Institutional Review Board (IRB) before they can start any kind of research activity. The IRB asks researchers to prepare a consent form that needs to be signed by their research participants. The consent form has some key clauses explaining the rights of the participants, the fact that they might be audio- and/or video-recorded, and the research project in general terms. If research participants don't wish to talk about a certain topic, they have the right to stop the recording at any moment, for example, as is usually noted in the consent form.

The collected narratives would lose all their research value and effectiveness if they were not gathered with sociocultural and ethical awareness. For example, for narratives emerging in interview settings, Briggs argues that

> [t]he context in which a question is posed often affects the respondent's interpretation of the query and the nature of his or her response. Resultant variations in the received data thus range from the interviewee's intentional omission or falsification of material to subtle differences in pragmatic indexical meanings.
>
> (Briggs, 1986, p. 45)

Furthermore, Briggs continues, if the notion of the interview itself is not shared by the culture under study, for instance, interviewees might "apply norms of interaction and canons of interpretations that differ from those of the interviewer" (Briggs, 1986, p. 48). Thus, both formal and informal conversations can take various directions also because research participants might feel anxious or compelled to answer certain questions, especially being aware of the presence of an audio or, even more so, a video recorder. These "transduction technologies," as Black (2017) defines them, can thus influence the trajectory of the storytelling event in significant ways.

In this respect, it is important to ask: what alternatives do researchers have if, once in their fieldsite, they realize that using their audio and video recorders to collect narratives would be inappropriate? These are key questions that scholars should keep in mind when they embark on a research project involving the collection of narratives through audio and video recording. As Briggs (1986) has suggested, it is better to wait and familiarize oneself with the new environment before collecting storytelling practices from research participants and other ordinary speakers. Recording narratives without respecting these ethical guidelines would be ethically questionable. As Black (2017) has noted, moreover, not using the audio recorder at particular times, as much needed as it was in his research, meant to be respectful of the sociocultural norms in the HIV community of practice he was studying and, ultimately, gain respect and trust among his research participants. Without an attentive look at their interactional nature and at the surrounding context, many salient points would be entirely missed in the collected stories.

4. Critiques and responses

Oral and digital narratives have been key methodological tools in linguistic anthropological data collection processes. Scholars have developed various definitions and ways of using narratives in their data. Several scholars have criticized narratives as they were used and analyzed by William Labov and Joshua Waletzky (1967), for example. It is important, however, to recognize that the Labovian model was revolutionary and that it is thanks to these theoretical advances that more pragmatic and discursive approaches to storytelling practices have emerged. During the 1960s, importantly, Labov and Waletzky (1967) elaborated their well-known narrative model positing that narratives need to contain six units indicating the "necessary" progression of a story. More specifically, the six Labovian narrative units are the *abstract*, the *orientation*, the *complicating action*, the *resolution*, the *coda*, and, finally, the *evaluation* (Labov & Waletzky, 1967). In Labov's perspective, (1) the *abstract* summarizes the content of the story, i.e., what the story is about. It is usually made of a couple of sentences at the beginning of a story. Narrators often offer a glimpse of the stories they are about to tell (e.g., *did you know what happened to me over the weekend?*). (2) In the *orientation*, the narrator offers some details about the characters, the location, and the time of the story. It is a contextualization of the upcoming story. (3) The *complicating action* is the main plot of the story, the most important events of the narrative. (4) The *resolution* represents the solution of the story, how the complicating action ends, positively or negatively. (5) The *coda* usually bridges the story with the present reality. The narrator might add a moral lesson to the story and thus might connect it to the present world. (6) In a story, the narrator might also add an *evaluation*, which is a personal perspective on the events presented in the story. This serves the function of orienting the listener to the key points of the story and to the lesson that the audience members should learn from the narrative (De Fina & Georgakopoulou, 2012, pp. 28–29; Labov & Waletzky, 1967; Labov 1972). For Labov, the evaluation can have various ramifications, given the key roles played by narrators when they "evaluate" their own stories.

While the Labovian model has been used by many analysts and has been praised for identifying the units of a narrative, linguistic anthropologists and sociolinguists have considered it too narrow and monologically-oriented in the sense that it does not include other speech participants' contributions during the storytelling event. Starting with what was named the narrative turn in the 1980s (De Fina & Georgakopoulou, 2012), many sociolinguists and linguistic anthropologists opted to consider narratives as interactional events in which, as they argued, the classic Labovian units were not sufficient to explain their pragmatic effects. From the classic Labovian model, in which narrative units are key elements for a narrative to be considered as such, to the more pragmatic and discursive approaches to narratives today, many theoretical advancements have been made in this field (De Fina, 2020; De Fina & Georgakopoulou, 2012; Perrino, 2021). In other words, as De Fina and Georgakopoulou (2012, p. 35) have contended, analyzing narratives through this model does not include "cases of systematic audience participation, co-construction of the story between teller and audience and many other phenomena that characterize the telling of narratives in interaction." Indeed, narratives are interactional events in which the classic Labovian units might not be applicable, or they might work only partially.

In this light, as Ingold (2011) usefully reminds us, it is difficult and unnatural to add boundaries around the beginnings and ends of stories. In his perspective, people's past stories can become part of the present here-and-now interaction. In this way, there is not a clear division between the past story and the present storytelling event, which, at times, conflates (Perrino, 2007, 2011). "To tell a story," continues Ingold, "is to relate, in narrative, the occurrences of the past, bringing them to life in the vivid present of listeners as if they were going on here and now" so that past and present experiences can serve as great teachings for novices and children if a story is told in a family context, for example. As he writes:

> There is no point at which the story ends and life begins. Stories should not end for the same reason that life should not. And in the story, as in life, it is in the movement from place to place – or from topic to topic – that knowledge is integrated. (Ingold, 2011, p. 161)

In this perspective, there are always continuous movements between past stories and present interactional moments. Like Ingold, many other scholars have started to embrace this more dynamic view of narrative in the last two decades. From Labov's narrative advancements, narrative studies have indeed shifted from a text-oriented to a practice-oriented perspective of storytelling (De Fina, 2013; De Fina & Georgakopoulou, 2012; Schiffrin, 1996; Schiffrin et al., 2010). Linguistic anthropologists and sociolinguists have studied narratives as performances embedded in their sociocultural context, and not as isolated, static texts (Bauman, 1977, 1986). Narratives are indeed performances in the sense that they are contextualized and dynamic: the relations between narrators, events, and the sociocultural contexts are as important as the content of a story. In this view, narratives are interactional events in which their sociocultural surrounding is always fluid and can influence the story in unpredictable ways as it unfolds in interaction (Wortham, 2001). As De Fina and Georgakopoulou (2012, p. 61) contend, "[a] significant consequence of the fact that stories are not told in a vacuum but by tellers to audiences in specific settings and for specific purposes is that the mechanisms through which performers contextualize meanings for their audience come to the forefront." Storytelling events are thus intricate and varied, since audience members not only become part of the story, but they also often influence and change it in the process – even silent audience members do. As Goodwin (1986) argued, in a storytelling event the structure of the ongoing conversation both molds and is molded by the audience. Inspired by Goffman's (1981) notion of participation framework, Goodwin thus emphasizes that the audience is a very intricate concept in the sense that "a group of recipients becomes an audience only when they orient to the storytelling through displays of attention and engagement" (De Fina & Georgakopoulou, 2012, p. 92). As Goodwin and others have demonstrated, the audience/storyteller binary is flawed by indicating how audience members can be storytellers too and, they can then influence the storied world of narratives. In this respect, the role of the audience is key in the interactional co-construction of these narrative practices.

5. Conclusions

Narratives are discursive and interactional events that can be easily incorporated in researchers' methodological tools. They indeed can be used and analyzed to unveil speech participants' fluctuating and emerging interactional patterns. In this respect, as I have argued in this chapter, researchers should consider narratives as *sociocultural practices* given their situatedness in context. Participants often recount personal stories during informal conversations and more formal interviews. Narratives developing in these interactional settings are thus more common than one would expect. Narratives are thus unpredictable as conversations and stories can be more or less engaging (Perrino, 2011, 2021). Research participants can talk for long stretches of time or just answer researchers' questions rapidly in a "yes-no" fashion, for example. Several unexpected patterns might emerge, too. Researchers should thus consider this context-related unpredictability in the various analyses they perform and in their ensuing outcomes. As De Fina and Perrino (2011, p.8) have emphasized, for example, scholars should thus be aware that the narratives that they collect in interview settings are always interconnected with speech participants' interactional roles in very complex ways.

By exploring how participants navigate through time and space in narratives, moreover, it is important to consider spatiotemporal configurations to examine the fluctuating character of narrative practices. Studying these emergent interactional movements is possible thanks to the versatility of the Bakhtinian chronotope, as I argued, which allows analysts to explore these patterns through multiple and varied spatiotemporal scales. I have described how the concept of chronotope, as it emerges in narrative practices, can assist analysts to unveil not only speech participants' denotational and interactional moves, but also the simultaneous (co)construction and solidification of their sociocultural, collective, and intimate identities. In these cases, multiple chronotopic alignments might occur, thus showing the complexity of these spatiotemporal configurations, which are prompted by various interactional moves. Multiple chronotopes can thus conflate in significant *cross-chronotope alignments*, as I named them, especially through processes of *participant transposition* (Perrino, 2007, 2021) as I show in the next chapter. These coeval alignments are very common in Senegalese storytelling practices, for example, and they can be unveiled through a close analysis of the spatiotemporal alignments of the various emerging chronotopes coupled with speech participants' discourse strategies (Gumperz, 1982), such as the use of the historical present and other particular tenses, subject and object pronouns and other deictics, laughter, and parallelistic structures.

In closing, paying careful attention to the interactional dynamics between speech participants, while their storytelling practices unfold, is as important as the information that is being exchanged and collected during these speech events. As I have contended, these interactional patterns can not only influence the content of the stories, or their denotational text, but they can also change and reorient the whole interaction in significant ways. Over the course of an interview, for example, speech participants can transform from passive to active actors (Perrino, 2022a; Wortham, 2001), and this becomes visible only through a careful analysis of both denotational and interactional texts. In closing, this chapter has demonstrated that narratives are very intricate venues as they offer the researcher access to the subtleties of participants' interactions at various levels. These dynamics thus emerge, unexpectedly, while collecting a great variety of narrative practices.

Funding

Chapters 11 and 12 are based on research that I conducted during twenty-two months of fieldwork in Senegal (West Africa) and Northern Italy (Europe) between 1999 and 2004, and research in Northern Italy during summer trips and continuous contacts with research consultants and ordinary speakers (2003–2022). I offer my deepest thanks to the many participants in Senegal and in Northern Italy who agreed to be video- and audio-recorded and who variously assisted me during my research. I acknowledge support from a Wenner-Gren Foundation Dissertation Fieldwork Grant (Grant Number 6957), the University of Pennsylvania's Penfield Scholarship in Diplomacy, International Affairs, and Belles Lettres, and the research funds that have been offered by the Department of Anthropology and the Linguistics Program at Binghamton University (SUNY) since 2015.

Acknowledgements

I wish to thank the Editor of this collection, Mehdi Riazi, first for inviting me to write two chapters in this timely volume, and then for his invaluable guidance during the writing and publication processes. I am solely responsible for any remaining mistakes and infelicities.

References

Bakhtin, M. M. (1981). *The dialogic imagination: Four essays.* Texas University Press.

Bauman, R. (1977). *Verbal art as performance.* Prospect Heights.

Bauman, R. (1986). *Story, performance, and event: Contextual studies of oral narrative.* Cambridge University Press.

Black, S. P. (2017). Anthropological ethics and the communicative affordances of audio-video recorders in ethnographic fieldwork: Transduction as theory. *American Anthropologist, 119*(1), 46–57.

Black, S. P., & Conley, R. (2022). Care as a methodological stance: Research ethics in linguistic anthropology. In S. M. Perrino & S. E. Pritzker (Eds.), *Research methods in linguistic anthropology* (pp. 97–124). Bloomsbury Academic.

Briggs, C. L. (1986). *Learning how to ask: A sociolinguistic appraisal of the role of the interview in social science research* (1). Cambridge University Press.

De Fina, A. (2013). Narratives as practices: Negotiating identities through storytelling. In G. Barkhuizen (Ed.), *Narrative research in applied linguistics* (pp. 154–175). Cambridge University Press.

De Fina, A. (2020). Doing narrative analysis from a narratives-as-practices perspective. *Narrative Inquiry, 31*(1), 49–71.

De Fina, A., & Georgakopoulou, A. (2012). *Analyzing narrative: Discourse and sociolinguistic perspectives.* Cambridge University Press.

De Fina, A., & Perrino, S. (2011). Interviews vs. 'natural' contexts: A false dilemma [Special Issue]. *Language in Society, 40*(1), 1–11.

Chapter 12. Narrative inquiry   203

Depperman, A. (2013). How to get a grip on identities-in-interaction: (What) does 'positioning' offer more than 'membership categorization'? Evidence from a mock story. *Narrative Inquiry*, *23*(1), 62–88.

Du Bois, J.W. (2007). The stance triangle. In R. Englebretson (Ed.), *Stancetaking in discourse: Subjectivity, evaluation, interaction* (pp. 140–182). John Benjamins.

Duranti, A., & Goodwin, C. (1992). *Rethinking context: Language as an interactive phenomenon.* Cambridge University Press.

Fontana, A., & Frei, J.H. (2004). Interviewing: The art of science. In N.K. Denzin & Y.S. Lincoln (Eds.), *The SAGE handbook of qualitative research* (pp. 361–376). Sage.

Goffman, E. (1981). *Forms of talk.* University of Pennsylvania Press.

Goodwin, C. (1986). Audience diversity, participation and interpretation. *Text and Talk*, *6*(3), 283–316.

Goodwin, C. (2015). Narrative as talk-in-interaction. In A. Georgakopoulou & A. De Fina (Eds.), *The handbook of narrative analysis* (pp. 197–218). Wiley-Blackwell.

Gumperz, J.J. (1982). *Discourse strategies.* Cambridge University Press.

Ingold, T. (2011). *Being alive: Essays on movement, knowledge and description.* Routledge.

Jaffe, A. (2009a). Introduction. In A. Jaffe (Ed.), *Stance: Sociolinguistic perspectives* (pp. 3–28). Oxford University Press.

Jaffe, A. (2009b). Stance in a Corsican school: Institutional and ideological orders and the production of bilingual subjects. In A. Jaffe (Ed.), *Stance: Sociolinguistic perspectives* (pp. 119–145). Oxford University Press.

Jaffe, A.M. (2009c). *Stance: Sociolinguistic perspectives.* Oxford University Press.

Jaffe, A. (2015). Staging language on Corsica: Stance, improvisation, play, and heteroglossia. *Language in Society*, *44*(02), 161–186.

Jakobson, R. (1957). Shifters and verbal categories. In L.R. Waugh & M. Monville-Burston (Eds.), *On language* (pp. 386–392). Harvard University Press.

Kohler, G., & Murphy, K.M. (2022). Audio-video technology for and in the field: A primer. In S.M. Perrino & S.E. Pritzker (Eds.), *Research methods in linguistic anthropology* (pp. 197–222). Bloomsbury Academic.

Labov, W. (1972). *Language in the inner city* (3). University of Pennsylvania Press.

Labov, W., & Waletzky, J. (1967). Narrative analysis: Oral versions of personal experience. *Journal of Narrative & Life History*, *7*(1–4), 3–38.

Lempert, M. (2008). The poetics of stance: Text-metricality, epistemicity, interaction. *Language in Society*, *37*(04), 569–592.

Perrino, S.M. (2005). Participant transposition in Senegalese oral narrative. *Narrative Inquiry*, *15*(2), 345–375.

Perrino, S. (2007). Cross-chronotope alignment in Senegalese oral narrative. *Language and Communication*, *27*(3), 227–244.

Perrino, S. (2011). Chronotopes of story and storytelling event in interviews. *Language in Society*, *40*(1), 91–103.

Perrino, S. (2015a). Chronotopes: Time and space in oral narrative. In A. De Fina & A. Georgakopoulou (Eds.), *The handbook of narrative analysis* (pp. 140–159). Wiley-Blackwell.

Perrino, S. (2015b). Narrating authenticity in northern Italian historical cafés. *Language and Communication, 40*, 82–91.

Perrino, S. (2015c). Performing extracomunitari: Mocking migrants in Veneto Barzellette. *Language in Society, 44*(2), 141–160.

Perrino, S. (2018). Exclusionary intimacies: Racialized language in Veneto, northern Italy. *Language & Communication, 59*, 28–41.

Perrino, S. (2019a). Narrating migration politics in Veneto, Northern Italy. *Narrative Culture, 6*(1), 44–68.

Perrino, S. (2019b). Recontextualizing racialized stories on YouTube. In A. De Fina & S. Perrino (Eds.), *Storytelling in the digital world* (pp. 261–285). John Benjamins.

Perrino, S. (2020a). Methods: Methodology in linguistic anthropology: Experiments. In J. Stanlaw (Ed.), *International encyclopedia of linguistic anthropology*. Wiley Blackwell.

Perrino, S. (2020b). *Narrating migration: Intimacies of exclusion in northern Italy*. Routledge.

Perrino, S. (2021). Narratives as discursive practices in interviews: A linguistic anthropological approach. *Narrative Inquiry, 31*(1), 72–96.

Perrino, S. M. (2022a). Interviews in linguistic anthropology. In S. M. Perrino & S. E. Pritzker (Eds.), *Research methods in linguistic anthropology* (pp. 159–195). Bloomsbury Academic.

Perrino, S. M. (2022b). Narrating pandemics across time and space. *Anthropology & Humanism, 47*(1), 264–272.

Perrino, S., & Kohler, G. (2020). Chronotopic identities: Narrating made in Italy across spatiotemporal scales. *Language & Communication, 70*, 94–106.

Perrino, S., & Wortham, S. E. F. (2022). Narrating heterogeneous identities in multilingual communities. In L. Fisher & W. Ayres-Bennett (Eds.), *Interdisciplinary perspectives on multilingualism and identity* (pp. 239–260). Cambridge University Press.

Sabaté-Dalmau, M. (2016). Migrant narratives of dis/emplacement: The alternative spatialization and ethnicization of the local urban floor. *Text & Talk, 36*(3), 269–293.

Schiffrin, D. (1996). Narrative as self-portrait: Sociolinguistic constructions of identity. *Language in Society, 25*(2), 167–203.

Schiffrin, D., De Fina, A., & Nylund, A. (2010). *Telling stories: Language narrative and social life*. Georgetown University Press.

Shohet, M., & Loyd, H. (2022). Transcription and analysis in linguistic anthropology: Creating, testing, and presenting theory on the page. In S. M. Perrino & S. E. Pritzker (Eds.), *Research methods in linguistic anthropology* (pp. 261–295). Bloomsbury Academic.

Silverstein, M. (1998). Improvisational performance of culture in realtime discursive practice. In K. Sawyer (Ed.), *Creativity in performance* (pp. 265–312). Ablex.

Tannen, D. (2007). *Talking voices: Repetition, dialogue, and imagery in conversational discourse*. Cambridge University Press.

Van De Mieroop, D., & Clifton, J. (2014). The discursive management of identity in interviews with female former colonials of the Belgian Congo. *Pragmatics. Quarterly Publication of the International Pragmatics Association (IPrA), 24*(1), 131–155.

Veronesi, D. (2019). "But you're gonna ask me questions, right?": Interactional frame and "for-the-record" orientation in language biography interviews. In K. Roulston (Ed.), *Interactional studies of qualitative research interviews* (pp. 181–200). John Benjamins.

Walton, S., & Jaffe, A. (2011). "Stuff white people like": Stance, class, race, and internet commentary. In C. Thurlow & K. Mroczek (Eds.), *Digital discourse: Language in the new media* (pp. 199–211). Oxford University Press.

Wortham, S. (2000). Interactional positioning and narrative self-construction. *Narrative Inquiry, 10*(1), 157–184.

Wortham, S. (2001). *Narratives in action: A strategy for research analysis.* Teachers College Press.

Wortham, S., Mortimer, K., Lee, K., Allard, E., & White, K. D. (2011). Interviews as interactional data. *Language in Society, 40*(1), 39–50.

CHAPTER 13

Narrative inquiry
Case studies from Senegal and Northern Italy

Sabina M. Perrino
Binghamton University

This chapter describes how narratives can be useful analytical and methodological tools through a close analysis of two narrative excerpts that I collected in Senegal and Northern Italy. Both examples examine how certain interactional patterns, such as participant transposition and the co-construction of individuals' identities and stances, are enacted and sustained in storytelling practices. These patterns would not emerge if narratives were not considered as situated speech events in which speech participants' interactional moves ("interactional text") are as important as the narrative content ("denotational text"). It is thanks to this narratives-as-practices approach, versus the more traditional narratives-as-texts approach, that scholars are able to unveil participants' interactional dynamics. The two case studies, moreover, are fully contextualized and situated.

1. Introduction

In this chapter, I offer an overview of the study and will comment on the value and applicability of the methodology that I used. I will also examine the challenges faced and the various ethical issue that usually emerge in these research settings (ethical matters are described in the previous chapter as well).

In July 2006, I conducted an interview with Mamadou, a research consultant, on the value and functions of storytelling practices in Senegal, West Africa. During our conversation,[1] he emphasized the importance of the audience in storytelling practices:

---

1. In Senegal, French, the former colonial language, is still used together with Wolof, the vehicular language, and other languages, including Pulaar, Sereer, Diola, and Mandingo (Irvine, 1989; Perrino, 2002).

https://doi.org/10.1075/rmal.6.13per
© 2024 John Benjamins Publishing Company

> In Senegalese narratives, the audience immediately becomes a participant in the narrative itself. This means that the audience has some very important roles in the narration [process]. It is only part of the storytelling, but it also becomes characters in the story. This is very typical in Senegal. The audience participates as audience and as character of the story as well. If the audience is not part of the story, the story cannot be told.[2,3]　　　　　　　　　　(Mamadou, July 2006)

As Mamadou describes, Senegalese narratives cannot be considered as such if the audience members are not part of the story. Senegalese storytellers include participants in their stories through a practice that they metapragmatically define as "démarche participative," or as I named it, *participant transposition* (Perrino, 2005, 2007). As I show in the first example that I examine in this chapter, participant transposition often emerges in narrative practices in various sociocultural settings, including interviews. This interactional strategy, in Gumperz's (1982) terms, would not become visible, moreover, if researchers were to limit their analysis to the plot of the story only. Thus, participants' moves would also remain veiled if their analysis were based exclusively on their content, or the "denotational text" (Silverstein, 1998), as I argued in my theoretical chapter.

The case studies that I analyze below are inspired from a chapter, published by Bloomsbury Academic, entitled "Interviews in Linguistic Anthropology" (Perrino, 2022), as part of a collection entitled *Research Methods in Linguistic Anthropology* (Perrino & Pritzker, 2022). I decided to use these narrative excerpts because they persuasively illustrate how the interactional dimensions of narratives are primary methodological and analytical research tools. The narratives excerpts that I present in this chapter are extracted from data that I collected in my two main fieldsites: Senegal and Northern Italy. The narrative excerpts were fully audio-recorded and carefully transcribed following the insights of linguistic anthropological methodologies and ethical tenets, as I discussed in the previous chapter (Perrino & Pritzker, 2022). Both examples examine how certain interactional patterns, such as participant transposition and the co-construction of individuals' identities, are enacted and sustained in narratives. These patterns would not emerge if narratives were considered abstractly. It is thanks to a narratives-as-practices approach that scholars can unveil participants' interactional dynamics.

---

2. Original French version: "Dans les histoires sénégalaises le public devient immédiatement partie de l'histoire. Ça signifie que le public a des rôles très importants dans la narration. Il ne fait pas seulement partie de la narration, mais il devient aussi un personnage de l'histoire. Cela est très typique au Sénégal. Le public participe comme public et comme personnage de l'histoire aussi. Si le public ne fait pas partie de l'histoire, l'histoire ne peut pas être racontée" (Mamadou, July 2006).

3. All translations from French, Italian, and Wolof to English are mine.

Before analyzing my two case studies, I offer a brief contextualization for each of them by describing the location and situation in which these storytelling practices emerged.

2. An overview of the study

In the study I will discuss in this chapter, I examined how Senegalese ethnomedical modernity emerges in actual interaction and how this modernity is localized both in Senegal and in Northern Italy. More specifically, I studied how reflexive cues were used by healers, patients, and ordinary speakers in interactions to performatively make manifest the "modern" against a background of objectified "traditional" medicine (Perrino, 2006). By examining this medical hybridity in Senegal, and its ramifications in Northern Italy, my study contributed to our understanding of how Western biomedicine could be locally interpreted and changed. Collecting narratives on these topics allowed me to learn about these "multiple," "alternative" or "vernacular" modernities as ways to reinterpret the global in local spaces. At that time, I focused on the domain of medicine since I wanted to further my understanding on the heterogeneity of the category of "alternative modernities." Besides studying the many and diverse semiotic articulations of Senegalese ethnomedical practices, I considered what motivates this modern hybridity and what interests are at stake for different social actors. In this vein, I studied the various local reflective formulations of ethnomedical practices in multiple sites and in relation to larger scalar projects and processes.

Besides collecting storytelling practices, in this study I used other linguistic anthropological methods (Perrino & Pritzker, 2022), such as the collection of data through audio- and video-recording, transcription and analysis of narratives in interactions and of interactions more generally, and the writing of copious field-notes while engaging in participant observation. To show how some of these methodologies work, I analyze two excerpts of narrative practices that I collected in Senegal and in Northern Italy. More specifically, in the first example, extracted from an interview that I conducted in Thiès, a small town in Senegal, I show how and why Senegalese narratives are complex interactional events in which the audience members play pivotal roles. I especially focus on an interactional positioning strategy that I name participant transposition (Perrino, 2005, 2007). The second example includes a narrative that I collected in the small town of Treviso, in Northern Italy. In her moving story, Veronica, one of my research participants, changes her position by using some specific narrative and discourse strategies (Gumperz, 1982) throughout her stories. Methodologically, this chapter thus shows how analyzing narratives as discursive practices adds significant layers

Chapter 13. Narrative inquiry: Case studies from Senegal and N. Italy **209**

of understanding to the many facets of storytelling. Importantly, I demonstrate that narratives are key interactional events that should be studied as such to be able to fully capture the fluid and dynamic relationships between speech participants as their stories unfold.

Example 1.

Example 1 features a narrative excerpt of a Senegalese research consultant in which these interactional patterns are not only metadiscursively discussed, but they are also enacted. This example especially centers on how intimate stances can be performed through instances of participant transposition. These alignments clearly emerge in Example 1, in which speech participants enact intimate stances through various cases of participant transposition. I collected this narrative in Thiès (a small town in the vicinity of Dakar, the capital of Senegal), in June 2001, with Maimuna, a woman in her late forties at that time.[4] A combination of Wolof (the vehicular language of Senegal) and French (the former colonial language), which is a typical combination in urban centers in Senegal, emerged during our conversations which were often centered on healers' use of plants in their medical recipes and on their illness stories. Maimuna recounted three personal narratives in which she engaged in participant transposition five times. In one of her illness narratives after thirty-five minutes into our conversation, for example, she remembered that she had an unbearable pain in her legs and entire body one night and that her family wanted to take her to the healer.[5] In this excerpt, Maimuna enacted five cases of participant transposition:

Example 1. 'I couldn't move!'
(M: Maimuna; S: Interviewer)
First line: Original French and Wolof version[6]
Second line: English translation

```
1.  M: […] c'étai::t en novembre e:::n 1991
       […] it wa::s in November i:::n 1991

2.      mmhh e:::t j'étais très malade pendant la nuit d'un fin de semaine
        mhmm a:::nd I was very sick one might of a weekend

3.      je ne pouvais pas bouger et mes jambes me faisaient très mal=
        I couldn't move and my legs hurt badly=

4.  S:=Je suis désolée=
       =I am sorry=

5.  M:=merci… j'avais trè:::s peur d'être paralisée
       =thanks… I was ve:::ry scared of being paralyzed

6.      tout mon corps me faisait mal et tremblait, xam nga?
        my entire body hurt and was shaking, you know?
```

---

4. In this chapter, I use pseudonyms for all my research participants to protect their identity and privacy. All my research projects were approved by the Institutional Review Board (IRB).

5. In many Senegalese families, herbal remedies are used to cure many diseases at home before going to a healer or to a Western biomedical doctor.

210   Sabina M. Perrino

7.   S: waaw xam naa je peux imaginer la douleur
      <u>yes I know</u> I can just imagine the pain

8.   M: donc j'avais pris le palu, tu sais?
      so I got <u>malaria</u>, you know?

9.   avec la fièvre feebar haute
      with high fever <u>fever</u>

10.   amoon naa feebar, la fièvre était tell- tellement forte
      <u>I had a fever</u>, the fever was real- really high

11.   je ne pouvais pas dormir
      I couldn't sleep

12.   je ne pouvais pas bouger
      I couldn't move

13.   je ne pouvais pas même penser, t'as-vu?
      I couldn't even think, do you see?

14.   gis nga palu boobu
      <u>do you see the kind of malaria</u> [I had]?

15.   pendant la nuit je dis à ma sœur SABENA[7]
      during the night I say to my sister SABINA

16.   "Sabena, excuse-moi, je ne peux pas bouger"
      "Sabina, sorry, <u>I can't move</u>"
      |

17. S: @@@@=

18. M: =et Sabena:: ma sœur, elle dit
      =and Sabina:: my sister, she says

19.   "Maimuna, ñu ngiy dem chez le seriñ"
      "Maimuna, <u>let's go</u> to the <u>healer</u>"

20.   elle donc va chez le guérisseur
      she then goes to see a healer

21.   elle demande des médicaments pour mon palu mais les guérisseurs n'en donnent PAS!=
      she asks for some medicines [to heal] my malaria but healers DON'T give them out!=

22. S: =oui je le sais!
      =yes I know!
      |

23. M: Sabena xamuma@@@@
      Sabina doesn't know@@@@

24.   ella y va également les chercher pour moi
      she goes there to look for them for me anyway

25.   ma chère sœur Sabena [...]
      my dear sister Sabina [...]

After my initial questions about her healing habits and family's diseases, Maimuna naturally launches into a personal story. She starts her narrative with a classic Labovian "orientation" (Labov, 1972; Labov & Waletzky, 1967) to contextualize the disease she underwent when she was younger (lines 1–2). She indeed situates her

---

6.   See Appendix for transcription conventions.

7.   In Senegal, my first name, [Sabina], was often pronounced as [Sabɛna].

Chapter 13. Narrative inquiry: Case studies from Senegal and N. Italy   **211**

story in a precise spatiotemporal configuration: she was sick in her bed, and it was a weekend in November 1991. She recounts that one night she couldn't even move in her bed since her legs were in terrible pain (line 3). After I instinctively show my sympathy for her by latching with her in line 4, she confesses that she was in fear of being paralyzed in her bed that night (line 5). Her entire body was in terrible pain (line 6). Interactionally, Maimuna tries to find sympathy with her interviewer, me, from line 6 until the end of her story. Intertextually, she often ends her lines with rhetorical questions for me, such as 'you know?' (lines 6, 8), 'did you see?' (line 13), and 'do you see the kind of malaria [I had]?' (line 14) to find complicity, support, and understanding. After I show my sympathy with her in line 7, she asserts that she feared to have contracted malaria, palu[8] in Wolof, in line 8, since she also had a high fever. Maimuna also codeswitches from French to Wolof after line 6 and emphasizes the fact that she might have contracted malaria given the high fever and the pain that her body experienced. As a discourse strategy (Gumperz, 1982), codeswitching[9] can change speakers' participation roles and can thus project various interactional meanings (Heller, 1988; Bailey, 2000; Woolard, 1995), such as more connection with the surrounding audience members who are believed to understand both codes (Perrino, 2015). Soon after these codeswitches to Wolof in lines 8 and 10, Maimuna codeswitches back into French and starts describing the terrible high fever she had that night. By codeswitching back to Wolof in line 14, she emphasizes, again, the gravity of her disease, and wants to make sure that I understand what she went through ('do you see the kind of malaria [I had]?' [line 14]).

Maimuna's interactional stances emerge even more clearly in lines 11–13, when she repeats the negative form of the French modal verb "pouvoir," conjugated in the first singular person, followed by three different verbal constructions: 'I couldn't sleep' (line 11), 'I couldn't move' (line 12), and 'I couldn't even think' (line 13). This poetic form of repetition in speech has been studied as parallelism by several linguistic anthropologists. Parallelism can be simply defined as repetition with variation in discourse and has been examined extensively especially for its discursive intertextual effects (Silverstein & Urban, 1996; Wilce, 2001, p. 191; Tannen, 2007). These parallelistic structures emerge several times in this inter-

---

8. The Wolof term palu, which is widely used to indicate any disease with malaria-like feverish symptoms, derives from the French paludisme, 'malaria'. Unlike the French term (paludisme), however, Senegalese use the term palu not only to refer to cases of malaria, but also to other ranges of diseases as different as having a high fever, being unconscious or hallucinated, having a bad cold, and suffering from extreme fatigue.

9. While codeswitching takes many forms and involves different units, such as inter-sentential versus intra-sentential, when I mention this discourse strategy in this chapter, I only refer to its sociocultural and pragmatic functions in interaction.

view, especially when I do not seem to be emotionally involved in Maimuna's storytelling details. She tries to keep my attention focused on the hardship of her past self by repeating certain structures. I add my remarks to her storylines only three times, in lines 4, 7, and 22, thus acknowledging my attention. The dynamic nature of the interview emerges at every turn thus demonstrating that these speech events are unique in that participants often co-construct, moment-by-moment, their stories.

It is precisely after Maimuna's second instance of codeswitching from French to Wolof in line 14, where she asks me if I realize the kind of malaria she had, that she engages in the first instance of participant transposition. By explicitly addressing me as if I were present in her past story in line 15 ('[...] I say to my sister SABINA'), she inserts, or transposes, me into her past self and I thus unexpectedly become one of her past addresses, her sister precisely. This transformation of me into one of her intimate family members indexes the level of interactional closeness that is enacted through her narratives. At that moment, she gets my attention: I start laughing in line 17 by being surprised of becoming, all of a sudden, her sister in her story. In this way, I am part of Maimuna's reported speech, or "constructed dialogue" in Tannen's (2007) terms, in line 16, when she repeats that she cannot move from her bed. Through this narrative move, I thus become a witness of her serious health conditions. In these lines, Maimuna aligns her past self with the present interaction between the two speech participants.

Maimuna sustains this case of participant transposition at every line from line 15 until line 25. At line 18, moreover, Maimuna reiterates my participant role as her sister who witnesses her immobilization and pain in her bed. With a wit of irony, indexed by her raised volume in line 21 and by four bursts of laughter in line 23, Maimuna recounts how, wrongly, my past self visited a healer to look for some medicines for her (lines 21, 23), even though my past self claims to know this fact in line 22. To keep my full attention focused on her story, Maimuna questions my real knowledge of Senegalese ethnomedical rituals. Healers usually don't dispense medicines; one needs to go to the pharmacy or to a Western biomedical doctor to find them. Through these discourse strategies (Gumperz, 1982), Maimuna finally captures all my attention since I have become one of the main protagonists of her narrated event, a very close member of her family, her sister. At the same time, she also actively constructs a closer relationship between us. At line 25, indeed, she expresses an intimate stance by adding the adjective 'dear', "chère" in French, when she refers to her "sister Sabina." Notably, four more instances of participant transposition followed,[10] providing us with more oppor-

---

10. Due to space limitations, in this chapter, only the above case of participant transposition is presented and analyzed.

tunities to enact and co-construct an even closer relationship. Narrative practices are thus sites where interactional moves can take different directions depending on participants' multiple and various stances and on the surrounding sociocultural context. The next example, centered in Northern Italy, continues to illustrate these patterns in which spatiotemporal configurations play key roles in the co-construction of speech participants' stances and identities.

Example 2.

My second example is extracted from an interview that I collected in the small town of Treviso, in Northern Italy, in May 2003. At that time, I was studying the transnational circulation of Senegalese ethnomedicine in Italy, as well as researching migration more generally. Veronica, the narrator, is an Italian schoolteacher who was in her fifties, and she had a lot of experience as a volunteer assisting children, and occasionally migrants, in northern Italian hospitals during her free time. Our conversation, which lasted almost two hours, focused on the issue of how Italian hospitals and hospital personnel had been reacting to the new waves of migrants in Italy (Perrino, 2020). At a certain point, however, when she was talking about the relationship between Italian doctors and migrant patients, she launched into three personal narratives. In one of them, Veronica recounted the experience she had with a physician who directed the neurology department where her father had been hospitalized for possible brain cancer a couple of days before. Her narrative began with a description of how Veronica had gone to the neurology department to hear about her father's diagnosis after the doctors had performed a CAT-scan on him. In Italy, doctors do not usually talk directly to patients about their diagnoses if they are serious. Rather, they first communicate with a close family member and leave the choice to that family member as to what, or how much, of the diagnosis to convey to the sick patient. As one of the daughters of this patient, then, Veronica was allowed to go to the doctor to hear her father's diagnosis results. Anxiously, as she recounted, she rushed to the hospital to hear the verdict about her father's brain problems.

Example 2. 'Here everyone has problems!'
(V: Veronica; S: Interviewer)
First Line: Original Italian Version
Second Line: English Translation

```
1. V: ehmm io- eh c'era mio padre ricoverato
       ehmm I- uh there was my father [who was] hospitalized

2.     che aveva un tumore al cervello
       who had a tumor at his brain

3.     e io ero andata il giorno dopo che gli avevano fatto la TAC
       and I went that day after they performed the CAT on him

4.     per sapere di quale:- quale era il problema di cui era affetto
       to know of wha:t- what was the problem by which [he] was affected

5.     e:h e avevo mio figlio Mauro a casa con mia sorella
       u:h and [I] had my son Mauro at home with my sister
```

6. e *io non lo potevo lasciare mio figlio quindi è stata* uhm
    and *I couldn't leave my son so [it] was* uhm

7. sì mia sorella era in grado di fare determinate manovre pe:::rché lui eh
    yes my sister was able to take certain steps be:::cause he [i.e., her son] eh
                        |

8. S: per lui
      for him

9. V: e:h però:: io naturalmente ero venuta via col cuore in mano=
      u:h bu::t I of course had gone away with my heart in my hands=

10. S: =eh
       =eh

11. V: perciò ero- mordevo anche un po' il freno
       so [I] was- '[I] was also a bit in a rush[11]

12.   guardavo l'orologio
       [I] was looking [continuously] at my watch

13.   ero ansiosa e preoccupata sia per mio figlio sia per mio padre *perché non sapevo-*
       [I] was anxious and worried both for my son and for my father *because [I] didn't know-*

14.   e questo medico::: al quale io ho chiesto
       and this docto:::r to whom I asked

15.   "scusi professore ma Lei" dico
       "sorry professor but you [formal]," [I] say

16.   "pensa di poterci:: eh spiegare quanto prima
       "[you] think [you] can explain to us as soon as possible

17.   sa ho dei problemi avrei dei problemi
       [you] know [I] have some problems [I] might have some problems

18.   posso anche spiegarLe"
       [I] can also explain [them, i.e. the problems] to you [formal]"

19.   "qua problemi ne abbiamo tutti"
       "here everyone has problems"

20.   mi ha risposto mi ha inveito
       [he] responded to me, [he] railed against me

21.   nel corridoio dicendo che lì: lì lavoravano
       in the hallway [he was] saying that there: there they were working

22.   non è che:: stessero lì a grattarsi i cosiddetti
       it is not tha::t [they] were staying there scratching their you-know-what

23.   e ehmm e questo mi ha trattato veramente in maniera:: molto molto aggressiva
       and uhmm and this [doctor] treated me really in a very very aggressive manne::r

24.   cosa che io non gli ho mai perdonato
       something that I have never forgiven to him

25.   e dopo che appunto ci ha spiegato, illustrato la situazione
       and after that [he] actually explained, illustrated the situation to us

26.   che era drammatica appunto ho detto
       which was actually tragic, [I] said

27.   "guardi:::: Lei si ricordi comunque ecco che è un esser umano anche Lei
       "liste:::n [you should] remember anyway well that you are a human being as well

28.   che non debba mai provare le situazioni che io sto provando in questo momento
       [I wish] you never experience the situations that I am experiencing in this moment

29.   perché allora capirebbe" […]
       because at that point [you] would understand" […]

30. ho preso e me ne sono andata
     [I] got together and [I] went away from there

31. e non mi ha più visto questa persona
     and this person never saw me again

In this short, yet intense, narrative, Veronica seems to be eager to tell me her personal experiences concerning her interactions with an Italian neurologist who was overseeing her father's care. At the beginning of her narrative, Veronica keeps her past story separate from our present interaction. The two events, the narrated event (or denotational text) and the narrating event (or interactional text) (Jakobson, 1957; Perrino, 2015, 2022a; Silverstein, 1998; Wortham, 2000, 2001) are kept distinct and distant. Like Maimuna in Example 1, Veronica begins her story with a classic Labovian orientation, in which she briefly outlines the context of the story that she is about to tell. In lines 1–2, moreover, Veronica informs me that her father had been hospitalized for brain cancer. The fact that this tragic statement is in the very first lines of her narrative indicates her disposition to emotionally involve me right at the outset of her story. Indeed, as Veronica continues in lines 2–3, at that point in her past story, she didn't know whether her father had brain cancer or not. The day after the CAT-scan was performed on her father, she explains, Veronica went to the hospital to hear what the outcomes were (lines 3–5). Even though in the first 5 lines of the orientation, Veronica sets up a very dramatic situation, I seem to remain unresponsive verbally, mostly silent. At line 6, Veronica then adds even more dramatic information when she states that, for that occasion, she had left her son at home with her sister. At first, this line does not seem to add anything dramatic or tragic to the story; however, if one looks at the interactional history between Veronica and myself, things become more intricate. Indeed, during our previous conversations, Veronica had mentioned that her 1-year son, Mauro, had been very ill for more than a year, and that she could not leave him alone (line 6), not even for ten minutes.[12] If one looks at the interactional text then, one notices that Veronica accelerates the pace of her speech[13] in line 6 when she says 'I couldn't leave my son so this was uhm', which suggests a sense of anxiety in remembering those moments through her storytelling event.

These interactional moves become more prominent after I overlap with Veronica at line 8. In line 7, Veronica explains that she left her son with her sister, who, at the time, was the only person who was able to help her son with his medical care. It is precisely at that point that I cooperatively overlap with her (Tannen, 1984,

---

11. Literally, '[I] was also biting the brake a bit'.

12. Later I learned from Veronica that, after a couple of months, her 1-year son tragically passed away.

13. Wavy underline indicates a fast(er) speech pace – see Appendix.

2007, 2012) to show not only solidarity with her past dramatic situation, but especially awareness of it at the moment of the narrated event. Soon after my overlap, moreover, Veronica adds more emotional details to her description when she says 'of course I had gone away with my heart in my hands', in line 9. She uses the Italian metaphor "col cuore in mano" ('with my heart in my hands') to show how much she cared that I understand the gravity of the situation when she left her son behind to go the hospital. She then recounts how much in a hurry she was when she was waiting for the doctor at the hospital: in line 11, she uses another metaphoric phrase, "mordevo un po' il freno," which literally means 'I was biting the brake a bit'. This tropic phrase is followed by a further explanation when she says that she was continuously checking her watch and that she was worried for both her son at home and her father at the hospital (lines 12–13). It is at this point of her narrative (at line 14) that Veronica aligns her past story with our present interaction by using certain discourse strategies (Gumperz, 1982) to continue her story.

As in the Senegalese interaction between Maimuna and myself discussed earlier, Veronica's narrative alternates between moments of alignment between past and present and moments in which she keeps her past story more distant from the present interaction (especially in the beginning of her narrative). The storytelling practice becomes emotionally more involved and dynamic in relation to shifts between Veronica's past narrative moments that she recounts and our present interaction when she accelerates her speech pace. By using the Italian proximal deictic demonstrative adjective questo ('this') when referring to the doctor in her narrated event in line 14, for example, Veronica brings her past experiences back to the present, to her narrating event. Her narration is marked by rapid shifts that create the impression of back-and-forth space-time movement. Soon afterward, indeed, still in line 14, by using the past tense (passato prossimo) of the Italian verbum dicendi "chiedere," that is "io ho chiesto" ('I asked'), her story is temporally relocated into her remote past. Past and present become, again, two separate realms. The two spatiotemporal realms conflate, again, in line 15, however, when Veronica starts a long stretch of direct reported speech. Her narrated event is aligned, again, with our narrating event, the here-and-now interactional framework.

Direct reported speech, or, as Tannen (2007) usefully defines it, "constructed dialogue," always has interactional qualities when it is used in conversation. In her direct reported speech, starting in line 15, Veronica addresses the chief of the neurology department as if he were present in, and part of, our interactional text. As normally happens in Italian conversations between speakers who do not know each other or who have a different status, Veronica addresses the doctor by using the Italian polite form of address Lei. In the same line, moreover, she uses the historical present of the Italian verbum dicendi dire in the first-person singular form,

Chapter 13. Narrative inquiry: Case studies from Senegal and N. Italy   **217**

"dico" ('I say'), and this, again, further decreases the spatiotemporal boundaries between narrated event and narrating event.

In lines 15–18, Veronica maintains and projects a respectful and polite demeanor in her request to the doctor. In line 19, however, when she reports the doctor's response to her question to me, Veronica breaks register by saying "qua problemi ne abbiamo tutti" ('here everyone has problems'). By using the Italian proximal deictic qua, Veronica thus adds a negative connotation to the doctor's overall demeanor. Indeed, in standardized Italian, there are two proximal deictics for 'here', that is qui and qua. While qui and qua can be interchangeable (Renzi & Cardinaletti, 1988), ideologically, the use of qui is considered more sophisticated in Northern Italy. During a follow-up interview, for example, Veronica herself stated that qua is used in more dialectal situations than qui, especially in her northern Italian region, Veneto. Thus, by having the neurologist utter qua, she thus voices him negatively, as someone who is not as sympathetic as a doctor should be. In line 20, having completed her direct reported speech, Veronica shifts to the past tense again to reflect upon the doctor's behavior by saying, '[he] responded to me, [he] railed against me'. She first uses the verb "rispondere" ('to respond') which is a rather neutral verb, but soon afterward she uses the verb "inveire" ('to rail against') which is a much stronger verb indexing aggressiveness on the part of the other speaker (i.e., the doctor). Thus, Veronica seems to be completely dumbfounded by the doctor's response to her polite request, and she then gives more details about that particular moment by describing how he railed at her in the hallway of the hospital when he said that they were working very hard and that they didn't have any time to waste there (lines 21–22). She then adds 'this [doctor] treated me really in a very very aggressive manner', in line 23, where she uses the proximal demonstrative adjective "questo" ('this'), again, when she refers to the doctor. By using this proximal demonstrative pronoun, Veronica not only shifts back to the present narrating event and, again, makes the doctor be part of it, but also communicates her profound disrespect toward him to me.

If we look at the overall interaction, moreover, Veronica also undergoes an important change over the course of her storytelling events. Analogously to the transformations of the narrators described in Wortham's (2001) research, Veronica shifts from being remissive and polite to becoming unforgiving and embittered. After claiming that she would never excuse this doctor for his disrespectful behavior in line 24, Veronica continues her sad story by stating that the doctor finally explained the clinical situation of her father to her and probably to her siblings (line 25).[14] The diagnosis of her father was truly tragic, since she was

---

14. In line 25, the Italian pronoun ci ('to us') indicates that Veronica received the information about her father's disease together with her siblings or other relatives.

informed that he suffered of brain cancer. It is at this moment of the narrated event, at the very peak of her complicating action (Labov & Waletzky, 1967), that Veronica conflates the past with the present interaction again by resorting to a lengthy, uninterrupted, direct reported speech. She addresses the doctor by catching his attention with the polite form of the verb "guardare" ('to look'), which is conjugated in the present subjunctive (line 27). The Italian polite imperative "guardi," which I glossed in English as 'listen', is mainly used in two ways in Italian: to show understanding and sympathy to a listener (as in the sentence, "guarda, ti capisco benissimo," 'look, I really understand you'), or to start an argument, as in Veronica's case, in her direct reported speech. By addressing the doctor with "guardi" ('listen') and by lengthening the final vowel i, Veronica immediately sets the tone of her upcoming statements.

At line 28, she uses another polite imperative of the reflexive verb ricordarsi which is also preceded by the polite third person subject pronoun Lei: "Lei si ricordi comunque ecco" ('you [should] remember anyway well'). The explicit use of the polite third person subject pronoun Lei further increases Veronica's unfriendly tone, especially if one considers the fact that subject pronouns are optional in Italian, and they are often used to just add emphasis to one's speech. Veronica indeed uses the polite subject pronoun Lei repeatedly. In lines 27–29, she reminds him that even doctors are mortal, and thus challenges his status. In this way, through Veronica's direct reported speech, the doctor is not only part of her narrated event, the past story, but he has also become part of her narrating event, the present interaction. Veronica then suddenly ends her stretch of direct reported speech at line 30 when she recounts that after the above reported conversation with the doctor, she quickly went away, and this person never saw her again (lines 30–31).

The fleeting and ever-changing nature of storytelling events thus clearly emerges in this example as well. Like in my conversation with Maimuna in Example 1, Veronica and I engage in shifting interactional dynamics. While I overlap with Veronica only twice in the beginning of the her storytelling event, in lines 8 and 10, unlike my more involved participation with Maimuna's stories in Example 1, my silence during Veronica's storytelling indicates my sympathy, respect, and participation as well. Silence, as has been demonstrated (Basso, 1979; Ephratt, 2022; Nakane, 2012), should be analyzed as an interactional and discursive strategy (Gumperz, 1982), and can thus show involvement and intimacy instead of awkwardness or disinterest.

3. Why was narrative inquiry used?: How was it implemented?

The methodology that I used was implemented by collecting narrative practices as they emerged in conversations and interviews with my research participants. There was no elicitation on my part for these stories to be told. After the audio- or video-recording, moreover, I coded the collective narratives in a database for easy topical access before, during and after their transcription phase(s). During my fieldwork in Senegal, I mostly lived with an extended family and I had the chance to engage in many conversations with family members and acquaintances, depending on their availability. I collected almost one thousand hours of narratives. In Northern Italy, I collected stories from migrants and from Italians as well. I have continued to gather storytelling events from Northern Italians since 2003. During the COVID-19 pandemic, moreover, I started to collect storytelling practices through various digital platforms. Furthermore, I implemented this methodology by carefully and professionally transcribing many hours of storytelling practices before turning into their detailed analysis. While my two chapters do not focus on transcription as theory and method (Shohet & Loyd, 2022), storytelling practices need to be first transcribed and then carefully analyzed to find recurrent patterns and to confirm or refute theoretical hypotheses.

4. What challenges were faced?: How were the challenges addressed?

Scholars usually face many challenges during the various phases of their research. Collecting data often presents obstacles that were not expected, and researchers need to overcome them by finding contextualized solutions in situ and promptly as Briggs (Briggs, 1985, 1986) advocated. When I was in the process of collecting narratives in Senegal, for example, I often had to adapt to the wishes and needs of my research consultants. At times, healers didn't feel comfortable being asked questions or telling me their personal stories. Their preference was to be in control of the conversation and to teach me their ethnomedical recipes by offering their knowledge (xam xam in Wolof) in various forms. During these moments, I was able to ask questions related to some plants that they used in their healing practices. This was a new format for me, and I was thus able to learn more about plants and ethnomedical recipes thanks to this adaptation. Ethically, moreover, it was important to respect their wishes as much as possible, and not to interrupt them with other questions, as I discussed in my previous chapter.

Other times, there were some challenges in adjusting to Senegalese healers' wishes. Once, for example, I was able to talk to a healer in a village in inner Senegal, after several days of traveling in unsafe conditions. Once I arrived at his home, the healer asked me to stay at his door and to turn backwards so that he could see just my back. He of course did the same, he was turned the other way, facing his wall. We were not looking at each other. He agreed on all my research terms, he happily signed the consent form, and so forth, he only asked me to talk to him without looking at each other. Our conversation lasted longer than 3 hours and it was another new format for me.

As I mentioned earlier, another challenging aspect of this research methodology is to carefully transcribe the collected narratives, ideally while still in the field. It is indeed important to resolve immediately all possible questions that emerge while researchers transcribe. Transcription is thus a key methodological step for linguistic anthropologists. Inspired by Duranti's (2006) work, Shohet and Loyd argue that "transcripts are "like shadows on a wall": they are skeletal, selective representations of a rich phenomenal world that allow ethnographers to draw their audience's attention to specific features of that world, in order to make convincing claims about it" (Shohet & Loyd, 2022, p.262). All these and other challenges were variously addressed in my research as I explain in my two chapters.

5. Insights gained

As research on this topic has demonstrated, narratives are key sites to study participants' various interactional dynamics. In these conversational settings, narrators usually end up telling stories of their past, present, or imagined future. As I noted in my two chapters, during these speech events, participants can assume and reverse speech roles while they deliver their stories. Speakers' roles can shift, for example, from acting as a storyteller with full narrative authority, to being an audience member or a listener (De Fina & Georgakopoulou, 2012; Wortham, 2001). Storytelling practices are thus very intricate as they offer the researcher access to the subtleties of participants' interactions at various levels (Perrino, 2021a, 2021b). In these tellings, speech participants continuously align and misalign with the various topics of the story and with each other. In this way, they engage in interactional positionings thus demonstrating, once again, how narratives simultaneously shape and are shaped by their surrounding context (Duranti & Goodwin, 1992).

6. Conclusions

Why do researchers need to study the many, shifting interactional dimensions of storytelling practices? As I have argued in this and the preceding chapters, the developing interactional dynamics between speech participants, while their stories unfold, are constantly influenced by the various stances that they take vis-à-vis each other and the evolving narrative topics. In the first example described in this chapter, Maimuna, collapses time and space several times over the course of our interview. Through so doing, she enacts participant transposition at precise moments of our interaction. In particular, she collapses a chronotope of the past with a chronotope of the present to transpose me into her past biographical self. In this way, she is able to influence our interaction as well since, at first, I didn't seem to be too involved in her telling. After she transformed me in one of her family members, her sister precisely, however, the interactional patterns changed.

Similarly, in the second example, Veronica tries to keep my involvement in her storytelling event by using some discourse strategies such as fast speech pace, reported speech, the use of specific verbs and deictics, and thus rapidly shifts from her past self to the present interaction. At the same time, she makes significant claims about Italian hospitals and personnel and the way patients might be treated unethically despite their serious circumstances. In both cases, moreover, intimate relations are also foregrounded, showing how narratives can be transformed into intimate moments for speech participants. These two examples thus show how interactional dynamics in narrative practices can develop differently, depending on the various sociocultural contexts, speech participants, and, of course, the stories that are told during these events. In closing, a cross-cultural perspective is thus key in better understanding how interactional dynamics emerge in narratives. In this respect, the collection of narratives has proved to be a very effective methodological tool to navigate several discursive patterns in diverse sociocultural contexts.

References

Bailey, B. (2000). Social/interactional functions of code-switching among Dominican Americans. *Pragmatics, 10*(2), 165–193.

Basso, K. H. (1979). *Portraits of "The Whiteman": Linguistic play and cultural symbols among the western Apache.* Cambridge University Press.

Briggs, C. (1985). Learning how to ask. *Language in Society, 13*(1), 1–29.

Briggs, C. L. (1986). *Learning how to ask: A sociolinguistic appraisal of the role of the interview in social science research.* Cambridge University Press.

De Fina, A., & Georgakopoulou, A. (2012). *Analyzing narrative: Discourse and sociolinguistic perspectives.* Cambridge University Press.

Duranti, A. (2006). *A companion to linguistic anthropology.* Wiley Blackwell.

Duranti, A., & Goodwin, C. (1992). *Rethinking context: Language as an interactive phenomenon.* Cambridge University Press.

Ephratt, M. (2022). *Silence as language: Verbal silence as a means of expression.* Cambridge University Press.

Gumperz, J. J. (1982). *Discourse strategies*. Cambridge University Press.

Heller, M. (1988). *Codeswitching: Anthropological and sociolinguistic perspectives*. Mouton de Gruyter.

Irvine, J. T. (1989). Strategies of status manipulation in the Wolof greeting. In R. Bauman & J. Sherzer (Eds.), *Explorations in the ethnography of speaking* (pp. 167–191). Cambridge University Press.

Jakobson, R. (1957). Shifters and verbal categories. In L. R. Waugh & M. Monville-Burston (Eds.), *On language* (pp. 386–392). Harvard University Press.

Labov, W. (1972). *Language in the inner city*. University of Pennsylvania Press.

Labov, W., & Waletzky, J. (1967). Narrative analysis: Oral versions of personal experience. *Journal of Narrative & Life History, 7*(1–4), 3–38.

Nakane, I. (2012). Silence. In C. Bratt Paulston, S. F. Kiesling, & E. S. Rangel (Eds.), *The handbook of intercultural discourse and communication* (pp. 82–85). Wiley Blackwell.

Perrino, S. (2002). Intimate hierarchies and Qur'anic Saliva (Tëfli): Textuality in a Senegalese ethnomedical encounter. *Journal of Linguistic Anthropology, 12*(2), 225–259.

Perrino, S. M. (2005). Participant transposition in Senegalese oral narrative. *Narrative Inquiry, 15*(2), 345–375.

Perrino, S. M. (2006). *Senegalese ethnomedicine: A linguistic and ethnographic study of medical modernities between Senegal and Italy*. University of Pennsylvania.

Perrino, S. (2007). Cross-chronotope alignment in Senegalese oral narrative. *Language and Communication, 27*(3), 227–244.

Perrino, S. (2015). Performing extracomunitari: Mocking migrants in Veneto Barzellette. *Language in Society, 44*(2), 141–160.

Perrino, S. (2020). *Narrating migration: Intimacies of exclusion in northern Italy*. Routledge.

Perrino, S. (2021a). Narratives as discursive practices in interviews: A linguistic anthropological approach. *Narrative Inquiry, 31*(1), 72–96.

Perrino, S. M. (2021b). Embodied dread in COVID-19 images and narratives. *Life Writing, 18*(4), 579–592.

Perrino, S. M. (2022). Interviews in linguistic anthropology. In S. M. Perrino & S. E. Pritzker (Eds.), *Research methods in linguistic anthropology* (pp. 159–195). Bloomsbury Academic.

Perrino, S. M., & Pritzker, S. E. (Eds.). (2022). *Research methods in linguistic anthropology*. Bloomsbury Academic.

Renzi, L., & Cardinaletti, A. (1988). *Grande grammatica italiana di consultazione*. Mulino.

Shohet, M., & Loyd, H. (2022). Transcription and analysis in linguistic anthropology: Creating, testing, and presenting theory on the page. In S. M. Perrino & S. E. Pritzker (Eds.), *Research methods in linguistic anthropology* (pp. 261–295). Bloomsbury Academic.

Silverstein, M. (1998). Improvisational performance of culture in realtime discursive practice. In K. Sawyer (Ed.), *Creativity in performance* (pp. 265–312). Ablex.

Silverstein, M., & Urban, G. (1996). *Natural histories of discourse*. University of Chicago Press.

Tannen, D. (1984). *Conversational style: Analyzing talk among friends*. Oxford University Press.

Tannen, D. (2007). *Talking voices: Repetition, dialogue, and imagery in conversational discourse*. Cambridge University Press.

Tannen, D. (2012). Turn-Taking and intercultural discourse and communication. In
C. B. Paulston, S. F. Kiesling & E. S. Rangel (Eds.), *The handbook of intercultural discourse and communication* (pp. 135–157). Wiley Blackwell.

Wilce, J. M. (2001). Divining troubles, or divining troubles? Emergent and conflictual dimensions of Bangladeshi divination. *Anthropological Quarterly, 74*(4), 190–200.

Woolard, K. A. (1995). Changing forms of codeswitching in Catalan comedy. *Catalan Review, IX*(2), 223–252.

Wortham, S. (2000). Interactional positioning and narrative self-construction. *Narrative Inquiry, 10*(1), 157–184.

Wortham, S. (2001). *Narratives in action: A strategy for research analysis.* Teachers College Press.

Appendix.   Transcription and abbreviations conventions

|| Utterances starting simultaneously.

| Overlapping utterances.

=   Latching, or contiguous utterances, with an interval of less than one tenth of second between lines.

(00.00)   Time intervals within and between utterances (length of pauses in seconds, tenths and hundredths of seconds).

::   Syllable lengthening.

:::::   Prolonged syllable lengthening.

-      Syllable cut-off.

.   Stopping fall in tone.

,   Continuing intonation.

?   Rising intonation.

!   Animated tone.

____   Words with underline indicate stress.

CAP   Words in capitals indicate increased volume.

(...)   Talk between parenthesis indicates the transcriber's best guess at a stretch of discourse that is unclear on the original tape.

(???)   Question marks inside parenthesis indicate uncertain or unclear talk.

[...]   Three dots between square brackets indicate that some material of the original transcript has been omitted.

[[ ]]   The material inside double square brackets indicate transcriber's comments.

Regular font = French or Standard Italian.

Underlined Italics: Wolof.

Italics: English Translation.

Bold: Portions of transcripts discussed in the analysis.

CHAPTER 14

Repertory grids

Myles Grogan
Osaka Ohtani University

Repertory Grid Technique (RGT) derives from Personal Construct Psychology. The technique aims to understand how participants view objects, events, or people chosen as a kind of thematic sample by comparing them against each other, revealing the participant's constructs. After introducing the "fundamental postulate" and corollaries developed by its founder, George Kelly, the chapter explores how this technique may be applied in the field of SLA or language education. After discussing how this highly adaptable technique has been used, the chapter shows how researchers can gain qualitative and quantitative data on research questions relating to change over time or how different members of a group perceive a phenomenon. Although this technique presents some challenges for generalization, the chapter concludes by showing how data may be analyzed and used productively.

1. Introduction

The Repertory Grid Technique (RGT) is a tool originating in Personal Construct Psychology. In its simplest form, the technique asks research participants to explain, in their own terms, the way they might sort a sample of people, situations, or things concerning a central focus or research question. In the sorting process, the participant explains their thinking in terms of personal constructs, which they articulate and display in a grid. This grid uses a "linking mechanism" (Easterby-Smith, 1980, p. 4), such as a Likert scale (perhaps ranging from 1–5), to show how each person, situation, or thing from the sample connects to the constructs that an individual gives. A Repertory Grid, therefore, shows what might, in other research approaches, be called a cognitive map, a mental model, or a set of schema for an individual (Tan & Hunter, 2002). While each person construes in a different way, collections of individual grids may be analysed and used to enhance understanding and inform decision-making.

Repertory grids have been in use in one form or another for more than 60 years. RGT has been successfully used in health (Blundell et al., 2012; Brophy,

https://doi.org/10.1075/rmal.6.14gro
© 2024 John Benjamins Publishing Company

2015), business and marketing (Fassin et al., 2015; Lemke et al., 2011), tourism (Kerr & Kelly, 2019; Kotsi & Pike, 2021), and many other disciplines. It has been used within general education for some time (Bezzi, 1999; Pope & Denicolo, 1993). While some forms of the technique are beginning to appear (e.g., Gardiner et al., 2021), it seems to remain underdeveloped in language education and second language acquisition.

RGT allows researchers to generate and analyse both qualitative and quantitative data. Typically, though, RGT is referred to as a qualitative technique, as it was originally designed for clinical use with individuals. More recently, however, it is being seen as a potential "hybrid" (Bazeley, 2018) or "advanced" (Fetters, 2019) approach for integrating qualitative and quantitative data in mixed methods research. A variety of statistical analyses and choices have made the technique much more versatile and flexible since its inception.

This chapter aims to explain RGT and the thinking behind it in simple terms, and to explore how it might be used in second language education and acquisition.

2. Theoretical foundations

RGT is a method developed over a long career by George A. Kelly, and is based on Personal Construct Theory (PCT), also known as Personal Construct Psychology (PCP). The Repertory Grid and other techniques from PCT use an idiographic approach, meaning that researchers focus on the individual and their uniqueness, and expect people to be more different than similar. Because of its emphasis on difference, PCT is less focused on broad-based validity and reliability in the psychometric sense. The goal of PCT is to understand the way a person construes the world at a given time, allowing for action. As Kelly (1991) stated, "usability, rather than accuracy, per se, is the minimum standard of a good clinical test. One might even argue that usability is a good operational definition of accuracy" (p.142).

Unlike a nomothetic approach, an approach that seeks to make broad statements that apply to a larger population, "the grid is not a psychometric procedure dependent on a set of standardised norms" (Jankowicz, 2019, p.94). For example, features such as standardised wording may be construed differently by different people, and tend to be avoided. Nonetheless, PCT does allow for some shared construal, and some studies – particularly in the field of business (see, e.g., Fassin et al., 2015) – have supplied constructs to all participants.

Kelly's PCT was originally outlined in 1955, with a more closely edited version released in 1963. The theory he proposed centred around his fundamental postulate, stating "A person's processes are psychologically channelized by the ways in which he anticipates events" (Kelly, 1991, p.32). This means that people try to understand the world around them by making hypotheses in order to predict (or anticipate) events in much the same way a scientist might. Kelly called these hypotheses constructs, and RGT helps to unveil how these hypotheses or constructs work and interact.

Following the fundamental postulate, the way in which a person creates their constructs is further explored in 11 corollaries, each dealing with a different aspect of the construct system. These are covered in detail in many guides (e.g., Denicolo et al., 2016; Jankowicz, 2004), but are presented briefly here. The names of specific corollaries are given in italics, with quotations from the corollaries themselves where appropriate. The priority or salience of these corollaries may depend on the focus of the research, and the order of presentation may change slightly in some publications.

The first corollary (*construction* corollary) holds that people actively make a system of constructs by finding regularities based on their experience. This system is not imposed or inherited in any way, although the way people make their system is limited inasmuch as it is "channelized." The system is made of sets of opposites (*dichotomy* corollary). As a result, an individual construct is principally an axis or continuum, and is referred to as being *bipolar*. While a simple concept, such as *dark* or *sweet*, may stand alone in a "dictionary" sense, in a construct system, *dark* may contrast with *light*, and *sweet* may contrast with *sour*. An experience may then be interpreted through this axis, with a particular thing being more light than dark, or more sour than sweet.

In interaction, such as a research interview, the participant shares a verbal description of the construct, which may more or less accurately describe any particular construct the participant has (Fransella, 2015). Rather than being a logical or dictionary opposite, poles are constructed by the person who holds them. They have a "focus of convenience" or "range of convenience" (*range* corollary), meaning a person may apply them in some case but not others. While the word a participant uses to describe one end of a pole may be similar, it may contrast with different ideas as part of different constructs. *Dark* may be contrasted with *light* when talking about lumination, with *sweet* when talking about chocolate, or even *light-hearted* when talking about humour. Despite the common label at one end of the pole (*dark*), these may be different constructs with a different focus of convenience.

Because the construct system is hierarchically organised, the same person may apply different constructs at different times for seemingly the same thing. The *fragmentation* corollary suggests that "inferentially incompatible" constructs are possible because the system is not a totally integrated system and varies according to circumstances and the roles we are playing at the time. For example, a person may see themselves as a law-abiding citizen, but regularly break the speed limit if they are in a hurry (thus breaking the law), without seeing the apparent contradiction.

The system of constructs changes through successive experiences (*experience corollary*). New experiences may cause us to change our constructs. However, some constructs may linger, despite evidence to the contrary. The *modulation* corollary builds on the experience corollary, stating that change is limited by the "permeability of the constructs within whose range of convenience the variants lie." For example, the experience of burning one's fingers may cause one to stop touching a hot surface. However, in spite of negative effects (such as weight gain), a bad habit such as eating too many sweets may persist. The negative evidence is not strong enough to "permeate" the benefit (such as comfort) obtained.

As the name Personal Construct Psychology suggests, constructs are unique to the individual (*individuality* corollary). While people may share similar constructs, it is not common events or experiences in and of themselves that give people similar constructs. However, a similar construct system may lead people to interpret events in a similar way (*commonality* corollary). Two teachers could have the same qualification from the same institution and even have worked in the same school for years. Their common experience, however, does not predict a similar set of constructs. They may be very different. Further, one of the teachers may have a very similar system to a third person they know only distantly.

One's ability to understand another person depends on the ability to "construe the construction processes of another" (*sociality* corollary). When interacting with a child, an adult does not need to "become" a child or assume a socially defined role as an "adult" (Bannister & Fransella, 2021, p.34). Returning to the "scientist" image of the fundamental postulate, each interlocutor creates a model of the other's thinking – often subconsciously – and tests hypotheses through the response of the other (Fransella et al., 2003).

The result of the fundamental postulate and the corollaries is a practical basis for understanding the world. Kelly was strongly influenced by pragmatists and by Dewey in particular (Butt & Warren, 2015). The pragmatism of PCT and techniques such as the Repertory Grid resonate with a pragmatic approach to Mixed Methods Research (MMR). In a pragmatic MMR approach, the focus is on answering the research question rather than using a particular methodological or theoretical approach (Tashakkori et al., 2020). In other words, it is the research question that determines the kind of data and analysis required. Kelly's processes have been further developed in so far as more sophisticated statistical techniques have expanded the horizons and applications of the theory. This development has got to the point where MMR researchers such as Bazeley (2018) and Fetters (2019) have considered the Repertory Grid a natural iterative integration of the qualitative and quantitative investigation.

3. Methodological orientation

3.1 Principles and affordances

Although other principles or processes may be seen in RGT literature, the steps for carrying out RGT given here follow those that are applied in the common texts on the topic, such as given in Jankowicz (2004), Shaw and McKnight (1981), and Denicolo et al. (2016), as well as the author's own practical experience.

The key principle in most PCT research is to try to understand the world from the participants' perspective. This usually involves recording the constructs that participants use to interpret their world using their own words as much as possible. In the Repertory Grid Technique, the researcher elicits a sample of people, situations, or things relating to the research focus. The researcher typically gives a category (such as asking a teacher for "learning activities in a reading class"), and participants choose something from that category with which they are familiar (such as class discussions or learner journals). These are called *elements* in the RGT literature, and the participant's choice of an element from a broader category is a part of the process.

The main principle in RGT is that the participant compares elements from the broader categories and differentiates between them. A participating teacher may give several "activities in a reading class," with each one having different affordances. These differences form the basis of a construct that can be elicited. A participant looks at a small subset of elements (typically three) to identify how they differentiate between them. Following the dichotomy corollary, the constructs elicited should be bipolar rather than simply negated. Once a construct has been articulated for the subset, the participant and researcher will see if the other elements fit the construct. This is usually done by placing the poles of the construct at either end of a Likert scale. In the event that another element from the overall set of elements does not fit the scale, that element may be omitted or the construct may be discussed and developed further. Once the first construct has been completed, the process is repeated, and a different construct is elicited.

Findings from Repertory Grid research do not compare people against "established normative data" (Bannister & Fransella, 2021, p. 51), and this can make the comparison of participants difficult. To overcome this problem, a researcher may give common elements or constructs that all participants may have some experience of. For example, the researcher may give a teacher a common activity from the setting (such as a required activity), or give a common construct that all teachers may be familiar with (such as whether an activity is for long-term or short-term development).

The interview may continue until it is felt that all possible constructs have been thoroughly explored. This can be seen when the participant cannot think of a new construct, the elicited constructs tend to become similar, or the participant becomes tired. The process of exploring constructs and putting them into words requires a lot of concentration and mental resources. Participants may need extra time to verbalize these processes and check that they have done so in a manner the researcher can understand. Care should be taken to exhaust the list of possible constructs rather than exhausting the participant.

This may seem abstract to readers unfamiliar with RGT, and so a concrete example follows to illustrate the principles involved. A researcher wants to explore how different teachers in a school believe that activities from a reading class contribute to student reading development. These activities may form a category from which elements can be drawn. In collaboration with one particular teacher, they produce the Repertory Grid shown in Figure 1.

Repertory Grid

Topic: The uses and effects of classroom activities in a reading class
How do the activities in a reading class contribute to student development?

Two the same Score: 1	E1 Common vocabulary quizzes (MC)	E2 speed reading (fluency quiz)	E3 Main text search activities	E4 Group discussions of articles	E5 Extended reading quizzes	E6 Class journal	One different Score: 5
C1 Answers mostly unambiguous	1	1	2 (0)	5 (×)	1 (0)	5	More room for personal opinion
C2 Less complex interaction	1	1	3	4	2	5 (×)	More complex interaction
C3 Can be developed/extended	5	5 (×)	3	1 (0)	4	1 (0)	More time pressure
C4 More from textook	1 (full-context elicitation)	1	2	5	2	3	More direction from teacher
C5 Focused	1	1	3	5	3	5	Multi-skill
C6 Shorter term goal	1	2	2	5	3	5	Longer-term goal

Figure 1. An example of a completed repertory grid

Note: In the example, the research participant compares one activity provided by the researcher and five activities from their class. These represent the elements of the grid, and are designated E1-E6. By comparing these activities, the participant produces constructs – pairs of ideas that form an opposite (C1-C6). These are then linked with a Likert scale. The different process used for eliciting constructs are explored in Section 3.3.

The researcher gives one element to allow comparison with other teachers in the setting. This is a "Common vocabulary quiz" (E1), and the participant gives five activities they use in their class as elements (E2–6). The participant compares and considers the set of elements (classroom activities), and tries to articulate the different ways that the elements may contribute to students development. The participant expresses these attributes as constructs (Jankowicz, 2004, p. 282). These are C1 through C5 in Figure 1. The researcher provides construct C6, "Shorter-term goal – Longer-term goal" as a common construct, allowing comparison between teachers in the project.

The first construct the teacher expressed (C1) contrasts "Answers mostly unambiguous" with "More room for personal opinion." The contrasting poles of the construct are recorded on either side of the grid. Each of the activities making up the elements is then rated on a Likert scale, with the aim of providing an ordered ranking. The score provided is neither "high" nor "low" – it is simply a description showing which end of the scale the element is closer to on the construct. The process would have worked equally well if the labels for the pole and the scores for the construct were reversed, with E1 scoring 5 instead of 1, and E6 scoring 1 instead of 5. The relative positions would remain the same, allowing comparison with other constructs.

RGT is principally exploratory, and Kelly used it to gain "a preliminary list of clinical hypotheses" (Kelly, 1991, p. 152). Because it relates to the way people think, it has been used in research on teacher cognition (Borg, 2015). It has also been used in multicomponent designs, alongside questionnaires on student assessment procedures (Oscarson & Apelgren, 2011), or alongside more extensive measures such as classroom observation, reading speed measures, and c-tests to monitor the use of data-driven learning in stimulating lexicogrammatical knowledge (Hadley & Charles, 2017).

The goal of RGT is to "subsume another's construing" (Fransella, 2005, p. 41), meaning that the researcher is trying to put aside their own worldview as much as possible and to see the world as the participant does. A core feature of the RGT interview is referred to as the "credulous approach" (Denicolo et al., 2016) or "credulous listening" (Fransella, 2005). As a result, researchers need to be prepared to unexpectedly meet ideas they strongly disagree with and suspend their own values – a task easier said than done. It may be reasonable for the researcher to ask questions to check that they understand the perspective of the participants. However, even if the interviewer hears strange or unusual ideas, "never mind; accept them" (Jankowicz, 2004, p. 46). The point is that the participant's point of view is privileged in RGT research.

The advantages afforded by RGT were recognised by early advocates of practitioner research. Block (1997) preferred techniques like RGT to questionnaires when gathering classroom data, as "while the former allows the student to define and evaluate using his/her own terms, the latter acts as a corset, asking him/her to agree with or disagree with pre-fabricated items" (p.355). More broadly, in practitioner research, the desire to subsume and understand the construing of colleagues or students is clearly present in the collaborative philosophies of Exploratory Practice (Mann & Walsh, 2017). Practitioners of Exploratory Practice propound "prioritising understanding over solutions, and emphasising the importance of *agency* [emphasis in original], of learners as well as teachers, in the learning/teaching enterprise" (Hanks, 2017, p.3). Helping learners or teachers become aware of their own frameworks (and respecting these once they are uncovered) is a necessary pre-cursor to implementing positive change, and RGT allows the explicit awareness that teachers or students must come to the fore before even deciding if change is necessary.

RGT is particularly effective where other techniques may not be available. In situations with low numbers, for example, conventional interviews or questionnaires may be less effective. This may be the case with specialised programs. Yildrim and Akcayoglu (2019) investigated perceptions of what made a good language learner with two gifted learners and two of their teachers to see the degree to which these matched. They chose RGT as it allowed participants to express constructs without interference from the researchers, as well as being amenable to both qualitative and quantitative forms of analysis. Participants were asked to choose three effective learners, three typical learners, and three ineffective learners as elements. The two student participants were asked to include the anchor elements of "self" and "ideal" as language learners, allowing a comparison between present and possible future selves. Interestingly, the gifted learners did not seem to perceive themselves as effective learners, but both teachers and learners had many similar constructs, allowing a specific characterisation of "what giftedness in foreign language learning entails" (p.99), as well as identifying possible needs for professional development of the teachers. RGT thus addressed an area where large-scale study was challenging because of the small numbers involved.

3.2 Types of RQs addressed by repertory grid

RGT is generally exploratory in nature, and so published RGT studies may have favoured stating general research focus rather than specific research questions. Within second language research, RGT has two main applications. Firstly, RGT may address questions of change in outlook over time. Sendan and Roberts (1998), for example, used RGT to report how a student teacher's ideas about teacher effectiveness changed over 15 months. Teacher education has adapted both RGT and other techniques from PCT for this purpose (Pope & Denicolo, 1993). A second focus of RGT in second language research addresses questions concerning how a group understands a phenomenon. Constructs elicited from multiple participants are reviewed in an open-ended form of content analysis (see Jankowicz, 2004) to form categories of constructs shared by many participants. This content analysis is included as part of the RGT process in many texts.

Adapting RGT for young learners, Boye et al. (2021) explored how younger learners perceive the language classroom in order to "learn more" about the extent and types of learner engagement. The findings highlighted a gap between the pedagogic purposes of teachers and the purpose of the students. Though the research featured only 16 learners, it suggested many possible ways that students engage in the classroom above the behavioural or cognitive level commonly addressed in research. This supported the need for a more ecological approach to research and teaching.

An example of adapting Repertory Grids for exploration in the classroom, allowing for a group participatory research approach, comes from Kramsch (1983). She had found that cultural "facts" ("Germans close their office doors," p.438) presented in language courses, though interesting, were not helping students to understand how people from different backgrounds might think or react. She used the Repertory Grid as a "psychic mirror of cultural attitudes and values" (p.438). She presented an English grid to American graduate students and grids in French and German to graduate students from those countries. Students populated their grids with elements representing figures who would be familiar to both English speakers and non-English speakers (a TV star, a teacher, a business person). Using data from RGT, she and her class explored how constructs were similar or different based on the nationality and first language of the respondent, inviting discussion of the results as a class activity. The combined reflections with students allowed a rich view of how people in different cultures viewed certain figures. This project showed many of the features of Exploratory Practice, and helped to create deeper learning in a non-threatening way. In particular, moving past the "cultural facts" and looking at the common ground or the reason for cultural norms presented in the course helped students reach a broader understanding and appreciation of each other on both individual and group levels.

While Repertory Grid studies are highly effective where only a small number of participants are available, studies with larger numbers of participants are also possible. Richter and Lara Herrera (2017) investigated student teachers' perspectives on what made a good EFL instructor. The 116 participants came from either Mexico or several Southeast Asian countries. Teaching in the countries involved had been characterized by views of pedagogy regarded as conservative, meaning "synthetic, teacher-centred, forms-focused, and examination driven" (p.181). Participants chose six language teachers from their learning experience as elements.

Two of the language teachers were regarded by the learners as "great," two "average," and two "poor." Also included in the sort were the participant themselves and the participant "after some professional growth" (p.185). This mammoth effort gained 1206 constructs. The set of constructs produced by all participants was then analysed as a whole, through a content analysis procedure, allowing researchers to identify common themes and ideas through the participants' construing (see Section 3.3). In addition to broader results, a comparison was made between the Mexican and the Southeast Asian student teachers. Despite some differences, the findings reflected a similar outlook, suggesting a move away from conservative pedagogical ideas, even in countries which may be thought of as being more traditional. While the ability to generalize is limited in this study, it reflects a positive trend towards a broader application of RGT within language education research.

RGT may also contribute to a broader study in phenomenological or thematic analysis research (Denicolo et al., 2016). Hadley (2017) suggests using RGT at the beginning of Grounded Theory research, as it may be more effective than unstructured interviews when trying to understand the perspective of collaborating participants. This again shows the pragmatic nature of RGT in resolving research issues. The result is that RGT may therefore sometimes appear as part of a multi-component study to address particular aspects of a research focus.

3.3 Procedures of data collection and analysis

The most common form of data collection in RGT tends to be a one-on-one interview, particularly where the focus of the grid is research rather than as a training or reflective tool (see, for example, Korthagen, 1992). An effective introduction to the RGT interview will explain the goals and value of the research, the ethical procedures associated with it, and details such as the confidentiality protocol, contact, and withdrawal procedures. Denicolo et al. (2016) suggest including a practice with something easily understood. In their case, the "something" is a physical thing, in the form of different kinds of biscuits (cookies). Also, allowing sufficient time is important for success in any endeavour, but this is especially true for the Repertory Grid interview. Interviews of between 60 to 90 minutes may not be unusual. Ensuring that participants are aware of the demands on time is essential.

The first step of the data-gathering procedure is to elicit the elements. The elements are the sample of people, places, or things that participants will be considering in relation to the research focus. They are usually described to the participant in general or categorical terms (e.g., "a teacher I respect," "an activity that makes classes go well," or "a book that seems popular with students"). The participant then chooses a specific example that fits the description with which they are familiar and uses it for the procedure. Participants should choose elements that are "easy to keep in mind and manipulate" (Denicolo et al., 2016, p. 62). In the example from Section 3.1, the teacher was asked to give classroom activities that they regularly use in a reading class. One element was supplied (E1: Common vocabulary quizzes).

To keep interviews manageable, researchers tend to work with between 5 and 8 elements (Jankowicz, 2004; Shaw & McKnight, 1981). The elements are recorded in two places. The first is an interview record sheet, such as that in Figure 1, used for recording the results of a sort. The second place is a set of cards or papers, which the participant will use for the sorting task (Hadley, 2017). Figure 2 shows the elements from the interview in Section 3.1, designated E1 to E6, listed on sorting cards, and ready for the interview. Presenting the elements to the participant on cards allows the participant to compare elements more tangibly, thus lowering the cognitive demand and improving the quality of the interview.

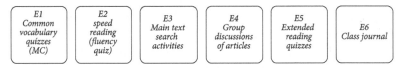

Figure 2. Sample elements from a repertory grid

After elements have been elicited, construct elicitation begins. The most common technique, known as triadic elicitation, involves the interviewer presenting three elements to the participant for comparison. Using the cards shown in Figure 2, three elements can be picked at random. Alternatively, the interviewer may follow a pre-decided sequence. The interviewer simply asks the participant to describe a way in which two of the elements are similar yet different from the third in a way that is connected to the focus of the research. Figure 3 shows how the participant in the example sorted the cards for elements E3, E4, and E5. The participant decided that E3 (Main text search activities) and E5 (Extended reading quizzes) were similar in that "answers are mostly unambiguous," while E4 (Group discussion of articles) left "more room for personal opinion." The comparison of elements, therefore, successfully yielded a bipolar construct, which was recorded in the first row of the record sheet as construct C1.

Before comparing the remaining items to the construct, preparation is made for a Likert scale to link the construct and the elements. The two similar items (E3, E5) initially receive the same score (in this case a 1), and are always displayed on the same side (the left, in our example). The single element scores 5 and is placed on the right. This score is neither high nor low, but represents a tendency to one end or other of the construct scale. This convention avoids a tendency for partici-

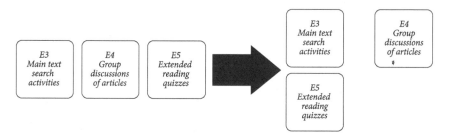

Figure 3. An example of triadic elicitation

pants to focus on "good versus bad" when describing constructs, even when it may not be relevant (Jankowicz, 2004).

The remaining elements (E1, E2, and E6) can now be compared using construct C1. Using the cards makes this process simple and easier to manipulate and change. In the example, the participant believed that E3 had more room for ambiguity than elements E1 and E2, and therefore changed the score to a 2 for the E3 element. The final scores for the example were then recorded on the interview record sheet, as shown in Figure 4.

Two the same Score: 1	E1 Common vocabulary quizzes (MC)	E2 speed reading (fluency quiz)	E3 Main text search activities	E4 Group discussions of articles	E5 Extended reading quizzes	E6 Class journal	One different Score: 5
C1 Answers mostly unambiguous	1	1	2　0	5　x	1　0	5	More room for personal opinion

Figure 4. Initial ranking of elements on the Likert scale

Sometimes, one or more of the remaining elements may not fit the construct from the initial three elements in triadic elicitation. As mentioned in Section 2, constructs have a range or focus of convenience, and the remaining elements may be outside the range of the construct elicited. Interviewers may negotiate with the participant to decide if the construct is important, in which case the element may be omitted from the scale. Alternatively, the participant and interviewer can discard the construct, and explore similarities and differences further.

Having elicited the first construct, the interviewer then tries to elicit a new construct. This can be done a) with the same elements, b) with a new set of three elements, or c) by using an alternative elicitation technique. Triadic elicitation is a good starting point for an interview, but can be tiring if it is the only approach used. Many researchers also seem to use full or whole context elicitation (Denicolo et al., 2016, p.64), in which a researcher simply asks the participant to illustrate any construct that they want to explain. This may be done near the end of the interview, by asking the participant if there are any further constructs that might be missing from the set. Finally, the researcher was also interested in whether the activity was aimed at short- or long-term development, and thus asked the participant to use the construct "Shorter-term goal – Longer term goal." As with the common element, this common construct allows a degree of comparison between the participants in the analysis stage.

Some conventions in RGT are not necessary but are helpful. In the example record sheet in Figure 1 and in Figure 4, the elements used for triadic elicitation received a symbol which was recorded under the Likert scores. The elements sorted received either a "O" (for the two items deemed to be similar in terms of the construct elicited) or a "X" (for the item deemed to be dissimilar). This provides a kind of audit trail for elements selected for elicitation (Hadley, 2017; Shaw & McKnight, 1981). If an item has not been used for elicitation, the interviewer can see at a glance. Similarly, if an item has been used often, it may be replaced in later sorts.

In the final stages of the interview, both the researcher and the participant review the completed grid. Reviewing may simply mean the researcher checking that the constructs are recorded properly, and the participant double-checking the scores they have given. If two constructs seem similar – semantically or in terms of score – the researcher may want to explore whether they are aspects of the same construct, or whether they differ in some respect. After reviewing, if possible, it is a good idea to give the participant a copy of the recorded grid, enhancing the collegiality of the process.

Analysis may begin by reviewing elicited constructs in a broad sense. Some will be more central to behaviour than others. When characterizing constructs, Jankowicz (2004) suggests that some "core" constructs may not be obvious to researchers at first, appearing more "peripheral." It may be that some constructs are subordinate to others from the interview. Other constructs may simply be descriptive ("propositional"). An additional consideration is what the construct describes. Constructs describing behaviour may be observable, referring to actions such as timekeeping or test scores. However, describing activities as "engaging" or "easy" suggests an evaluation on the part of the participant. The participant's description should be respected as part of a credulous approach, but corroboration for some claims may be available in the transcript of an interview.

An initial "eyeball" analysis of the quantitative data helps researchers become more familiar with their content, consistent with good practice in Thematic Analysis or Grounded Theory (Braun & Clarke, 2012; Charmaz, 2014). Data from Likert scales is, at best, ordinal. The difference between a score of 1 and 2 may not be the same as the difference between a 2 and a 3. Nonetheless, comparing quantitative details such as a column total, arithmetic mean, or standard deviation makes patterns or tendencies within the data obvious "at a glance."

To compare two elements, the easiest way is to compare the difference between scores. In our example, by subtracting E2 from E1, and rendering any negative numbers as positive, we can see how many points of difference there are. In this case, the two elements differ only by a single point on a single construct. If we checked the degree of movement between E2 and E4, we would see that there is a 23-point difference. This score is known as the "sum of difference."

An eyeball view of constructs is slightly more complex, as the poles are elicited randomly. Had the eliciting process been different (for example, had a different triad been used) the poles may have been reversed. It is therefore worth reversing the scores to see if other similarities appear. A table of similarity can be made to show how similar or different constructs are from each other using this system. A detailed overview of this process can be obtained in Jankowicz, (2004).

Dedicated software for analysis of grids is available. For those new to the field, analysis can be done using a plug-in from the R package, such as the OpenRepGrid package (Heckmann, 2016). However, learning how to use R while also learning how Repertory Grids work can be demanding. For this demonstration, a simpler "plug and play" alternative was used in the form of WebgridPlus (2020), which has both a downloadable version or an online version.

WebGrid Plus allows one to input the data from a grid and see several forms of visual output relatively easily. The first of these is through focused cluster analysis, which is shown in Figure 5. The chart produced looks like what might be found on an eyeball analysis, but constructs will be reversed automatically if required. Constructs and elements may be re-ordered in terms of similarity by the system. This is visible in Figure 5, where the fourth construct is listed at the top. Also visible is a dendrogram, which shows construct-to-construct similarities, in the form of connections linked to a scale on the right-hand side. For constructs, C3 and C5 are shown as similar, as are the elements E1 and E2. This makes gauging similarity between constructs or elements much easier.

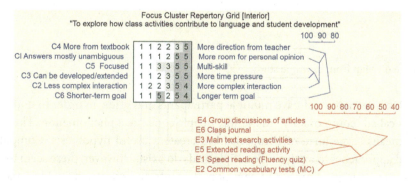

Figure 5. Cluster grid from example study

A second common visual aid from the WebGrid software is called a "PrinGrid Map" on the website. It shows the results of a Principal Component Analysis and is shown in Figure 6. This process shows elements and constructs in a more organized grouping. In Figure 6, two axes are shown, representing the "components" that explain the most variance. Elements and constructs are displayed with reference to the components. As can be seen in Figure 6, the supplied construct (C6) behaves differently from many of the other constructs supplied by the participant, and the journal and group discussions are on opposite sides of the graph from vocabulary quizzes and speed reading, with main text search activities being between the two.

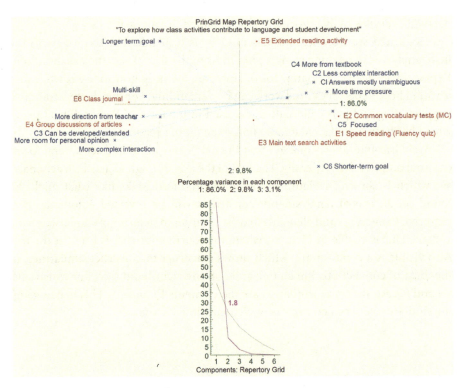

Figure 6. Map from example study

Most research will have multiple participants and grids, in order to find what Kelly called "commonality" in the way people construe a phenomenon. This usually means some form of comparison to create a useful hypothesis. Computer-based approaches to analysing multiple grids do exist. However, these seem to rely on having a larger number of common elements and constructs, which may be contrary to the exploratory nature of RGT.

A more useful approach is based on a form of content analysis, to show how two constructs are performing similar roles, or how systems of constructs might be hierarchically organized. Having an independent perspective in the form of a third party helps to improve the relatability of the research (Lincoln & Guba, 1985; Miles, Huberman, & Saldana, 2014). However, it needs to be planned for early in the research process and design. While common strategies for content analysis require researchers to prepare a rule before analysis and compare the results of several researchers in preparing that rule (Krippendorff, 2018; Neuendorf, 2016), such strategies may not be appropriate for RGT, and a more discovery-based approach is usually needed.

In a process described by Jankowicz (2004), the researcher provides a relevant outline of the goal of the research and the constructs obtained to the third party researcher, clarifying any questions they may have. Using cards labelled with the constructs, the researcher and third party independently create categories and sort the cards into those categories. In our example, a possible category might be "Demonstrating progress," including assessments that can easily be graded to show progress (tests, etc.). Another category might be "Agency," relating to who is responsible for the learning.

Once finished, the researcher and third party explain their categories. A table comparing the categories is then made. Similarities and differences between categories and membership of categories are explored together. For example, the researcher may have a category they named "demonstrating progress," while the third party may have a category with the label "visibility," and the two categories may contain many of the same constructs. Alternatively, one person may have used several categories to finely delineate an idea where the other party created a single category. Discussion of the processes and reasoning is helpful in making explicit some of the assumptions that both are using in their interpretation of the construct sets.

Independently re-organizing and re-categorizing ideas a second time helps both the researcher and third party try the ideas presented in the previous discussion. The second re-organization is likely to see more commonality in the structure of constructs. The key to successful analysis is to try to reach an agreed upon condition and level of similarity, which Jankowicz (2004) gives as 90%. The process will therefore help to ensure that the reasoning underlying the final agreed-upon categories and organization of the constructs provided by participants is not overly esoteric.

3.4 Ethical issues

An RGT interview is a non-trivial undertaking. While some research methods have the capacity for complete anonymity, with RGT this is not the case, and the participant will be sharing personal details which may make them identifiable. For this reason, confidentiality in research is something that needs to be carefully addressed, much as it would for any in-depth qualitative research (Miles et al., 2014). This may be particularly true if colleagues at the same institution are participating, where one participant may be in a position of power or responsibility to another.

On a related note, Denicolo et al. (2016) note that some participants may be reluctant to have interviews recorded electronically or digitally. There may be times when handwritten notes may have to suffice. Typically, researchers must follow institutional guidelines from ethics committees, which may help to reassure participants with regard to the privacy of their interview. This may include restricitons on who sees the data, how long the data is stored for, and where it is stored. For example, storing data online or in computers outside a designated area may be prohibited. Handling and storage of data should therefore be considered in concert with confidentiality.

Because constructs are personal, the participant may end up "addressing deep issues" (Denicolo et al., 2016, p.125), perhaps unexpectedly. Some issues, such as the way people teach or learn, may reach into a participant's core, and it is possible for interviewers to stumble on areas that are unexpectedly emotional or painful (Walker & Crittenden, 2011). There is no way to take back such discoveries after the fact. Fransella (2005) emphasizes that PCP is not a "party trick" (p.45). For this reason, it is important to allow participants to withdraw from any area of questioning, or even the whole interview. A prepared phrase, such as "I would prefer not to cover this," should be decided and respected. Although it may be frustrating to the researcher, it is better than causing harm. Such precautions make the research experience more positive for all involved.

A final noteworthy point is that because of the time and energy given by the participant, good practice regarding follow-up in research is particularly important. Researchers should try to meet participants' expectations about any promised follow up. This is one reason why giving the participant a copy of the interview record sheet helps. Depending on the scale and scope of the study, providing participants with a clear schedule or result from a research project may be challenging. While it may be impractical to keep participants up to date with every step of a multistage study, participants may be interested to hear how their voices have impacted a particular section of that study, and to know that their views are represented reasonably. Being clear with participants about what will and will not happen, as well as establishing and keeping clear schedules, are an important part of "doing no harm" in RGT as other aspects of the research ethics.

4. Critiques and responses

For those new to RGT, the biggest immediate challenge may be the variety of forms that the grid may take. In part, this is a response to certain formats or constraints of delivery and design. This means that certain aspects that may appear in many guides are subject to change. While the Likert scale seems to be common, Boye et al. (2021) used a more binary approach, to accommodate younger participants. Kramsch (1983) was working with a more classroom-style activity, and asked students to work with three elements at a time rather than all the elements. Such adaptations are also to be found in larger, group-based applications of the grid (Donaghue, 2003; Korthagen, 1992). The large number of these adaptations has resulted in a situation where "no such creature as 'The Grid' exists" (Pope & Keen, 1981, p.37), and understanding some of the choices in research design requires some practice in reading and interpreting previous research. This can be confusing for those new to the field, but is worth the effort.

RGT excels in areas that emphasize difference, even though studies tend to be relatively small scale. Where more global generalization is needed, RGT may be of limited value. Johnson and Nádas (2012) pointed out several problems in using RGT for studies involving larger-scale educational assessment. Because the processes are so adaptable, combining studies and making broader generalizations is problematic. Many of these issues with the studies examined stemmed from differences in the underpinning theoretical framework, the goals of the studies that were being combined, and the practices of implementation. Such differences can be addressed, but would require considerable planning and collaboration. Nonetheless, within the field of assessment, RGT has been used in highlighting specific instances of issues, such as comparability of grading methods between departments in higher education (Bloxham et al., 2015).

From a practical point of view, RGT can be complicated to use well, especially when getting familiar with the technique (Hadley, 2017). Getting to the core of the issue being addressed takes practice (Jankowicz, 2004). In addition, the current lack of research in SLA using the technique means that exemplars of results showing how qualitative or quantitative data may be derived and used is sparse. In short, it is a technique that requires some effort to master. The best way to become familiar with it, however, is to try it. In addition to those studies within language learning and teaching, the author strongly encourages readers to look at studies outside of the field. Not only do studies outside of SLA show different uses of RGT, they also present new ideas and perspectives on broader methodological issues that research users and authors may find beneficial. This may incude epistemologies or ethical considerations in fields such as health, management, or design. Reading accounts or attending presentations of RGT studies may help us to reconisdier our own work and to communicate to a broader audience, improving the image of SLA as a field.

5. Conclusions

This chapter introduced RGT regarding its underlying theory and philosophy and its methodological orientation. The pragmatic nature of the approach means that not all the underlying principles and corollaries need to be "true" to be helpful, and the framework of the corollaries offers a useful structure for exploratory studies. PCT prioritizes the research participant perspective, and allows a highly flexible and respectful approach to inquiry about teaching and learning a second language. Although it can be used on a broad scale with complex statistical techniques (such as principal component analysis), it is also highly adaptable, and can be simplified for collegial processes or research projects with students. RGT does not necessarily need to be used to "solve" a particular problem, to promote a particular viewpoint, or to find data to justify implementing specific actions. Along with Exploratory Practice, it is a technique which promotes a better understanding as an end in itself. Although it may be under-represented in second language literature, it appears often enough for readers to be able to begin interacting with it, and to see how it can be adapted. The next chapter shows how RGT can be applied in a specific context. It is hoped that readers will feel more fully able to engage with – and, hopefully, adopt – the Repertory Grid in their own future endeavours.

References

Bannister, D., & Fransella, F. (2021). *Inquiring man: The psychology of personal constructs* (3rd ed.). Routledge.

Bazeley, P. (2018). *Integrating analyses in mixed methods research*. Sage.

Bezzi, A. (1999). What is this thing called geoscience? Epistemological dimensions elicited with the Repertory Grid and their implications for scientific literacy. *Science Education, 83*(6), 675–700. https://doi.org/10.1002/(SICI)1098-237X(199911)83:6<675::AID-SCE3>3.0.CO;2-Q

Block, D. (1997). Learning by listening to language learners. *System, 25*(3), 347–360.

Bloxham, S., Hudson, J., den Outer, B., & Price, M. (2015). External peer review of assessment: An effective approach to verifying standards? *Higher Education Research & Development*, *34*(6), 1069–1082.

Blundell, J., Wittkowski, A., Wieck, A., & Hare, D. J. (2012). Using the repertory grid technique to examine nursing staff's construal of mothers with mental health problems: MBU staff's construal of mothers with mental health problems. *Clinical Psychology & Psychotherapy*, *19*, 260–269.

Borg, S. (2015). *Teacher cognition and language education: Research and practice*. Bloomsbury Academic.

Boye, S., Gardiner, I. A., & Littlejohn, A. (2021). 'Makes head hurt': School-aged learners' perceptions in the language classroom. *System*, *100*, 102560.

Braun, V., & Clarke, V. (2012). Thematic analysis. In H. Cooper, P. M. Camic, D. L. Long, A. T. Panter, D. Rindskopf, & K. J. Sher (Eds.), *APA handbook of research methods in psychology, Vol 2: Research designs: Quantitative, qualitative, neuropsychological, and biological.* (pp. 57–71). American Psychological Association.

Brophy, S. (2015). Humanizing healthcare. In D. A. Winter & N. Reed (Eds.), *The Wiley handbook of personal construct psychology* (pp. 293–305). John Wiley & Sons.

Butt, T. W., & Warren, B. (2015). Personal construct theory and philosophy. In D. A. Winter & N. Reed (Eds.), *The Wiley handbook of personal construct psychology* (pp. 9–23). John Wiley & Sons.

Charmaz, K. (2014). *Constructing grounded theory: A practical guide through qualitative analysis* (2nd ed.). Sage.

Denicolo, P., Long, T., & Bradley-Cole, K. (2016). *Constructivist approaches and research methods: A practical guide to exploring personal meanings*. Sage.

Donaghue, H. (2003). An instrument to elicit teachers' beliefs and assumptions. *ELT Journal*, *57*(4), 344–351.

Easterby-Smith, M. (1980). The design, analysis and interpretation of repertory grids. *International Journal of Man-Machine Studies*, *13*(1), 3–24.

Fassin, Y., Werner, A., Van Rossem, A., Signori, S., Garriga, E., von Weltzien Hoivik, H., & Schlierer, H.-J. (2015). CSR and related terms in SME owner–managers' mental models in six European countries: National context matters. *Journal of Business Ethics*, *128*(2), 433–456.

Fetters, M. D. (2019). *The mixed methods research workbook: Activities for designing, implementing, and publishing projects*. Sage.

Fransella, F., Bell, R., & Bannister, D. (2003). *A manual for Repertory Grid technique* (2nd ed.). Wiley.

Fransella, F. (2005). Some skills and tools for personal construct users. In F. Fransella (Ed.), *The essential practitioner's handbook of personal construct psychology*, (pp. 41–56). John Wiley & Sons.

Fransella, F. (2015). What is a personal construct. In D. A. Winter & N. Reed (Eds.), *The Wiley handbook of personal construct psychology* (pp. 1–8). Wiley Blackwell.

Gardiner, I. A., Littlejohn, A., & Boye, S. (2021). Researching learners' perceptions: The use of the repertory grid technique. *Language Teaching Research*, 136216882110136.

Hadley, G. (2017). *Grounded theory in applied linguistics research: A practical guide*. Routledge.

Hadley, G., & Charles, M. (2017). Enhancing extensive reading with data-driven learning. *Language Learning & Technology, 21*(3), 131–152.

Hanks, J. (2017). Integrating research and pedagogy: An exploratory practice approach. *System, 68*, 38–49.

Heckmann, M. (2016). OpenRepGrid: An R package for the analysis of repertory grids. R Package Version 0.1.10. https://cran.r-project.org/package=OpenRepGrid

Jankowicz, D. (2004). *The easy guide to repertory grids*. Wiley Blackwell.

Jankowicz, D. (2019). Sociality and negotiation in the research grid interview. *Personal Construct Theory and Practice, 16*, 94–99. https://www.pcp-net.org/journal/pctp19/jankowicz19.pdf

Johnson, M., & Nádas, R. (2012). A review of the uses of the Kelly's repertory grid method in educational assessment and comparability research studies. *Educational Research and Evaluation, 18*(5), 425–440.

Kelly, G. (1955). *A theory of personality: The psychology of personal constructs*. W. W Norton & Company.

Kelly, G. (1991). *The psychology of personal constructs, Volume One: Theory and personality*. Routledge.

Kerr, G., & Kelly, L. (2019). Travel insurance: The attributes, consequences, and values of using travel insurance as a risk-reduction strategy. *Journal of Travel & Tourism Marketing, 36*(2), 191–203.

Korthagen, F. A. J. (1992). Techniques for stimulating reflection in teacher education seminars. *Teaching and Teacher Education, 8*(3), 265–274.

Kotsi, F., & Pike, S. (2021). Destination brand positioning theme development based on consumers' personal values. *Journal of Hospitality & Tourism Research, 45*(3), 573–587.

Kramsch, C. J. (1983). Culture and constructs: Communicating attitudes and values in the foreign language classroom. *Foreign Language Annals, 16*(6), 437–448.

Krippendorff, K. (2018). *Content analysis: An introduction to its methodology*. Sage.

Lemke, F., Clark, M., & Wilson, H. (2011). Customer experience quality: An exploration in business and consumer contexts using repertory grid technique. *Journal of the Academy of Marketing Science, 39*(6), 846–869.

Lincoln, Y. S., & Guba, E. S. (1985). *Naturalistic inquiry*. Sage.

Mann, S., & Walsh, S. (2017). *Reflective practice in English language teaching: Research-based principles and practices*. Routledge.

Miles, M. B., Huberman, A. M., & Saldaña, J. (2014). *Qualitative data analysis: A methods sourcebook*. (3rd ed.). Sage.

Neuendorf, K. A. (2016). *The content analysis guidebook* (2nd ed.). Sage.

Oscarson, M., & Apelgren, B. M. (2011). Mapping language teachers' conceptions of student assessment procedures in relation to grading: A two-stage empirical inquiry. *System, 39*(1), 2–16.

Pope, M. L., & Denicolo, P. (1993). The art and science of constructivist research in teacher thinking. *Teaching and Teacher Education, 9*(5–6), 529–544.

Pope, M. L., & Keen, T. R. (1981). *Personal construct psychology and education*. Academic Press.

Richter, K. G., & Lara Herrera, R. (2017). Characteristics and pedagogical behaviours of good EFL instructors: The views of selected Southeast Asian and Mexican SLTE students. *RELC Journal, 48*(2), 180–196.

Sendan, F., & Roberts, J. (1998). Orhan: A case study in the development of a student teacher's personal theories. *Teachers and Teaching, 4*(2), 229–244.

Shaw, M. L. G., & McKnight, C. (1981). *Think again: Personal problem-solving and decision-making*. Prentice Hall Direct.

Tan, F. B., & Hunter, M. G. (2002). The repertory grid technique: A method for the study of cognition in information systems. *MIS Quarterly, 26*(1), 39.

Tashakkori, A. M., Johnson, R. B., & Teddlie, C. B. (2020). *Foundations of mixed methods research: Integrating quantitative and qualitative approaches in the social and behavioral sciences* (2nd ed.). Sage.

Walker, B. M., & Crittenden, N. (2011). The use of laddering: Techniques, applications and problems. In P. Caputi, L. L. Viney, B. M. Walker, & N. Crittenden (Eds.), *Personal Construct Methodology* (pp. 69–87). John Wiley & Sons.

WebGrid Plus. (2020). http://webgrid.uvic.ca/

Yıldırım, R., & İspinar Akcayoglu, D. (2019). A study of young gifted learners' and their teachers' perceptions of effective EFL learners. *Journal for the Education of the Gifted, 42*(1), 85–104.

CHAPTER 15

Repertory grids
How grades might be interpreted

Myles Grogan
Ohtani High School, Osaka

Recent literature suggests that classroom-based assessment should perhaps work from a different set of assumptions than large-scale testing. This idea is explored through RGT by asking how seven teachers, each with a unique approach to teaching and assessment, create their grades in a multi-faculty undergraduate EFL course in Japan. In an interview, the researcher asked each teacher to compare a sample of their own students achieving different grades, demonstrating the teachers' constructs for teaching and assessment. These were then analyzed, and subject to a form of content analysis used in RGT. The process revealed that, although the assessment approach used by each teacher differed, the grade reflected similar underlying teaching values that seemed to be legitimate expressions of the framework provided by the institution.

1. Introduction

Many of us have experiences of being assessed by a classroom teacher. Following such experiences, we may carry with us personal assumptions about what our grades mean and what they are for, making assessment an emotional subject. This chapter explores the assupmtions – the personal constructs – that teachers may have with regard to assessment and pedagogy in an EFL setting.

Recent scholarship is giving more consideration to classroom-based assessment as a unique phenomenon, distinct from large-scale testing and operating under a different set of constraints (Fulcher & Davidson, 2007; Shepard, 2020; Turner, 2012). Understanding these constraints involves understanding how different people operate in different contexts. Settings vary enormously in terms of teachers' and students' background, time available to study, the concreteness of desired outcomes, and so on. This need for greater contextual understanding is an area in which Repertory Grid Technique (RGT) excels, and the study presented and discussed in this chapter used Repertory Grids to reverse engineer the mean-

https://doi.org/10.1075/rmal.6.15gro
© 2024 John Benjamins Publishing Company

ing of grades by comparing the classroom behaviour of students through the eyes of their teachers. This chapter explores how RGT methodology was used as part of a case study in a private university in Japan (Grogan, 2021), allowing an exploration of what particular classroom grades may mean when compared to a formal curriculum, and attempted to summarize how a particular class grade might usefully be interpreted.

As in some other Asian countries, Japanese university mission statements and publicity often seem to contain references to a global outlook and communicative ability, and many university programs in Japan require courses in English as a Foreign Language (EFL), regardless of students' major. However, specific course goals in EFL classes may have to be broad enough to accommodate the varied ability of the students entering compulsory language courses. Though student populations in Japan may appear relatively homogenous compared to some other settings, they carry a diverse range of ability and – perhaps more importantly – attitudes towards English classes. For those assessing students in the classroom, this creates an issue of equity and fairness, especially with regard to students' prior opportunities to learn (Kunnan, 2018; Moss et al., 2008). Overly rigid assessment in EFL classes, which may be relatively unrelated to the students' chosen discipline (science or liberal arts), may prevent them from graduating.

At the time of the case study, most high school leavers in Japan were at the A1/A2 level in the Common European Framework of Reference (MEXT, 2018). Students attending university after graduating may still have had a relatively low level of English, but had successfully graduated high school and been accepted onto programs with their current level of English. For the teachers of required EFL courses at Japanese universities, many of whom are part-time, the level of supervision and support varied "from strictly controlled syllabi to complete freedom" (Butler, 2018, p. 30). The differing starting point of students, practical issues of day-to-day management, and the goal and desires of different groups within the university may have made defining assessible outcomes challenging. Consequently, teachers faced with balancing these different issues may have had to make many on-the-spot decisions, and adapt assessment to meet different stakeholder interests.

The study presented in this chapter is one of a broader collection of four studies (Grogan, 2021) exploring what factors, both content and non-content based, might impact upon grades in a compulsory first-year EFL speaking and listening course at a single Japanese university. The larger collection of studies used a Qualitative Data Analysis approach, borrowing from Thematic Analysis (Braun & Clarke, 2012) and Grounded Theory Methodology (Bryant, 2017; Charmaz, 2014; Hadley & Hadley, in this volume). While information from students, faculty, and administration had suggested several factors, both academic and non-academic, that may have been impacting assessment, specific details of how grades were made and what information such grades might convey was lacking. RGT methodology addressed this lack by asking teachers to consider students awarded different grades on one particular course, and to reflect on how classroom experience and the values reflected in the university environment were transformed into specific letter grades.

2. An overview of the study

The project aimed to "reverse engineer" (Fulcher & Davidson, 2007), the concept of what a particular letter grade for a particular EFL speaking and listening course might mean to students or other stakeholders. In the context of the study, grades were being reported using a five-letter grade system (S as the highest grade, followed by A, B, and C, and D being a failing grade). Given the number of factors involved in the management and teaching of the course, a simple reading of a grade denoting a specific level of language proficiency or other simplistic outcome seemed unlikely. This study aimed to explore and understand possible alternative interpretations of the letter grade based upon the perspective of the teachers awarding those grades.

The university where the data were collected is a relatively large institution with several campuses. This study focused on one required first-year listening and speaking course. Roughly 6,000 students took the course annually, in just over 200 instances of the class, with between 70 and 80 teachers responsible for teaching the course in any given year.

Students from the same faculty took the EFL course together. Classes were formed through a third-party placement system. Those scoring in the top 15% on the placement test were automatically placed in an advanced class, without regard to the score or any external criterion such as the Common European Framework of Reference. Likewise, those scoring in the lowest 15% were placed in a beginner class. The rest (70%) were placed in an intermediate class. Further details concerning the classes are provided in Table 1.

The goals of the speaking and listening course were broad. A list of example activities, such as shadowing or note-taking, as well as possible textbooks were provided to teachers, but linguistic objectives were left to the teacher. Scoring for each component of a teacher's classroom-based assessment followed the numeric outline shown in the final column of Table 1. However, teachers were free to choose both how they taught textbook content and how they interpreted the assessment of each component, with the exception of the common test material (20% of the total grade). One teacher could use a listening comprehension for a

Table 1. Guide to content and scoring system

Nominal level (placement test score)	Class size (students)	Grades awarded (by population)	Components of classroom-based assessment
Advanced (Highest 15%)	30	S: 20–30% A or B: 50–70% C or fail (D): 0–30%	
Intermediate (Middle 70%)	40	S: 10–20% A or B: 60–80% C or fail (D): 0–20%	20% – Common test material 10% – Short tests 20% – Midterm test 20% – Final test 30% – In-class activity
Beginner (Lowest-scoring 15%)	30	S: 0–10% A or B: 70–90% C or fail (D): 0–30%	

Note. The S grade was the highest grade, scoring above an A grade. Grades were awarded based on a percentage of the class population. For example, 20–30% of the advanced class (meaning between 6 and 9 people for a class of 30) had to be awarded the S grade. Similarly, no more than 30% could be awarded a C or a failing grade (D).

midterm, while another might use a group discussion, and a third could ask for presentations, and yet each student would receive a grade for the same course.

Seven teachers agreed to be interviewed. Each teacher chose one or two students from each letter-grade as elements for the Repertory Grid process. Teachers compared the students in terms of their classroom behaviour, their abilities, or their English level. By comparing the students at each letter-grade level, a picture of what might be inferred from each letter grade was developed for each individual teacher. These were then compared across participating teachers to create a broader image of what might be inferred from each letter grade at a broader, more course-wide level.

Following the process for RGT suggested by Jankowicz (2004) and outlined in the previous chapter, Content Analysis showed seven different categories of constructs that may have affected the grading outcome. However, most individual Repertory Grids revealed two components accounting for most of the variance. Reflection on these two data points suggested that the grade may reflect both language domain skills and a broader academic apprenticeship. The constructs and categorizations were combined to produce an overview of how each grade may be interpreted in this light.

3. Why was repertory grid technique used?: How was it implemented?

The RGT study was the final in a series of four studies, conducted as part of an overall case study of course assessment in the setting. The second and third studies had suggested that there was a great difference between teacher approaches to both teaching and assessment, and ways to interpret the possible meanings of a grade remained elusive (Grogan, 2021). RGT seemed to offer a way to account for teacher difference with concrete data on the grading process. It also fit the underlying Qualitative Data Analysis (QDA) research approach (Burr et al., 2014; Denicolo et al., 2016), which had been used for the previous studies.

The project needed a composite picture of what a specific grade might mean through the teachers' eyes, without inadvertently privileging a particular style or image of what assessment should be. RGT has been shown to uncover tacit knowledge, and has been used to make elusive professional or skills-based knowledge more concrete in fields as diverse as risk-management (Rad et al., 2013) or wine-tasting (Herdenstam et al., 2018). This ability to reach this tacit knowledge used by teachers was another factor in choosing the methodology.

RGT allowed teachers to explain their own system of grading, "freeing them from the intrusion of questions derived from the researchers' worldview" (Hadley, 2017, pp. 94–95). It avoided a specific view of assessment on the part of the researcher, and also avoided any implicit criticism of participants whose persepctive differs from that view. It provided both qualitative and quantitative data with regard to how teachers construe grades and grading in terms of the constraints placed on them by the institution, the classes they teach, and their own value structures.

In addition, the possibility of coding interviews and comparing different constructs provided by participants also provided additional data for use in Constant Comparison (Glaser, 1978) in the series of studies. RGT is regularly recommended to gather data for Phenomenological, Thematic Analysis, or Grounded Theory projects (Denicolo et al., 2016; Hadley, 2017). The processes involved in RGT lead to a high level of understanding of the setting, which in itself may be a useful result when researching a particular setting (Hanks, 2017).

In summary, RGT was chosen for the study as it fit the overarching QDA approach of the broader case study, it provided both quantitative and qualitative data, it offered the potential to access tacit teacher knowledge, and privileged the perspective of the informant. It would also help to provide a broader understanding of the setting, and contextualize the grading process.

The interviews were implemented in the second semester of the academic year. Each interview was recorded on video, with the teachers' consent. The seven participating teachers were asked to choose representative students from a single class they had already assessed in the first semester, but were still teaching. This provided a concrete point of reference for the discussion of student behaviour, ability, or level. Following the consent procedure, the interviews began with an outline of the procedure, and the participants gave a brief overview of their personal background with regard to language learning and teaching, an outline of the class they taught (assessment strategies and personal goals), as well as an anonymous description of the students provided as elements. This gave the interviewer context and background through which to begin to "subsume" the participants construing of the elements (Fransella, 2005), as required by RGT.

Participants generally chose two students from each of the passing letter grades to compare and to identify their constructs in the elicitation process. To make the elicitation of constructs easier, pre-prepared cards were used to allow participants to physically show the rankings and to reflect upon while producing constructs. Students were coded using the letter grade (S, A, B, or C, and D if appropriate), a number showing their sequence in the grade sample order, and their gender (M or F). Thus, S1M referred to the first S grade student (who was male), and S2F to the second S grade student (who was female). Similarly C1M refers C grade student 1, (male). These codes were used in later analysis with a participant number. Constructs were also coded according to the participant and the order of elicitation.

From the set of students provided by the participant teachers, three students were chosen at random. Participants were asked how two of the students might be seen as similar, and different from the third in terms of their classroom behaviour, their abilities, or their English level. Eliciting using three elements in this way is called triadic elicitation. For example, Participant 5 found S1M and A1M to be "Sociable with classmates," while S2F was "Shy." After eliciting the construct using three elements, the participant used the two poles of the construct as the two ends of a Likert scale (1 to 5), on which to place the remaining elements. This scale linked the elements and constructs. S1M and A1M scored 1, as the similar constructs, while S2F scored 5 as the dissimilar construct.

After several constructs had been elicited, participants gave a general speaking level, listening level, and overall English level for each element as additional common construct. Finally, participants were asked to give any constructs they felt were missing. At the conclusion of the interview, participants were offered copies of their interview record sheet, containing their scores and constructs, for their personal records.

After the interview, the elicited constructs were numerically compared to the grades, with the S grade scoring 1 and the C grade scoring 4, and where a participant provided a D-grade student, this was given a score of 5. This order reflects the order of elicitation in the interview. An example of this process is shown in Figure 1, using the first elicited triad, "Sociable with classmates – Shy," labelled P5:C01 (*Participant 5: Construct 01*). The scores from the Likert scale were subtracted from the grade scores (second row) and totalled to provide the "Sum of Difference" (SoD) score, which totalled 11. Because the same construct may have been reversed if it was elicited with a different triad, a "reverse" SoD score is also shown (final row), subtracted from the reversed scores (third row). As mentioned in the previous chapter, the practice of putting the similar scores on the same side prevents a tendency to think only in terms of "good" or "bad" constructs.

EXPLICIT (1)	S1M	S2F	A1M	A2F	B1M	B2M	C1M	C2M	Implicit (5)
Grade S	1	1	2	2	3	3	4	4	*Grade D*
Rev S	5	5	4	4	3	3	2	2	*Rev D*
P5:Co1 Sociable with classmates	1	5	3	1	3	4	3	1	Shy
SoD	0	4	1	1	0	1	1	3	11
SoD Reversed	4	0	1	3	0	1	1	1	11

Figure 1. The first construct elicited in an RGT interview
Note. The row marked SoD (Sum of Difference) shows the difference between the focus of the research, represented by the grade (for a value given in bold), and the elicited construct. The score is shown in the right-hand side of the chart. Because the poles could have been elicited in opposite order, a "reversed" score is also given.

Using a procedure outlined in Jankowicz (2004), the Sum of Difference was translated into a score that showed similarity to the grades awarded to each student in the group of elements, known as a similarity score. Figure 2 presents the sum of difference scores and the similarity scores for each construct as given by participant 5 (P5). These similarity scores are on the right of Figure 2, and were labelled as *high*, *mid*, and *low* similarity. This technique, proposed by Honey (1979), can be used when comparing multiple participants' ideas about a central construct. This relatively simple method of comparison preserves the participant's raw scores, and can be done on an Excel spreadsheet.

	EXPLICIT (1)	S1M	S2F	A1M	A2F	B1M	B2M	C1M	C2M	Implicit (5)		
	Grade S	1	1	2	2	3	3	4	4	*Grade D*		
	Rev S	5	5	4	4	3	3	2	2	*Rev D*		
P5:Co1	Sociable with classmates	1	5	3	1	3	4	3	1	Shy		
	SoD	0	4	1	1	0	1	1	3	11	31.3	Low
	SoD Reversed	4	0	1	3	0	1	1	1	11		
P5:Co2	Usually motivated in groupwork	1	2	1	2	1	5	1	3	Not usually engaged in groupwork (Chatting / sleeping)		
	SoD	0	1	1	0	2	2	3	1	10	37.5	Low
	SoD Rev	0	3	2	1	2	1	2	2	13		

Chapter 15. Repertory grids

Figure 2. *(continued)*

	EXPLICIT (1)	S1M	S2F	A1M	A2F	B1M	B2M	C1M	C2M	Implicit (5)		
P5:Co3	Responds actively and quickly	1	1	2	1	2	3	5	5	Delayed response / reluctance		
	SoD	4	4	2	3	1	0	3	3	20		
	SoD Rev	0	4	1	0	1	1	2	4	13	18.8	Low
P5:Co4	Late	5	5	3	3	3	5	1	1	There before teacher		
	SoD	4	4	1	1	0	2	3	3	18		
	SoD Rev	0	0	1	1	0	2	1	1	6	62.5	Mid
P5:Co5	Takes notes in class listening, good recall, and plus alpha	1	1	2	1	2	3	5	5	No notes: Incorrect / no answer to text questions		
	SoD	0	0	0	1	1	0	1	1	4	75	High
	SoD Rev	4	4	2	3	1	0	3	3	20		
P5:Co6	Seems to enjoy school life	1	2	2	4	2	4	5	4	Seems to have negative pressure / effect in private life		
	SoD	0	1	0	2	1	1	1	0	6	62.5	Mid
	SoD Rev	3	1	1	2	2	4	0	2	15		
P5:Co7	Seems to worry about grade	1	1	2	2	2	2	5	5	Seems easy-going about grade		
	SoD	0	0	0	0	1	1	1	1	4	75	High
	SoD Rev	4	4	2	2	1	1	3	3	20		
P5:Co8	Self starter- independent study	1	1	2	2	2	2	5	5	Expends minimum energy: Seems to think presence is enough		
	SoD	0	0	0	0	1	1	1	1	4	75	High
	SoD Rev	4	4	2	2	1	1	3	3	20		
P5:Co9	Bright – high energy level	1	2	3	2	3	4	5	5	Zombie		
	SoD	0	1	1	0	0	1	1	1	5	68.8	Mid
	SoD Rev	4	3	1	2	0	1	3	3	17		
P5:ES	Better overall English speaking ability	1	2	3	1	2	3	5	4	Poorer overall English speaking ability		
	SoD	0	1	1	1	1	0	1	0	5	68.8	
	SoD Rev	4	3	1	3	1	0	3	2	17		
P5:CEL	Better overall English listening ability	2	2	3	1	2	4	5	5	Poorer overall English listening ability		
	SoD	1	1	1	1	1	1	1	1	8	50	
	SoD Rev	3	3	1	3	1	1	3	3	18		
P5:CEo	Better overall English ability	2	1	2	1	2	5	3	4	Poorer overall English ability		
	SoD	1	0	0	1	1	2	1	0	6	62.5	
	SoD Rev	3	4	2	3	1	2	1	2	18		

Figure 2. The completed repertory grid with similarity scores

While the technique described by Honey (1979) focused on similarity to a common construct – the grade, in this case – the way that individual constructs interact with others becomes more obvious using images such as the cluster diagram shown in Figure 3. The application used here (*WebGrid Plus*, 2020) re-organizes the constructs in terms of their similarity to each other, even reversing the constructs if appropriate. The degree of similarity is shown in a dendrogram, connecting the constructs together along a scale on the top right of Figure 3, with scores ranging from 100 to 70 in this case. A useful feature of the dendrogram is that constructs with identical scores, such as P5C08 and P5C07, are joined by a vertical line. Such similarity may be missed in an eyeball analysis.

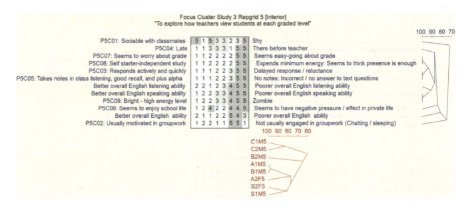

Figure 3. A cluster map of elements and constructs from an RGT interview

The data can also be viewed in a visual representation of a principal component analysis (PCA), shown in Figure 4. PCA simplifies the data available into the smallest possible "components" to explain the variance. In Figure 4, we can see the variance listed below the graph. The X and Y axes of the graph show the strongest components, and constructs (shown as lines) and elements (shown as points) are organized in relation to them. Items close together are similar, so the constructs which scored the same in Figure 3 track the same path. One of these pairs (P5C03 and P5C05) track a path very close to the strongest component, hinting at what the component may consist of for that participant. The figure also shows how constructs such as speaking, listening, and overall English ability match the elements, giving an indication of how well grades track linguistic ability.

Seven participants gave a total of 47 constructs. In addition to coding of interviews and further analysis of the data provided, a content analysis was undertaken to see how the elicited constructs might fit together, following a procedure outlined by Jankowicz (2004). A research assistant was briefed fully on the goals of the study and the procedure to be followed. The constructs were provided to the

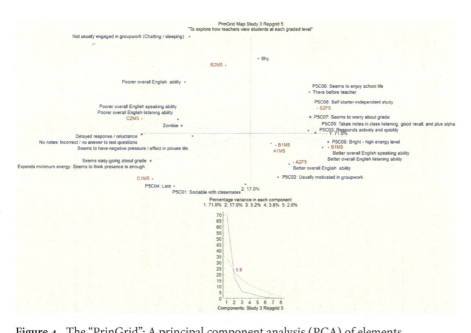

Figure 4. The "PrinGrid": A principal component analysis (PCA) of elements and constructs

research assistant, and were reviewed so that any questions could be asked and clarifications given. Both the main researcher and the research assistant then created categories for constructs independently. Both people produced seven categories that were relatively similar. In the first try, 54% of the constructs were to be found categorized in a similar way. Following the process, both researchers discussed why constructs had been placed similarly or differently, and the procedure was repeated independently. This resulted in a higher level of agreement, and was followed by more discussion. After the second try, the two researchers collaborated, resulting in a joint categorization covering 45 of the 47 constructs. The remaining two constructs were excluded because they were ambiguous and could have been assigned to multiple categories in the final joint model. The final results are shown in Table 2.

The resulting set of categories was believed to show some overarching trends in the grading process, and some homogeneity started to become visible in the differing approaches to assessment. Through a further process of Constant Comparison and memoing, this homogeneity was refined into a possible outline of what the characteristics of learners at each letter grade might be. These are shown in Table 3. The result is both a greater understanding of possible constructs at work in grading, as well as a clearer understanding of what grades may represent.

Table 2. Results of content analysis of rep grid constructs

Classwork	Placement and level	Out of class preparation	Autonomy and attitude	Group	Energy and sociability	Traits and habits
P4Co3: Soon writes on board / Slow to write on board (94)	P7Co4: Has grammatical knowledge / Lacks grammatical knowledge (78)	P1Co2: Prepare for speaking test / Performs poorly on test (83)	P7Co7(R): Positive towards learning / Negative towards learning (84)	P2Co2: Helpful to others, facilitates speaking in others / Minimal interaction. One-sided, no back & forth (94)	P6Co3: Focused / Sleepy (75)	P7Co3: Confident / Hesitates (76)
P1Co6: Strong in dictation / Poor in dictation (83)	P3Co6: Grammatical ability (Textbook) / Weaker textbook grammar (60)	P2Co1: Came to all classes, did all assignments / Missed classes or assignments (75)	P4Co1: Motivated to do tasks / Absence of motivation (82)	P3:Co2 Helps partners: Interactive, Independent / Doesn't show enthusiasm, or willingness to interact (80)	P7Co6(R): Sociable / Doesn't interact easily (72)	P5Co4(R): There before teacher / Late (75)
P4Co4: Listens carefully to CD / Sleeps during listening (69)	P1Co5: Strong background in English / Weak background in English (50)	P1Co4(R): Completed task (Common unit) / Failed to complete tasks (67)	P5Co5 Takes notes in class listening, good recall, and plus alpha – / No notes, incorrect or no answer to text questions (75)	P2Co4: Others respond – invites response. Supportive to conversation. / Minimal interaction. More conversationally passive. Doesn't invite response (63)	P5Co9: Bright – high energy level – Zombie (69)	P5Co7: Seems to worry about grade – Seems easy-going about grade (75)
P2Co5 (R): Used a variety of target phrases (actively integrating class phrases in class uptake) / Not integrating class phrases in class uptake (63)	P1Co3: *Level higher than class / Suitably placed* (8.33)	P4Co5: Seemed well-prepared for test / Seemed unprepared for test (63)	P5:Co8 Self-starter, independent study / Expends minimum energy, seems to think presence is enough (75)	P6Co6 Speaks to classmates in English / Wouldn't speak English to classmates (56)	P3Co4: Enthusiastic (Using English) / Seemed shy (limited English) (60)	P7Co5(R): Well-organized / Forgetful (73)
P1Co1: Focused on class / Doesn't pay attention (50)		P2Co6: Performed well on Common unit / Didn't perform well / complete Common unit (63)	P7Co1(R): Ready to participate / Needs a push (73)	P5:Co2 Usually motivated in groupwork / Not usually engaged in groupwork (38)	P5Co6: Seems to enjoy school life / Seems to have negative pressure, effect in private life (63)	*P3Co3: Less memorable / More memorable* (30)

Table 2. *(continued)*

	Classwork	Placement and level	Out of class preparation	Autonomy and attitude	Group	Energy and sociability	Traits and habits
	P5C03 (R): Responds actively and quickly / Delayed response, reluctance (19)		P6C04 (R): Usually does homework / Usually doesn't do homework (63)	P3:C07 Observes (Learns from others' performance) – Self-centred. (Wants to finish quickly without observing others) (60)	P6C05 Gets confidence only in a group / Confident on their own (13)	P3C08 Sociable, talkative, energetic personality / More socially withdrawn, calm (50)	P7C02(R): Better at memorizing. less creative / Better at improvising, creative (28)
				P2C03 (R): Trying to engage at a class level. Not standing back. / Reluctant to volunteer. Not going above minimum. (63)		P6C01 : Serious face, serious character in class / Social in class (44)	
				P3:C05 Autonomous, didn't need the teacher to proceed / Waited for instructions, just sat there, existed (40)		P5C01: Sociable with classmates/Shy (31)	
						P4C02: Stands out/ Plain, doesn't stand out (6.0)	
Total Construct	6	4	6	8	6	9	6
	4	3	4	5	4	S	3
Participants in set							

Excluded constructs:
P3:C01 Does all tasks beyond average / Doesn't meet teacher's stated expectations (80)
P6:C02 Fighting to answer, eager / Won't answer easily (69)
Bold = Most closely follows grade profile for a participant
Italic = Least similar to grade profile for a participant

Table 3. Integrated description of student performance at each grade level

Grade	Description
S	Completed all compulsory work and assignments, and appeared disciplined (P4, P7) and active in meeting/exceeding expectations (P3). They appeared to take the class seriously (P1, P6). Often friendly, collaborating with and supporting others (P2, P7). However, some preferred to work independently (PT5, P6). Additionally, these students seemed to be entering the class with a high level.
A	Generally co-operative and "easy to teach." Some scored in S range, but were "relegated" owing to the quota – the "Lowest of the high" (P2). Others have low ability or English background, but invested in the class by doing most assignments and preparing for class (P1, P7). Higher ability students getting an A may be invested elsewhere, but not in English class (P6). Dependable (P3), these students did not stand out (P4) or failed to seek help (P5).
B	Almost all teachers believed that students at this level needed more effort in at least one area. Students may not have tried to understand their mistakes (P5), or were weak in a specific (rather than general) area of work, such as listening (P4) or speaking (P2). They may have misunderstood or failed to check instructions somewhere or be missing some grades, such as compulsory vocabulary (P7).
C	Generally performed enough to pass, despite a lack of engagement and missed assignments. The problems tend to be systematic, such as attentional (P1) or energy (P6) issues. In some cases, teachers were surprised the student had enough points (P5), but accept the pass. In other cases, the students failed on points (P3, P4), but the teacher felt they had performed to a standard where a pass was reasonable. Some should perhaps have been placed in a class at a lower level (P2).

Note. P = Participant number, showing the origin of the data used to infer the meaning for the grade.

4. What challenges were faced?: How were the challenges addressed?

The first major challenge in the project was recruitment. While recruitment is an issue for most research projects in second language acquisition, the typical 60–90 minutes interviews caused several potential participants to decline due to lack of time. The course under investigation was taught by 70 to 80 teachers to around 6,000 students every year. Having only seven participants was disappointing. However, this low number was slightly compensated for by getting participants from multiple campuses and multiple faculties.

Part-time teachers may only come to campus once or twice a week, while also working at many other universities in the larger metropolitan area. They also have personal lives with additional responsibilities. Both of these factors may make participation prohibitive for some participants more than others, potentially skewing the data. Some who did participate were those who were particularly interested in second language research, which may have caused another trend within the data. With the under-representation of busy teachers and the over-representation of more research-oriented members, the participants could not be described as a complete or thorough cross-section of the teaching population. RGT, however, is an exploratory technique. In this respect, the data could be sampled to test possible theories (Charmaz, 2014), allowing for a process of Constant Comparison within interviews, between participants, and with information for the broader case study. This was in line with Kelly's original aim for of "a preliminary list of clinical hypotheses" (Kelly, 1991, p.152). Although more participants would have been preferred, the data were sufficient to create a plausible image of the grading process.

Checking findings with participants is a common step within Qualitative Data Analysis to help ensure its integrity and worth (Bazeley, 2013; Miles et al., 2014). Sharing the interview sheet at the end of the session provides a kind of built-in member check with regard to the individual interview. However, at a broader level, the interview process was spread out over several weeks – partly as a result of difficulties in recruitment – and the chance to feedback broader findings to participants was not available. The Content Analysis procedure outlined by Jankowicz (2004) somewhat compensated for this by providing a cross-check on the categories of construct observed, perhaps restoring some of the integrity.

A report of the findings in RGT should honour the voice of the participant, using their words as much as possible. The labels for constructs that participants used are representations of constructs (Fransella, 2005). While they reflect the participant's world view, and make sense to a researcher increasingly familiar with the context, the language used may not be clear to a wider audience. For example, P5:Co5 has as its explicit pole "Takes notes in class listening, good recall, and *plus alpha*." The Japanese expression "plus alpha," in this case meaning to go above and beyond the minimum, may be unfamiliar to some readers of this research, though most stakeholders in the setting would be familiar with it. Striking the balance between preserving the voice of the participant and labelling constructs that readers of the research may understand was an ongoing challenge.

A related challenge lay in the basic skill of implementing the RGT interview. As Denicolo et al. (2016) suggest, making in-time decisions, such as deciding when to ask for clarification and when to give the participant space, and being able to use language the participant can relate to are very much skills that takes time to develop. The author followed several practice procedures from Jankowicz (2004) to prepare for the procedure, and two interviews unrelated to the project were undertaken before a pilot for this project was conducted. However, acquiring interview skills was made more challenging by the fact that, although the participants were all proficient, most of them were not native speakers of English. Occasional code-switching was common in the interviews, and one interview was conducted in Japanese as the participant's preferred medium of communication. With the exception of a single interview, at least one person (either the interviewer or the research participant) was speaking a second language. Transcribing the interviews, re-watching the video recording of the interviews, and making memos allowed opportunities for reflection on the specific skills of implementing a RGT interview. While early interviews generally took longer, the author felt that the interview process became gradually more focussed and efficient as the interview schedule progressed.

5. Insights gained using repertory grid technique

The process of RGT includes interviewing, analysing individual grids, and the content analysis of the set of constructs. The first insight to arise from the interviews relates to the general aim and process of research. In some cases, research risks being a process in which the researcher's needs dominate. Although the researcher may be aiming to contribute to the profession in the long term, during the research exchange, the participant gives and the researcher takes. However, the participants reported finding RGT personally and professionally rewarding. Being able to hand the participants their interview record sheet and seeing it valued made the research process feel like a "win-win" situation, in that both parties tangibly benefitted. This caused the author to reflect on how this win-win approach might be implemented in other research approaches.

The interviews generated a large amount of information. The seven different participants presented very different interpretations of the course guidance and the assessment process, yet each seemed to fit the nature of the class. This helped to reinforce the idea that the vagueness of the course guidance allowed teachers to negotiate the course and the assessment process for the students that they taught. While the participants differed widely in terms of types and level of student, assessment activity, and pedagogical approach, eliciting bipolar sets of constructs revealed teacher thinking in more depth. This in turn helped the researcher find commonality among participant approaches to teaching and assessment in terms of acquiring language skills and trying to implement behaviour that would lead to success. Hadley (2017) comments that RGT can act as a kind of self-coding interview, and this reflects the author's experience. Although additional codes could be generated from the interview transcripts, the process of the interview resembled coding with participating teachers, and was extremely helpful.

With regard to the Content Analysis presented in Table 2 (see Section 3), the discussion between the researcher and research assistant proved fruitful as a reality check to make categories clearer in terms of their scope, and more communicable to users of the research. For example, grades were impacted by institutional factors like the level of the class or the textbook (*Placement and level*). Both *Classwork* and *Out of class preparation*, however, may be more amenable to change, whether through coaching or a change of approach by the teacher. In contrast, *Autonomy and attitude* were seen as being more in the domain of the student. This category was more flexible than their *Traits and habits*. Similarly, *Groupwork* was generally more visible in the classroom than the more evaluative category of *Energy and sociability*. The Content Analysis aspect of RGT therefore proved to be an important factor in the success of the preject.

Becoming familiar with data (Miles et al., 2014), Theoretical Sampling (Charmaz, 2014), and Constant Comparison (Glaser, 1978) are a regular part of Qualitative Data Analysis approaches. The richness of data created through RGT allowed a provisional image of the grade in spite of a relatively small number of participants. The results of possible interpretations for the meaning are provided in Table 3, taken from Grogan (2021). The diverse range of activities undertaken in classrooms, which had looked so disparate at the beginning of the project, seemed to have a set of underlying values and principles in it that would not perhaps have been accessible without a technique like RGT.

6. Conclusions

RGT was chosen for this study because it provided both qualitative and quantitative data, it privileged the perspective of the informant, and had the potential to uncover tacit principles at work in the environment. In these respects, the methodology proved successful, while providing a research experience directly of value to both the researcher and participant. It also successfully uncovered possible interpretations of the letter grade in the particular setting, especially in terms of the process of acquiring language skills and in a broader academic apprenticeship in the university setting. Finally, it provided a rich source of data consistent with approaches such as Thematic Analysis or Grounded Theory, which could be applied as part of a broader case study.

Universities are becoming increasingly competitive. While using some kind of standardised test to measure linguistic development may seem attractive, doing so may represent issues of fairness for students in terms of their previous opportunities to learn. In addition, universities may choose to promote themselves in terms of a broader learning ethos rather than a specific standard of achievement in a non-major subject. The approach used here allows for a deeper examination of classroom grading as a multi-faceted process, focussing on far more than simple proficiency. Rigid application of criterion-referenced assessment may well be useful in some settings, but the diversity of levels, student needs, and teaching approaches made such a system impractical in this context. RGT as a methodology allows multiple perspectives, and may yet help to provide alternative ways of understanding classroom-based assessment as a distinct field within the literature, and help all stakeholders negotiate learning outcomes with respect and a broader commitment to learning. It is the authors' hope that this research will help readers to understand both methodology and to perhaps view assessment in broader terms than simple testing.

References

Bazeley, P. (2013). *Qualitative data analysis*. Sage.

Braun, V., & Clarke, V. (2012). Thematic analysis. In H. Cooper, P. M. Camic, D. L. Long, A. T. Panter, D. Rindskopf, & K. J. Sher (Eds.), *APA handbook of research methods in psychology, Vol. 2: Research designs: Quantitative, qualitative, neuropsychological, and biological.* (pp. 57–71). American Psychological Association.

Bryant, A. (2017). *Grounded theory and grounded theorizing: Pragmatism in research practice*. Oxford University Press.

Burr, V., King, N., & Butt, T. (2014). Personal construct psychology methods for qualitative research. *International Journal of Social Research Methodology, 17*(4), 341–355.

Butler, C. (2018). The ronin teacher: Making a living as a full-time part-timer at Japanese universities. In C. C. Hale & P. Wadden (Eds.), *Teaching English at Japanese universities* (Kindle).

Charmaz, K. (2014). *Constructing grounded theory: A practical guide through qualitative analysis* (2nd ed.). Sage.

Denicolo, P., Long, T., & Bradley-Cole, K. (2016). *Constructivist approaches and research methods: A practical guide to exploring personal meanings*. Sage.

Fransella, F. (2005). Some skills and tools for personal construct users. In F. Fransella (Ed.), *The essential practitioner's handbook of personal construct psychology* (pp. 41–56). John Wiley & Sons.

Fulcher, G., & Davidson, F. (2007). *Language testing and assessment: An advanced resource book*. Routledge.

Glaser, B. G. (1978). *Theoretical sensitivity: Advances in the methodology of grounded theory*. Sociology Press.

Grogan, M. (2021). Making the grade: An investigation into the creation and meaning of grades in university EFL classrooms in Japan (Unpublished doctoral dissertation). Kansai University Graduate School of Foreign Language Education and Research.

Hadley, G. (2017). *Grounded theory in applied linguistics research: A practical guide*. Routledge.

Hanks, J. (2017). *Exploratory practice in language teaching: Puzzling about principles and practices.* Palgrave Macmillan.

Herdenstam, A. P. F., Nilsen, A. N., Öström, Å., & Harrington, R. J. (2018). Sommelier training – Dialogue seminars and repertory grid method in combination as a pedagogical tool. *International Journal of Gastronomy and Food Science, 13*, 78–89.

Honey, P. (1979). The repertory grid in action: How to use it to conduct an attitude survey. *Industrial and Commercial Training, 11*, 452–459.

Jankowicz, D. (2004). *The easy guide to Repertory Grids.* Wiley Blackwell.

Kelly, G. (1991). *The psychology of personal constructs, Volume One: Theory and personality.* Routledge.

Kunnan, A. J. (2018). *Evaluating language assessments.* Routledge.

MEXT. (2018). Heisei 29-nendo eigodjikara chōsa kekka (kōkō 3-nensei) no gaiyōHeisei 29-nendo eigodjikara chōsa kekka (kōkō 3-nensei) no gaiyō [Outline of Heisei 29 English proficiency research result (third grade of high school)]. Retrieved on 24 July from http://www.mext.go.jp/a_menu/kokusai/gaikokugo/__icsFiles/afieldfile/2018/04/06/1403470_03_1.pdf

Miles, M. B., Huberman, A. M., & Saldaña, J. (2014). *Qualitative data analysis: A methods sourcebook.* (3rd ed.). Sage.

Moss, P. A., Pullin, D. C., Gee, J. P., Haertel, E. H., & Young, L. J. (2008). *Assessment, equity, and opportunity to learn.* Cambridge University Press.

Rad, A., Wahlberg, O., & Öhman, P. (2013). How lending officers construe assessments of small and medium-sized enterprise loan applications: A repertory grid study. *Journal of Constructivist Psychology, 26*(4), 262–279.

Shepard, L. A. (2020). Should "measurement" have a role in teacher learning about classroom assessment? In S. Brookhart & J. A. McMillan (Eds.), *Classroom assessment and educational measurement* (pp. 192–205). Routledge.

Turner, C. E. (2012). Classroom assessment. In G. Fulcher & L. Harding (Eds.), *The Routledge handbook of language testing* (pp. 64–78). Routledge.

WebGrid Plus. (2020). Retrieved on 24 July 2023 from http://webgrid.uvic.ca/

CHAPTER 16

Challenges and contributions
of less frequently used methodologies

A. Mehdi Riazi
Hamad Bin Khalifa University

This concluding chapter is organized into four sections. The first section, the introduction, discusses the purpose of compiling the volume. In the second section, I highlight some of the challenges faced by the researchers when they used each methodology and the insights they gained. Thirdly, I will provide a synthesis of the main ethical issues discussed in the chapters and will attempt to relate them to the current discussions of ethics in AL research. Finally, I will elaborate on how these methodologies can inform research on current and new language-related problems in the world we live in. I hope these discussions will be the readers' take-home message if they consider employing these methodological orientations in the future.

1.   Introduction

The purpose of this edited volume was to profile and discuss research methodologies that are less frequently used in Applied Linguistics (AL). Equally important as more frequently used methodologies, these methodological approaches can help AL researchers expand their research topics and research achievements.

A unique feature of the volume is that each methodology is discussed in two chapters: As it is already noticed, the first chapter on each methodology discusses the theoretical aspects, while the second chapter presents a showcase of the methodology in action, making the two chapters complementary. The discussion in each of the two chapters is intended to help readers understand the methodological affordances of the methodology in focus in terms of the research questions they can address, the type of data they can work with, the appropriate data analysis procedures they can use, and the inferences researchers can make from the data and analyses. The two chapters can thus give readers a coherent and balanced understanding of the methodology, that is, its theoretical underpinnings, its design structure, its affordances and challenges, ethical issues involved, and its feasibility.

https://doi.org/10.1075/rmal.6.16ria
© 2024 John Benjamins Publishing Company

2.   Challenges faced; insights gained

One of the recurring challenges mentioned by the researchers was data collection. In any research project, data collection is a crucial and challenging step since it is the data, and subsequently, its analysis, that allows researchers to make valid and credible inferences. Adequate, valid, and relevant data can thus play a significant role in the research process. However, data collection is rarely a straightforward process. Several of the chapter authors referred to the challenges they faced in the data collection process.

In the multiperspective approach (MPA), for example, the researchers referred to the fact that they needed to collect a large and diverse range of data to represent different perspectives. Such a demand, the authors mentioned, required detailed planning, preparatory meetings with different participants, and an examination of the site of engagement to determine what data could be collected and when.

Similarly, data collection turned out to be a challenge in multimodality research. The researchers found themselves working with a relatively large set of data. Collecting such a large amount of data was considered labor-intensive and required subsequent qualitative analytical methods. They also reported that despite the theoretical advancements in multimodality, there was not a set of agreed instruments that could help with the required empirical data. In narrative inquiry, the challenge of data collection was facing unexpected obstacles, especially in unfamiliar contexts. The researcher had to think about and find in situ solutions. For example, after several days of traveling in unsafe conditions and getting to the research site, the healer participant asked the researcher to stay at his doorstep and to turn back. The healer participant also did the same and turned back to face the wall. All through the interview, the researcher and the participant were not looking at each other.

Another related challenge mentioned by the chapter authors was choosing appropriate analytical methods. Given the variety of data sources usually collected in these methodological approaches, researchers must familiarize themselves with sometimes unfamiliar analytical methods. For example, authors of the Multiperspectival Approach (MPA) found that MPA was oriented less to methodological traditions, such as conversation analysis, ethnography, or action research, and more open to potentially eclectic configurations of analytic methods, such as content (keyword) analysis, transitivity analysis, and thematic analysis. These analytical methods are drawn from diverse methodologies, such as corpus analysis, systemic functional analysis, and linguistic ethnography. Such analytical methods helped researchers tailor their understanding of the insights emerging from their exploration of the multiple perspectives. This challenge was reported in other methodological approaches in one way or another. As such, early career researchers who will be using these methodologies will need to attend to the challenge of choosing appropriate analytical frameworks.

Notwithstanding the challenges researchers raised, they also referred to insights they gained when using the methodology. Multimodality researchers, for example, provided additional empirical evidence that communication involves more than language. This led them to conclude that analyses that only take account of linguistic meaning will never capture the complex nature of human communication. As such, the value of a multimodal analysis lies in its inclusive use of a fuller range of meanings made in the research site. The gained insight is that multimodal analysis offers a way to describe and discuss how the semiotic choices work together to express specific meanings in particular contexts. The multimodal analysis, as the authors highlighted, 'makes visible' the semiotic resources that are typically neglected but are meaningful in communication. This led the authors to argue that multimodal analysis enables researchers to provide a more comprehensive account of communication across various contexts. This aspect of multimodal analysis has given certain affordances to the methodology to be used in other disciplines and fields. Readers might be interested to read some of these studies (see, e.g., Bernad-Mechó, 2021; Kuttner et al., 2021; Malinverni et al., 2019).

Regarding conversation analysis, the researcher developed a shift in approach due to the insights developed working on the methodological orientation. He had originally thought that an ethnographic notion of context could legitimately be used to supplement a conversation analysis. However, he found that a more nuanced analysis of how the participants were oriented to the practices of turn-taking, repair, sequence, and preference organizations as they produced the talk could legitimately be used to supplement a conversation analysis. This led the researcher to understand that the interlocutors in the conversation were, in fact, pursuing different agendas during their talk. In this context, the researcher was able to move away from a concern with the relative truth value of one of the interlocutor's claims in the turns and to focus instead on developing a granular analysis of how the interlocutors actually developed their competing agendas on a moment-by-moment basis.

The grounded theory (GT) researchers appreciated the creativity aspect of the methodology and how it complements a researcher's theoretical sensitivity and imagination. As researchers, they felt free to create a new theoretical terminology to better describe and identify the social interactions that emerged from their study. They coined the term "avidization" to describe the various trajectories participant readers went through to become more intentional extensive readers. In other words, they created the term avidization to refer to the processes through which a certain activity becomes meaningfully integrated within one's professional, social, or personal life. By creating this new term as a placeholder concept, the researchers created an interconnected framework linking earlier motivational studies with their novel descriptions of social processes in extensive reading.

The insights gained through the phenomenological approach were also interesting. Before considering and using phenomenology for their study, the researchers considered phenomenology as a unified research methodology. It was by further explorations and the need to use the methodology that they realized they had to align their study with either transcendental or interpretive phenomenology. They noticed they had to decide whether to go with descriptive or interpretive phenomenology. They also realized that the philosophical underpinnings of phenomenology helped them to make a shift from theory-driven to data-driven studies. In narrative inquiry, the researcher noticed that speakers' roles could shift, for example, from acting as a storyteller with full narrative authority to being an audience or a listener. This helped the researcher to attend to the participants' interaction subtleties at various levels. This was because, as reflected by the researcher, in storytelling events, speech participants continuously align and misalign with the various topics of the story. In other words, the participants in narrative inquiry engage in interactional positioning and demonstrate how narratives simultaneously shape and are shaped by their surrounding context. In line with what was discussed earlier in MPA, the researcher in the narrative inquiry had also to wait and familiarize herself with the new environment before interviewing research collaborators and other ordinary participants. The researcher thus shared a broader insight that ethnographers collecting interviews need to familiarize themselves with the sociocultural and ethical aspects of the research site. Otherwise, interviews, and the narratives enclosed in them, would lose their value and utility.

Through the repertory grid technique (RGT), the researcher reflected that he needed to develop a familiarity with some concepts mostly used in grounded theory. These concepts were data, theoretical sampling, and constant comparison analysis. While this might pose some challenges to some researchers, it helped the RGT researcher to gain a broader perspective of qualitative data analysis. Again, this resonates with what was also discussed earlier by MPA authors. That is, the need to learn about different methodological approaches and the insights gained from that familiarity.

In short, the methodologies discussed in this volume have their own challenges and gains. Researchers, therefore, must be ready to face the challenges and use appropriate strategies to face those challenges. For example, they must not only have a carefully planned data collection protocol, but must also have a plan B, and be ready to make appropriate in situ decisions. Having a plan B will help researchers to avoid big surprises they face when their original plan may not work. In addition, and in congruence to new data sources, researchers need to choose appropriate analytical methods that for the new data sources. This is especially important for less experienced researchers. In a sense, those who are going to use any of the methodologies discussed in this volume need to be innovative in one way or another. They need to be innovative in choosing sites of research, potential data sources, and appropriate analytical frameworks. It is this innovative approach that can equip researchers to draw more valid inferences and more comprehensive conclusions.

3. Ethical issues

Another important focus of the methodological orientations was related to ethical issues and how they might be conceptualized and addressed when designing and conducting research. Typically, when ethics in research is discussed, immediately the ethics approval from Institutional Review Board (IRB) occurs to us. Following codes of ethics and applying to relevant IRBs for ethics clearance is now globally established. Ethics guidelines require all researchers to strictly adhere to the codes of ethics before, during, and after the study. The guidelines cover respect for participants, observing their rights, giving participants the opportunity to provide informed consent and participate voluntarily, the confidentiality of the data, and so on. However, an important ethical issue in AL and social sciences, more broadly, is the philosophical and theoretical underpinnings of ethics when it comes to human participants. This aspect of ethics was discussed in some of the chapters and is worth considering.

The methodologies included in this volume, and even some of the more frequently used methodologies, require new conceptualizations of ethics compared to the conceptualizations that are common in (post)positivist approaches. Two issues related to the new conceptualizations will be discussed. The first is related to researchers' conceptualization of the role of language in accomplishing research outcomes, and the second is the IRB's orientation toward less frequently used methodologies.

The first is related to the ethical issue raised in some of the chapters. This issue is the role of language and its ethicality. As discussed in the multiperspectival chapters, an aspect of this issue is using language to accomplish ethical functions rather than the ethicality of functions researchers may accomplish using language. The focus here is less on the ethicality of functions that we may accomplish using language (for example, obtaining consent forms or collecting data). The focus is more on the language that we use in accomplishing these functions. For example, a question can be raised about the ethicality of a request or the judgments that are implied by the language in which the request is made. In other words,

Chapter 16. Challenges and contributions of less frequently used methodologies 269

there is reciprocity when language is used to communicate with others (including participants and other stakeholders). In a sense, this alludes to Giddens' (1987, pp. 20–21) "double hermeneutics." This is because, in social sciences, including AL, researchers study people and their social interactions. In most studies, the focus of the study is on how people understand their world and how what they do is shaped by their understanding. Participants interpret their worlds and communicate their interpretation and understanding (first hermeneutics) with researchers, and researchers interpret participants' understandings through relevant analyses and produce some inferences (second hermeneutics).

As foregrounded in MPA, as researchers, we not only use language with others; the language of others reciprocally constitutes the medium and focus of our collaborations with them. At the same time, we make it our business to make claims about the meaning of language that we use with others. Crichton and Hocking (in MPA chapters) call this a "double accountability" for the applied linguist, in which researchers not only make judgments about others (participants) through their interpretations but also make judgments about participants' interpretations (judgments). Crichton and Hocking (Chapter One) cite Sarangi (2015), who considered language and discourse as context-specific and raised the question of whose description and interpretation of context should prevail. As Crichton and Hocking (Chapter One) rightly observe, failing to acknowledge ethical accountability is particularly acute for Applied Linguistics. This is because AL researchers'

> attention to the language of participants and its remit and to make claims about meaning in their lives, creates quintessentially ethical risks for those involved: for example, trust may be jeopardized, mutual understanding compromised, expertise and experience misrepresented, and identities put on the line.
>
> (p. 30 this volume)

A solution to this potential issue is the researcher's positionality and reflexivity. Researchers may explain their positionality in the research project and use reflexivity to clarify their epistemological position regarding the research phenomenon. This will help them to be more mindful of their reciprocal relationship with the participants and their accountability to the ecological validity of the study, as Crichton and Hocking also observed. Weninger et al. (this volume) also attended to reflexivity when it comes to the analysis and interpretation of participants' semiotic activities. They recommended that researchers exercise greater reflexivity not to trap in the overinterpretation of participants' data.

The second ethical issue is related to the IRBs and their approach to reviewing less frequently used methodologies. Conventionally, IRB members and reviewers have a more (post)positivist perspective, and sometimes this creates problems for researchers whose research projects do not follow those guidelines. For example, Hadley and Hadley (this volume) cited Hammersley and Traianou's (2012) concept of "ethicism". Hammersley and Traianou reflected on ethicism as a situation where the term "ethics" might lead to intellectual censorship and enforced conformity to post-positivist beliefs about what constitutes proper research. From this perspective, research proposals that do not conform to ethical guidelines informed by (post)positivism may be looked at with suspicion and led to disapproval. Some negotiations with the IRB members regarding other methodologies and even diversifying IRB membership will prove helpful. The editor of this volume's experience as an IRB member and his discussion of other methodologies with the IRB members attests to this solution.

4. Methodological contributions

Overall, the seven less frequently used methodological orientations presented and discussed in this book contribute to the methodological discussion in AL.

The methodologies discussed in this volume are prominent in addressing research questions that are "multi" in several respects. The multiplexity of research questions addressed by these methodologies covers multi-layered, multimodal, multi-element, and multi-level analytical frameworks. For example, in Multi Perspectival Analysis (MPA), the research questions focus on themes that are relevant to different stakeholders. Each participant will react to the themes from their own perspective, providing the researcher with a more comprehensive understanding of the research issue. This will, indeed, require the researcher to draw on relevant theoretical frameworks when analyzing different data sources. In other words, the methodology will enable the researcher to look at the research problem from different lenses, drawing on different data sources, different theoretical frameworks, and different analytical frameworks. As Hocking and Crichton explain in their chapters, "the discursive interdependence of the textual, social action, socio-historical, and participant and researcher perspectives can be explained" through MPA. The outcome of such methodological orientation will absolutely be more comprehensive than when a routine methodology is used to investigate the research problem.

In multimodal methodology, researchers get the chance to analyze different modes of communication and how these different modes help to make meaning in specific contexts. For example, in recent classroom settings, teachers and students draw on a variety of resources like oral and written language, gestures, web resources, and so on to jointly create knowledge and enact their social roles in the classroom. As the authors of the multimodal analysis chapters discussed,

Chapter 16. Challenges and contributions of less frequently used methodologies

conventional productive skills like speaking and writing are now expanded to embrace multimodal sources of producing language. When it comes to researching productive skills, the researchers are no more focusing on one mode of communication, but rather an array of such modes. The outcome of multimodal methodological orientation will thus expand the traditional perspectives on communication and meaning-making to embrace more semiotic sources and provide more comprehensive perspectives.

The multiplexity feature in Conversation Analysis (CA) alludes to multiple analytical elements. The multiple analytical elements in CA include turn-taking, adjacency pairs, sequential order, and repair. Each of these elements draws on unique theoretical underpinnings and requires the researcher to consider them when analyzing the element. The multiplicity of the elements and analytical frameworks enable CA researchers to study conversations in context and how such conversations are opened, continued, and ended. The naturalistic nature of conversation analysis (studying naturally occurring conversations) requires conversation analysts to attend to the multiplicity of the elements (turn-taking, adjacency pairs, sequential order, and repair) involved in specific conversations between specific speakers in specific contexts. This will help conversation analysts to present an explanation of how conversations start, continue, and end to achieve a purpose. Other methodologies cannot afford such an explanation.

The Grounded Theory Methodology (GTM) also lends itself to the multiplexity concept. The methodology seeks to understand and theorize what human beings do and say in particular contexts. Drawing on a variety of data sources (e.g., activities and discourses in social contexts), the GT researcher uses three levels of coding to reach data-driven inferences about the phenomenon. The three levels of coding are open coding, axial coding, and selective coding. The multiplexity of the coding procedure provides evidence to readers as to how the researcher explored themes and patterns related to the phenomenon. The inductive nature of GTM enables researchers to look for the main processes involved in the phenomenon under study. Through constant comparative analysis, that is, the back-and-forth movement between the data and emerging theoretical explanation of the phenomenon, more focused questions are developed. These questions usually relate to the properties, conditions, trajectories, problems, and solutions surrounding the processes explored in the phenomenon under study.

The concept of multiplexity in phenomenological research and narrative inquiry can also be traced in intersubjectivity in these methodologies. Interpretive phenomenology focuses on "lived experiences" and intends to inductively explore participants' perceptions of their lived experiences. As such, interpretive phenomenology entails a joint effort on the researcher's and participants' part through intersubjectivity to uncover the lived experiences of the participants.

Interpretive phenomenology thus goes beyond subjectivity (an individual participant's perspectives and perceptions) to embrace intersubjectivity. Intersubjectivity allows for a joint effort to co-construct the participants' lived experiences. Similarly, in the narrative inquiry, researchers study participants' identity (co)construction as it is linked to their interactional dynamics. In narrative inquiry, researchers and participants engage in long conversations in which several personal narratives emerge.

Finally, the Repertory Grid Technique (RGT) investigates how participants conceive the already defined constructs. In other words, RGT seeks to explain how a group of participants understand a phenomenon. The multiplexity concept can be applied to the multiplicity of constructs created by participants. As such, RGT shares features with grounded theory and phenomenological studies and may even be used as a technique for data collection in those methodologies. For example, Hadley (2017) suggested using RGT at the beginning of GT research, as it may be more effective than unstructured interviews when trying to understand the participants' perspectives.

Given the affordances of the less frequently used methodological approaches included in this volume, they can open up new horizons to AL researchers enabling them to investigate and address more complex and sophisticated research phenomena and research issues. While the book may serve more experienced researchers who aspire to address more novel and/or complex research issues in AL, it can also be used as a resource for research methodology courses in postgraduate programs. The unique feature of the book with showcase studies will hopefully help prospective researchers to decide if any of these methodologies can assist them with their future research projects.

References

Bernad-Mechó, E. (2021). Combining multimodal techniques to approach the study of academic lectures: A methodological reflection. *Journal of the Spanish Association of Anglo-American Studies, 43*(1), 178–198.

Giddens, A. (1987). *Social theory and modern sociology.* Polity Press.

Hadley, G. (2017). *Grounded theory in applied linguistics research: A practical guide.* Routledge.

Kuttner, P.J., Weaver-Hightower, M.B., & Sousanis, N. (2021). Comics-based research: The affordances of comics for research across disciplines. *Qualitative Research, 21*(2) 195–214.

Malinverni, L., Schaper, M.M., & Pares, N. (2019). Multimodal methodological approach for participatory design of full-body interaction learning environments. *Qualitative Research, 19*(1), 71–89.

Sarangi, S. (2015). Experts on experts: Sustaining "communities of interest" in professional discourse studies. In M. Gotti, S. Maci, & M. Sala (Eds.), *Insights into medical communication* (pp. 25–50). Peter Lang.

Index

A
a priori theory 90
action research 128, 133
American pragmatism 129
ATLAS 139
authenticity 166
axial coding 271

B
Bakhtin 15, 192, 193
Bhatia 32
Blumer 130
Bourdieu 20
bracketing 163, 165, 168

C
Candlin 15, 21
Charmaz 132, 136, 137, 142, 171, 259
Cicourel 14, 15, 23
codes of ethics 268
collaborative interpretation 22
communicative language teaching 97
Computer Assisted Qualitative Data Analysis Software (CAQDAS) 139
confirmation bias 137
constant comparative analysis 271
constant comparison analysis 137, 139
Corbin 132, 136
corpus analysis 19
credibility 166, 173
Cresswell 185
Creswell 136, 176

D
data-driven inferences 271
data-driven understating 165
denotational moves 194
denotational text 194, 195
Denzin 128
descriptive phenomenology 162

Dewey 227
dichotomy corollary 226
discursive strategies 194, 195, 196
double hermeneutics 269
Durkheim 132

E
ecological validity 14, 14, 18, 20
empirical sociology 130
epistemological investments 12
epoche 163
epoché 168
ethical awareness 192
ethicism 141, 270
ethnography 133
ethnomethodology 19, 83, 85
evidence-based approach 174

F
Fairclough 15, 15
focused investigation 137
Foucault 20
functional linguistics 19
fusion of horizons 165

G
Gadamer 165
Garfinkel 19, 26, 84
Geertz 133
Giddens 20, 269
Glaser 130, 131, 138, 142, 143, 261
Goffman 19, 85, 200
grand theories 131
Gumperz 194, 195, 211

H
Habermas 20
Halliday 50, 51
Heidegger 163, 165
hermeneutic phenomenology 162
hermeneutic researcher 165
hermeneutics 164
Husserl 163, 164, 165
hypothetical explanations 136

I
idiographic approach 225
imaginative variation 168
informed consent form 172
initial codes 135
institutional review board 197
Institutional Review Board 103, 268
institutional review boards 140
institutional talk 85
intentionality 167
interactional dynamics 195, 197
interactional sociolinguistics 19
interactional text 191, 195
interaction-as-ritual 85
interdiscursive 16
interdiscursivity 15
interpenetrating contexts 14
interpretive perspective 167
interpretive phenomenology 171, 271
interpretivism 163
intersemiosis 53
intersubjectivity 169, 176, 271
intertextual analysis 19

J
Jakobson 195
Jefferson 95

K
Kelly 225, 227, 259
Kramsch 241

L
Labov 198, 210
language as social semiotic 51
Layder 20, 21, 34, 142
layered approach 4
life experiences 195
Lincoln 128, 141
linguistic anthropology 193, 196
lived experience 164, 166, 176
lived experiences 271

M
Marx 132
MAXQDA 139, 152
Mead 130
member checking 171, 174, 175
membership categorization
   analysis 19
memo writing 137
memos 136
memo-writing 135
metaphor analysis 19
methodological awareness 1
methodological turn 1
middle-range theories 132
modulation corollary 227
motivational relevancies 18
multimodal turn 4
multimodality 49

N
narrative analysis 194
narratology 19
natural attitude 167, 176
NVIVO 139

O
objectivity 173
open codes 135
open coding 271
open exploration 134

P
participants' perspective 18
Personal Construct Psychology
   225, 227

phenomenological attitude 167,
   168
positionality 269
positivist paradigm 162
post-positivist 143
practical ontology 12, 32
practical relevance 18
purposive sampling 170

R
range corollary 226
transcendental
reflexive awareness 165
reflexive methodology 15
reflexivity 269
reliability 173
researcher reflexivity 163
researcher's perspective 18

S
Sacks 85, 92, 123
Schegloff 85, 86, 92, 94, 101
scientific legitimacy 174
scientific method 163
scientific methods 167
selective coding 271
snowball sampling 182
social action perspective 19
social semiotics 50
sociality corollary 227
socially distributed cognition 103
sociolinguistics 196
storytelling practices 196, 198
Strauss 130, 136
subjective experience of
   participants 18

subjectivity 169, 176
substantive theories 132
symbolic interactionism 19, 130,
   134
systemic functional grammar 50
systemic-functional semiotics 61

T
text and genre analysis 19
textual perspective 19
theoretical codes 139
theoretical construction 138
theoretical frameworks 270
theoretical sampling 137, 171, 183
theoretical saturation 170
theoretical sensitivity 143
thick description 133, 163, 164,
   166, 174
thought experiment 11
thought experiments 10
transcendental 163, 164
transcendental approach 165
transcendental perspective 167
transcendental phenomenology
   171
triangulation 15
trustworthiness 166

V
validity 164, 175, 185
Venn diagram 16

W
Weber 132
Wodak 41